Alberto Hijazo-Gascón
Moving Across Languages

Applications of Cognitive Linguistics

Editors
Gitte Kristiansen
Francisco J. Ruiz de Mendoza Ibáñez

Honorary editor
René Dirven

Volume 47

Alberto Hijazo-Gascón
Moving Across Languages

―

Motion Events in Spanish as a Second Language

DE GRUYTER
MOUTON

ISBN 978-3-11-126618-3
e-ISBN (PDF) 978-3-11-072107-2
e-ISBN (EPUB) 978-3-11-072109-6
ISSN 1861-4078

Library of Congress Control Number: 2021939085

Bibliographic information published by the Deutsche Nationalbibliothek
The Deutsche Nationalbibliothek lists this publication in the Deutsche Nationalbibliografie; detailed bibliographic data are available on the Internet at http://dnb.dnb.de.

© 2023 Walter de Gruyter GmbH, Berlin/Boston
This volume is text- and page-identical with the hardback published in 2021.
Typesetting: Integra Software Services Pvt. Ltd.
Printing and binding: CPI books GmbH, Leck

www.degruyter.com

To Nieves and Carmelo, my parents

Αυτό ήταν. Η πρώτη μου γλώσσα είναι ένα καρδιοχτύπι. Η δεύτερη μια σκέψη. Η πρώτη γεννιόταν από τα σωθικά μου, η δεύτερη στον εγκέφαλο. Το πρόβλημα ήταν πώς να τις παντρέψω.
[Θοδωρής Καλλιφατίδης *Μια ζωή ακόμα*. Theodor Kallifatides *Another life*]

En ese momento lo entendí. Mi primera lengua es palpitación. La segunda, cavilación. La primera brotaba de mis entrañas, la segunda de mi cerebro. El problema era ensamblarlas.
[Theodor Kallifatides *Otra vida por vivir*. Translated from Greek into Spanish by Selma Ancira]

At that moment, I understood. My first language is a heartbeat. My second language is a thought. The first arose from my gut, the second from my brain. The problem was to put the two of them together.
[My translation from Spanish into English]

Acknowledgments

I am extremely grateful to many people who have supported me, academically and emotionally, during the process of writing this book. I started writing the draft during a period of study leave, for which I thank the University of East Anglia (United Kingdom). I am also thankful to the different agencies that have funded my work, specifically the Spanish National Research Agency (AEI) and the FEDER funds (CONESSO Project, FEDER/AEI: FFI2017-82460-P), the Government of Aragón (Psylex H11-17R) and the UEA Faculty of Arts and Humanities (Publications Fund).

I am incredibly lucky to have encountered excellent professionals that have helped me and inspired me during my research career. *Eskerrik asko*, thank you, to Iraide Ibarretxe-Antuñano, my PhD supervisor, who passed on her enthusiasm, knowledge and fascination about languages and linguistics. Her teachings made me the researcher I am today. I am also grateful to Marianne Gullberg for encouraging me to look into the differences between Romance languages and for her advice in research methods, *tak!* My warm gratitude and a big *¡gracias!* and *tak for sidst!* is also to Teresa Cadierno for all her guidance and advice on the field of second language acquisition. A special mention to Luna Filipović, my colleague and research mentor in the UK, for all our discussions, her support and her invaluable comments on the draft of this book, *hvala!* I feel honoured and privileged to have learned so much from these wonderful researchers.

I am thankful to the editors of this series for their trust in me and this project, especially to Gitte Kristiansen for her encouragement every time we met at conferences. I am also grateful to the editing team of Mouton the Gruyter. I would like to thank the participants who took part in the linguistic experiments reported here. I am grateful to the comments, discussions and contributions I had with many colleagues on different aspects of this book. They are, in alphabetical order, Maria Andriá, Andrea Ariño-Bizarro, Chris Bishop, Laura Costa, Vera da Silva-Sinha, Mayte Fernández, María Gómez-Bedoya, Manuel Hartmann, María Hernández, Moiken Jessen, Elsa Liste-Lamas, Reyes Llopis-García, Sara Luna, Chris Skedgel, Leslie Tixier, Valeria Tosi and Meike Wuenn. Finally, I am immensely thankful to my family and friends, for all their support and love.

Contents

Acknowledgments —— IX

List of figures —— XV

List of tables —— XVII

List of abbreviations —— XIX

Chapter 1
Introduction —— 1
1 Introduction —— 1
2 One mind with several languages: Overcoming the monolingual bias —— 2
3 Conceptual transfer and cross-linguistic influence —— 5
3.1 A brief overview of transfer research —— 7
3.2 Types of cross-linguistic influence —— 9
3.3 Conceptual transfer and psychotypology —— 11
4 Cognitive Linguistics and second language acquisition —— 13
4.1 Usage-based approaches to SLA —— 13
4.2 Cognitive Linguistics theoretical models applied to SLA —— 15
5 Moving across chapters —— 20

Chapter 2
Motion events: Semantic typology and its acquisition —— 22
1 Semantics of motion —— 22
2 The typology of motion: Verb-framed and satellite-framed languages —— 27
3 Thinking for speaking hypothesis —— 29
4 Main debates about the typology of motion events —— 40
4.1 Boundary-crossing constraint —— 41
4.2 The notion of satellite —— 44
4.3 Broad nature of semantic components —— 46
4.4 A third typological group? Equipollently-framed languages —— 49
4.5 Intra-typological differences —— 54
4.6 Intra-lingual differences —— 58
5 Acquisition of motion events in a second language —— 59
5.1 Inter-typological studies on motion and second language acquisition —— 60

5.2	Intra-typological studies on motion and second language acquisition —— 64	
5.3	Other lines of research in SLA related to motion events —— 67	
5.4	Main results of the literature on the acquisition of motion events —— 69	

Chapter 3
Inter- and intra-typological differences —— 72

1	Intra-typological differences and genetic families —— 72	
1.1	From Latin into Romance motion events —— 73	
1.2	Motion events in minority Romance languages —— 77	
2	Motion Events in French, Italian and Spanish —— 81	
2.1	Motion verbs in Romance languages —— 82	
2.2	Manner in Romance languages —— 88	
2.3	Path in Romance languages —— 103	
2.4	Deixis —— 125	
2.5	Cause —— 132	
2.6	The position of French, Italian and Spanish in the typology —— 135	
3	Motion events in German —— 142	
3.1	German lexicalization patterns —— 142	
3.2	Thinking for speaking in German —— 147	
3.3	The position of German in the typology —— 151	
4	Diatopic variation in the expression of motion —— 154	

Chapter 4
Typological study: Motion events in French, German, Italian and Spanish —— 159

1	Introduction —— 159	
2	Research questions and hypotheses —— 160	
3	Methodology —— 161	
3.1	Experimental design —— 161	
3.2	Material for data elicitation —— 162	
3.3	Procedure —— 163	
3.4	Participants —— 163	
4	Transcription and coding —— 166	
4.1	Transcription —— 166	
4.2	Classifying motion verbs —— 166	
4.3	Methodological challenges and potential solutions —— 168	
5	Analysis —— 170	
6	Statistical methods —— 172	

7	Results of the typological study: Motion verbs —— 172
7.1	Spanish motion verbs —— 173
7.2	Italian motion verbs —— 173
7.3	French motion verbs —— 174
7.4	German motion verbs —— 175
7.5	Motion verb comparison —— 176
8	Results of the typological study: Manner —— 177
8.1	Manner verbs —— 178
8.2	Total manner expression —— 181
8.3	The owl scene —— 183
8.4	The boundary-crossing constraint —— 184
9	Results of the typological study: Path —— 189
9.1	Satellites and pseudo-satellites —— 189
9.2	Minus Ground vs. Plus Ground —— 191
9.3	Minus Ground vs. Plus Ground in the narratives —— 192
9.4	Minus Ground vs. Plus Ground in the falling scenes —— 198
9.5	Falling scenes with Slobin's Spanish data —— 205
9.6	Deixis —— 207
9.7	Specific aspects of Path in the four languages of the study —— 211
10	Results: Causative constructions in Romance languages —— 212
11	Results: Event granularity —— 214
12	Conclusions on the typological study —— 215

Chapter 5
Acquisition study of motion events in L2 Spanish —— 219

1	Introduction —— 219
2	Research questions and hypotheses —— 220
3	Methodology —— 221
3.1	Methodology to identify cross-linguistic influence —— 221
3.2	Experimental design, material for data elicitation and procedure —— 223
3.3	Participants —— 224
4	Transcription and coding —— 226
5	Analysis —— 226
6	Statistical methods —— 227
7	Results: Motion verbs —— 227
7.1	L1 Italian learners of L2 Spanish —— 228
7.2	L1 French learners of L2 Spanish —— 229
7.3	L1 German learners of L2 Spanish —— 230
7.4	Comparison of motion verbs —— 231

8	Results: Manner —— 232
8.1	Manner verbs —— 233
8.2	Total Manner expression —— 235
8.3	The owl scene —— 236
8.4	The boundary-crossing constraint —— 237
9	Results: Path —— 240
9.1	Satellizations in L2 Spanish —— 241
9.2	Minus vs. Plus Ground in the whole narratives —— 243
9.3	Plus Ground with 2 or more elements —— 246
9.4	Minus vs. Plus Ground in the falling scenes —— 247
9.5	Deixis —— 253
10	Results: Causative constructions in L2 Spanish —— 255
11	Results: Event granularity —— 257
12	Conclusions on the L2 acquisition study —— 258

Chapter 6
Conclusions and future directions —— 263

1	Introduction —— 263
2	Conclusions in relation to the typology —— 263
3	Conclusions in relation to second language acquisition —— 268
4	Moving forward: Applications of this research —— 273
4.1	Pedagogical approaches to teaching typology —— 274
4.2	Focus on meaning: Pedagogical translation and mediation —— 275
5	What is next? Future research —— 279

Appendix 1: Motion verbs in Spanish, Italian, French and German *Frog Stories* —— 283

Appendix 2: Motion verbs in L1 and L2 Spanish —— 289

References —— 293

Subject index —— 321

Author index —— 325

List of figures

Figure 1	The dog scene —— 34	
Figure 2	The beehive scene —— 35	
Figure 3	The boy scene / The owl scene —— 35	
Figure 4	The deer scene —— 36	
Figure 5	Romance languages in the Path salience cline —— 125	
Figure 6	Evolution of Path lexicalization from satellite- to verb-framed languages. (Adapted and translated from Goschler and Stefanowitsch, 2009: 113) —— 145	
Figure 7	Evolution of Path Lexicalization in German. (Adapted and translated from Goschler and Stefanowitsch, 2009: 114) —— 145	
Figure 8	Percentage of Manner verbs in L1 —— 180	
Figure 9	Percentage of Total Manner Expression in the L1s —— 182	
Figure 10	The owl scene —— 183	
Figure 11	The jar scene —— 186	
Figure 12	Plus Ground Percentage in L1s —— 194	
Figure 13	Percentages Plus Ground with 2 or more elements in L1s —— 197	
Figure 14	Dog scene —— 198	
Figure 15	The beehive scene —— 199	
Figure 16	Boy scene —— 200	
Figure 17	Deer scene —— 201	
Figure 18	Percentage of Plus Ground in the falling scenes in L1s —— 204	
Figure 19	Percentage Plus Ground with two or more elements in the falling scenes in L1s —— 205	
Figure 20	Percentage Plus Ground in falling scenes in L1s (Slobin's data) —— 207	
Figure 21	Percentage of Manner verbs in L2 Spanish —— 235	
Figure 22	Percentage of Total Manner Expression in L2 Spanish —— 237	
Figure 23	Percentage Plus Ground in L2 —— 245	
Figure 24	Percentage Plus Ground in the falling scenes in L2 Spanish —— 251	
Figure 25	Percentage of Plus Ground in falling scenes with Slobin's data —— 252	

List of tables

Table 1	Types of cross-linguistic influence. Adaptaded from Jarvis and Pavlenko (2008: 20) —— 10	
Table 2	Semantic classification of motion verbs (translated from Morimoto 2001: 50) —— 85	
Table 3	Types of Trajectories according to telicity (translated from Morimoto 2001: 121) —— 94	
Table 4	Manner verbs and boundary-crossing in a Verb-Framed Language (Iacobini and Fagard 2011: 163) —— 100	
Table 5	Different possible expressions of boundary-crossing events in VF and SF languages (Iacobini and Fagard 2011: 167) —— 101	
Table 6	Verb-particle constructions in English and Italian (Iacobini and Masini 2007b: 161) —— 104	
Table 7	Implication scale of verb-particle expressions expressing displacement in verb-framed languages (Iacobini and Fagard 2011: 165) —— 117	
Table 8	Path prefixes in French (Kopecka 2006a: 87) —— 118	
Table 9	Hierarchy of Grounds Lexicalised in COME (adapted from Lewandowski 2014: 46) —— 130	
Table 10	Types and tokens of motion verbs —— 177	
Table 11	Types (and tokes) of motion verbs in L1s —— 177	
Table 12	Manner verbs for the four language groups —— 178	
Table 13	Descriptive statistics Manner verbs —— 180	
Table 14	Descriptive statistics Total Manner Expression —— 182	
Table 15	Owl scene description in the L1s —— 184	
Table 16	Expression of Boundary-crossing events for the jar scene —— 187	
Table 17	Percentages of Boundary-crossing events for the jar scene —— 187	
Table 18	Plus Ground and Minus Ground in L1s —— 193	
Table 19	Descriptive statistics % Plus Ground —— 194	
Table 20	Statistical descriptions Plus Ground 2 or more elements —— 197	
Table 21	Dog scene in L1s —— 199	
Table 22	The beehive scene in the L1s —— 200	
Table 23	The boy scene in the L1s —— 201	
Table 24	Deer scene in the L1s —— 202	
Table 25	Total results from the falling scenes in L1s —— 202	
Table 26	Comparison % Plus Ground whole narrative vs. falling scenes —— 203	
Table 27	Descriptive statistics % Plus Ground in falling scenes —— 203	
Table 28	Descriptive statistics % Plus Ground 2 or more elements in the falling scenes —— 204	
Table 29	Descriptive statistics % Plus Ground in Falling Scenes with Slobin's data —— 206	
Table 30	Deictic motion verbs in *The Frog Story* —— 209	
Table 31	Event granularity. Deer scene in 6 segments in L1s —— 214	
Table 32	Event granularity. Deer scene in 4 segments in L1s —— 215	
Table 33	The four types of evidence for cross-linguistic influence (Jarvis 2010: 182) —— 222	

List of tables

Table 34	Types and tokens of motion verbs in L1s and L2 Spanish ——	231
Table 35	Types and tokens of motion verbs in L2 Spanish ——	232
Table 36	Manner verbs in L2 Spanish ——	233
Table 37	Descriptive statistics for Manner verbs in L2 Spanish ——	234
Table 38	Descriptive statistics for Total Manner Expression in L2 Spanish ——	236
Table 39	Boundary-crossing tokens in the jar scene ——	239
Table 40	Percentages Boundary-crossing in the jar scene ——	239
Table 41	Percentages of the boundary-crossing in L1s ——	240
Table 42	Minus and Plus Ground in L2 Spanish ——	243
Table 43	Descriptive statistics Plus Ground ——	244
Table 44	The dog scene in L2 Spanish ——	248
Table 45	The beehive scene in L2 Spanish ——	248
Table 46	The boy scene in L2 Spanish ——	249
Table 47	The deer scene in L2 Spanish ——	249
Table 48	Total results from the falling scenes in L2 Spanish ——	250
Table 49	Descriptive statistics Plus Ground in the falling scenes in L2 Spanish ——	250
Table 50	Descriptive statistics percentages in the falling scenes in L2 Spanish with Slobin's data ——	251
Table 51	Plus Ground comparison between L1 and L2 ——	253
Table 52	Deictic verbs used in L2 Spanish ——	254
Table 53	Deictic verbs used in L1s ——	254
Table 54	Event granularity. Deer scene with 6 segments in L2 Spanish (and L1s) ——	257
Table 55	Event granularity. Deer scene in 4 segments in L2 Spanish (and L1s) ——	258

List of abbreviations

1	First person
3	Third person
ABL	Ablative
ABS	Absolutive
ACC	Accusative
ADVP	Adverbial pronoun
ALL	Allative
AUX	Auxiliary
CAH	Contrastive Analysis Hypothesis
CASP	Complex Adaptive System Principles for SLA
CEFRL	Common European Framework of Reference for Languages
CL	Clitic
CONN	Connective suffix
COP	Copula
DAT	Dative
DECL	Declarative ending
DEF	Definite
DIM	Diminutive
EVI	Evidentiality marker
F	Feminine
FUT	Future
GER	Gerund
IMP	Imperative
INF	Infinitive
L1	First language
L2	Second language
LA	Language acquisition
M	Masculine
N	Neuter
NEG	Negation
NON	Non-unidirectional
NOM	Nominative
PCIC	Plan Curricular del Instituto Cervantes [Curricular Plan of the Cervantes Institute]
PFV	Perfective
PL	Plural
PRE	Prefix
PRS	Present
PST	Past
PTCP	Participle
REFL	Reflexive

SBJ	Subject marker
SBJV	Subjunctive
SG	Singular
SLA	Second language acquisition
UNI	Unidirectional

Chapter 1
Introduction

1 Introduction

Multilingual people and language learners often find that concepts and words do not always match one another across languages. In most cases they realize they have to change the patterns of their first language to sound natural in the second language. The influences of one language on another are part of the second language acquisition process and can occur at different language proficiency levels. We all have experienced the traces of a first language phonological system in the accent of a foreign speaker of our language. Spanish speakers of English are easily identified by their difficulties in pronouncing an /s/ before a consonant at the beginning of a word, inserting an additional /e/ as we do in our language. Similarly, English speakers of Spanish are easily recognizable in their pronunciation of Spanish /t/ not articulated in the teeth and with an aspiration. When learning an additional language, we try, consciously or not, to adapt our words from the first language into the second, with mixed levels of success. Any language learner who has been immersed in that linguistic environment remembers anecdotes of language learning difficulties with false friends and misunderstandings due to the attempts to "force" the first language into the "costume" of the second.

This phenomenon, often called interference or transfer, is the focus of this volume, in particular at a conceptual level. Transfer happens when the relationship between one language and the other entails a restructuring of conceptual categories and not just individual lexical items. Pavlenko (2014: 302) explains that the relation between one's language and the material world may shatter in the encounter with a new world with new categories that are not equivalent to those of the L1. She illustrates this with an example by Otheguy and García (1993). These researchers noticed that Spanish-speaking migrants in New York replaced the word *edificio* 'building' in L1 Spanish with the borrowing *bildin*. This seemed contradictory, since *building* and *edificio* are translation equivalents. However, in the interviews with the speakers they found that when they arrived they were surprised to find that what in their Latin American countries would be called *edificios*, i.e. two- or three-floor buildings, are called *houses* in New York. The skyscrapers in New York were a new category for them, so they borrowed the term *bildin* for these items and kept *edificio* for two- and three-floor houses and *casas* 'houses' for smaller structures. This shows how learners can experience a cognitive dissonance when they try to map new words into the concepts of their language. In this sense, second language acquisition (henceforth SLA) can be seen as cognitive restructuring.

The cognitive category under study in this book is motion. Speakers of all languages describe how they and other entities move. Therefore, motion is of crucial importance and is ubiquitous in the discourse of any speaker in any language. Yet the way motion is encoded in different languages is very different. Indeed, motion has been identified as a semantic domain where conceptual transfer is likely to occur (Jarvis and Pavlenko 2008). The theoretical framework followed here is Cognitive Linguistics and, in particular, Talmy's (1991, 2000a, 2000b) semantic typology of motion events. This typology classifies languages depending on the encoding of the semantic component of Path (including trajectory and direction of the movement) in the main verb of the event (verb-framed languages, e.g. Spanish *salir* 'exit') or in a nonverbal element (satellite-framed languages, e.g. English *go out*). The consequences of motion encoding in discourse, memory and attention have been widely studied under the complementary hypothesis of thinking for speaking (Slobin 1991, 1996a, 1996b, 1997a, 1997b).

Before delving into the explanations on conceptual transfer and how this phenomenon has been approached from different perspectives, some concepts on bi/multilingualism and second language acquisition will be discussed to offer a review of the field.

2 One mind with several languages: Overcoming the monolingual bias

How two (or more) languages coexist in the human mind has been one of the main research questions in the language sciences. Bilinguals are defined in linguistics as speakers who use two or more languages in their everyday lives, simultaneously -in bilingual contexts- or sequentially -as migrants or students in a different country-. These definitions can be also applied to multilingual speakers (see Pavlenko (2014: 20–25) for a review on bilingualism and the key terms in the field). Bilingualism has attracted the attention of linguists, although they have often looked at the phenomenon of second language acquisition with a monolingual bias. Bilingualism (and multilingualism) was for a long time considered an imperfection. Bilinguals were far from the ideal speaker proposed in certain theoretical models, and an exception to the norm of monolingualism. This monolingual or fractional view on bilingualism, as explained by Grosjean (1989), implies the belief that bilinguals have two separate and isolated language competencies similar to those of monolingual speakers. The main negative consequence of this view is to consider that the perfect bilingual is someone who shows monolingual-like competences in their both languages.

However, the overwhelming majority of bilinguals are not like that. Multilingual speakers have different needs and different social functions for their languages. This led Grosjean (1997, 2010) to elaborate the *complementary principle*, which claims that bilinguals usually acquire and use languages for different purposes, in different domains of life and with different people. This principle is coherent with his *bilingual/holistic view of bilingualism* (Grosjean 1989). In other words, he considers that a bilingual is not the sum of two monolinguals. Bilingual speakers develop their language competences to the extent required by their needs and those of the environment. They are not equal in their language proficiency and their communicative competence cannot be evaluated by considering only one of their languages (see also Grosjean 2008, 2010).

Another important concept put forward by Grosjean (2012: 12) is language mode, defined as the "state of activation of the bilingual's languages and language processing mechanism at a given point in time". In other words, bilinguals can switch between monolingual and bilingual modes depending on how many of their languages are active at the utterance point. This is a crucial concept that should be taken into account before making claims about bilingual competence, as the activated mode can influence the bilingual's speech. Unfortunately, language mode has been overlooked in traditional views on bilingualism, which considered bilinguals' speech to be imperfect and even inferior to monolingual speakers.

Based on Grosjean's ideas, Cook (1991, 1994, 2012) coins the term *multicompetence*. His first definition of *multicompetence* is "the compound state of a mind with two grammars" (Cook 1991), redefined as "the knowledge of more than one language in the same mind" (Cook 1994). He regards the L2 user in all their complexity and not as a monolingual native speaker. He considers that the native speaker does not have a particular status and argues that bilingualism is the norm for most individuals in larger areas of the world. Cook (2016) uses Selinker's (1972) well known concept of *interlanguage*, which claims that learners create their own language out of the resources they have available to them: learning strategies, language teaching provision, and the first language, instead of considering learners as speakers of an imperfect L2. The sum of the L1 and the *interlanguage* in the mind of the user compose the *multicompetence*. Therefore the *multicompetence* concerns the total system for all the languages in a single mind (or in a community) and their inter-relationships.

Other models are closely related to this notion of multicompetence. For example, the Dynamic Systems Theory (de Bot 2015), which considers that the language system is always in a state of flux, and that it is fluid and changeable.

The fluidity of the language system has been also noticed in L3 acquisition research, which shows that the multilingual system is constantly changing and that language attrition appears more often in multilingual than in bilingual speakers (Jessner, Megens, and Graus 2016). In the same vein, the Dynamic Model of Multilingualism (Herdina and Jessner 2002) accounts for transfer as a dynamic process.

Multilingualism seems to offer several advantages over monolingualism in terms of language competencies and cognitive and social development. In fact, it seems that multilingual speakers acquire a new set of skills including metacognitive strategies on how to learn a language and an enhancement of linguistic awareness (see Bialystok (2007) for an overview of studies that report cognitive advantages of bilinguals).

In recent years, considerable advances have been made in overcoming the traditional monolingual bias in bilingualism studies. However, this bias persists in the related field of second language acquisition (SLA). As Ortega (2010, 2013) explains, since the 90s the field of SLA has evolved to include a social turn and epistemiological diversity, but it fails to address the monolingual bias. Ortega (2013) claims that the social turn has been completed with the increase of new theoretical frameworks and the growing attention to social phenomena in different models. However, the field of SLA still needs to address the monolingual bias and the problem of nativeness (Ortega 2010, 2013, 2014). Most studies still see monolingualism as the norm and measure the acquisition of a second language in monolingual native-like terms. This monolingual bias sees SLA as the efforts by monolingual adults to add on to their L1 a monolingual-like command of an additional language, but the language faculty is not monolingual itself. It is indeed much more complex and dynamic.

Ortega (2010) argues for a bilingual turn for SLA. This reorientation means that some of the pervasive aspects of SLA should be changed. First, the birth privilege should be substituted by empirical focus on experience. Second, monolingualism should not be regarded as the norm, and non-normative comparisons should be established with multilingual natives and with other diverse multiple language learning profiles. Finally, bilingualism should not be established as a hidden reality and the multilingual dimension of participants should be visible.

Research into this bilingual turn would support other attempts in order to understand better SLA and multilingualism. According to Ortega (2014) the field should replace the research question of why late bi/multilinguals are not like native speakers, by trying to understand the processes that lead to becoming a bi/multilingual speaker. This should be done by shifting the focus on birth to a new focus on the history and experience of the speaker. The main hypothesis is that linguistic development is driven by changes in exposure. This involves variation in brain activity, in working memory, and in the ability to judge grammaticality. In fact, Muñoz and Singleton (2011) show how different studies suggest that age does not deserve the prominent role that has traditionally played in the literature.

What is more, the bilingual turn is not only exclusive to acquisition research but it is also growing in the study of language and cognition as noted by Pavlenko (2014). Her studies on language and cognition attempt to understand the relation between cognitive processes (attention, perception, memory, etc.) and language. However, the fascination with the nature of bilingualism is not new. Pavlenko (2014) explains how both Humboldt and Whorf considered that language learning is a way to transcend the boundaries of the first language. In this sense, Pavlenko clarifies that the so-called Sapir and Whorf Hypothesis was never formulated as such by Sapir or Whorf, but by R.Brown and Lenneberg (1954), who redefined their works in terms of a testable hypothesis, ignoring the multilingual awareness present in Sapir's and Whorf's works. As a result, the controversial hypothesis with two versions and which is articulated in monolingual terms has been in the focus of heated debates for decades. Pavlenko (2014) argues that the language-mediated effects found in cognitive processes (memory, attention, etc.) lose relevance when they are considered for monolingual speakers. They become more intriguing when we go back to Humboldt and Sapir and Whorf's ideas of L2 learning as a way to transcend the boundaries of the L1 and try to understand when and why such effects persist and how they may be destabilized (Pavlenko 2014: 301).

The research project presented in this book builds on these foundations. It presents a multilingual perspective on motion events, with the focus on linguistic thought, considered by Pavlenko (2014: 35) as the cognitive processes fully or partially mediated by language. The research presented in this book aimed to avoid the monolingual bias in SLA and to this effect, comparisons were not limited to native speakers *vs.* L2 groups. The results from different L2 user groups are contrasted and all our informants were in a comparable immersion context, which ensured maximum L2 exposure. Additionally, the performance by the same speakers in both languages is also contrasted. In this way, we avoid the monolingual bias.

3 Conceptual transfer and cross-linguistic influence

One of the main aspects of research on second language acquisition entails understanding the influence of one language on another when a speaker that knows both communicates in one of them. The phenomenon of transfer can be defined as "the influence resulting from the similarities and differences between the target language and any other language that has been previously (and perhaps imperfectly) acquired" (Odlin 1989: 27). Several terms have been used to refer to this phenomenon, such as transfer, linguistic interference, role of the mother tongue, influence of the native language, and language mix (Odlin 2003). The term *interference* has been less used in more recent literature, as it is considered that it leads to negative connotations and ignores cases in which the influence of the first language is positive and eases language learning (see Odlin 2016b for a detailed explanation of the evolution of the field). Interference was substituted by the more neutral term of *transfer*, although this is not free of controversy. For example, Cook (1991: 24) concludes that transfer is not the right word to explain this phenomenon as it restricts L2 users to the position of cumulative monolinguals and it disregards the richness of the bilingual mind. The alternative and more neutral term *cross-linguistic influence*, put forward by Sharwood Smith and Kellerman (1986), reflects the interplay between earlier and later acquired languages and has been extensively used in later literature in the field. Without disregarding the disadvantages of using these terms, in this book the terms *transfer* and *cross-linguistic influence* will be preferred, as they are the terms that are more widely used in the literature.

Research on transfer does not originate in second language acquisition studies, where it has received more attention, but in sociolinguistics. Odlin (2003) explains that the first linguist who identifies this phenomenon is Weinreich in *Languages in Contact* (1953). This author studies the cases of *interference*, i.e. cases in which the mother tongue causes difficulties in second language discourse. This shows the strong interest in transfer from other fields, such as sociolinguistics, contact linguistics and creole linguistics. The phenomenon is also relevant to translation, although it is worth explaining that even though many cases of lexical transfer involve some translation, not all transfer behaviours involve translation (Odlin and Yu 2015).

The focus here will be on the role of transfer in SLA, where all theories have acknowledged it as an important aspect in second language acquisition, although there is some variation with regard to the extent of its relevance in the language acquisition process. In fact, transfer should be understood as complementary to other processes in second language acquisition that are not due to the L1 or any of the other languages acquired by the speaker. These phenomena that are shown in the L2 but are not caused by L1 transfer are identified in the literature as *learner varieties* and are originated by general cognitive processes (R. Ellis 1994, Perdue 2000).

3.1 A brief overview of transfer research

The history of transfer can be traced back for centuries. As explained by Jarvis (2015), even before modern linguistics, Ancient Greeks were aware of transfer. This should not surprise us. After all, anyone who has learnt a second language has at some point become aware of how the knowledge of one language affects the other. Odlin and Yu (2015) and Odlin (2016) explain the history of transfer research in modern linguistics and discuss the origin of the notion of the Contrastive Analysis Hypothesis (henceforth CAH). The Contrastive Analysis Hypothesis was based on Lado's (1957: 2) assumption that the linguistic elements that are similar to the first language will be easy for the learner and that those elements that are different will be difficult. It is commonly believed that Lado (1957) formulated the CAH, that the notion of language transfer comes from behaviourist psychology and that Weinreich introduced the term transfer to L2 research.

However, Odlin (2016) challenges these beliefs and moderates some of the common assumptions in transfer research. He explains that there are some preliminary definitions of transfer and contrastive analysis that show that there was intellectual interest in transfer before Lado's work. He traces the use of transfer in linguistics in the 19th century. The term is used in English by William Dwight Whitney in 1881 and by Aaron Marshall Elliott in 1885. Both authors studied Philology in Germany and use transfer and inference as translations for *hinübertragen* 'transfer' (used by Wilhelm von Humboldt from Latin 'transferre' in 1836) and *übertragen* 'carry over' (used by Ahlqvist (1875) and Schuhardt ([1884] 1971) cited in Odlin (2016). Shuchardt also uses *Einfluss* 'influence' in 1884 in relation to German and Italian varieties in contact with Slovenian. Therefore the use of this terms stems from German linguistics and not from American psychology as was previously thought. The differentation between positive and negative transfer also occurred after the first use of the term transfer itself in German linguistics and not thanks to behavioural psychology.

These studies constitute the very beginning of a systematic study of transference, evolving from the first notes on this phenomenon in the 19th century philological tradition (especially German as seen above) into the behaviourist theories of language acquisition and the consolidation of Generative Grammar as the mainstream theory in Linguistics in the 50s. As R. Ellis (1994) points out, the term interference was central in the late 50s and 60s, when Contrastive Analysis was the main trend in Applied Linguistics. Scholars in the 60s followed this line of research, hand in hand with the CAH, looking for differences between European language pairs that would lead to the production of errors.

In the 70s, researchers started to consider that the difference between two languages did not automatically mean that it would be a source of difficulty in acquisition. First, evidence suggested that many errors were not necessarily due to transfer, but to other phenomena in the language acquisition process. Second, contrastive analyses predicted certain errors that did not always take place in the learners' productions. Finally, the rise of generativism as the main trend in Linguistics implied a shift in the aims of language acquisition research. The focus changed to general acquisition processes and, consequently, the importance given to first language influence was diminished. According to Jarvis (2016), although there was less research on transfer in the US during these years, European researchers continued to study this area, mainly Ringbom (1976, 1978) and Kellerman (1977, 1978). Jarvis (2016) explains that historically transfer had been seen as an independent variable, as the main obstacle to understanding second language acquisition. However, after the 1970s, transfer became a dependent variable, worthy of its own research on its own merit, and with its own independent variables such as language distance and L2 proficiency. The research questions moved from the number of errors triggered by transfer towards the causes of transfer and the factors that can prevent it.

In the 80s and 90s, theories of SLA were proposed to explain how, when and why transfer is produced and what types of transfer occur. More specific and testable hypotheses were put forward and tested. For example, Andersen (1983) formulated the *transfer to somewhere principle*, which consists of two parts. First, any element of the L1 should be compatible with the general principles of acquisition to be transferred to the L2, and second, the input in the L2 should facilitate the generalization of an element of the L1. Transfer is likely to happen when these conditions are fulfilled. This explains why English speakers tend to transfer their word order in French and produce mistakes like **Je vois le* 'I see him' instead of *Je le vois*, whereas French speakers do not produce the reverse mistake: it is unlikely that they will transfer and say **I him see*, as this is not compatible to the language order in the input they receive.

However, for certain authors, Andersen's (1983) principle falls short, as it only takes into account the similarities between the L1 and the L2. In order to complement Andersen's work, Kellerman (1995: 137) proposed the *principle of transfer to nowhere*, which states that transfer is not necessarily caused by similarity to the L2. This type of transfer occurs while completely ignoring the way the L2 works. For example, he shows how Dutch learners of English judged intransitive uses of break like *The cup broke* as less acceptable than transitive uses of break, like *He broke his leg*. While beginner learners accepted all the intransitive cases, intermediate and advanced learners did not. This was not due to the input received in the L2, but because they perceived the intransitive construction as less prototypical and "too Dutch" so they tried to avoid transferring it. It is important to note that this principle does not refer as much to differences in the grammar forms as to the way speakers conceptualize experience. Kellerman (1995) illustrates its principle with the thinking for speaking hypothesis (Slobin 1991, 1996a), which captures how linguistic thought works when we are verbalising experience using lexical and grammatical categories of our language(s). Slobin (1993) considers that the thinking for speaking patterns are very difficult to restructure in a second language and this is assumed by Kellerman too, who considers that his principle presupposes that thinking for speaking is inaccessible to the individual consciousness (Kellerman 1995: 141).

In the 21st century, the focus of transfer research is in finding explanations related to how the phenomenon takes place in the brain (Jarvis and Pavlenko 2008). Connections between bilinguals' languages are found in long-term memory and may offer underlying explanations for transfer. Research has identified how these connections are formed, changed and kept. There is also evidence for how languages are activated in the brain and how the knowledge of a language can activate and interfere with the use of another language (see Jarvis and Pavlenko 2008).

3.2 Types of cross-linguistic influence

Some of the main problems found in transfer studies stem from overlooking its complexity and from approaching this phenomenon from a simplistic perspective. Odlin (1989) explains that transfer is not a consequence of linguistic habits, nor the mere interference between two linguistic systems, because we can find different outcomes in the form of positive and negative transfer. Besides, transfer does not always follow the same direction. The second language can influence the first language or a second language can influence a third. Although cross-linguistic influence is generally identified via lexical items and false friends, it can also help in cognate facilitation (Helms-Park and Dronjic 2016). Importantly, transfer can occur at any language level and it is not exclusive to lexical items.

Odlin (1989) classifies transfer depending on the language level in which transfer is produced. For example, transfer can occur at a discourse level in politeness issues in relation to the interlocutors' face in speech acts such as requests, apologies and greetings. Transfer is also related to pragmatics when the conversation and narrative styles are transferred from the L1. At the semantic level, Odlin recognizes both positive and negative transfer. The ability to recognize cognates (terms that are similar in form and meaning in the L1 and the L2) can have beneficial effects in the language acquisition process, for example in reading comprehension. However, the best-known case of transfer is probably false friends, i.e. words that are similar in form but different in meaning. Transfer seems to be less frequent at morphological level, but syntactic transfer can be found in simoultaneous and sequential bilinguals. For example, Yip and Matthews (2007) show Cantonese word order transfer in bilingual children. In other cases, syntactic transfer can be positive, in areas such as the acquisition and use of articles or relative sentences. Finally, phonetics and phonology are areas in which transfer occurs more clearly and where it is more difficult to overcome.

R. Ellis (1994: 302) distinguishes between the type of transfer according to the effect on the second language of the learner. He argues that there are four types of transfer. The first one is negative transfer. This has received most of researchers' attention, as they attempt to determine whether errors are due to cross-linguistic influence or to general processes of language acquisition. The second type of transfer is facilitation (positive transfer). In this case, the influence of the mother tongue can also be beneficial for the learner. This does not mean that errors will not be produced, as they are part of the acquisition process. Rather, this means that the cases of positive transfer have as a result a minor proportion of mistakes in a given aspect. The third type of transfer is avoidance, which refers to cases in which speakers avoid the use of certain constructions because they find them difficult due to the language contrasts. The effects of this type are not translated into errors, but into omissions. Finally, the fourth type of transfer is overuse, i.e. the use of a structure with excessive frequency. R. Ellis (1994: 305) points out that overuse can be due to a general cognitive process, but he also admits that in some cases it can be due to transfer.

Jarvis and Pavlenko (2008) provide a comprehensive classification of transfer. They develop a detailed account of the different types, which attends to a range of factors.

Table 1: Types of cross-linguistic influence. Adaptaded from Jarvis and Pavlenko (2008: 20).

Dimension	Types of Cross-Linguistic Influence
Area of language knowledge/use	phonological, orthographic, lexical, semantic, morphological, syntactic, discursive, pragmatic, sociolinguistic
Directionality	forward, reverse, lateral bi- or multi-directional
Cognitive level	linguistic or conceptual
Type of knowledge	Implicit or explicit
Intentionality	Intentional or non intentional

Table 1 (continued)

Dimension	Types of Cross-Linguistic Influence
Mode	Productive or receptive
Channel	Aural or visual
Form	Verbal or nonverbal
Manifestation	Overt or covert
Outcome	Positive or negative

Research on transfer has traditionally focused on transfer from the L1 into the L2. However, the L2 can also influence the L1 or the L3, etc. Jarvis and Pavlenko (2008) use three terms: forward transfer, reverse transfer and lateral transfer to define these possibilities. The L1 has a special status, however, some studies on reverse transfer show that it should not be understood as unchangeable but rather as variable (Gullberg 2011).

3.3 Conceptual transfer and psychotypology

Jarvis and Pavlenko (2008) highlight the importance of distinguishing between linguistic and conceptual transfer, especially between semantic and conceptual transfer. The first deals with phenomena that are related to the linguistic system, particularly with meaning. They give the example of cases like *He bit himself in the language* instead of *He bit his tongue* in English by a native speaker of Finnish. This transfer is produced because in Finnish there is only one form, *kieli*, that covers these two meanings 'tongue' and 'language'. This is a case of semantic transfer because it is at semantic but not at conceptual level.

However, conceptual transfer is defined as the influence that one language can exert on another at a cognitive level. In this sense, conceptual transfer is related to Slobin's (1991, 1996a, 1996b) theory, which includes two dynamic entities: *speaking* and *thinking*, and also the specific type of thinking that is carried out in the process of speaking, the *thinking for speaking*. According to the literature, cross-linguistic influence is produced in the *thinking for speaking* and the *thinking*. For example, Jarvis and Pavlenko (2008: 120) explain that when an L1 English learner of Russian asks for a *chashka* 'cup' in relation for a plastic cup, transfer is semantic but also conceptual, because she does not know the contents of this conceptual category. In Russian this type of liquid container belongs to the category of glasses (*stakany*), whilst in English plastic and paper containers for drinks are peripheral members of the category of cups. Therefore even though both languages have equivalents for its translation, conceptual categories are mediated by these words being different in their peripheral members. Jarvis and Pavlenko (2008) claim that the acquisition of an L2 includes restructuring the conceptual categories existing in the L1. Conceptual transfer originates from conceptual representation, even though it has implications for semantic representations, i.e. unions between concepts and words. It is important to highlight that conceptual transfer does not exclude peripheral members of categories. Jarvis and Pavlenko give other examples such as the differences between *ser* and *estar* 'be' in Spanish and their uses by L1 English speakers. In any case, Cognitive Linguistics understands semantics as conceptual, and therefore the differences between semantic and conceptual transfer would be more understood as a matter of degree than a clear-cut distinction from our cognitive postulates.

Jarvis and Pavlenko (2008) identify eight semantic domains that are prone to cross-linguistic influence and which are all basic for communicating our experience and about our environment. These are objects (in relation to prototypes), emotions, personality (in relation to participants' roles and social distance), grammatical gender, number, time, space and motion. As will be further explained in the next chapter, there are several studies on the expression of Manner and Path of motion, following Talmy's (1991) typological classification of languages based on how motion events are verbalized and Slobin's thinking for speaking hypothesis (1991, 1996a). Jarvis (2007) himself links conceptual transfer and the thinking for speaking hypothesis. He considers that conceptual transfer includes thinking for speaking and goes beyond it. In this sense, thinking for speaking and neo-Whorfian assumptions about the effect of language on thought are not the only factors that can lie behind cross-linguistic influence. However, both are interrelated and conceptual transfer is crucial in studies which focus on thinking for speaking in a second language (Cadierno 2004) or re-thinking for speaking (N. Ellis and P. Robinson 2008).

Conceptual transfer is closely related to prototypicity, i.e. the speakers' perceptions of the degree to which a structure or meaning is more or less prototypical. Learners' perceptions of their own language can lead them to consider some constructions as non-transferable because they feel these constructions are too similar to their L1 and therefore non-acceptable in the L2. These perceptions are related to prototypicity and what speakers consider to be very specific of their own first language. This has been studied, for example, in relation to the meanings of *break* and its Dutch equivalent *brekken* (Kellerman 1978), and English prepositions (Ijaz 1986; Alonso Alonso, Cadierno, and Jarvis 2016).

A concept closely related to protoypicity is the perception of language distance. Ringbom (2016) also notes that if both languages are closely related, their formal similarities allow for bases for at least minimal comprehension before learning. It is natural to connect new information in the L2 with prior knowledge, especially of forms. When the target language items are semantically transparent, equivalences are more easily established, while having vocabulary knowledge helps text comprehension. The learning burden is then lighter than for learners of distant languages. Kellerman (1977) coins the concept of psychotypology and refers to the perceptions that speakers have about the language distance between the first and the second language. According to Kellerman, learners have a psychotypology, i.e. a set of perceptions about the language distance. It is this that causes (or rejects) potential transfer rather than the actual distance between the languages.

4 Cognitive Linguistics and second language acquisition

Cognitive Linguistics focuses on the relation between language and cognition, including psychological, anthropological and cultural aspects. Cognitive Linguistics includes several theoretical models that share three main tenets (Geeraerts and Cuyckens 2008; N. Ellis and Cadierno 2009; Ibarretxe-Antuñano and Valenzuela 2021). First, language is integrated with other human cognitive abilities, such as memory, attention and categorization. Second, language is symbolic and motivated: the relations between the form and the meaning are not arbitrary but motivated. Finally, language acquisition is usage-based and thus our knowledge of language is based on the abstraction of symbolic units extracted from the regular use of language.

4.1 Usage-based approaches to SLA

It is important to note that when dealing with Usage-Based approaches we do not think of a unified theory, but rather of different approaches that share interest and basic tenets. N. Ellis (2003) reviews the relationship between Cognitive Linguistics and Second Language Acquisition. He explains that different directions in usage-based linguistics represented by emergentists, functional linguists and cognitive linguists share the same views about language: that it is usage-based and it develops according to functional needs. Instead of considering grammar to be innate, they consider that language emerges from significant linguistic experiences. In other words, they think that the regularities in syntax emerge from the intermodal evidence collected when using and understanding language throughout the learner's life (N. Ellis 2003: 66). In this process *chunks* play a fundamental role. They are the result of memorizing frequent collocations. When speakers learn the formula an associative frequency learning takes place.

It has been observed that native speakers of a language know a lot about their sequences at all levels, i.e. what is more likely to be produced after a given phoneme or word. N. Ellis (2003, 2008) explains how psycholinguistic experiments show that we can easily grasp regularities, because we process more easily and more quickly the linguistic elements that meet our expectations. These expectations come from the unconscious analysis of the probabilities that we find in the input. In this sense, the most frequent sequences are perceived as chunks. As a result, short-term memory is larger for the regular sequences that have been experienced in the language (L1 or L2) than for irregular sequences. It is thus considered that chunking is one of the learning mechanisms to acquire meaning. This consists of joining a set of chunks that are already formed in memory and insert them in a higher unit (N. Ellis 2003: 78).

A more recent cognitive approach to second language acquisition is the Complex Adaptive System Principles for Bilingualism (CASP) model put forward by Filipović and Hawkins (2013, 2019). They propose a set of principles for a multi-factor model of bilingual language acquisition and use, including SLA. The model explains how multiple factors, linguistic, psycholinguistic and sociolinguistic, interact in different ways on different occasions of use resulting in different outputs by the same bilingual speaker, or the same outputs by different speakes. These authors consider that the non-occurrence of transfer is as relevant as its occurrences, and that the interrelation of multiple factors is what determines (i) what is and what is not possible in the interlanguages of the learners, and (ii) when transfer should (or should not) occur. One of the most important implications of this model is that positive transfer is maximized in the learning process. The properties of the L1 that are also present in the L2 are learned more easily and with less effort. They are therefore good for learning and processing and enhance the expressive power and communicative efficiency. However, all the features that are common in both languages are not necessarily transferred, since other factors, such as frequencies of use of a specific item may not be matched in the two languaes and this would impact the frequency of input or exposure in the L2.

In the case of negative transfer, Filipović and Hawkins consider it to be a consequence of a complex mechanism that involves a push-pull relationship among different principles: the desire to maximize expressive power and communicative efficiency and, at the same time, to minimize learning and processing effort. In other words, negative transfer is not maximized, unlike positive transfer, but it still does occur because L2 speakers aim to achieve expressive power and communicative effects in their L2 just like they would do in their L1.

In the later version of the model Filipović and Hawkins (2019) argue that both positive and negative transfer are driven by the same mechanism, and they formulate this as the principle of "Maximize Common Ground". They explain that both types of transfer are actually motivated by the need to facilitate learning and processing, which the bilingual mind tries to achieve by bringing the two languages closer together. How closer they come will depend on the three types of factors identified: linguistic (typological proximity/distance), internal-psycholinguistics (e.g. proficiency levels) and external-sociolinguistic (e.g. conversation with a monolingual vs. another bilingual, or formal vs. informal setting). The Maximizing Common Ground principle predicts that when the two languages share an element and its processing mechanisms they will be used more frequently in both languages. However, if the languages do not share a construction, word meaning or grammatical rule and its associated mechanisms, the common ground will be created by the introduction of a new shared entity preferably within the limits of the grammatical and usage conventions of the languages. When these conventions are violated the cause will be due to internal (psycholinguistic) or external (sociolinguistic) factors.

4.2 Cognitive Linguistics theoretical models applied to SLA

Cognitive Linguistics is a very relevant approach for second language acquisition, as it considers language an integral part of cognition. It does not present a clear dichotomy between grammar and lexis nor between linguistic and encyclopaedic meaning, which are considered clines rather than clear-cut dichotomies.

The lack of imposed dichotomies helps in the study of second language acquisition and teaching. Previous linguistic approaches were focused on these dichotomies and on ideal speakers, and their theories constrained SLA and bilingualism. In this sense, Cognitive Linguistics brings a new perspective that is easily applicable to SLA. In fact, this application can be seen from the number of collective volumes, handbooks and books in relation to the subject. Some of the most relevant ones are Pütz & Niemeier (2001) *Applied Cognitive Linguistics I: Theory and Language acquisition* and Pütz, Niemeier and Dirven (2001) *Applied Cognitive Linguistics II: Language Pedagogy*; Achard and Niemeier's (2004) *Cognitive Linguistics, Second Language Acquisition, and Foreign Language Teaching*; Boers and Lindstromberg's (2008) *Cognitive Linguistic Approaches to Teaching Vocabulary and Phraseology*; de Knop and T. de Rycker's (2008) *Cognitive Approaches to Pedagogical Grammar*; P. Robinson and N. Ellis's (2008) *Handbook of Cognitive Linguistics and Second Language Acquisition*; Littlemore's (2009) *Applying Cognitive Linguistics to Second Language Teaching*; Holme's (2009) *Cognitive Linguistics and Language Teaching*; de Knop, Boers and A. de Rycker's (2010) *Fostering Language Teaching Efficiency through Cognitive Linguistics*; and Tyler's (2012) *Cognitive Linguistics and Second Language Learning*. The applications of Cognitive Linguistics have also inspired a number of publications: the special section in the *Annual Review of Cognitive Linguistics, Constructing a Second Language* edited by N. Ellis and Cadierno (2009), the special issue on Applied Cognitive Linguistics in SLA and Teaching in the *AILA Review* edited by Littlemore and Juchem-Grundmann (2010), the special issue on *Applying Cognitive Linguistics: Figurative Language in Use, Constructions and Typology* by Piquer-Píriz and Alejo-González (2016), republished in 2018. In this section an overview of the application of the different perspectives within Cognitive Linguistics is presented, with a special focus on the acquisition of Spanish as a second language.

Cognitive Linguistics is a model that includes different theories that share the main tenets that were introduced at the beginning of this section: language as an integrated part of cognition, language as motivated and symbolic, and a usage-based approach to language acquisition. The main theories under the umbrella of Cognitive Linguistics are the Theory of Conceptual Metaphor (Lakoff and Johnson 1980), Cognitive Grammar (Langacker 1987), Cognitive Semantics (Talmy 1985, 2000a, 2000b), the Theory of Mental Spaces and Conceptual Blending (Fauconnier 1994), Frame semantics (Fillmore 1977) and Construction Grammar (Goldberg 1995). All these models have been successfully applied to the acquisition of second languages, mainly in relation to English as a foreign language. In the case of the acquisition of Spanish as a foreign language, Cadierno and Hijazo-Gascón (2013) and Hijazo-Gascón and Llopis-García (2019) show that the development of the field has focused mainly on Cognitive Grammar and Cognitive Semantics, and consequently these will be theories featured here. For more recent developments, the reader can see the Special Issue of *IRAL* edited by Llopis-García and Hijazo-Gascón (2019) and the handbook of Cognitive Linguistics and Spanish as an L2/FL edited by Ibarretxe-Antuñano, Cadierno and Castañeda Castro (2019).

Cognitive Grammar is a Cognitive Linguistic theory that has been widely applied to L2 acquisition, in particular in relation to prepositions. In this view of language, for example, the human cognitive ability to shift attention can be reflected on language. Langacker (1987) exemplifies this by illustrating the use of the passive voice, showing that language can provide us with conventional means of directing attention or raising the profile of certain aspects of an event. Attention can be focused on the agent of the event if we use the active voice (*He broke the window*), or in the patient of the event if we use the passive voice (*The window was broken by him*). In the case of Spanish, this perspective has been used in the explanation of complex phenomena in the Spanish language such as the middle voice in Spanish, which would be a means of directing the attention to the end point of the event or the change of state, as in *se rompió la ventana* 'the window broke' (Maldonado 1999, 2019). This has been also used in relation to spatial prepositions, for example to explain the contrasts between *por* and *para* (Delbeque 1996; Mendo Murillo 2019).

Cognitive Grammar has also been applied to SLA. For example, Tyler and V. Evans (2003) and Tyler (2008) work on prepositions in English as a second language. Lowie and Verspoor (2004) also examine the role that input frequency has in relation to the acquisition of L2 prepositions. Coventry and Guijarro-Fuentes (2008) also focus on spatial language from this perspective. In the case of Spanish as a second language, Cognitive Grammar has been used to tackle some of the most challenging aspects for students of Spanish as an L2, including the temporal verb system (Ruiz Campillo 2005; Alonso-Aparicio and Llopis-García 2019), the uses of *se* (Maldonado 2019), verbal aspect (Castañeda Castro 2006), the contrast *ser* and *estar* 'be' (Castañeda Castro and Ortega Olivares 2019), the subjunctive mood (Llopis-García 2010), articles (Montero Gálvez 2019), comparative constructions (Alhmoud, Castañeda Castro, and Cadierno 2019) and prepositions (Llopis-García 2015), in particular for *por* and *para* (Lam 2009; Mendo Murillo 2019). Some general overviews of the advantages of using Cognitive Grammar for the teaching of Spanish as a foreign language can be found in Castañeda Castro (2012), Llopis-García, Real-Espinosa, and Ruiz Campillo (2012) and Castañeda Castro (2014). The productive research on this approach has led to the creation of pedagogical materials that are well known in the Spanish as a Foreign Language teaching sphere, such as Alonso Raya et al.'s (2005) *Gramática básica del estudiante de español* and Chamorro et al.'s (2006) *El ventilador*.

Cognitive semantics and its relation to Cognitive Linguistics is applied to SLA mainly in relation to Talmy's semantic typology of motion events (Talmy 1985, 1991, 2000a, 2000b) and also in relation to the thinking for speaking hypothesis (Slobin 1991, 1996a, 1996b). As will be extensively explained in the next chapter, the thinking for speaking hypothesis consists of the effects of the language one speaks on memory and attention during the process of verbalization. The question for SLA researchers in this area is to determine whether it is possible or not to have a different thinking for speaking in an L2 (Cadierno 2004) or *re-thinking for speaking* (P. Robinson and N. Ellis 2008). In this sense, as Cadierno and Hijazo-Gascón (2013) point out, research on thinking for speaking in an L2 is closely related to the studies on transfer or cross-linguistic influence mentioned earlier. Several books have been published on this topic, such as Han and Cadierno (2010) and Pavlenko (2011), see also Cadierno (2017) for an overview. In the case of Spanish as a foreign language, several studies have analysed the change in thinking for speaking patterns in Spanish by English speakers (Montrul 2001; Negueruela et al. 2004; Hohenstein, Eisenberg, and Naigles 2006; Stam 2006; among others, see Hijazo-Gascón, Cadierno, and Ibarretxe-Antuñano 2019 for an overview). Also noteworthy are the pioneering contributions of Cadierno (2004, 2008; Cadierno and Ruiz 2006) on Spanish by Danish learners. Latest developments have drawn the interest of scholars into other areas of motion, such as motion and aspect (Bylund 2011a, 2011b; Bylund and Jarvis 2011) and caused motion, particularly placement events (Cadierno, Ibarretxe-Antuñano, and Hijazo-Gascón 2016; Ibarretxe-Antuñano, Cadierno, and Hijazo-Gascón 2016). An overview of motion events and thinking for speaking and its applications to SLA will be provided in detail in the following chapter.

Although Cognitive Grammar and Semantic Typology have been the main areas of development in Cognitive Linguistics and SLA, in recent years interest has increased regarding the application of other cognitive approaches to the acquisition and teaching of Spanish as a second language, namely the theory of Conceptual Metaphor and Construction Grammar.

The Theory of Conceptual Metaphor (Lakoff and Johnson 1980) is a good example of this pre-eminence of figurative meaning, as it considers metaphor as a cognitive device to express abstract meaning and not just an ornament of literary language. In this sense, metaphor is a key concept for Cognitive Linguistics. It is produced according to specific linguistic and cultural preferences, through the concept of embodiment of our physical experiences. For example, we say that *we are fuming* when we are angry, by using the metaphor ANGER IS FLUID BOILING IN A CONTAINER, because of our experiences how our body temperature rises and our faces redden when we are feeling angry. As tools for abstract semantic domains, metaphor and metonymy is an interesting starting point when studying questions related to semantics, pragmatics, discourse competence and communicative strategies. Examples include the studies in Cameron and Low (1999) and the work by Piquer-Piriz on children's L2 acquisition (Piquer-Píriz 2008). Work on conceptual metaphor has led some authors to put forward theoretical concepts such as metaphorical competence (Danesi 1988), which can be defined as the ability to identify how the L2 uses metaphor to codify and represent abstract concepts. Others have pointed out the importance of metaphors in relation to learning strategies (Littlemore 2001). The application of conceptual metaphor to Spanish language acquisition is still in its initial stages, but there have been some contributions in this line (Acquaroni 2008; Hijazo-Gascón 2011b; Gómez Vicente 2013; Lantolf and Bobrova 2014; see also Suárez-Campos and Hijazo-Gascón 2019 and Suárez-Campos, Hijazo-Gascón, and Ibarretxe-Antuñano 2019 for an overview).

Finally, Goldberg's (1995) Construction Grammar has been also applied to second language acquisition. A general overview of how the model can be applied can be found in Goldberg and Casenhiser (2008). In the case of Spanish, there are several studies that contrast English and Spanish. Gonzálvez-García (2009, 2019) has extensively worked on these contrasts from a more theoretical perspective. Gras (2011) studies different types of independent constructions introduced by subordinate markers in Spanish. He also examines insubordinate *que*-constructions in detail (Gras 2016). Valenzuela and Rojo have studied different constructions in L2 English by Spanish learners, such as the ditransitive construction (2008a) and the transitive, ditransitive, caused motion and resultative constructions (2008b). There is a growing interest in exploring the potential of Construction Grammar for second language acquisition and teaching: for example see the studies collected in de Knop and Gilquin (2016). In the case of Spanish, initial work on this area has focused on different types of constructions, such as pedagogical proposals for the acquisition of the caused motion construction (Hijazo-Gascón, Cadierno, and Ibarretxe-Antuñano 2016), and the acquisition of constructions with verbs of change, such as *ponerse, volverse, hacerse*, etc. (Ibarretxe-Antuñano and Cheikh-Kamis 2019).

As we have seen in this section, the use of Cognitive Linguistic theories in SLA is increasing their relevance. Most studies focus on English as a Foreign Language. However, research into the acquisition of Spanish as a second language is also part of this trend and, as a consequence, there is increasing interest in applying Cognitive Linguistics to Spanish Second Language Acquisition. This can be seen in the establishment of the first panel on Cognitive Linguistics and Spanish as a Foreign Language at the AELCO Conference 2016 in Alcalá de Henares, and the subsequent special issue in *IRAL* edited by Llopis-García and Hijazo-Gascón (2019). The publication of handbooks on Cognitive Linguistics in Spanish (Cuenca and Hilferty 1999; Ibarretxe-Antuñano and Valenzuela 2012) has contributed to a wider dissemination of Cognitive Linguistics in the Hispanic World. The new volume on Cognitive Linguistics and Acquisition of Spanish as a Foreign Language edited by Ibarretxe-Antuñano, Cadierno, and Castañeda (2019) will pave the way for future applications of different Cognitive Linguistics models.

5 Moving across chapters

The structure of this volume is as follows. There are six chapters, including this first introductory chapter in which the main tenets of transfer research and Applied Cognitive Linguistics have been explained. In Chapter 2 the semantic typology of motion events by Talmy (1985, 1991, 2000a, 2000b) and the thinking for speaking hypothesis by Slobin (1991, 1996a, 1996b, 1997b, 2000, 2004) are presented. The second part of that chapter concerns how these theoretical concepts relate to the field of second language acquisition and bi/multilingualism.

Chapter 3 offers a detailed literature review on the specificities of motion events in each of the languages under study, namely Spanish, Italian, French and German. It is important to have a deeper understanding of the commonalities and differences between the languages from a typological point of view before embarking on a study on conceptual transfer and second language acquisition. The motivation for this typological research is driven by two main research questions. First, is it really true that all Romance languages behave as a monolithic group? Assuming that there are differences among these languages, the second research question is: Do inter- (German vs. Spanish) and intra-typological (French vs. Italian vs. Spanish) differences trigger conceptual transfer in the acquisition of Spanish as a second language?

The choice of these languages is deliberate. As will be explained in Chapter 3, most research focuses on contrasts between English and Spanish. However other satellite-framed languages seem more prototypical than English (see for example Pavlenko (2014) on her claims that Russian is a more prototypical satellite-framed language). German, a Germanic language with less influence of Romance languages than English, presents in this sense an interesting point of contrast with Romance languages. The differences among Romance languages have been noted in the literature, but without a focused empirical study like the one presented here. Finally, this volume is also an original contribution in that the focus of the acquisition study is a verb-framed language, while most of the studies on this area prefer to use satellite-framed languages as the target languages. However, as shown by the results presented here, conceptual transfer is also present when verb-framed languages are the target languages, even when the first language is also verb-framed and even genetically close.

Chapter 4 contains a typological study in which French, German, Italian and Spanish motion events are compared. This is an innovative study in that not only inter- but also intra-typological differences are found. A contrastive study between the four languages involved was carried out in order to shed light on these contrasts and is presented in Chapter 4. The results of this study show that languages belonging to the same typological group and genetic family (Romance in this case) can present interesting differences that should not be overgeneralised.

The study in Chapter 4 prepares the ground for a second study on the crosslinguistic influences from these languages into Spanish as a second language. This study is presented in Chapter 5 and shows how the inter- (German vs. Spanish) and intra-typological (French vs. Italian vs. Spanish) differences have an impact on cross-linguistic influence and conceptual transfer. The analysis reported in Chapter 5 includes contrasts between the different groups and also between the same speakers in both their languages. Since it does not rely exclusively on the comparison with the native speaker, this methodology is coherent with the multilingual turn in second language acquisition research (Ortega 2010, 2013). It is also congruent with the rigor of the methodological proposals for transfer research (Jarvis 2000, 2010).

Finally, Chapter 6 summarizes the main findings of both studies and provides insights into how these findings can contribute to a better understanding of how the processes of conceptual transfer work in a bi/multilingual mind. The aim of this chapter is also to propose a practical application of the theoretical findings of the study for the foreign language classroom. Very often these sorts of semantic contrasts have been ignored in language learning training and the focus has been either on grammar and syntax or in communication. The pedagogical proposal involves more attention to be paid to semantics in the foreign language class. This will include a focus on language contrasts in meaning in order to prevent negative transfer and foster positive transfer when appropriate.

The results presented in this monograph are not only relevant for the theories of Language and Cognition and Multilingualism. This book also makes a contribution for pedagogical translation, as an approach that enables semantics to be dealt properly with in the foreign language classroom. Semantics has largely been neglected in modern foreign language curricula and teaching materials even though it plays a key role in how we conceptualize and categorize the world using our languages. Overall, the aim of this volume is to shed light on how our concepts and categories are reshaped in the process of acquiring a new language.

Chapter 2
Motion events: Semantic typology and its acquisition

1 Semantics of motion

Motion is probably one of the most studied areas in semantics. The European linguistics tradition noticed very early cross-linguistic contrasts between motion verbs in French and German. Tesnière (1959: 307–310) distinguishes between movement (*mouvement* in French) and displacement (*déplacement* in French). Movement is intrinsic and is related to the properties of the subject (e.g. differences between *walk* and *run*), while displacement is extrinsic and involves a change of place (e.g. *enter*, *exit*). The focus of this distinction is thus not as much in the subject moving as in the space. According to Tesnière (1959), German verbs tend to express movement, the very action of motion, whereas French verbs tend to express displacement in the same way that German particles do. This classification has been used in later studies (Cifuentes Honrubia 1999; Morimoto 2001; Wälchi 2006; among others). Bally (1965: 349) also compares German and French and points out that movement penetrates all German syntax, while that of French gives the impression of rest, of immobility. He also examines the relationship of German particles with French verbs. These were the first authors to notice what would develop into a broad field of study. However, as Talmy explains in Ibarretxe-Antuñano (2005: 327), even though Tesnière and Bally observe the differences of what he will call Path and Manner between German and French, they did not establish a systematic framework of this phenomenon.

Other perspectives have also tackled the expression of motion, for example Fábregas (2007) and Nikitina (2008) following Generative Grammar. One of the main theories in this area is Jackendoff's Conceptual Semantics (1983, 1987, 1990). It consists of a modular conception of grammar with three levels of structure: phonological, syntactic and conceptual. Jackendoff (1990) considers concepts as mental representations that serve as the meaning of linguistic expressions. This mental representation is common to all natural languages. According to this author, there is not an exact correspondence between conceptual and syntactic categories, but they are connected by means of correspondence rules. This model has been very successful, especially in research focusing on the relationship between verb and argument (Levin 1993; Levin and Rappaport Hovav 1995, 2005). However, the focus in this book will be on Talmy's perspective of conceptual semantics (1991, 2000a, 2000b) because it has been adopted on multiple studies on language and cognition in monolingual and bilingual contexts. Talmy's model is also focused on cross-linguistic differences and the focus of this research is the study of typological contrasts and their effect in SLA.

Talmy's conceptual semantics stems from two main ideas. First, language is the vehicle of meaning. Second, language is the window that allows us to observe how speakers of a certain language conceptualize reality. Therefore, the linguistic meanings observed in a language are a reflection of the conceptual structure, that is, the mental representations that speakers have of the surrounding reality. This conceptual structure consists of a limited set of schematic systems. This is the "architecture" to support the conceptual content expressed by the lexicon. These core schemes are the *configurational system*, which imposes the spatial and temporal structure on a scene and divides it into actions and participants; the *perspective system*, which specifies the point of view from which the scene is observed; the *attentional system* that directs the attention to one or several parts of the scene; the *force dynamics system* that presents the interactions between participants in terms of force, and the *cognitive state system*, which presents the elements forming the mental state of an agent.

Talmy (2000b: 215) considers that the human mind in perception or conception can extend a boundary around a portion of what would be a continuum, such as space or time. This portion achieves the property of being a single unit entity by the operations of very general cognitive processes, namely *conceptual partitioning* and *ascription of entityhood*. This new category is thus perceived or conceptualized as an event. In other words, according to Talmy (2000b), an event is a type of entity that includes within its limits a continuous correlation between a part of the qualitative domain that identifies and a part of the temporal continuum. These events can be unitary or complex. Unitary events are represented by a simple sentence and their conceptualization consists of components that are not events themselves. Complex events are represented syntactically by complex sentences and in their conceptualization are formed by a main and a subordinate event. In some cases an event can be understood as complex due to its conceptualization but represented as unitary, i.e. with only one sentence in syntax. This is a general cognitive process called conceptual integration of events. The result of this integration is a macro-event, represented by a simple sentence, but with a structure and conceptual content similar to that of complex events. This is the case with (1), which can be paraphrased as (2) (Talmy 2000a: 217):

(1) *The candle blew out*

(2) *The candle went out because something blew on it*

These macro events have two parts: the *framing event* and the *supporting event*. The framing event is the main one and can be applied to different domains: motion or location in space events, contouring in time (aspect) events, events of change or constancy among states, events of correlation among actions and events of fulfillment or confirmation in the domain of realization. Each of these events presents the following features: (i) an entity working as a Figure, i.e. the physical object involved in the event, (ii) Ground elements, which indicate the location of the Figure, (iii) an activation process by which the Figure transits or is fixed in relation to the Ground, and (iv) an association function, by which the Figure is associated with the Ground elements. In the case of motion events, the activation process is the Motion component, that is, the process by which the Figure moves or remains static in relation to the Ground. The association function would be the Path component, which places the Figure in relation to the selected Ground elements. Precisely because of the fact that this association function is performed by the Path component, this is considered the *core schema*, i.e. the nuclear component of the event. Meanwhile, the supporting event adds other circumstances to the framing event. The main ones are Manner and Cause.

According to Talmy (1985: 60), motion events are "situations containing movement or the maintenance of a stationary location". He explains that "the basic motion event consists of one object (the 'Figure') moving or located with respect to another object (the reference object or 'Ground')". He states that four compulsory components are needed in a motion event. First, the Figure, which is the object that moves or could move. Second, the Ground, which is the reference point with respect to the trajectory or the location of the Figure. Third, the Movement itself is another component. Finally, the component of Path is the trajectory of the Figure with respect to the Ground. In Talmy (2000b: 53), three components of Path are defined: Vector, Conformation and Deixis. The Vector includes the departure, trajectory and arrival that a Figure performs in relation to a Ground. The Conformation is a geometrical complex that relates the Ground schema in a motion-aspect formula to the schema of a Ground object. For example, in English, if the movement is performed from a closed Ground, *out of* will be used. If the Ground is a surface, *off* will be used instead. Finally, the Deictic component presents two options: motion towards the deictic center or away from the deictic center. Sign languages can also present two components of Path: Contour and Direction.

There are two other components that are not compulsory but can appear in a motion event: Manner and Cause, as respectively shown in (3) and (4):

(3) He ran out of the room

(4) The wind blew the paper to the ground

Talmy (1985, 1991, 2000a, 2000b) establishes two typologies. He points out (in Ibarretxe-Antuñano 2006b), that both typologies are complementary, since they study meaning and linguistic expression from two different perspectives. The main difference between both classifications lies in the fact that the first typology is focused on the semantic components of the verb that are lexicalized in the verb, while in the second typology languages are classified according to the encoding of the semantic component of Path.

Talmy (1985) aims to examine the relations between form and meaning and how associations are made according to lexicalization patterns. In this sense, motion events enable him to detect differences among languages in how they create these form-meaning associations. He considers that all languages fall into one of the three types of lexicalization patterns that he identifies. Talmy (1985: 62) considers that in all languages one of these types will be the most characteristic, but not necessarily the only one that each language contains. In order to be considered the most characteristic pattern, this lexicalization pattern must be (i) colloquial and not literary, (ii) frequent in use and not occasional, and (iii) dominant in language, i.e. that other semantic notions are expressed in the same way.

The first Talmian typology is that of motion verbs, depending on the components of motion that are encoded most frequently in the main verb. There are three main groups:

A. Motion + Manner/Cause

The verb root is associated to the components of Motion and one of the optional components, either Manner or Cause. This applies to agentive and non-agentive verbs, as can be seen in the following examples from Talmy (1985: 62):

(5) *The rock rolled down the hill* (Motion + Manner, non-agentive)

(6) *I rolled the keg into the storeroom* (Motion + Manner, agentive)

(7) *I twisted the cork out of the bottle* (Motion + Cause, agentive)

(8) *The pencil blew off the table* (Motion + Cause, non-agentive)

This is the most characteristic lexicalization pattern in most Indo-European languages (excepting the Romance languages) and in Mandarin Chinese. The compulsory Path component is expressed in these cases in a Prepositional Phrase, as in (6) *into the storeroom*, or in what Talmy defines as satellite, as in (5) *down*, in (7) *out*, and in (8) *off*. As will be explained below, the notion of satellite is one of the most controversial issues in Talmy's framework. He defines it as a constituent of the verb root, which is not an auxiliary, nor a nominal or prepositional phrase. The verb and the satellite form what he calls verb complex. These satellites can be free words or affixes. Some examples are the English particles, the separable and inseparable German prefixes, Latin verbal prefixes, Mandarin verbal compounds, among others. It is worth remembering that being the most common lexicalization pattern does not imply being the only one present in a language.

B. Motion Path

In this type of lexicalization the verb root expresses two basic components: Motion and Path. If Manner of Cause is added, this must be done by means of a Prepositional Phrase, an Adverbial Phrase or a gerund. Talmy (1985: 69) illustrates this lexicalization type with Spanish examples:

(9) *La botella entró a la cueva flotando*
 The bottle enter.3SG.PST to the cave floating
 'The bottle entered the cave by floating'

(10) *Metí el barril en el almacén rodándolo*
 put.1SG.PST the keg in the storeroom rolling.it
 'I put the keg in the storeroom by rolling it'

(11) *Saqué el corcho de la botella retorciéndolo*
 take.1SG.PST the cork of the bottle twisting.it
 'I took the cork of the bottle by twisting it'

This type of lexicalization is the most characteristic one in Romance, Semitic and Polynesian languages. However, this does not imply that other types are not present in these languages. For example, Manner can be lexicalized in Spanish in cases like (12) even though this is not the most frequent pattern:

(12) *La pelota rodó hasta el final de la calle*
 The ball roll.3SG.PST until the end of the street
 'The ball rolled up to the end of the street'

C. Motion + Figure

The last type of lexicalization pattern encodes Motion and Figure in the verb. This lexicalization pattern can occur in some cases in English, as in (13):

(13) *It rained through the bedroom window*

This is not a very frequent lexicalization pattern in Indo-European languages, but it is the main lexicalization pattern in some American languages such as Navajo and most Hokan languages. Talmy studied one of the latter, Atsugewi, which was spoken in Northern California. This language shows verbal roots like *–lup-* 'move or be located in the case of a spherical, small and shiny object', used with candles and hailstones, *-caq-* 'move or be located in the case of a viscous object', used with frogs or excrement.

Talmy acknowledges that there are other types of lexicalization that are possible in different languages, but they are not the most characteristic pattern in any of them. This is the case with some English verbs which lexicalize Motion and Base (*to plane, to house*), Motion, Base and Path (*to box, to shelve*) or Motion, Figure and Path (*to powder*).

2 The typology of motion: Verb-framed and satellite-framed languages

The second typology proposed by Talmy classifies languages according to where the Path component is encoded. He defines conflation patterns as the fusion of conceptual elements. It is important to bear in mind that the union of semantic elements and superficial elements does not correspond one-to-one. A syntactic element can present several semantic elements in the conflation and vice versa.

In the case of motion events, it is considered that the core schema is formed by Motion and Path. Talmy (1991, 2000a, 2000b) establishes this typology based on the most characteristic pattern in which the conceptual structure of the macro event is projected onto the syntactic structure. If the core schema is projected onto a satellite, as in (14), and this is the most characteristic pattern in a language, this language is classified as a satellite-framed language. This is the case with English,

Latin, Mandarin Chinese or Atsugewi. If on the contrary, the core schema is frequently projected on the verb, as in (15) this language is a verb-framed language. The criteria to define if it is the most characteristic pattern are the same as the ones explained above for the first typology.

(14)   *The bottle floated out of the cave*

(15)   *La botella salió de la cueva flotando*
         the bottle exit.3SG.PST of the cave floating
         'The bottle exited the cave by floating'

In (14) the Path component is expressed in the satellite out, whereas in (15) this component is encoded in the verb salir 'exit', which is the main verb of the event. Since this typology was proposed, several studies and publications have been devoted to determining whether a given language belongs to the satellite-framed or to the verb-framed group. An exhaustive list is provided in Ibarretxe-Antuñano (2004d: 405) and reproduced here:

> Verb framed languages:
> Romance languages (Portuguese, Galician, Spanish, Catalan, French, Italian, etc.), Semitic languages (Arabic, Hebrew), Turkish, Basque, Korean, Greenlandic, Chantyal, Cebuano, Malay, Tagalog, Squliq, Saisiyat, American Sign Language and Dutch Sign Language

> Satellite framed languages:
> Germanic languages (German, Danish, English, Icelandic, Dutch, Swedish, Yiddish, etc.), Slavonic languages (Czech, Polish, Russian, Serbo-Croatian, etc.), Finnish, Hungarian, Mandarin Chinese, Walpiri

This dichotomy has inspired other researchers to test whether the two-way distinction is exhaustive and applicable to all languages. These studies focused first on how languages express motion, especially in relation to first language acquisition. This is the case with the studies collected in Berman and Slobin (1994) on German, Spanish, Hebrew, English and Turkish, which established a strong research methodology, followed later in other studies, such as the ones collected in Strömqvist and Verhoeven (2004). The results of these papers show crucial differences in terms of attention, language acquisition, rhetorical style and narrative building, depending on the affiliation of the first language of the speakers to the satellite-framed or the verb-framed group. These cross-linguistic differences have proved to be crucial for translation, cross-linguistic influence between the first and the second language, and the possible effects of lexicalization patterns in language processing and its potential influence in cognition in non-linguistic tasks. Despite its success and acceptance, this framework is not free of controversial debates, such as the notion of satellite and the difficulty in classifying some languages into one group or the other. These challenges for the typology and Talmy's responses (2012) will be explained in detail in Section 4. In the following section the focus will be on this typology's main implications for cognition and narrative effects.

3 Thinking for speaking hypothesis

Talmy's conceptual semantics and its typology of verb-framed and satellite-framed languages are the perfect illustration for Slobin's thinking for speaking hypothesis (1991, 1996a, 1996b, 2003). He puts forward this notion from a psycholinguistic angle, in relation to language acquisition. Thinking for speaking is "the special kind of thinking that is intimately tied to language –namely the thinking that is carried out, on-line, in the process of speaking" (Slobin 1991: 11). This mental activity involves selecting the characteristics of events that fit some conceptualization of the event and are readily encodable in the language (Slobin 1991).

The relation between language and thought was already present in 19th century linguists' debates, including von Humboldt, Sapir and Whorf. The interpretation of their writings led to the formulation of the Linguistic Relativity hypothesis. Its strong version, which is refuted today, is called linguistic determinism and considers that the language one speaks determines different conceptual structures and cognitive effects. The "weak" version, linguistic relativism, considers the relationship between language and thought in terms of influence (Lucy 1992). Relativism started hand in hand with the study of American languages and Linguistic Anthropology. Franz Boas argued for the need to have access to a people's language to understand their culture. He was fascinated by the different ways of classifying the world in different languages, for example the terms related to snow in Eskimo. His disciple Sapir paid more attention to linguistic structures and criticized the attempts to classify languages as more or less primitive. Whorf, Sapir's disciple, studied the Hopi language and aimed at describing the worldview of different peoples. He formulated the linguistic relativity principle (Whorf 1956) that considers that speakers of different languages are led to different observations and evaluations of these observations, such that they reach different points of view about the world.

After the rise of generativism and its postulates on Universal Grammar at the end of the fifties, the studies from the relativistic perspective were abandoned. It was not until years later, that this topic would receive some renewed attention, in response to the studies carried out by Berlin and Kay (1969) on color terms and by Lakoff and Johnson (1980) on conceptual metaphor. For example, Roberson and Davidoff (2000) show that verbal codes are crucial for categorial preception for colors. According to Regier and Kay (2009: 445), research shows: "that language affects color perception primarily in the right visual field probably via activation of language region of the left hemisphere, and that color naming reflects both universal and local determinants".

Cognitive Linguistics accepts linguistic relativity, i.e. the consideration that each language may have some influence on cognitive processes, but rejects the deterministic idea that our way of thinking and conceiving reality changes depending on the language one speaks. This perspective is known as *neo-relativism* (Lucy 1992) and has led to interesting results on the relationship between language and cognition, for example Boroditsky (2001) on time perception, Boroditsky, Schmidt, and Philips (2003) on the relation between grammar gender and cognition, and Levinson (2003) on absolute, relative and intrinsic frames of reference in different languages that affect how speakers navigate in space.

Choi and Bowerman (1991) claim that children use their language spatial terms appropriately from a very young age. In their study, Korean-speaking and English-speaking children did not categorize spatial situations according to a set of universal semantic principles, but according to the special categories present in their first language: English-speaking children distinguish consistently the notions of container and surface in their first uses of the prepositions *in* and *on*, whilst Korean-speaking children differentiate very early between fit tightly and fit loosely in correspondence with the Korean verbs *kkita* and *nehta*.

Slobin (1991, 1996b) considers that the classical conception needs to replace the static notions of *language* and *thought* by two dynamic notions: *speaking* and *thinking*. He claims that a part of the thinking is closely related to language. This would be the thinking activity that is carried out while speaking. Thinking for speaking is thus understood as the form of thinking that is mobilized during communication. In other words, it is the type of mental activity that works while utterances are formulated. The main difference with regard to Humboldt and Whorf's writings that inspired relativistic ideas is that Slobin considers that the concepts do exist in the mind independently of the language, while for the earlier authors the concept's existence depends on the linguistic structure.

Slobin (2003: 23) explains that the speakers of a given language adopt a perspective with respect to events and experiences when they talk about them, depending on the availability of linguistic resources. The development of this perspective adoption training begins in childhood and is resistant to changes in the second language acquisition process in adulthood. For example, Turkish has two different morphological markers (*-di* and *-mış*) to indicate whether the speaker was a witness or not of the information she is giving, as in the case of (16), taken from Özturk and Papafragou (2005: 1):

(16) *Çocuk oyun oynaidi*
      child game play.PST.EVI
      'The child played a game (I saw it)'

(17) *Çocuk oyun oynaimış*
      child game play.PST.EVI
      'The child played a game (I heard it/I was told → I inferred it)

The closest mechanism to express these degrees of evidentiality (Chafe and Nichols 1986; Willet 1988; Aikhenvald 2004) in Indo-European languages would be something like *It seems that the child played with a game* or *Apparently the child played with a game*. However, presenting this information in English is optional, while in Turkish it is compulsory as it is grammatically codified. These differences have discourse implications in each language, leading to a different rhetorical style, one of the key concepts in Slobin's framework.

These contrasts are present in several domains. For example, the Spanish tense and aspect system distinguishes between perfective, imperfective and progressive, but this distinction does not exist in Hebrew or in German (see Berman and Slobin 1994). In the case of spatial description, satellite-framed languages can easily encode the optional component of Manner in the main verb. However, verb framed languages do not tend to encode this component unless it is particularly relevant for discourse.

The thinking for speaking hypothesis was tested in different languages using the Frog story illustrations as the experimental stimuli. This is a well-known elicitation tool, used for the first time by Bamberg, one of Slobin's students. Speakers of a language are asked to describe the story in the children's book *Frog, where are you?* by Mercer Mayer (1969). The aim of the experiment is to obtain natural oral descriptions about how the characters move. This book was chosen because there is no text and the story is rich in motion events, which are depicted in the pictures. It is the story of a boy who has a frog in a pot and it runs away. They boy and his dog look for it in different places and they find several animals until they find it. During their search they go into places, they leave others, they fall from different places, etc.

Berman and Slobin's (1994) project used this elicitation tool in speakers of five different languages in four age groups: 3, 5, 9 years old and adults to observe the development of lexicalization patterns in the first language. The choice of languages allowed for cross-linguistic and inter-typological comparisons since two of these languages are satellite-framed (German and English) and the other three are verb-framed (Spanish, Turkish and Hebrew). The results show that speakers are closer to their first language than previously thought. This meant a growth in studies from this perspective, taking into account different languages and the implications for the study of first language acquisition, typology and rhetorical style.

Some of these studies are collected in Strömqvist and Verhoeven (2004), following the methodology and objectives in Berman and Slobin (1994) and covering fourteen languages: Aranda, Spanish, Basque, Greenlandic, Hebrew, English, Icelandic, American Sign Language, Japanese, Swedish, Thai, Turkish, Tzeltal and Walpiri. These contributions on different languages from different genetic families and different modalities (sign languages) have been crucial in improving and strengthening the theory and identifying some of the controversial issues that will be explained later. These studies show that what is not typically encoded in the grammar of the language tends to be ignored, while all the categories that are grammatically encoded in the language are persistently expressed from the age of three years old (Slobin 1996b).

Slobin (2003: 2) states that the effects of thinking for speaking do not have strong implications for perception and conceptualization. In other words, there is no difference in how a Turkish-speaker and an English-speaker perceive an event. However, studying the effects of thinking for speaking is relevant for the study of language in use. These effects are also related to effects in selective attention or in memory. Thinking for speaking includes all forms of language: production (talking, writing, signing) and reception (listening, reading, seeing) and the related mental processes (understanding, imagining, remembering). Motion events are an excellent semantic domain to study this hypothesis. These events are frequently codified in languages, as expressing how entities move is basic in every language, and at the same time, there are important differences in how each organizes the information, encoding semantic components in different formal elements.

Therefore, the thinking for speaking hypothesis has developed together with the typology of satellite and verb framed languages. Slobin (1991, 1996a, 1997a, 1997b, 2003; Özçalışkan and Slobin 2003) studies how the fact that satellite framed languages can easily encode Manner implies greater attention to this semantic component by speakers of these languages. In the case of speakers of verb-framed languages, they do not compensate for the expression of Manner in their discourse, because the linguistic elements they could use to express it are syntactically more complex. As a result, they tend to omit this component, and they express it only when it is of special relevance for discourse. There are other differences in the case of Path, despite this being a compulsory semantic component. Speakers of verb-framed languages encode it in the verb, expressing each part of the trajectory in a different sentence. However, speakers of satellite-framed languages produce more detailed trajectories, as they are expressed by means of different satellites and prepositional phrases. Finally, Slobin points out that verb-framed language narratives include more descriptions of the physical setting, leaving the Path to be inferred, while narratives by speakers of satellite-framed languages seem to be more focused on the action, producing more dynamic descriptions in which what is inferred is the physical setting.

Slobin considers that the existence of a linguistic mechanism to express a given concept favors its salience in rhetorical style. The typological frame of the motion event enables and limits the means of expression of the semantic components in a language. In this sense, whereas in English there is a broad array of possibilities to encode Manner in a verb (e.g. *prance, tiptoe, dash, trudge* . . .), in Spanish the number of Manner verbs is limited and restricted to general Manner verbs. Normally finer-grained distinctions need to be expressed in adverbs, gerunds or prepositional phrases, which make Manner less salient. Slobin's main hypotheses are that lexicalization patterns have consequences for the focalization of certain components and that this has an impact on the lexical choices and syntax of the narrative style.

The different levels of analysis carried out by Slobin (1996a) have established a research methodology and are followed by other authors for several languages, including the studies presented in this book. Therefore it is important to provide a detailed explanation of how these analyses are carried out. There are four main analyses:

1. Verbs. Slobin analyzes the total number of motion verbs used by speakers, including voluntary and caused motion verbs. He examines the number of types in each language, with a special focus on those encoding Manner. It is expected that satellite-framed languages have a larger number of verbs, both general motion and Manner of motion verbs. He also considers the addition (or not) of locative phrases to the verbs. He defines as bare verbs those cases in which the verb occurs without a locative addition. In these cases Path is elaborated only in the directionality encoded in the verb. This seems to be the most frequent pattern in verb-framed languages. Although both types of languages can add locative phrases to express the origin and/or the goal of the movement, it seems that satellite framed language speakers do add them more frequently than verb-framed language speakers.

Some studies using the Frog Story elicitation materials scrutinize all the verbs used throughout the narrative while some others performed the analyses only on elicited descriptions of the falling scenes in the story, because they are considered the richest source of in motion event descriptions. These key scenes are that of the dog, the beehive, the boy and the deer (see Figures 1 to 4).

Figure 1: The dog scene.

One of the scenes that has been widely used and focused on is that of the owl (Figure 3), in which an owl flies out of a tree and scares the boy who falls to the ground. This scene has been frequently analyzed to observe whether speakers use Manner or Path verbs to describe this motion event. As will be explained later, while all speakers express Path in some way, speakers of certain languages will not even mention Manner when describing the scene, neither in the verb nor in other linguistic elements.

2. Phrases. In the previous analysis, the verb-satellite combinations do not count as a bare verb and this has important implications. On the one hand, it is problematic because verb-framed languages do not have this category. On the other hand, the addition of a satellite does not mean a higher elaboration of Path, e.g. *fall* and *fall down* would both equate to the Spanish verb *caer(se)*. This is the main reason why Slobin presents the analysis between Minus Ground (including bare verbs and verb-satellite combinations) and Plus Ground (when verbs and satellites are accompanied by one or more pieces of information that specify

3 Thinking for speaking hypothesis — 35

Figure 2: The beehive scene.

Figure 3: The boy scene / The owl scene.

the Ground of the movement). This Ground can refer to the origin, the medium or the goal of motion. It seems that speakers of satellite-framed languages pay more attention to Path so they tend to include more Plus Ground cases, being Minus Ground infrequent. Speakers of verb-framed languages seldom include Plus Ground, as the Path component tends to be inferred.

3. Journeys. This concept designates a Complex Path, that is, an event in which several aspects of Path (origin, medium, and/or goal) are included. Journeys can be expressed in one or several sentences. Complex Paths are easily encoded in one sentence in satellite-framed languages, as exemplified by Slobin (1996a) in (18):

(18) *He [the deer] tips him off over a cliff into the water*

In verb-framed languages Complex Paths tend to be segmented in different sentences. This is coherent with the typology since Path information tends to be encoded in the verbs. Slobin hypothesizes the possibility that the reason why verb-framed language speakers produce fewer cases of Plus Ground might be because they use several sentences to express Complex Paths. In order to test this possibility he analyses the deer scene, in which the deer runs with the boy, stops on the edge of a cliff and throws the boy into the water below (see Figure 4).

Figure 4: The deer scene.

Slobin (1996a) divides the scene into six narrative segments to check if this compensation is made: (a) the deer starts running, (b) the deer runs, carrying the boy, (c) the deer stops on the edge of the cliff, (d) the deer throws the boy, (e) the boy and the dog fall, (f) the dog and the boy land on the water. His results show that Spanish speakers mention fewer narrative segments than English speakers. Therefore it seems that speakers of satellite-framed languages tend to express jouneys more frequently than verb-framed languages speakers.

4. *Settings*. Slobin considers that there are differences in relation to the description of the settings in which the motion event takes place. Speakers of satellite-framed languages leave the setting to be inferred, whereas speakers of verb-framed languages elaborate more complex setting descriptions. Spanish-speakers, for example, give information about the Ground, but they do it in different sentences from the sentence with the main verb of the motion event. They mainly use relative sentences.

All these analyses are coherent with the contrasts in rhetorical style. The main conclusions taken from Slobin's work are: (i) satellite-framed languages tend to use a wider variety of motion verbs, especially Manner verbs, (ii) verb-framed languages present more cases of bare verbs and Minus Ground, whereas satellite-framed languages tend to elaborate more Path descriptions, (iii) satellite-framed languages present more cases of journeys and verb-framed languages tend to leave them inferred, and (iv) verb-framed languages describe the setting with more detail and satellite-framed languages leave it inferred.

The conclusions of the analysis of the data collected from the Frog Story are consistent with data elicited using other methodologies. For instance, Slobin (1996b) analyzes several novels in English and Spanish. He selects randomly twenty motion events, that is, descriptions of movement of a character from one place to another. The English novels show a greater lexical diversity of Manner of motion verbs and more detailed Path descriptions. Spanish novels tend to use relative sentences to give information about the Path component. In this paper he also analyzes translations of English novels into Spanish and vice versa. Translators into English tend to keep the original Path description, but translators into Spanish reduce Complex Path constructions. They normally segment the English structure into two Spanish constructions, as in (19):

(19) *She walked to the park along the avenue*

(20) *Cruzó el parque y paseó a lo largo de la avenida*
cross.3SG.PST the park and walk.3SG.PST to the long of the avenue
'She crossed the park and she walked along the avenue'

Slobin highlights that this is not a matter of grammaticality, as there are resources in Spanish to express Path. However, Spanish writers (and translators) do not use these resources due to issues of rhetorical style. In the case of Manner, translations into English tend to add Manner to the target text. Translators into Spanish need to decide whether to omit Manner information encoded in English or to add this Manner to another linguistic element, consequently giving more narrative importance to this component than it has in the source text.

Slobin (1997b, 2005) also contrasts motion events in the translations of *The Hobbit* from English into three satellite-framed languages (German, Dutch and Russian) and five verb-framed languages (French, Spanish, Italian, Portuguese and Hebrew). Satellite-framed languages encoded more Manner, both in verbs and in other elements. Verb-framed languages texts showed fewer Manner verbs, as in (21) in the case of Spanish and English (Slobin 1997b: 458):

(21) *deslizarse* = creep, glide, slide, slip, slither
escabullirse = scurry off, scuttle away/off, slip away
saltar = bound, dive, hop, jump, leap, spring
tropezar = stumble, trip, tumble

In the same vein, studies contrasting English and Turkish (Özçalışkan and Slobin 2000, 2003; Özçalışkan 2009) demonstrate that speakers tend to express as much semantic information as possible in the simplest syntactic form. These authors note Manner expression in the events in which Turkish speakers could encode Manner and Path in a single verb: *kovala* 'chase', *tırman* 'climb up', and events in which they could not lexicalize it (and English speakers could, for example in the owl scene). Overall Turkish speakers preferred to encode Manner+Path rather than only Path when they had the choice. However, it is harder to encode Manner in the main verb in the owl scene (due to the boundary-crossing constraint, see Section 2.4.1.). In the descriptions of this scene, Manner was not expressed at all, without occurrences of elements expressing Manner. In both languages there was a preference for syntactically less complex constructions. From the perspective of first language acquisition, Turkish children encode only Path verbs, and start using Manner+Path verbs in adulthood. By contrast, English-speaking children used more frequently the construction Manner verb + satellite and adults used at the same level this construction with Manner+Path verbs. Özçalışkan and Slobin also notice that Manner elements outside the verb have different functions in English and Turkish. These elements are adverbial expressions, psyche descriptions, and setting descriptions. In English these accompany Manner verbs, whilst in Turkish they qualify verbs that do no encode Manner. In this sense there is some sort of compensation for the lack of Manner in the main verb in verb-framed languages.

Even so, verb-framed language speakers conceptualize the domain of Manner of motion in a much more restrained way.

This distinction can be seen even at the level of gesture. Studies on motion events and gestures have focused on two main questions: whether gestures are used to encode components that are not present in speech and whether speakers synthesize Manner and Path components in one gesture or produce separate gestures for each component. McNeill (2000, 2005, 2009) and McNeill and Duncan (2000) notice how verb-framed language speakers tend to perform different gestures in Path description. They segment this component when gesturing, much more than satellite-framed language speakers. In boundary-crossing situations (e.g. *He ran out of the house*, see Section 2.4.1.) Spanish reduces iconicity and English keeps it, while it is the other way round when there is no boundary-crossing situation. Spanish speakers tend to produce what McNeill calls "Manner fogs", that is, Manner gestures that do not correspond with the speech. Conversely, English speakers gesture to modulate Manner. Since they always encode Manner, the gesture helps to differentiate Manner with communicative weight and without: when Manner is not communicatively relevant it is minimized by expression of Manner in speech and encoding of Path in the gesture; when Manner is communicatively relevant it is reinforced by a Manner gesture. However, Özçalışkan, Stites, and Emerson (2017) explain that most other research provides evidence for an augmentative role of gesture, that is, where gesture forces the patterns found in speech. In the case of verb-framed languages, Gullberg, Hendriks, and Hickmann (2008) for Fench, Özçalışkan 2015 for Turkish and Wieselman Schulman (2004) for Spanish show that adult speakers primarily express Path of motion in their co-speech gestures like they do in their speech.

With regard to packaging information in gesture, research (Kita and Özyurek 2003; Özyurek et al. 2005) has shown that satellite-framed language speakers tend to synthesize Manner and Path, whereas verb-framed languages produce separate gestures for each component. Some of these studies have used the so-called *Canary Row* as an elicitation tool. This consists of eight short clips of Tweety cartoon. Participants were asked to describe what they saw in the clips and their narratives were video-recorded in order to analyse their speech and gesture production. A classic example of the verb- and satellite-framed gesture patterns is the description of the scene in which the cat rolls down the street. Speakers of verb-framed languages perform a Manner gesture first and a Path gesture afterwards, while speakers of satellite-framed languages combine both components in the same gesture. Some authors have claimed the importance of gesture as part of thinking for speaking and rhetorical style. Adapting gesture patterns to a second language is probably one of the most difficult parts of the motion event expression to adapt to a second language (Gullberg 2009a, 2009b, 2011).

Other authors have focused on the question of whether speakers of different languages categorize differently their conceptual representations of motion. In other words, do speakers of a satellite-framed language pay more attention to Manner when categorizing motion events in non-verbal tasks? Some studies no effects of language were found, for example in Papafragou, Massey, and Gleitman (2002). Gennari et al. (2002) did not find effect of language in their recognition memory task and they only found effect of language in the similarity tasks after verbal encoding, which suggests that language-specific regularities may mediate the speaker's performance in specific tasks. In a similar vein, Montero-Melis and Bylund (2017) found that cross-linguistic differences were present when use of language was possible, but they disappeared when use of language was hindered. They suggest that the role of language in event conceptualization is dynamic. In a different study, Montero-Melis et al. (2017) attempt to answer this research question in an experimental study with participants who are native speakers of seven satellite-framed languages and twelve verb-framed languages. Their results suggest that there is no relativity effect, and that the typology of a native language does not lead motion events to be categorized in terms of Path and Manner. These authors conclude that there is great variation within the typological groups (contrasting one verb-framed and a satellite-framed language could lead to different answers to the research question, depending on which are these languages) and support considerations for this semantic typology to be viewed in terms of a cline, as will be explained below.

The expressions of motion events discussed so far, including Manner, Path and description settings reflect prototypical linguistic behaviors of verb-framed and satellite-framed language speakers. However, the main issues with this framework will be explained in the next section, contextualized with the relationship between this specific language typology as proposed by Talmy and to its psycholinguistic application. The solutions given to these problems have helped to improve, define and develop further the theoretical proposals with regard to the relationship between the conceptualization and the verbalization of motion events.

4 Main debates about the typology of motion events

Talmy's typology of motion events (1985, 1991, 2000a, 2000b) and Slobin's thinking for speaking hypothesis (1991, 1996a, 1996b, 1997b, 2000) have inspired many scholars to pursue further research into these areas. However, these proposals have also received some criticism and theoretical problems have been identified, as explained below. Although some of these issues are still open to debate, in most cases the identification of theoretical gaps has led scholars to carry out more research to redefine these areas and on the whole strengthen the framework. In their review on motion event studies, Filipović and Ibarretxe-Antuñano (2015) identify and group the main critics of the framework. They consider that several of these issues are related to the failure of the typology to account all possible motion structures. This is the case with the boundary-crossing constraint (Section 4.1), the notion of satellite (Section 4.2.) and the broad nature of the proposed semantic components (Section 4.3). The second group of critics focuses on the different types of variation between and within the groups, including inter-typological (Section 4.4.), intra-typological (4.5.) and intra-lingual variation (4.6). The main criticisms of the theory will be outlined here, following Filipović and Ibarretxe-Antuñano's (2015) grouping, but with a particular focus on the issues that are relevant for the languages studied in this volume, namely Spanish, French, German and Italian.

4.1 Boundary-crossing constraint

This is probably the earliest noticed phenomenon that did not fit into the initial studies on motion. Aske (1989) was the first author to note this semantic restriction in Spanish, and then Slobin (1996a, 1997b, Slobin and Hoiting 1994) coined the term "boundary-crossing constraint" and expanded its scope to verb-framed languages.

Aske (1989) points out that Path telic sentences that express the end of the trajectory of the Figure (e.g. *He ran into the house*) cannot have a Manner verb as the main verb of the event in Spanish. If a Manner verb is used, for example *correr* 'run', there are two possible interpretations, either that the Figure moved towards the goal but did not cross the border, as in the case of (22), or that the Figure moved in a given location, as in (23):

(22) *Corrió a la casa*
    run.3SG.PST to the house
    'She ran towards the house'

(23) *Corrió en la casa*
    run.3SG.PST in the house
    'She ran inside the house'

The closest version to the English examples would be (24) in which a Path verb is used, *entrar* 'enter, go into', and Manner is expressed (when necessary) in a gerund, *corriendo* 'running'.

(24) *Entró en la casa corriendo*

Contrarily to Talmy (1985)'s position, Aske (1989) points out that the use of Manner verbs as main verbs is not always problematic in Spanish. In fact, some examples following the "English lexicalization patterns" can be seen in (25)-(27). These utterances are totally natural and colloquial:

(25) *Juan bailó hasta la puerta*
Juan dance.3SG.PST up.to the door
'Juan danced up to the door'

(26) *La botella flotó hacia la cueva por el río*
the bottle float.3SG.PST towards the cave by the river
'The bottle floated towards the cave along the river'

(27) *Empujamos el coche hasta el final de la calle*
push.1PL.PST the car up.to the end of the street
'We pushed the car towards the end of the street'

The incompatibility comes when a Manner verb is combined with an element that indicates a boundary-crossing, because the default interpretation is locative. Aske (1989) considers that the interpretation of Path is possible if the Ground is not lexically expressed but determined by context, as in (28):

(28) *Nadaron dentro de la cueva*
swim.3PL.PST inside the cave
'They swam inside the cave'

(29) *Nadaron adentro*
swim.3PL.PST into/inside
'They swam into [the inner part of somewhere]'

Aske (1989) concludes that Spanish can express Path outside the verb when the directional sentences are not telic, as in English *Pat swam into the cave*. In Spanish only a locative interpretation is possible as in (30), or sentences in which the final location is not predicated, i.e. non-telic sentences (*Patricia nadó hacia la cueva*), even though the final location can be implied.

(30) *Patricia nadó en la cueva*
Patricia swim.3SG.PST in the cave
'Patricia swam in the cave'

(31) *Patricia nadó hacia la cueva*
Patricia swim.3SG.PST towards the cave
'Patricia swam towards the cave'

This restriction does not seem to be exclusive to Spanish. Slobin and Hoiting (1994) find that this restriction is characteristic of all verb-framed language, and coin the term "boundary-crossing restriction", i.e. the impossibility of combining a Manner verb with a Path complement that implies a change of state. According to Slobin (1997b: 441), verb-framed languages conceive a spatial boundary as a change of state, which needs an independent predicate. This can be seen when comparing (32) and (33):

(32) *She went downstairs and out of the house*

(33) *Bajó las escaleras y salió de la casa*
descend.3SG.PST the stairs and exit.3SG.PST of the house
'She went down the stairs and she went out of the house'

However, there is no problem with using a single predicate when there is not a boundary-crossing situation and only a locative interpretation is possible, as in (34) and (35):

(34) *I went up the great stairs toward her*

(35) *Subí las grandes escaleras hacia ella*
ascend.1SG.PST the great stairs towards her
'I went up the great stairs toward her'

A few studies have focused on the effects of this typological constraint (Gennari et al. 2002) to find that, when faced with boundary-crossing situations, speakers of verb-framed languages use Path verbs and speakers of satellite-framed languages use Manner verbs. Özçalışkan (2015) shows some fine-grained differences in her study comparing English speakers and Turkish speakers talking about boundary-crossing situations in a free speech talk and in a guided talk when asked to use a Manner verb. She finds that there are several factors that influence their use of Manner verbs. It seems that Manner verbs are categorically avoided when the activity is temporally extended (e.g. *running*, *crawling*), but the restriction can be violated when the verb expresses very rapid or instantaneous crossing (e.g. *diving into a pool*), especially when the boundary is two-dimensional and unenclosed (e.g. *a carpet, a beam*) and can only be crossed *over*. It is less likely that the restriction will be violated when the boundary is three-dimensional and enclosed (e.g. *a house*) and must be crossed *into* or *out* of a place. Therefore, two factors emerge as relevant for the use of Manner verbs in boundary-crossing situations by verb-framed language speakers, namely the type of event (sudden vs. temporally extended) and the type of boundary (two dimensional vs. enclosed). She also finds that Turkish speakers segment the event significantly more than English speakers. In her interpretation of results, she explains her findings with Slobin's idea that verb-framed language speakers use verbs to encode change of state verbs. When forced to use Manner verbs, Turkish speakers either used as an adjunct (in a gerund form) or they segmented the event, by using the Manner verb as an activity towards a boundary and then either marking the boundary-crossing with a Path verb or leaving it inferred. The boundary-crossing constraint is still one of the areas relevant for the typology and several studies are still being carried out to compare how this restriction can have consequences for different areas of the expression of motion events such as gestures, languages acquisition and translation.

4.2 The notion of satellite

Probably the most controversial issue in Talmian typology is the notion of satellite. Talmy (2000a: 102) conceives satellites as follows: "It is the grammatical category of any constituent other than a noun-phrase or prepositional-phrase complement that is in a sister relation to the verb root". He claims that it is related to the verb root as a dependent element, even though it can be a different word or an affix. Therefore the category of satellite includes concepts that traditionally have been classified as different categories, such as English verb particles, German separable and inseparable verb prefixes, Latin or Russian verb prefixes, Mandarin verb complements, non-head "versatile verbs" in Lahu, incorporated nouns in Caddo and polysynthetic affixes in Atsugewi.

Several authors (Filipović 2007a; Beavers, Levin, and Tham 2010; Croft et al. 2010) have criticized the concept and consider that its definition is confusing. In fact, Talmy (1985) himself takes care to differentiate satellites from prepositions and prepositional phrases. He considers that in some languages such as Latin, Classical Greek, and Russian it is easier to distinguish satellites and prepositions, because satellites are verb prefixes, whilst prepositions precede nouns. In other languages, for example in English, satellites and prepositions can occur together and sometimes share form, which can lead to confusion. However, they are very different because when the prepositional phrase is omitted, the satellite remains in the sentence. There are some elements that are not common to either category. For example, *from* and *toward* are always prepositions and never satellites, while *together*, *apart* and *forth* are satellites that can never be prepositions. When satellites and prepositions share the form they normally present prosodic differences.

Talmy considers that satellites tend to express Path, although they can encode other components. For example Ground and Path, as in *She drove home*. This type of satellites is common in American languages. For example, Atsugewi has around fifty forms with this encoding pattern: 'into a liquid', 'into a volume enclosure (e.g. a house)', 'into a fire', etc. (see Talmy 1985: 108 for more information). Satellites can also encode Figure and Base, as in Caddo, Manner as in Nez Perce and Cause (or Instrument) as in Atsugewi. Talmy (1985) states that satellites are used beyond the expression of motion and can be used for other semantic domains, such as aspect: *away, over, on, off*, etc.

However, the notion of satellite has been the target of the main critics of the typology. From a generative linguistics perspective, Fábregas (2007) studies the lexicalization of directional complements in Spanish and identifies prepositions as encoders of Path. In the same line, Beavers, Levin, and Tham (2010) consider that the distinction between satellites and prepositions is problematic and propose the inclusion of prepositions in the category of satellites. Croft et al. (2010: 205–206) also notice that there is no semantic difference in the encoding of the components of an event when the form is a preposition or when the form is a satellite:

(36) *The bird flew into the cave / *The bird flew into*

(37) *The bird flew over the house / The bird flew over*

According to Talmy's definition, *into* would not fit into the category of satellite but *over* would, even though both of them encode Path. Croft et al. (2010) consider that the solution to this problem is the establishment of cross-linguistic valid criteria, based on how function is expressed in the morpho-syntactic form.

However, as Ibarretxe-Antuñano (2017b) points out, if prepositions are included as satellites, the category becomes too wide and impossible to use to explain cross-linguistic differences, as verb-framed and satellite-framed languages would not show differences in lexicalization patterns. Other authors (Ibarretxe-Antuñano 2004a, 2004b; Iacobini and Masini 2007a, 2007b; Noonan 2003; Porquier 2001) acknowledge that verb-framed languages may have elements similar to satellites. They can share some properties of satellites but they are not as frequent and easy to combine as satellites. This is why some authors have proposed the term "pseudo-satellite" to treat them as a different category (Hijazo-Gascón and Ibarretxe-Antuñano 2013a, 2013b).

4.3 Broad nature of semantic components

As Filipović and Ibarretxe-Antuñano (2015) claim, this refers to the unclear subdivision of Talmy's main components (Path and Manner). Several authors have made more finer-grained contrastive comparisons among languages that allow for more precise cross-linguistic comparisons.

Manner is probably the semantic component that has raised more debate among scholars. Slobin's main tenet with regard to Manner is that it will be expressed in a finer-grained way and with more distinctions in the languages that have more linguistic resources to encode it. Consequently, satellite-framed languages tend to have more resources and therefore express Manner more frequently. He supports this claim using different methodologies: the Frog Story, narrative texts in novels, translations and journalistic texts. The Manner component covers several aspects such as motor patterns (*jump*), speed (*run*), force dynamics (*step*), attitude (*stroll*), instrument (*ski*), etc. Manner is optional in both types, but in satellite-framed languages it is easier to encode it in the main verb (as Path is added in the satellite).In these languages, adding Manner has a lower discourse processing cost, which has as a consequence a more varied Manner lexicon and ease of creating neologisms to distinguish Manner subcomponents.

A well-known example in English is the San Diego Zoo sign cited in Slobin (2006: 1):

> Do not tread, mosey, hop, tramble, step, plot, tiptoe, trot, traipse, meander, creep, prance, amble, job, trudge, march, stomp, toddle, jump, stumble, trod, spring, or walk on the plants.

This sign with all these Manner of motion verbs would pose a challenge to a translator into a verb-framed language. Most of these verbs need to be paraphrased in translation into Spanish. For example *trudge* could be translated as *caminar con dificultad* 'walk with difficulty', or *mosey* as *caminar sin prisa* 'walk without a hurry'. In verb-framed languages, Manner needs to be encoded in subordinate elements, which means a higher processing cost of this component and consequently it is encoded only when it is relevant for discourse. In this typological group, Manner can be encoded in verbs that encode both Manner and Path, for example *tırmanmak* in Turkish and *trepar* in Spanish 'climb up'. Another possibility is the expression of Manner adverbs. Özçalışkan and Slobin (2003) find that the additions of Manner are done differently in both typological groups. Whereas in Turkish Manner is added to Path verbs, in English they are added to modulate Manner verbs.

Slobin (2004, 2006) suggests some factors that facilitate the encoding of Manner and that can lead to a more frequent presence in discourse of this component: (i) expression by a finite rather than a nonfinite verb form, e.g. in satellite-framed and equipollently-framed (see Section 4.4. for a detailed definition of this third typological group) it is easily encoded in the main verb of a simple sentence; (ii) expression by an uninflected coverbal element rather than an inflected coverbal form. This is the case with Manner co-verbs in equipollently-framed languages that are not inflected in contrast with expressions combining Path and Manner in Turkish, which are inflected, and (iii) expression by a single morpheme rather than a phrase or a clause. This is the contrast between English *tiptoe* and Spanish *ir de puntillas* 'go on the tip of the toe'.

Slobin (2006) also considers the cognitive consequences of Manner encoding patterns, for example on mental imagery. In an experiment, monolingual English and Spanish speakers and bilinguals in both languages were asked to retell a text taken from a novel in which a very detailed motion description is described. English speakers tend to include Manner verbs in their descriptions, while Spanish speakers did not talk about Manner but gave clear images of the physical surroundings of the scene. They even reported at times having seen a series of static images like photographs. Interestingly enough, bilingual speakers adapted to give more Manner or Path details depending on the language in which they were telling the story. In the case of memory, K. Oh (2003) shows that English and Korean speakers had similar results when remembering details about Path or the clothes of the characters of video clips, but they differed with regard to Manner, English-speakers being better at remembering Manner details.

It being clear how different the encoding of Manner can be in verb-framed and satellite-framed languages, one of the issues that has attracted researchers' attention is that of the different types of Manner and what should be understood by Manner. Slobin (1997b: 459) proposes a two-tiered classification of Manner verbs lexicon. The first-tier includes the neutral, everyday Manner verbs like *walk* and *fly*. More expressive and exceptional verbs, like *dash* and *scramble*, comprise the second tier. Malt et al. (2008) used a naming task to inquire into Manner of motion in different languages. They found diversity of Manner verbs in satellite framed languages, for example the use of different Manner verbs in satellite-framed languages like *hop, skip, jump, leap*, whereas only one verb, namely 'jump', was used in verb-framed languages to cover all these situations. These findings are coherent with previous results elicited from narratives and translations.

Slobin et al. (2014) designed a study that aimed to confirm that speakers of languages that encode Path outside the main verb have more Manner verbs and at redefining the component of Manner. They prepared different stimuli considering different subcomponents of Manner and analyzed and clustered the results according to the encoding of Manner in the verb or in other expressions. The participants were speakers of English, Polish, French, Spanish and Basque. Slobin et al. conclude that there is a greater lexical density of Manner of motion verbs in satellite framed languages and give evidence that Manner of motion is particularly salient to speakers of satellite-framed languages. They also show coherent results with Özçalışkan and Slobin (2003) in that the use of Manner complements is different in both typological groups: in verb-framed languages it compensates for the lack of Manner in the main verb, in satellite-framed languages it modulates the Manner information in the verb. They also show two canonical gait patterns: walking and running, although speakers also attended to other factors such as non-canonical postures, rhythmic patterns, and arrhythmic gaits. In all five languages there were some regularities regarding the basic underlying concepts, e.g. velocity, but they differed in the granularity and the type of structure to codify it. Slobin et al. consider that the speakers showed continua of rate and force dynamics. It is also interesting to note that in all five languages an aspect of fine-grained Manner was the inner state of the person who is moving, with cross-linguistic degrees to its categorization. For example some distinctions in English do not differ in the motor pattern but on the evaluation of the moving Figure, like *saunter*, *stroll* and *amble*.

The broad nature of the semantic components has also been discussed with regard to Path, particularly in relation to Deixis. As explained in Section 1 of this chapter, Talmy considers three subcomponents of Path, namely Deixis, Conformation and Vector. However, some scholars (Matsumoto 2003; Matsumoto, Akita, and Takahashi 2017) have highlighted the importance of Deixis in some languages, like Japanese, and claim that this should be a component on its own, different from Path. In fact, in some languages Deixis has its own morpho-syntactic slot for deictic verbs and there are deictic verbs independent of the richness of Path verbs (Matsumoto, Akita, and Takahashi 2017). As these authors claim, the functional nature of deictic verbs involves an interactional relationship between the speaker and the moving person.

These debates have resulted in new proposals and redefinitions of the typology. Some of them can be regarded as an evolution of the typology, such as the clines of salience of Manner and Path proposed by Slobin (2004) and Ibarretxe-Antuñano (2004b, 2009) respectively. Others can be regarded as a more radical redefinition of the framework, since they change the terms and the criteria for the establishment of a typology of motion events. All these redefinitions will be explained in the following sections.

4.4 A third typological group? Equipollently-framed languages

One of the issues that directly challenges the typology is the existence of languages that do not fit into any of the two groups proposed by Talmy (1991, 2000). Zlatev and Yangklang (2004) and Ameka and Essegbey (2013) show that the languages they study (Thai and Ewe respectively) cannot be considered satellite or verb-framed languages and therefore argue for the creation of a third typological group. Slobin (2004) coins the term equipollently-framed languages to cover these languages in which, for different reasons, the lexicalization patterns do not fit with the two initial groups. This third typological group has been generally accepted in the field, although some authors do not agree with the creation of this type. Talmy himself rejects the third group and argues that these languages can be included in one of the two already established main groups (in Ibarretxe-Antuñano 2005 and Talmy 2009).

Slobin and Hoiting (1994) were the first authors to notice the difficulty in ascribing some languages to one of the two original groups, when studying motion events in Sign Languages. These languages use Manner+Path verbs at the same level of importance, so it is very difficult to determine which one is the main verb of the event. They encode Path in a verb that can occur independently, so they should not be considered satellite-framed languages. At the same time, their Manner verbs can also work in boundary-crossing situations. These languages present some events with two main verbs simultaneously, so at a discourse level their treatment of Manner and Path is very similar. Slobin and Hoiting consider that these languages, together with languages which present similar patterns, should be considered as "complex verb-framed languages".

Thai is another of these languages that are difficult to assign to one typological group. Zlatev and Yangklang (2004: 165) explain that serial constructions like Manner verb > Non-Deictic Path verb > Deictic Path verb are very frequent in this language. They explain that more verbs can be added only if the final position is occupied by a deictic verb:

(38) chán dəən khâw paj
      I walk.INF enter.INF go.INF
      'I walk in [towards a place far from deictic centre]'

It has been argued that these Path verbs could be considered as a deverbal adverb, a homophone of the Path verb. This would allow the inclusion of Thai in satellite-framed languages. However, Zlatev and Yangklang (2004) maintain that: (i) there is no semantic difference between the "adverb" and the verb, as is the case in grammaticalization processes; (ii) several Path verbs can occur in this construction and it would be strange to consider all of them as satellites; (iii) all verbs in a serial construction can be affected by negation.

Moreover, it is proposed that some verbs should not be considered pure Manner verbs, but Manner+Path verbs instead. This would include the category of verbs that imply going through a landmark, e.g. *thîm* 'puncture', *thalú* 'pierce'; those indicating downwards motion, e.g. *tók* 'fall' and *lâj* 'chase', also indicating the direction and Manner. It is interesting that these verbs constitute not only a semantic category but also a syntactic one, as they should be placed after a Manner verb and before the Path verb. Zlatev and Yangklang (2004) consider that the Thai equivalent to fall implies a lack of the Figure's control. This has meant that the equivalents of fall in different languages have been considered as encoders of Manner+Path in the studies of motion events in different languages.

In the Thai data elicited with the Frog story, Thai speakers describe Path less frequently than verb-framed language speakers, but the characteristic narrative is in between those of verb-framed and satellite-framed speakers, as the expression of Manner is similar to Germanic languages. This difficulty in determining whether Thai is a verb-framed or a satellite-framed language leads these authors to defend the creation of a third type to include serial languages. It is similarly difficult to classify the African language Ewe as verb-framed or satellite framed (Ameka and Essegbey 2013). This language has also serial constructions. These constructions can be also included in different families: Niger-Congo, Hmong-Mien, Sino-Tibetan, Tai-Kadai, Mon-Khmer and (some) Austronesian (Slobin 2004).

Given the results of these studies, Slobin (2004) proposes the equipollently-framed languages category. The term indicates the equality of elements in which Manner and Path are encoded. Slobin (2004) calls attention to another language which is difficult to fit into the two-group typology: Mandarin Chinese. Talmy (1991, 2000b) had considered this language as a satellite-framed language because he interprets the Manner verb as the main verb and the Path verb as a satellite. However, Slobin (2004) claims that in the process of first language acquisition of Mandarin Chinese, Path is present at all ages and the combination of Path and Manner increases with age. Children aged 3 do not use the Path+Manner combination, children aged between 4 and 7 use it in 22% of the occurrences and children over 9 and adults use it 73% of the time. Therefore, its position as satellite-framed is not as clear as previously thought. Later studies on Chinese (Chen 2007, Chen and Guo 2009) agree with the classification of Mandarin Chinese as an equipollently-framed language.

Jaminjung, an Australian language, is also difficult to classify (Shultze-Berndt 2000). In this case, this language has compulsory generic verbs, such as *-ijga* 'go', and *-ruma* 'come' that mainly encode deixis (also caused motion and accompaniment) and aspect. In a way these verbs can be considered as Path verbs and Jaminjung should be considered as a verb-framed language, though not a prototypical one. In this language, the only encoding devices for Manner are preverbs, a sort of satellite that encodes Manner information but also direction. Schultze-Berndt (2000) concludes that Manner expression is accessible in Slobin's sense (2004), but not as salient in discourse as in satellite-framed languages. Manner is expressed only when there is an intention to foreground it in discourse. This language also follows the boundary-crossing restriction. As a consequence, it does not fit with the characteristics of verb-framed nor satellite-framed languages. The first consideration was to include Jaminjung in the equipollently-framed group. However, other studies (Schultze-Berndt 2007, Hoffmann 2012) show that speakers use non-flexive Path verbs twice as often non-flexive Manner verbs. Hoffman (2012) shows that the construction Manner coverb + Path coverb + flexive verb is not very frequent, unusual even. Minus Ground is also more frequent in its speakers' narratives, which makes this language closer to verb-framed languages. This leads Schultze-Berndt (2007) to include Jaminjung in this group and raises awareness of the importance of clarifying the categories of verb and satellite, beyond the "main verb of the event" and "a member of an open class". In Jaminjung verbs are a members of a closed class.

As explained above, the proposal for the third group has received acceptance by most authors working on the typology of motion events and thinking for speaking. However, Talmy (see Ibarretxe-Antuñano 2005 and Talmy 2009, 2012) disagrees and prefers the binary typology. He defends the ascription of polysynthetic and serial languages as satellite-framed languages and of co-verb languages as verb-framed languages. First, in the case of polysynthetic languages, Talmy (2009) argues with examples from Atsugewi that these languages have a defined verb root (expressing Motion and Figure) and Path tends to be expressed in a satellite. Second, he claims that, in serial verb languages, the verb that presents more factors to be considered the main verb is the Manner verb, and he illustrates his points with examples from Lahu and Mandarin. Finally, he uses his explication of different subcomponents of Path (Vector, Deixis and Conformation) to explain that in co-verb languages the main verb encodes the Deixis subcomponent of Path and the second verb encodes the Conformation subcomponent of Path. He considers that Jaminjung is similar to Japanese and Korean, in which deictic verbs are frequently accompanied with gerunds to express Manner or Conformation of Path. In Talmy (2012), a revised version of Talmy (2009), the equipollent group is rejected. He claims that the studies challenging the binary typology focus only on two of the components of the motion event (Path and the co-event), they also treat Path as a unitary component when it has three parts, and they treat the co-event only as Manner, disregarding

Cause. However, he admits that the problem might lie in the fact that the criteria used for judging what is a main verb have been too few. He proposes an extended set of criteria to determine whether a linguistic element should be considered the main verb of the event or not. These criteria are of diverse types: morphological, syntactical, related to co-occurrence patterns, semantic, phonological and related to the class size. He applies them to English, Atsugewi, Lahu, Mandarin and Jaminjung and concludes that there is no reason to create a third typological group. He considers that even in the cases that equipollence could be applied it would still be a rare phenomenon.

The classification of certain languages as members of one group or the other is still a controversial issue. This has led several authors to propose other variants or redefinitions of the typology. For instance, Matsumoto (2003) considers that using "verb" or "verb-framed" is problematic and argues that it is better to talk about "heads", because all satellites are by definition not heads, but not all the non-head elements are satellites, like prepositions or noun phrases. One of the advantages of this reformulation is to avoid relating the typology to verb lexicons in the languages, since some verb-framed languages (e.g. Hindi, Tswana) seem to have a broad lexicon of Manner of motion. He also believes that Manner expression should not be tied to the typology. Japanese illustrates this point with the presence of ideophones that allow fine-grained Manner distinctions despite it being a verb-framed language.

Croft et al. (2010) is another study that revisits the lexicalization pattern typology. The main problems they identify are: (i) that there should be more types and (ii) that the typology applies to specific types of complex events within a language and not as much to languages themselves. They propose different types (Croft et al. 2010: 208) like verb-framed, symmetrical framed, satellite-framed and double-framed and they argue for a morpho-syntactic scale of different constructions parallel to a semantic scale. In this case it is important to remember that Talmy (1985, 1991, 2000a, 2000b) always insists on determining which pattern is the most characteristic and he never claims that this is the only lexicalization pattern available in the language.

Wälchli (2006) claims that data should be examined before creating a theory which includes all languages in the world. He recommends some methodological questions, like the inclusion of languages from all continents to avoid macro-area features, and that the typology should be examined language by language to avoid assumptions that related languages have similar lexicalization patterns. Wälchli (2006) puts forward a more detailed typology following Tesnière's idea of displacement (1959). He distinguishes three *loci* for the expression of displacement: verb encoding, adnominal encoding and adverbial encoding.

Filipović (2007a) also considers that aspect should be taken into account when determining typological preferences and restrictions. She proposes a focus on the different means that language has for the expression of different types of situations that are characterized in terms of space (boundary-crossing, boundary-reaching and non-boundary-crossing) and time (change, moment of change and no change). She showed that languages may have different preferred patterns in different situation types. For example, when describing a boundary-crossing/moment-of-change situation type, such as "He was limping into the house when I saw him", Manner verbs cannot be used in Serbo-Croatian because of *morphological blocking* (Filipović 2007a) and Path verbs need to be used instead, which reflects a verb-framed pattern rather than the satellite-framed one assigned to Serbo-Croatian.

In the same vein, Bohnemeyer et al. (2007) propose a different typology to deal with event segmentation, i.e. the distribution of information about an event across the parts of an utterance. Their starting point is the Macro-Event property (MEP), which is a property of constructions that presents the event in terms of a unique initial, terminal boundary, in a unique position in the time line. They classify languages into three groups. Type I languages allow the integration of sub-events for source, goal and route in a single macro event (for example *He went from London across the channel to Paris*). Type II languages permit the integration of the departure and the arrival but require a separate macro event for some passing events (as in *He went from London to Paris, crossing the channel*). Finally, Type III languages need to encode each change of location in a macro event expression.

Aware of the issues of the typology, Slobin (2008) proposes a reformulation with the Path-in-verb constructions (PIV) and Path-in-nonverb constructions (PIN) to acknowledge that Path can be encoded in elements that are not satellites. Depending on which of these constructions is preferred by speakers, a given language will be considered a PIV or a PIN language. In a more specific proposal, Grinevald (2011) focuses on Path and proposes a "working typology". Her proposal considers Path independently from motion and the definition of other semantic components.

The debates on intra-typological differences will be particularly relevant for the studies presented in this book. Despite all the issues mentioned, the Talmy-Slobin framework is still considered a pertinent framework to study motion events and most scholars keep working in this framework. In this book the typology of verb-framed and satellite-framed languages will be used, while keeping awareness about all the issues mentioned in connection with this dichotomous classification. The results of the studies presented in chapters 4 and 5 of this book give more evidence to support the existence of the clines with regard to habitual Manner and Path verbalization in different languages.

4.5 Intra-typological differences

Another of the main discussions around the typology is related to the variation within the typological groups. Several studies have noticed that languages can be more or less prototypical with regard to the rhetorical style that corresponds to their belonging to a typological group. There are several factors that should be taken into account, both cultural and structural. These differences affect satellite and verb framed languages. We will focus on intra-typological differences in satellite-framed languages first.

Even in closely related languages differences can be found. For example, Icelandic shows a greater variety of Manner verbs than Swedish. Icelandic speakers also describe Path in a more detailed way than Swedish speakers (Ragnasdóttir and Strömqvist 2004: 126–127). This difference could be due to the fact that Icelandic keeps the cases from old Nordic, while Swedish lost this linguistic resource. An example of this difference can be seen in the examples (39) in Icelandic and (40) in Swedish:

(39) *Og svo datt hundurinn og strákurinn ofan-í sjó*
and then fall.PST dog.DEF and boy.DEF up-into sea.ACC
'And then the dog and the boy fell from above into the sea'

(40) *Pojken ramla ner*
boy fall.PST down
'The boy fell down'

Icelandic presents more restrictions, which makes their speakers use more phrases than particles, whereas the opposite is the case in Swedish. In this sense we could say that Icelandic is "more satellite-framed" than Swedish, and Swedish is more than English. As Cadierno (2004) points out when contrasting English and Danish, English presents a broad range of vocabulary of Latin origin that is not present in Scandinavian languages. These observations are coherent with Slobin's hypothesis that the presence of linguistic resources in a language to express a certain semantic component makes it more accessible and therefore it becomes more frequently expressed by the speakers.

Filipović (2007a: 76–77) notices important pattern differences between Germanic and Slavonic languages even though they are both classified as satellite-framed languages. She shows that the use of Serbo-Croatian (and some other Slavonic) prefixes is affected by certain morphosyntactic restrictions that are not present in the English particles grammatical system where all prepositions freely combine with all Manner verbs. Although these prefixes should be considered satellites according to Talmy's definition, they are bound morphemes whose use is limited by the combinatory potential restriction, which does not allow all of the prefixes to combine with all of the prepositions that must follow the manner verbs. In these cases, one possibility is to use a Path verb instead and add a Manner adjunct, as is more commonly done in verb-framed languages. Filipović and Vidaković (2010: 264) illustrate this with the Serbo-Croatian translation of an original sentence in English, reproduced here in (41) and (42):

(41)   *They danced onto the balcony*

(42)   *Izašli su na balkon plešući*
       'They exited onto the balcony dancing'

Another option, especially if the Path is complex, is to use a manner verb prefixed with the deictic prefixes *od-* 'from' and *do-* 'to' because these prefixes can combine with all the other prepositions and many prepositions can be added to a single deictic verb, expressing different directions. However, this latter option means adding deictic information in translation that is not present in the original source text, as illustrated in (43) and (44), taken from Filipović (2007a: 121):

(43)   *He ran across the field and through the woods into the neighboring village*

(44)   *Otrčao je preko polja i kroz šumu u susedno selo*
       From-the-speaker/scene-run-PST-PFV-3SG-M be-COP across field and through woods into neighboring village

Therefore it seems that there is some degree of variation in the description of both Manner and Path within satellite-framed languages. This variation is even greater in the case of verb-framed languages.

One of the main differences is the codification of Posture. The expression of the position of the Figure seems to be crucial for thinking for speaking in certain languages. Some Mayan languages, for example Tzeltal (P. Brown 2004: 46), encode it in specific markers. In (45) the position of the Figure is encoded in the marker *jawal* 'face up':

(45)   *ch'ay koel jawal niwan ek*
       fall.3SG down face.up maybe too
       'He also falls down with face up'

Another important difference is the degree of elaboration of Path. For example, the Sino-Tibetan language Chantyal (Noonan 2003) presents a small set of verbs that lexicalize Path, corresponding to *wõ-* 'enter', *tho-* 'exit', *hya-* 'go', *kha-* 'come', and *tho-* 'arrive'. This is not common in verb-framed languages, nor is the frequent use of directional satellites as happens in this language. Chantyal speakers tend to specify origin and goal of motion in a way that resembles that of satellite-framed speakers.

In Basque (Ibarretxe-Antuñano 2004a, 2004b, 2006a, 2009) a more detailed elaboration of Path is also common in the narratives produced by the speakers. Ibarrtexe-Antuñano (2004a) coins the term Complete Path Construction for a frequent pattern in this language. In this construction the origin and goal of motion are mentioned and at times a redundant directional adverb is also added. An example is (46):

(46) *Danak amildegitikan behera erori zian ibai batera*
      all.ABS cliff.ABL.LOC below.ALL fall.PFV aux river one.ALL
      'All of them from the cliff down into the river'

This is an optional construction, as the expression with only one Ground or the bare verb is not agrammatical. Ibarrtexe-Antuñano (2004a, 2009) argues that the reasons for this preference may be the availability of linguistic resources to codify motion (cases, postpositions, locative nouns), word order with a final position for the verb or the possibility of omitting the main verb.

One of the languages that causes debate about the group in which it should be classified is Modern Greek. This language presents verb-framed language encoding but it also has a set of prefixes that can be combined with Motion verbs, in a clear satellite-framed language lexicalization pattern. The main difficulty noticed by scholars working on Greek is that these parallel verb and satellite-framed structures are present in equally frequent contexts (Soroli 2012). Papafragou, Massey, and Gleitman (2006) and Talmy (2007) consider Greek a clearly verb-framed language, despite the considerable presence of satellite-framed constructions. However, Soroli (2012) gives evidence of how this language is not clearly verb-framed. In an experiment with production, verbal and non-verbal categorization tasks, Greek speakers showed shared preferences with English speakers. While French speakers preferred Path in all categorization tasks, Greek and English speakers preferred Manner as the criterion for categorization in the verbal categorization task, and they showed no preferences in the non-verbal categorization task. Soroli (2012) claims that Greek should be better placed in an intermediate position in the typological continuum. In this vein, Soroli and Verker (2017) compare English, French and Greek through different analysis and conclude that Greek prefixes had more productivity than French prefixes. Coding these preverbs as Path satellites or as part of the verb-root had an impact in the analysis of motion in Greek. They also found complex constructions of motion, with spatial information distributed over several clauses, a pattern that was not found in English or French.

Finally, other differences have been noticed in relation to the elaboration of Path in Italian (Hijazo-Gascón and Ibarretxe-Antuñano 2013a, 2013b). The study of minority languages has proven very relevant in this sense, observing interesting differences in the expression of motion events among more standardized Romance languages and minority Romance languages (Berthele 2004 on Romasch; Ibarretxe-Antuñano, Hijazo-Gascón, and Moret-Oliver 2017 on Aragonese and Catalan). These intratypological differences among Romance languages will be explained in more detail in the following chapter.

Basque, together with other verb-framed languages such as Japanese (Akita 2017), also shows variability in the description of Manner (Ibarretxe-Antuñano 2004a, 2004b, 2006a). It has extra resources to express Manner, such as ideophones or sound symbolism, i.e. linguistic elements in which there is a more or less motivated relation between sound and meaning. For example, *ttxoko-ttxoko ibili* 'walk slowly' in Basque and *noro-noro aruku* 'walk slowly' in Japanese. The presence of ideophones does not challenge Talmy's typology, as they encode an optional component. However, they do contradict some of Slobin's claims. Despite having these resources available, some languages do not use them very frequently. Therefore more factors other than the existence of linguistic resources should be considered to explain the frequency of Manner in the speech of some languages and not in others (Ibarretxe-Antuñano 2004a, 2004b).

An interesting case is that of the Western Austronesian languages studied by S. Huang and Tanangkingsking (2005), namely Squliq, Tsou, Saisiyat, Cebuan, Tagalog and Malay. They conclude that Cebuan and Tagalog clearly fit in the typology as verb-framed languages, as well as Tsou as equipollently-framed. The other three languages are verb-framed but not prototypical, as they tend to express Manner much more than canonical verb-framed languages.

In other cases the difference lies in the dynamicity of the descriptions. Greenlandic does not seem to follow Slobin's (1996a) conclusion that verb-framed languages express fewer phases of the journey, with more static descriptions of the scene and leaving Path inferred. Engberg-Pedersen and Blytmann-Trondhjem (2004) find that in this polysynthetic language speakers present some patterns of verb-framed languages and some patterns of satellite-framed languages. They have four locative cases and five ways of expressing Path and Ground outside the main verb. However, they prefer to express motion with bare verbs. They prefer Minus Ground even less than Spanish speakers. However they elaborate much more the different phases of the journey in the deer scene. They do not mention

Path components, but they mention a complex series of events and actions. Therefore they behave like verb-framed language speakers with regard to the details regarding Path, but their descriptions are less static and more dynamic, similar to satellite-framed language descriptions. This also happens in Aranda in relation to the deer scene (Wilkins 2004).

Other verb-framed languages encode more information, as revealed by Slobin and Hoiting (1994) in their study of Dutch sign language and Galvan and Taub (2004) for American sign language. These sign languages encode Path in the verb and follow the boundary-crossing constraint like verb-framed languages, but they convey more information even than satellite-framed languages. It is important to note that sign languages have specific characteristics and also encode meaning via facial expression, different degrees of distance in the gesture or repetition of the gesture. Deixis also plays a crucial role in these languages as it is paramount when signing.

This debate on intra-typological differences has led some authors to revisit the typology. Instead of a binary static typology, Slobin (2004, 2006) proposes the idea of regarding the typology as a cline. He puts forward the cline of Manner salience (2004, 2006) and Ibarretxe-Antuñano (2004b, 2009) proposes the cline of Path salience.

4.6 Intra-lingual differences

Diatopic variation is the last issue mentioned by Filipović and Ibarretxe-Antuñano (2005) in their account of controversial issues for the typology. Although this is not a very well studied area and further research is needed, it is important to note the importance of intra-lingual variation in typology. Berthele's (2004, 2006) pioneering work highlights differences between Swiss German and standard German and compares these varieties with Romansch and French. The Muotathal dialect proves to be of special relevance, since despite being a variety of a satellite-framed language, it presents a scarce description of Manner. On the other hand, it elaborates Path in more detail than Standard German.

Ibarretxe-Antuñano and Hijazo-Gascón (2012) also find differences in Path descriptions among Spanish speakers from two Northern Peninsular varieties (Spanish from the Basque Country and Aragón) in contrast with the varieties from Madrid, Chile and Argentina. The differences among German and Spanish varieties will be further explained in the next chapter, in the sections deoted to those languages. Finally Yiu (2014) focuses on differences in the expression of motion among Chinese dialects. Overall these studies remind researchers to be careful with overgeneralizations. Typologists' task involves generalization of features across languages. However, when looking closer into the varieties within a language, interesting findings can be observed, which can be relevant for the theoretical frameworks.

As a conclusion, it can be stated that the study of motion events typology and thinking for speaking has benefited from the intense debate on all the issues covered. Despite the various criticisms that this framework has received, scholars have proposed solutions and moved forward to account for the lexicalization of motion across languages and its consequences in rhetorical style. These critics have strengthened and validated the theory that has inspired applications to different fields, such as first language acquisition, translation and interpreting (Slobin 2005; Ibarretxe-Antuñano and Filipović 2013; Rojo and Cifuentes-Férez 2017) and second language acquisition, the focus of the next section.

5 Acquisition of motion events in a second language

Linguistic relativity and thinking for speaking have increased considerably their influence in applied linguistics, particularly in the field of SLA. A number of studies have focused on the issue, especially in relation to Cross-linguistic influence and transfer and bi- and multilingualism. Some books have focused the attention of researchers on this topic, for example those by Jarvis and Pavlenko (2008), Cook and Bassetti (2011) and Pavlenko (2014) and the edited volumes by Han and Cadierno (2010) and Pavlenko (2011). Since the formulation of the hypothesis, thinking for speaking has been very closely related to motion, and this is also the case with second language acquisition. However, thinking for speaking has been also applied to other domains, among others, spatial relations (Coventry, Valdés, and Guijarro-Fuentes 2010), grammatical gender (Boroditsky, Schmidt, and Philips 2003) and colors (Athanasopoulos 2009).

In a comprehensive review of literature on thinking for speaking and Second Language Acquisition, Cadierno (2017) states that the main questions that researchers have attempted to answer are the following:
(i) Are adult learners of an L2 able to learn the L2 thinking for speaking (verbal and gestural) patterns?
(ii) To what extent is this learning influenced by L1 thinking for speaking patterns?
(iii) Can the L2 influence the already established L1 thinking for speaking patterns?

She notes that the studies on motion events and second language acquisition differ with regard to three main aspects: (i) type of motion: voluntary or caused-motion, (ii) type of participants (early bilinguals or adult learners), (iii) type of data (production, gesture and reception). Her analysis focuses on the mainstream body of research. That is, studies focusing on voluntary motion, adult learners and production data (with and without gesture analysis) and she produces a very clear table with the studies classified according to three criteria: type of transfer (from L1 to L2, L2 to L1 or bidirectional), focus on inter or intra-typological differences between the L1 and the L2, and level of proficiency.

The outcomes from her analysis are quite clear (Cadierno 2017): Most of the studies carried out so far are mainly unidirectional, i.e. they focus on transfer from the L1 into the L2. Studies whose target language is verb-framed tend to analyze only production and not gesture, whereas studies on L2 satellite-framed languages have analyzed both production and gesture. Studies focused on intra-typological differences do not take gesture into account, whilst bidirectional transfer studies always consider gesture. Finally there are not many studies focusing on the acquisition of motion events at a beginner level.

In this section the focus will be on the main studies that have been carried out in relation to the acquisition of Spanish as a second language, and those related works on other languages that have been built on to this research. The studies will be presented in two sections. First the studies in which the first and the second language are not typologically similar, for instance one of them being verb-framed and the other being satellite-framed. Second, studies in which both the first and the second language belong to the same typological group.

5.1 Inter-typological studies on motion and second language acquisition

The first studies on motion and second language acquisition were inter-typological, that is, with one satellite-framed language and the other verb-framed. Their main aim was to determine whether the cross-linguistic differences in thinking for speaking (Slobin 1991, 1996a, 1996b) had consequences in the acquisition of a second language, since typological differences could easily cause transfers and even fossilizations (Gullberg 2011). These first studies focused mainly on the difficulties faced by speakers from one of the typological groups when they were acquiring a second language from the other. Most of these studies also looked closely into gesture as an indicator of cross-linguistic influence Even in cases in which oral speech is correct in the L2, the gestures can show the persistence of conceptual patterns from the L1 (Gullberg 2009b, 2011). First, the results from studies in which the target language is satellite-framed will be presented, being some of them bidirectional. Second, studies with a verb-framed language as a target language will be discussed.

5.1.1 Satellite-framed languages as the target language

One of the first studies focuses on English and Japanese (Inagaki 2001). In a bidirectional study it is shown how L1 Japanese speakers accept L2 English Manner verbs with goals of movement, even at intermediate levels. At the same time, L1 English speakers learning Japanese, even at an advanced level, do accept this type of construction in their second language, which would be correct in English but not in Japanese, which follows the boundary-crossing constraint. Montrul (2001) finds that Spanish-speaking learners of English under-generalize Manner verbs in comparison with English native speakers. Nicoladis, Brisard and Clark (2002) find important differences in the encoding of motion events and gestures by English-French early bilingual children. Gestures seem to play a crucial role in this area, as the study by Kellerman and van Hoof (2003) points out. These authors analyze the differences between L1 Spanish and L1 Dutch speakers' productions in their L2 English. In their first language, Spanish speakers performed the motion gesture during the utterance of the verb, whilst Dutch speakers did it by mentioning the satellite. Interestingly enough, both groups placed the gesture in the verb when speaking in the L2, which can be interpreted as cross-linguistic influence only in the case of Spanish speakers.

The results of these first studies can be applied to the English and Spanish pair, which has received most of the attention. Negueruela et al. (2004) show two-way cross-linguistic influence at an advanced level in both L2 English and L2 Spanish. Spanish native speakers tend to use gestures and verbs to express Path but avoid Manner both in their L1 and L2. They used Manner gestures when the component is not encoded in the verb. By contrast, native English speakers struggled to find the adequate verb to meet their communicative needs, as in (47):

(47) El sapo entró, bueno saltó, como dentro del saxofón
      the toad enter.PST.3SG well jump.PST.3SG like inside the saxophone
      'The toad entered, well jumped, like inside the saxophone'

Negueruela et al.'s results also showed that English native speakers use more Manner gestures in their L2 than in the L1, which is attributed to a compensation strategy for the lack of Manner verbs in Spanish.

Hohestein, Eisenberg, and Naigles (2006) also give evidence of conceptual transfer between speakers of English and Spanish. In their bidirectional study they add the age of acquisition factor into the equation. Their results show that speakers had bidirectional lexical transfer, that is, from their L1 to their L2 but also from their L2 into their L1. However, grammatical transfer seems to be only in one direction, from the L1 into the L2. Differences were also found between speakers who acquired the L2 at an early age and those who acquired it as adults, the latter being those with higher levels of cross-linguistic influence.

Following the number of studies contrasting English and Spanish, Stam (2006, 2010) has worked extensively on this pair with a special focus on gesture patterns. Stam (2006) shows that advanced learners of English still keep their gesture patterns coherent with the thinking for speaking in their first language, despite their speech being grammatically accurate in the L2. She concludes that their L2 English thinking for speaking is in between the thinking for speaking of monolingual English and Spanish speakers. They do not overload discourse with Path verbs and they use satellites, but not as many as native speakers. Advanced learners used the same verbs as natives do, while intermediate learners use constructions that are not grammatically incorrect but reveal their first language lexicalization patterns. She considers that the inconsistent use of satellites and the low frequency of Manner verbs are clear signs of transfer from their L1 thinking for speaking. She also points out that their gestures show that they did not fully acquire the second language thinking for speaking. Stam's (2006) results are supported by Choi and Lantolf's (2008) findings in a bidirectional English-Korean study, in which learners changed their speech and gesture patterns regarding Path but not regarding Manner. Stam (2010) reports the result of a longitudinal study of speech and co-speech gestures of Rosa, a Mexican English learner. She shows that Rosa's gestures did not change from 1997 until 2006, when Path gestures were less segmented and closer to English. In a follow up study with the same learner in 2011, Stam (2015) notices that the participant's speech in her L1 did not change but her L1 gestures were influenced by the L2 gesturing pattern. In her L2 there were changes in her speech particularly in Path expression (she used satellites from 2006), and there were changes in her Path and Manner gestures. She showed a combination of the L1 Spanish and the L2 English thinking for speaking patterns. In another longitudinal study with another L1 Spanish L2 English learner in a language classroom environment, Li, Eskildsen, and Cadierno (2014) find similar difficulties in speech at the initial levels of proficiency.

Other studies have contrasted other language pairs using different stimuli etc. and they have supported the existence of cross-linguistic influence in the acquisition of motion events in a satellite framed by speakers of a verb-framed language. For example, Goschler (2009) shows transfer on L2 German learners by L1 Turkish speakers. Liste-Lamas (2016a, 2016b) studies the difficulties of Spanish learners of L2 German in encoding Path. In particular, in Liste-Lamas (2015), she focuses on German deictic prefixes *hin-* and *her-* and their acquisition by speakers of L1 Spanish at three different levels of proficiency. Her results show the difficulty of restructuring the complex domain of deixis in the second language. Finally, the difficulties in overcoming the boundary-crossing constraint have been also examined in L2 acquisition of English by Spanish learners (Alonso Alonso 2016).

5.1.2 Verb-framed languages as a target language

Other scholars have focused exclusively on verb-framed languages as the target language, emphasizing the challenges for learners whose first language is satellite framed. Cadierno (2004), Cadierno and Lund (2004), Cadierno and Ruiz (2006) analyze the acquisition of Spanish as an L2 by Danish learners, at an intermediate and advanced level. These studies show that cross-linguistic influence is not homogeneous in the narratives of Danish learners of Spanish. In some aspects it is particularly salient, as in the degree of complexity of Path. Danish learners use more Ground complements than native speakers and they even present some cases of what Cadierno calls "satellization" as in (48):

(48) *El niño fue arriba de una roca*
 The boy go.PST.SG up of a rock
 'The boy climbed onto a rock'

This satellization consists of the use of abnormal constructions incorporating Path particles (in this case *arriba* 'up'). These constructions tend to be redundant and are not present in the narratives of native speakers (Cadierno 2008a: 261). However, there is no cross-linguistic influence in the expression of journeys (such as *The deer dropped the boy off a cliff into the water*). Cadierno concludes that the absence of this in her data is due to the difficulty of conveying such constructions in the Spanish language. She also considers the possibility of the impact of psychotypology (Kellerman 1995), that is, the perceived distance between the characteristic patterns of two languages. In Cadierno and Lund (2004) several hypotheses are proposed with regard to the language contrasts between Danish and Spanish motion events. First, they note that Spanish speakers acquiring Danish as an L2 might pay less attention to Manner, with a lower use of verbs of this kind. Second, it is predicted that Spanish learners of Danish will not use Manner verbs in boundary-crossing situations, at least in the first stages of the acquisition process. In the case of Danish speakers learning Spanish, they think it probable that Danish speakers will add Manner information in their Spanish narratives, even in boundary-crossing situations.

Looking back at the English and Spanish contrasts, but with the focus on the acquisition of Spanish as an L2, Navarro and Nicoladis (2005) see that their

English-speaking participants have virtually acquired the motion event lexicalization patterns of Spanish in oral narratives. This is particularly so in the case of Path encoding. They find some influence of English in the higher presence of verbs followed by a phrase, while the native speakers preferred bare verbs. Regarding Manner, the native speakers presented more cases of the encoding of this component in complements than in verbs. The English learners presented the opposite trend, with more Manner verbs and fewer Manner complements. Taking into account the factor of an immersion context, Lewis (2012) focuses on speech and gesture of L1 English learners of Spanish. The results show that the majority of the participants showed L2 thinking for speaking patterns in their L2 after six months abroad. This confirms the possibility that thinking for speaking patterns can change and be restructured.

The boundary-crossing constraint has received special attention, as it is a specific feature of verb-framed languages. Larrañaga et al. (2011) show that English-speaking learners of Spanish at different levels tend to express Manner of motion in the main verb, without respecting the boundary-crossing restriction. Their participants produced examples like *El ladrón corre en el banco* 'The thief run in the bank' to express cases like *The thief runs into the bank*. These utterances would be interpreted as locative by native speakers. In the same way, Muñoz-Carrasco and Cadierno (2019) show bidirectional transfer between L1 and L2 learners at three different levels (A2, B1 and B2). They show that the L1 thinking for speaking patterns are kept in the L2 even at more advanced levels, shown in satellizations, less use of Path verbs and lack of awareness of the boundary-crossing constraint. According to their results, the higher the level of proficiency is, the greater is the influence from the second language into the first one. In contrast, Lewandowski and Özçalışkan (2021) found that L1 Polish learners of L2 Spanish could adapt to the L2 patterns in boundary-crossing events.

Deixis has also received some attention as an area prone for transfer in verb-framed languages acquisition. Yoshinari (2015) studies Japanese second language acquisition by learners of English and Mandarin Chinese, and shows the importance of Deixis in Japanese and the challenge it poses for learners of this language.

5.2 Intra-typological studies on motion and second language acquisition

The number of studies contrasting an L1 and L2 from the same typological group is much smaller than that of studies focused on inter-typological differences. However, there have been a few of them on both sides of the typology. In the case of satellite-framed languages, there are two studies contrasting Germanic and Slavonic languages. Filipović and Vidaković (2010) present a bidirectional study with English and Serbo-Croatian participants. They find that the results from the groups of learners are different from the results in the L1 and in the L2. In both cases, they have some specific influences from their first language, which shape their rhetorical style to a different degree. For example, English speakers do not tend to codify frequently Path information with boundary-crossing in the directional prefix of a Manner verb (as the Serbo-Croatian speakers do). They follow their own L1 pattern, by using a Manner verb and a preposition. Only speakers with the highest language proficiency follow the L2 pattern on certain occasions. Filipović and Vidaković (2010) also highlight the importance of several phenomena other than cross-linguistic influence, such as the economy of linguistic forms to ease the processing load. For instance, Serbian learners take to L2 thinking for speaking easily by using only prepositions to express Path, as this is a simpler pattern than the one in their L1 Path expression that requires verb prefixes as well as prepositions, and verb-prefix coordination (Filipović 2007a). In contrast, L1 English learners of L2 Serbo-Croatian acquire L2 motion expressions at a lower pace because they stick to their L1 simpler pattern of using prepositions and fail to also add the relevant prefixes as required by the L2 Serbo-Croatian. They also give importance to general knowledge about motion, conceptualized primarily as a change of location, which makes difficult the omission of Path, whilst Manner can be easily omitted. It is worth remembering that Manner is an optional component, even in satellite-framed languages because all languages can express the Path in the verb.

Hasko (2010) focuses on one of the main language contrasts between Russian and English. One of these contrasts is the use of unidirectional and non-unidirectional Manner verbs in Russian. Hasko (2010) explains that unidirectional verbs are characterized by: (i) indicating motion in one direction, (ii) continuously and (iii) at a particular moment, as in (49) taken from Hasko (2010: 43):

(49) *Nu vot, idu ia po ulitse Gor'kogo*
      so go-UNI.IMP I on Street Gorky
      'So, I am walking down Gorky street'

By contrast, non-unidirectional verbs refer to movement that is not in one single direction, not in one attempt and not at the same time at once. An example is (50) taken from Hasko (2010: 44):

(50) *Khozhu ia znakomyni zakoulkami po liubimonu tsentru*
      go-NON.IMP I familiar backstreets in favorite centre
      'I am walking up and down familiar backstreets in my favorite city centre'

Hasko (2010) finds that advanced learners overuse non-unidirectional verbs. Her results show that learners are not consistent with Russian thinking for speaking. The fact that both languages are satellite-framed causes the cross-linguistic differences to be subtler than in inter-typological contrasts. However they should not be disregarded as they constitute cases of conceptual transfer.

In other cases, the contrast has been made between two groups of learners with different mother tongues who are in the process of acquiring another language. For instance, Cadierno and P. Robinson (2009) look at the acquisition of L2 English motion events by Danish and Japanese speakers. They find out that Danish learners might benefit from a positive transfer in Plus Ground expression. They claim that the benefits of positive transfer for the thinking for speaking in the second language are related to the level of proficiency and the level of task complexity. Cadierno and P. Robinson (2009: 268) consider that productions which are more complex and closer to the L2 can be expected when the L1 is typologically similar to the L2. This happens especially in the case of cognitively complex tasks.

Cadierno (2010) reaches the same conclusions in a study of Danish as a second language by speakers of Russian, German and Spanish. As expected, German and Russian learners used more similar constructions to the L2, with a wider variety of Manner verbs, and they produced more motion verbs than Spanish learners. She also finds intra-typological differences, for example in relation to boundary-crossing events, German learners did better than Russian learners. Cadierno (2010: 25) considers the possibility that Russian learners might not be able to differentiate between Danish locative and traslocative Path particles. This distinction enables speakers to distinguish between boundary-crossing and non-boundary-crossing events. Germans are also better in the variety of motion verbs, but in this case the genetic links between German and Danish can explain this difference.

Czechowska and Ewert (2011) find that monolingual speakers of Polish pay more attention to Manner than English speakers, who focus more on Path. Polish-English bilingual speakers with less proficiency in the L2 start to change their lexicalization patterns, whereas bilinguals with higher levels of proficienty seem to restructure the conceptual domain. Lewandowski and Özçalışkan (2021) also find a mixed pattern, unlike the L1 and the L2, and an effect of the L1, in their study with Polish learners of L2 German. Vulchanova, Martínez, and Vulchanov (2012) explore the intra-typological differences between Norwegian and Bulgarian. Whereas Norwegian speakers tend to use prepositions in the encoding of Path, Bulgarian uses lexicon. In this study, advanced learners of L2 Norwegian whose first language is Bulgarian, do not present conceptual transfer in Path description, which supports the possibility of changing the L1 thinking for speaking patterns.

There has been also some work on Danish as a second language by speakers of German and Turkish (Jessen and Cadierno 2013). Jessen and Cadierno find conceptual transfer in the recategorization of motion verbs in the second language. For example, German speakers attempted to maintain certain distinctions that are not present in Danish but are relevant in their L1. The differences were of course larger in the case of Turkish learners of Danish. This maintenance of thinking for speaking patterns from the first language is also observed with regard to conceptual transfer in the description of Path (Jessen 2014b) and Manner (Jessen 2014a).

In the case of verb-framed languages acquired by speakers of verb-framed languages, Ibarretxe-Antuñano (2004c) shows that L2 Basque learners whose first language is Spanish do not present Path in the same detailed fashion as native speakers do. Cadierno and Ruiz (2006) compare Italian and Danish learners of Spanish as a second language. This study mainly focuses on the inter-typological differences. However, it is striking that Italian speakers did not present significant differences with regard to Manner expression nor type-token ratio. Danish speakers only used Manner verbs to express Manner and described Path in more detail by the addition of satellizations. They also had difficulties respecting the boundary-crossing constraint.

Hijazo-Gascón (2018) presents important differences in the acquisition of Spanish as a second language by speakers of French, German and Italian. He shows that Italian speakers transfer a more detailed elaboration of Path into the second language. French and Italian speakers also transfer certain caused motion constructions (make + infinitve) that are not present in the target language. The results of his study are expanded and reported in more detail in this volume. In a different study, of learners of L2 Spanish whose first languages are French, German and Italian, Hijazo-Gascón (2017) also shows difficulties in the use of *ir* 'go', *venir* 'come', *llevar* 'take' and *traer* 'bring', showing inter- and intra-typological transfer in the area of deixis. A replication of this study showed intra-typological differences in L2 Greek by L1 Spanish and L1 Spanish/Catalan learners (Andriá and Hijazo-Gascón 2018). Another study with a pedagogical intervention showed the benefits of explicit training in deictic verbs in L2 Spanish to L1 German and Italian learners (Colasacco 2019).

5.3 Other lines of research in SLA related to motion events

There are other areas of research into second language acquisition and motion events that look into different aspects of the motion event or that address the effects of thinking for speaking more in relation to cognition. The scope of this book is not to provide an extended revision of these studies but a few notes on their main findings are presented in this section.

One of the main bodies of research is that of motion and aspect. These studies explore the role of grammatical aspect in the encoding of motion event (Bylund 2008, 2009; Bylund and Jarvis 2011; Carroll and von Stutterheim 2003; Schmiedtová and Flecken 2008). Their main focus is on the differences between aspectual and non-aspectual languages. It seems that speakers of languages that can encode aspect in a progressive tense, e.g. Spanish or English, are less prone to mention the endpoints of the movement and segment the phases of the movement. These differences lead to cross-linguistic influence from the first language into the second, as noticed by Carroll and von Stuttenheim (2003) in English speaker learners of German. Bylund and Jarvis (2013) studied motion events from this perspective in the speech of Swedish-Spanish bilinguals. Their results showed that the endpoints are mentioned by this group more frequently than by native speakers.

Caused motion has also received some attention. This has been particularly studied in the case of the contrasts between French and English (Hendriks, Hickmann, and Demagny 2008; Hickmann and Hendriks 2006). Hijazo-Gascón (2018) also notes some intra-typological differences and consequent transfers in L2 Spanish by L1 French and Italian learners. A subset of caused-motion events that has been particularly salient in the analysis is that of placement events, mainly as a result of the application of the cross-linguistic differences analyzed within the PUT project of the Max Planck Institute for Psycholinguistics (Kopecka and Narasimhan 2012). Some examples of these differences can depend on force dynamics and intentionality, as in Spanish: *caerse* 'fall', *caerse* + dative 'drop (accidentally)', *dejar caer* 'leave fall, drop (intentionally)', *tirar* 'throw', *lanzar* 'cast', *arrojar* 'cast violently' (See Ibarretxe-Antuñano 2012). Similarly, in some Germanic languages the position of the Figure is key for conceptualization. For example in Dutch *zetten* 'set/stand' and *leggen* 'lay' (Narasimhan and Gullberg 2011). These cross-linguistic differences have consequences in second language acquisition, as shown by Viberg (1998) for Swedish as a second language, Gullberg (2009a) for English learners of L2 Dutch, Gullberg (2009b) in the case of Dutch and German learners of L2 French, Lemmens and Perrez (2010) on French learners of L2 Dutch, and Alferink and Gullberg (2014) on French-Dutch bilinguals.

Some studies have contrasted Danish and Spanish (Cadierno, Ibarretxe-Antuñano, and Hijazo-Gascón 2016; Hijazo-Gascón, Cadierno, and Ibarretxe-Antuñano 2016; Ibarretxe-Antuñano, Cadierno, and Hijazo-Gascón 2016). Danish and Spanish show important cross-linguistic differences in the encoding of these events. In Spanish, if the Figure is placed on a surface, the verbs *dejar* 'leave' and *poner* 'put (generally)' are used and *meter* 'put in' is used when the

Figure is placed in a container. In the case of Danish, the position of the Figure is crucial and should be encoded: *lægge* 'put horizontally' is used for horizontal positions and *sætte* and *stille* 'put vertically' for a vertical position. The direction of the movement is encoded in a satellite. The results of these studies show clear difficulties for learners in restructuring this domain in the second language, with cases of overuse of general verbs, underuse of particles and creation of non-native combinations.

Finally, one of the main criticisms of studies on motion events and second language acquisition is that researchers have mainly focused on verbalization and very little on cognition (Athanasopoulos and Bylund 2013). As Cadierno (2017) points out, Slobin (2003) states that the effects of thinking for speaking are in verbalization, but there can also be anticipatory effects and consequential effects. In this sense, Cadierno (2017) notes that there have been a few studies that have worked on anticipatory effects using eye-tracking methodology (Flecken 2011; Soroli 2012; Soroli and Hickman 2010), and others on the consequential effects of thinking for speaking (Filipović 2011; Hickman et al. 2017).

5.4 Main results of the literature on the acquisition of motion events

As Cadierno (2008b) points out, this line of research is particularly relevant for second language acquisition, not only from a theoretical acquisition perspective, but also from an applied pedagogical perspective, which will be explained in Chapter 6. It is also relevant for linguistic relativity, as it examines how adult learners adapt to the thinking for speaking patterns in the second language. The studies carried out to date are not completely homogeneous. Gullberg (2011) claims that some of these studies (Negueruela et al. 2004; Choi and Lantolf 2008 and Cadierno 2004) show instances of conceptual transfer from the first language thinking for speaking, even in advanced learners. In the case of the acquisition of a satellite-framed language, it seems that the difficulty is not as much the expression of Manner, as the fusion of Manner and Path (A. Brown and Gullberg 2008). When the target language is verb-framed, English speakers find ways to express Manner (Negueruela et al. 2004; Choi and Lantolf 2008), whereas it does not seem problematic for Danish speakers to omit this component (Cadierno 2004). However, they do show cross-linguistic patterns in the expression of Path by means of satellizations (Cadierno 2004). Gullberg (2011) concludes that these studies suggest difficulties in the reconceptualization of the motion domain in the L2. Independently of the typological direction, transfer from the first language is still present.

However, as noted by Gullberg (2011), none of the studies excludes the possibility that thinking for speaking can be changed. In fact, some studies show bidirectional cross-linguistic influence. This is the case with A. Brown and Gullberg (2008, 2010), who analyze speech and gesture in English and Japanese as L1 and L2. Their results show that the group of English speakers as L2 (Japanese L1) gestures differently from native speakers of English, but also differently from monolingual Japanese speakers. Similarly, Gullberg (2009b) finds conceptual transfer in French as a second language by German and Dutch learners in placement events. Learners reproduced the form of the object more than native speakers of French but less than monolingual Dutch speakers. Gullberg (2011) explains that these studies give evidence of a change into reconceptualization. This is what Cadierno (2004) defines as a *different thinking for speaking*, which later has been named *re-thinking for speaking* by P. Robinson and N. Ellis (2008). This would support the idea of the permeability of the L1 in relation to the L2, which involves revising the traditional idea of L1 conceptualization as invariable and impossible to restructure. It seems that all languages present in a speaker's mind interact. Hence the linguistic behavior of a speaker should be considered as dynamic and changing, depending on the situation and usage (Gullberg 2011: 160).

In her analysis of the literature on the acquisition of motion events by learners of a second language, Cadierno (2017) considers that the results from this whole body of research can be summarized into five conclusions. First, the studies show that there is cross-linguistic influence of the thinking for speaking patterns in the process of acquisition from the first language to the second. This happens both when the first language is satellite-framed and the second is verb-framed and vice versa. An example of this is the presence of satellizations in L2 Spanish narratives by Danish learners (Cadierno 2004; Cadierno and Ruiz 2006).

Second, the first language thinking for speaking patterns can be present in the form of gesture. The results of the studies taking the gestural component into account support the idea of a *manual accent* by Kellerman and van Hoof (2003). Third, advanced learners are able to develop L2 thinking for speaking patterns, but not always in the same way and in all aspects of the motion event. Cadierno (2017) gives the example of Choi and Lantolf (2008) in which advanced students of Korean L2 encoded Path according to the L2 patterns but still found difficulties with the encoding of Manner. The results presented in the acquisition study in this book are coherent with this result of the studies on motion, as the advanced learners will acquire some aspects of the motion event, but their first language thinking for speaking patterns will be present in some others.

Fourth, intra-typological contrasts can also be the basis for cross-linguistic influence. They can also present difficulties for the re-thinking for speaking, as shown in the case of Hasko (2010) for Russian and English speakers. The results of the study presented here show this pattern in the case of Italian and French learners of Spanish as a second language.

Finally, cross-linguistic influence also occurs from the second language into the first language. As Cadierno (2017) points out, the extensive work on English and Japanese by A. Brown and Gullberg (2008, 2010) shows evidence of convergence between the L1 and the L2 patterns. This is a pattern different to that followed by monolinguals of each language. These authors claim the support of these findings to give empirical support to Grosjean's (1989) theory that a bilingual does not equate to two monolinguals. They support Cook's (2012) idea of multicompetence, that is, the notion that the competences of multilingual and bilingual speakers are different to that of monolinguals and that they should not be treated as the same. Other studies also support this finding, such as Bylund and Jarvis (2013) on aspect in bilinguals.

The acquisition study presented here focuses mainly on voluntary motion and transfer from the first into the second language. The main results of the study are found with regard to inter- and intra-typological differences and how these lead to transfer into second language acquisition. They support these claims and contribute to give support to these notions of *multicompetence* and convergence patterns, as well as Filipović (2019b) principle of bilinguals maximizing common ground. In order to capture all the inter- and intra-typological differences among the languages present in the study, the next chapter focuses on French, German, Italian and Spanish and their lexicalization patterns for the motion semantic domain.

Chapter 3
Inter- and intra-typological differences

1 Intra-typological differences and genetic families

This chapter presents a deeper examination into the inter- and intra-typological differences with regard to the four languages included in this study, namely French, German, Italian and Spanish. A comprehensive understanding of how motion is encoded in these four languages will allow for a deeper analysis of the contrasts they show and of their impact on the acquisition of Spanish as a second language. As expected, the satellite-framed language of the study, German, shows interesting contrasts with the other three verb-framed languages. However, German also shows some similarities to Italian in the encoding of certain aspects. There are thus some intra-typological differences within the Romance language family. Indeed, the differences among languages belonging to the same typological group are one of the main topics of debate in the field. Within the satellite-framed group, Slavonic and Germanic languages, present differences with regard to morphological combinations (Filipović 2007a) or descriptions of Path (Ragnasdóttir and Strömqvist 2004). Even varieties of the same language have shown greater variation in the expression of Path, such as Swiss German and Standard German (Berthele 2004, 2006, 2013). In the case of verb-framed languages, major differences have been found in relation to the expression of Posture in Mayan languages, in particular in Tzeltal (P. Brown 2004). The expression of Manner also varies in its frequency and its encoding elements, such as the existence of ideophones in Basque (Ibarretxe-Antuñano 2004a, 2004b, 2006a) and Japanese (Akita 2017). The description of Path also allows for variation, for example with more detailed descriptions in Basque than in Spanish (Ibarretxe-Antuñano 2004a, 2004b). In all the above cases these languages are verb-framed but they come from very different genetic families. One of the novelties of this study is precisely the finding of intra-typological differences among languages that belong to the same genetic family.

This variation does not undermine the semantic typology of motion events, but helps to refine and develop the framework. Obviously, one of the main aims of typologists is to classify languages according to certain criteria, which inevitably involves some degree of generalization. However, the subtle differences among closely related languages address a number of theoretical and practical issues, which should not be overlooked. In the case of Romance languages, it is true that nearly all of them are verb-framed (with the exception of Rhaeto-Romance, as will be explained below) and to a greater or lesser degree they share the features proposed by Talmy (1985, 1991, 2000a, 2000b) and Slobin (1991, 1996a, 2000, 2004) for this type of languages. However, this chapter will explain how the presence of different linguistic devices in any language helps to create some differences in the rhetorical style of their speakers. In order to achieve a better understanding of how these languages differ, it is important to be aware of the evolution from Latin into Romance languages. Understanding the typological shift from satellite-framed into verb-framed patterns produced during this evolutionary process is also crucial to our understanding of the differences in the current state of Romance languages. The role of minority languages also helps us to identify the nature of the encoding of motion events within the Romance family, since they have been more isolated and evolved differently.

1.1 From Latin into Romance motion events

The basis of the intra-typological contrasts among Romance languages lies in the typological change produced during the evolution from Latin. This satellite-framed language evolved into Romance languages, which are mainly verb-framed. Latin has been considered a satellite-framed language since the original proposal of the typology. Talmy (1985) includes its prefixes as an example of his definition of satellite, for example *in-ire* 'go in', *in-gredi* 'go in' or incurrere 'run in'. An example of this satellite-framed pattern in Latin is (51) cited in Iacobini and Fagard (2011: 156):

(51) *Iuli-a flumen tra-nat-at*
 Julie-NOM.SG river.ACC.SG across-swim-PRS.3SG
 'Julie swims across the river'

There is common agreement with this classification of Latin as a satellite-framed language, although several authors (Stolova 2008, 2015; Ferrari and Mosca 2010; Iacobini and Fagard 2011; Iacobini 2012; Mosca 2017; among others) stress the complex nature of the encoding of motion events in Latin. For example, Ferrari and Mosca (2010) have pointed out that Path seems to be expressed by three linguistic devices in Latin, namely satellite prefixes, nominal cases and prepositions. These three linguistic elements present similar frequencies. The ascription of Latin to one typological group or the other goes beyond the scope of this study and we will assume its nature as a satellite-framed language, although its complexity is acknowledged (see the above mentioned literature for a more detailed description of Latin motion events). It is the evolution from this satellite-framed language to the modern verb-framed Romance languages which is of special interest for this study.

This transition from Latin to Romance languages is a complex phenomenon and does not just involve the substitution of one type by another (Ferrari and Mosca 2010; Mosca 2017; Stolova 2008, 2015). Other general tendencies in this evolution should be considered. For example Stolova (2015) explains that the complete loss of the category of deponent verbs[1] accounts for the disappearance of *egredi* 'go out', *ingredi* 'go in' and *degredi* 'go down', all of them deponent motion verbs. In Late Latin new phenomena appear such as the loss of compound motion verbs, the survival of the items that were perceived as monomorphematic, and the lexicalization of directed movement in terms of nouns and adjectives with spatial/deictic reference. Stolova (2008: 260) suggests this was an attempt to place the direction or path information in the foreground by incorporating it into the verbal stem. The loss of transparency and productivity of the Latin prefixes that acted as satellites resulted in the integration of Path in the main verb. This is the case of (52) for verbs meaning 'enter, come in':

(52) *in-ire*   *entrar* (Portuguese, Spanish, Catalan)
     intro-ire > *entrer* (French)
     in-trare   *entrare* (Italian)
               a intra (Romanian)

In the examples in (52) Path is encoded in the satellites *in-*, *intro-* and *intra-*, 'in' but in the evolution into Romance languages, this component is lexicalized in the verb root. Stolova (2008) focuses on Late Latin, which is crucial since this is the intermediate phase of this typological shift from satellite- to verb-framed languages. She foregrounds two change factors. First, the loss of productivity of the prefix system means that prefixed verbs were reinterpreted as monomorphemic, like *entrer*, *entrar*, etc. 'enter' in (50). Second, the creation of denominal verbs became a frequent morphological device. These trends led to the substitution of the most frequent lexicalization pattern in Classical Latin 'Motion + Manner/Cause' by that of 'Motion + Path'. According to Stolova (2008), the new verbs were created from nouns expressing a Ground, which suggest a movement towards them. For instance, stemming from *mons, -tis* 'mountain' the verb *montare 'ascend, go up' is created in late Latin which evolves into *monter* in French, *montare* in Italian, *montar* in Occitan and *muntar* in Rhaeto-Romance and Catalan. Similarly, the Catalan verb *pujar* 'ascend' stems from *podiare in Late Latin, which evolved from *podium* 'elevated place'. This phenomenon also applies to the opposite movement of descending, and a number of verbs are

---

[1] Deponent verbs are verbs that are conjugated with passive forms but have an active meaning

created from *vallis* 'valley', like *dévaler* in French, *davallar* in Catalan and *davalar* in Occitan, all meaning 'descend, go down'. Likewise, the origin of the French verb se *baisser*, the Portuguese *baixar*, the Catalan *(a)baixar* and the Spanish *bajar* 'descend, go down', comes from the late Latin **bassiare*, which stems from the adjective *bassus* 'short, low'. It is interesting to find that this tendency to create verbs from nouns with internal directionality also applies to borrowings from other languages. This seems particularly frequent in Romanian, due to its contact with Slavonic languages. In this language the verbs *a se coborî*, *a se pogorî* and *a se scoborî*, all meaning 'descend, go down' are related to the terms in Old Slavonic *pogorĭ* 'down', *pogorĭnŭ* 'head' and *podgorije* 'valley', *pogorije* 'range of mountains' and *gora* 'mountain' (Stolova 2008: 260).

In her thorough analysis on lexical change in motion events from Latin to Romance languages, Stolova (2015) examines these two trends further and shows how both formal continuity and formal change are at work in the evolution of the semantic field of motion. For instance, there is a high level of formal continuity between monomorphematic generic and Manner verbs is high. Most forms of *ire* 'go', *currere* 'run', *salire* 'jump', and *vadere* 'go' are kept in Romance languages. This also happens with other monomorphematic forms expressing Path, e.g. *venire* 'come', which remain in Romance languages. The most affected forms during his evolution process were those of polymorphematic verbs expressing Path through prefixes. Some of these survived because their prefix was reinterpreted as part of the stem. For instance, *exire* 'go out' evolved into Catalan *eixir*, Old Spanish *exir*, and Occitan *eissir*. According to Stolova (2015: 64) this should be understood as the historical outcome of communicative strategies to express Path with more transparency. She considers that there is a connection between the lexical continuity of some items, the loss of satellite-prefixes and the centrality of Path and its key role in human cognition. This process is apparently similar in the evolution of other languages such as English and North American languages and it is coherent with the results of experimental studies, research on memory and on child language acquisition. They all show the high relevance of Path in cognition.

Stolova (2015: 185) explains that the development from Latin to Romance needs to be understood as a complex combination of three different phenomena. The first of these is the shift from a satellite-framed system to a verb-framed one. This is accomplished by means of five different tendencies:
– The loss of the compound forms, such as *abire* 'go away'
– The retention of simple forms such as *venire* 'come', which evolves into *venir*, *venire*, etc. in different languages.

- The semantic change of verbs from other lexical fields that end up as motion verbs. The example she gives is *completere* 'fill', which evolves into Sardinian *lompi, crompi, lòmpere, cròmpere* 'come'
 - The word formation of new verbs of motion from nouns and adjectives. For example *bassus* 'short' > Catalan *baixar*, Spanish *bajar* 'go down'
 - The reanalysis of compound forms as simple ones (e.g. *exire* 'go out' > Italian *uscire* 'go out').

The second phenomenon is the reliance on satellites by combining prepositions and nouns, which evolve into verb-framed forms. For example, from Latin *ad* 'towards' and *ripa* 'shore' there is an evolution to Late Latin *adripare* 'come to shore' that culminates in French *arriver* 'come'. Finally, the third phenomenon is the creation of new compound verbs by combining prepositions, pronouns, and adverbs with different types of lexical items. For example, from *ambulare* 'walk', the pronoun *se* and the adverbial pronoun *inde* 'thence' > Italian *andarsene* 'go away'. It is important to note that Stolova considers the reflective pronoun *se* and the reflexes from adverbial pronoun *inde* (e.g. *ne* in Italian and *en* in French) as satellites.

According to Stolova (2015) only 8 out of 26 Latin motion verbs remain in practically all Romance languages. These are the reflexes from *ire* 'go', *venire* 'come', *ambulare* 'walk', *currere* 'run', *intrare* 'go in', *exire* 'go out', *ascendere* 'ascend' and *descendere* 'descend'. Other verbs prevail in the Romance lexicons but with different meanings. Latin *salire* 'jump' evolved from vertical movement, still present in Italian *salire* 'go up', to horizontal movement in Spanish *salir* and Portuguese *sair* 'go out'. In other cases, culture has proved to be crucial in the different evolution of Latin verb meanings. As Stolova (2015: 12) explains in detail, the verb *plicare* 'fold' developed a new motion meaning in some languages. In Portuguese and Spanish it turned into *chegar* and *llegar* respectively and in Romanian into *a pleca*. However the meaning could not be more different. In the Iberian languages the reflexes of *plicare* mean 'come', 'arrive', whilst the Romanian verb means 'go away'. Stolova suggests that in the Iberian societies the meaning derived from *plicare velam*, i.e. to 'fold the sail', which was a signal of the arrival into port. In Balkan shepherd society *plicare tentoria* 'fold tents' was an event related to the departure of speakers when they were about to move to a different place.

1.2 Motion events in minority Romance languages

Research on minority Romance languages has proved to be relevant for the typology (Vicario 1997; Berthele 2006, 2013; Ibarretxe-Antuñano, Hijazo-Gascón, and Moret-Oliver 2017). Speakers of these languages show divergence from the main patterns in the major Romance languages. Therefore their study provides interesting data, which challenge some of the main assumptions in the framework. The socio-politic situation of these languages varies greatly, but as claimed by Ibarretxe-Antuñano, Hijazo-Gascón, and Moret-Oliver (2017), minority languages share certain sociolinguistic features, such as linguistic conservatism, less accessibility and fewer possibilities of communication, situations of diglossia with pressure from dominant languages, lack of standardization, predominance of oral features. As will be seen, they also share some features in relation to the encoding of motion events. In this section the focus will be on Rhaeto-Romance (Vicario 1997; Berthele 2006, 2013), Aragonese (Hijazo-Gascón and Ibarretxe-Antuñano 2010; Ibarretxe-Antuñano, Hijazo-Gascón, and Moret-Oliver 2017) and to a lesser degree on Catalan, particularly in one of its Western variants (Ibarretxe-Antuñano, Hijazo-Gascón, and Moret-Oliver 2017). Examples from other varieties are also provided for comparison.

The use of satellite-framed lexicalization patterns with Path encoded outside the main verb seems to be very common in certain minority Romance languages, which contradicts previous claims based on generalizations taken from research on the main Romance languages. This satellite-framed pattern is particularly frequent in the case of languages that have not developed a standard variety and have been kept as oral languages. This is the case with Rhaeto-Romance, which comprises three large dialectal groups: Dolomitic Ladin and Friulan in Italy and Romansch in Switzerland. It seems that its most common lexicalization pattern is satellite-framed and not verb-framed, as would be expected in the case of a Romance language.

Vicario (1997) carries out an in-depth study on Friulan analyitic, some of which are used to express motion. These are defined as the verb category resulting from the union of a verb base and a modifier element, as in (53):

(53) *La mame 'e je lade su cumò*
'The mum went up (ascended) now'

In this example (Vicario 1997: 22) the component of Path is expressed in the particle *su* 'up' and not in the neutral verb *lâ* 'go'. This verb-particle combination means 'ascend', similarly to satellite-framed language patterns, e.g. *go up*. According to Vicario, these verbs are used for the expression of movement. In fact,

Vicario explains that one of the debates in the creation of a Friulan orthography was whether to write these elements with a hyphen. Vicario documents the presence of these constructions as early as the 9th Century and analyzes the current combinations of particles, like *vie* 'out', *jù* 'down', *fûr* 'out', *dentri* 'into', etc. with Deictic and Manner verbs, like *vignî* 'come', *corî* 'run', *saltâ* 'jump'. Ladin, the other Italian variant of Rhaeto-Romance, presents similar combinations with *jí* 'go' (Vicario 1997: 209). For example, *jí dlungia* 'go closer', *jí dô* 'go after, follow', *jí fora* 'go out', *jí ia* 'go away', *jí jö* 'go up', *jí sö* 'go down'.

Another Rhaeto-Romance variety is Romansch, spoken in Switzerland. Berthele (2006, 2013) has studied this language extensively from Talmy's and Slobin's perspective. In his studies he contrasts it with French, Swiss German and Standard German. He also points out the presence of these constructions involving the combination of a verb base and an additional particle:

(54) *al pövel d'aviöls es crodà giò per terra*
 the beehive of.bees be.AUX.PRS.3SG fall.PTCP down by ground
 'The beehive falls to the ground'

(55) *els von or aint igl gôt*
 they go.PRS.3PL out in the forest
 'They go out to the forest'

These examples, documented by Berthele (2006: 168), show how Path is encoded in the satellites *giò* 'down' and *or* 'out'. In (54) a redundant construction is present, similarly to *fall down* in English, since downward movement is described both in the verb and in the particle. In (55) a neuter verb *von* 'go' is combined with the directional particle *or* 'out'. His results in comparison with the other languages in his study (French and German) show that Romansch is a low-Manner salient language, with similar encoding of Manner to that of French speakers, but with a clear preference for encoding Path in a satellite. Berthele also shows that Romansch does not respect the boundary-crossing constraint, as boundary-crossing events can be expressed with a Manner verb and a prepositional phrase such as *or* 'out'. Berhtele (2006: 150) concludes that Romansch is a satellite-framed language.

Other minority languages present similar features. This is the case with Aragonese, a minority language spoken in the North of Aragón (Spain). Hijazo-Gascón and Ibarretxe-Antuñano (2010) find interesting cases of verb-particle combinations to express motion, even with non-motion verbs:

(56) *Fe-te ent'alto / ta dintro / ta baixo*
    make.IMP-you towards.up / to inside / to down
    'Go up', 'Come in', 'Go down'

The use of *fer* 'make' together with a directional adverb to express motion is similar to satellite-framed language constructions. This possibility is, in fact, a common feature of high Path-salient languages (Ibarretxe-Antuñano 2004b, 2009a). In a later study, Ibarretxe-Antuñano, Hijazo-Gascón, and Moret-Oliver (2017) gather data from the *Frog story* in different varieties of Aragonese and Western Catalan, which is spoken in the Eastern area of Aragón that borders with Catalonia. Their results reveal the presence of ideophones to encode Manner, especially in Aragonese, such as *a redolons* 'rolling', *patapimpatapa* 'bang', *cutio-cutio* 'quietly' and *bau* 'suddenly'. However, these specific linguistic devices do not translate to a higher frequency of this component and both languages are still low-Manner salient. The expression of Path resembles in some aspects Berthele's findings on Romansch, but in this case without direct contact with Germanic languages. This shows that speakers from smaller speech communities whose languages have been kept with orality features tend to share certain characteristics (Berthele 2013). Catalan and Aragonese speakers express Path more than French or Spanish speakers do and they use pseudo-satellites, in the same way as Italian speakers (see Hijazo-Gascón and Ibarretxe-Antuñano 2013a, 2013b, the following sections). For example (57) in Catalan and (58) in Aragonese:

(57) *Van caure damunt de l'aigua*
    AUX.3PL fall.INF on.top.of of the.water
    'They fell on top of the water'

(58) *El can blinca t'alto*
    the dog jump.3SG up.to-top
    'The dog jumps up'

Aragonese narratives also present several cases of Complete Path, i.e. motion events in which both source and goal of movement are expressed, as in the Aragonese example in (59). This is a prominent feature of other verb-framed languages, such as Basque (Ibarretxe-Antuñano 2004a, 2004b) and, according to Berthele (2013), it is a common feature in minority oral languages.

(59) *El can se cay de la ventana ta abaixo con o pote*
    the dog CL fall.3SG of window up.to below with the jar
    'The dog fell down from the window with the jar'

The presence of different linguistic devices in other Romance languages such as Romanian, Portuguese and Galician seems to vary as well, but more research is needed in order to have a fuller account of motion expression in these languages. There are similar analytical constructions with a verb and a particle although it seems that these occur in a less productive way than in Rhaeto-Romance. Vicario (1997: 211) gathers some examples from Romanian:

(60) *A se face încoace / încolo*
      REFL-make.INF close / far
      'come closer /go away'

This example uses a construction with a support verb, such as *face* 'make'. Vicario also explains that combining spatial adverbs with *ir* 'go' and *venir* 'come' is also possible in Portuguese: *vou dentro* 'I go in', *vou fora* 'I go out', *vou acima* 'I go up', *vou abaixo* 'I go down', *vou-me embora* 'I go away'. He claims that this use is acceptable but synthetic forms are preferred. It seems that there are also some analytic verbs in Galician, although Vicario (1997: 209) only documents cases with metaphorical meaning, such as (61):

(61) *Viñeronlle abaixo os seus ideais*
      come.PST.3PL.to him down the his ideals
      'He lost his ideals'

The analysis of Rhaeto-Romance, Aragonese and Catalan sheds light on intra-typological variation and challenges some theoretical assumptions. Rhaeto-Romance should be considered as a satellite-framed language, despite its genetic affiliation to Romance languages. Catalan and Aragonese cannot be considered satellite-framed but present different devices to express Manner and Path, which impact mainly in the detailed descriptions of Path. In this sense, the different degree of standardization seems to play a role for rhetorical styles and encoding of motion events as pointed out by Berthele (2006, 2013). Both Berthele (2006, 2013) and Ibarretxe-Antuñano (2009) refer to research on orality and literacy by Koch and Oesterreicher (1994) to explain some phenomena present in the narratives in Romansch, Swiss German and Basque. For Koch and Oesterreicher (1994) conceptual orality includes fewer items in the lexicon of some semantic domains, ellipsis, frequency of use of light verbs like DO or MAKE. Indeed, in his analysis of French, Swiss and Standard German and Romansch, Berthele (2013) concludes that the larger the speech community, the more Manner and Path verbs and the more Ground elements are included in the narratives. Complex Path elaboration seems to be more frequent in languages with fewer speakers. This illustrates how sociolinguistic features also play a role and how other minority Romance languages present divergences with regard to the evolution of motion encoding from Latin, their position in the typology and their thinking for speaking.

However, these intra-typological differences are not exclusive to minority Romance languages. Some of these patterns, such as verb-particle combinations, are also very frequent in Italian, as will be explained in Section 2.3.1. In the case of French and Spanish, these constructions seem to be considered very colloquial and are used only in oral speech. Pleonastic constructions such as *subo arriba* 'ascend up', *entro dentro* 'enter inside' are not considered normatively acceptable in Spanish, neither in French, nor Portuguese, whilst they are acceptable in Italian. Further studies on motion in these and other languages (e.g. Portuguese, Romanian, Asturian, Sardinian) are still needed for a deeper understanding of intra-typological languages. Moreover, sociological factors seem to play a role in the different ways of encoding motion events. Language contact, isolation from other related varieties, orality and late (or lack of) standardization seem to be key factors to take into account when contrasting Romance languages and its different outcomes in the typological shift and language evolution.

2 Motion Events in French, Italian and Spanish

Now that we have a better understanding of the typological shift from Latin into Romance and how motion is expressed in minority Romance languages, we can delve into the description of motion in the three major Romance languages that are present in our study. There are several aspects of motion in which these languages differ and which have caused heated debates among scholars about the extent to which they belong to the group of verb-framed languages. These cross-linguistic and intra-typological differences are tackled here in different sections focusing on Motion verbs, the description of Manner (through Manner verbs and their potential use in boundary-crossing situations), the encoding of Path (in verb-particle constructions, prefixes, and adverbial pronouns), the differences in meaning in Deictic motion verbs, and Caused motion. In the final sections the position of these three languages in the semantic typology of motion events will be revisited.

2.1 Motion verbs in Romance languages

Motion in Romance languages has been approached from different perspectives, the study of motion verbs and their syntactic and semantic properties being one of the most important. In this section an overview of different classifications of motion verbs is presented. This is mainly exemplified via Spanish, as it is the prototypical verb-framed language in Talmy's typology. The focus will then turn to Manner of motion verbs and their different semantic classifications. In this case Italian is the language that has received most attention, and as such will be foregrounded in this debate.

From a syntactic point of view, Spanish traditional grammar (Alcina and Blecua 1975) tends to consider Spanish motion verbs as a subgroup of intransitive verbs as seen in (62), although some of these verbs can also be transitive as in (63):

(62) *He subido a la planta de arriba en el ascensor*
have.AUX.1SG ascend.PTCP.1SG to the floor of up in the lift
'I went to the upper floor in the lift'

(63) *He subido las escaleras con mucha prisa*
have.AUX.1SG ascend.PTCP the stairs with a.lot.of hurry
'I have gone up the stairs hurriedly'

Mendikoetxea (1999: 1606–1607) distinguishes between inherent direction verbs like *ir* 'go', *venir* 'come', *descender* 'descend', *salir* 'exit', and verbs of manner of motion like *andar* 'walk', *nadar* 'swim' and *correr* 'run'. The inherent direction verbs that entail a movement endpoint can appear in absolutive constructions. For example *llegar* 'arrive':

(64) *Llegado Antonio, empezamos la fiesta*
arrive.PTCP Antonio, start.PST.1PL the party
'Once Antonio arrived, we started the party'

These verbs are unaccusative, that is, their only argument (the subject) receives the semantic function of theme or patient and they express states or achievements, as in *Manuel llega a casa* 'Manuel arrives home'.

In contrast, Manner of motion verbs cannot be used in absolute participle constructions:

(65) *Andado Antonio, empezamos la fiesta
    walk.PTCP Antonio, start.PST.1PL the party
    ?'Once Antonio walked, we started the party'

This type of verb is unergative, that is, their subjects receive the thematic role of agents, but when combined with an endpoint the agent changes to a theme affected by the change of place:

(66) Juan corrió a casa
    Juan run.PST.3SG to home
    'Juan ran home'

Mendikoetxea (1999: 1606–1607) claims that this difference is more evident in Italian than in Spanish because a different auxiliary verb is used for each type of verb. The past tenses of intransitive verbs are combined with the auxiliary verb *essere* 'be', whilst inergatives are combined with *avere* 'have'. This explains why (67) is not acceptable but (68) is:

(67) *Gianni è corso
    Gianni be.AUX.PRS.3SG run.PTCP
    'Gianni has run'

(68) Gianni è corso a casa
    Gianni be.AUX.PRS.3SG run.PTCP to home
    'Gianni has run home'

The use of *avere* 'have' as the auxiliary verb, *Gianni a corso*, makes (67) acceptable. The reason for this is that the sentence is an activity and thus Gianni is the agent in an inergative construction. The sentence in (68) is grammatical because Gianni receives the role of patient, with a change of state, in an inaccusative construction, similar to *Gianni è arrivato a casa* 'Gianni has arrived home'. This distinction in the auxiliary choice is not alien to the Spanish language, as it was a pertinent distinction until the 16th Century. Lapesa (1968: 256) gives this example by Juan de Valdés:

(69) Los moços son idos a comer y nos han dexado solos
    the lads be.AUX.PRS.3PL go.PTCP.PL to eat and pro have.PRS.3PL leave.PTCP.SG alone
    'The lads have gone to eat and they have left us alone'

The present perfect tense of *ir* combines with the auxiliary *ser* 'be' and produces the agreement of the past participle in gender and number with the subject of the sentence. Campos (1999) states that the distinction between auxiliaries is lost in other Romance languages too, like Catalan. Campos considers that inaccusative verbs can be distinguished because they allow the absolute construction, they do not admit the suffix *–dor* (e.g. **venidor* from *venir* 'come', but *andador* 'person who walks a lot' from *andar* 'walk'), they can be used in interrogative sentences starting with a complement of the subject, and they do not admit the impersonal *se* with the preterit tense: **Se llegó temprano a la oficina ayer* 'It was arrived early yesterday'. Cifuentes Honrubia (1999) supplies more evidence for the identification of the inaccusative Spanish verbs: for example they can be combined with *recién* 'just, recently', and they admit the absence of a determiner in the subject. The Spanish Royal Academy agrees with this in its grammar (RAE 2009: 3057) and considers that inergative verbs belong to several semantic classes, manner of motion being one of them.

Cifuentes Honrubia (1999), following the French tradition initiated by Tesnière (1959), differentiates between movement (which would correspond to Manner in Talmy's terms) and displacement (corresponding to Path). He determines several syntactic differences. For instance, displacement needs a compulsory adverbial, and therefore **Juan llevó a su primo* 'Juan took his cousin' is not acceptable, whereas movement verbs do not need this complement: *Juan bailó con su primo* 'Juan danced with his cousin'. Displacement verbs are combinable with adverbials indicating origin, goal or both: *Envió la pelota hasta el final* 'He sent the ball to the end', but they are not combinable with place adverbials indicating 'where'. An example of this is the difference between **Vamos en la Universidad* 'We go in the university' and *Bailamos en la Universidad* 'We dance in the university'.

Cifuentes Honrubia considers that the notion of direction is key in displacement. He highlights the importance of the component of Manner of displacement, as noted by Talmy (1985) and Slobin and Hoiting (1994). Cifuentes Honrubia (1999) presents some syntactic differences between displacement verbs and Manner verbs in Spanish. Some of these have been mentioned already, such as the possibility of participating in absolutive constructions, or in the choice of *ubi-* place locative adverbials. He also considers the possibility of using directional prepositions (Manner verbs only allow *hacia* 'towards' and *hasta* 'up to'), the possible combination of Manner gerunds with displacement verbs, and the combinability of displacement verbs with clitics. Moreover, displacement verbs can be combined only with origin, while Manner verbs cannot because they do not imply arrival: **corrió desde el parque* 'run from the park'. However, not all his differences seem to be applicable: for example the agrammaticality of *corrió desde el parque* is debatable.

Marimoto (2001) applies Jackendoff's framework (1983, 1987) to Spanish and distinguishes between displacement verbs and manner of motion verbs. The first group of verbs includes *ir* 'go', *venir* 'come', *entrar* 'enter', *salir* 'exit', etc. while the latter refer to manner. Their main characteristics are summarized in Table 2:

Table 2: Semantic classification of motion verbs (translated from Morimoto 2001: 50).

	Displacement	Trajectory	Manner of motion
Displacement verbs	Yes	Determined	No
External manner of motion verbs	Yes	Indetermined	Yes
Inner manner of motion verbs	No	No trajectory	Yes

Displacement verbs can be sub-divided into three categories depending on the type of trajectory. The first category is displacement verbs with trajectory type TO-WARDS, like *subir* 'go up', *bajar* 'go down', *caer* 'fall' and *avanzar* 'move forward'. The second category consists of displacement verbs with trajectory type FROM and/or TO. In this case they can be either without boundary-crossing (*venir* 'come', *llegar* 'arrive', *alcanzar* 'reach', *partir* 'leave') or with boundary-crossing (*entrar* 'enter', *penetrar* 'penetrate', *irrumpir* 'burst in', *salir* 'exit'). Finally the third category is formed by displacement verbs with trajectory of transit such as *pasar* 'pass', *atravesar* 'go through', *cruzar* 'cross'. Manner of motion verbs can be also divided into two subgroups: those verbs with external movement (*caminar* 'walk', *arrastar* 'drag', *correr* 'run' and *andar* 'walk') and those with inner movement (*tambalearse* 'stagger', *agitarse* 'shake', *temblar* 'shiver', *patalear* 'kick').

From a Cognitive Linguistics perspective, Cifuentes-Férez (2009) focuses on the comparison of motion verbs in English and Spanish. She used the data obtained from monolingual dictionaries to compare the lexicons of these two languages. She classifies those verbs according to the semantic components that are codified in each verb, based on Talmy (1995, 1991, 2000a, 2000b). Her classification for Spanish is outlined below.

In some cases, only the motion component is encoded: *mover(se)* 'move', *menear(se)* 'to (cause to) move oneself', *trasladarse* 'to (cause to move) from one place to another' and *mudarse* 'to go from one place to the other'.

Another possibility is Motion + one component. There are three types depending on the nature of the second component:

- Motion + Ground. This is the case with some denominal verbs such as *atajar* 'go somewhere by taking a short cut' (*atajo* 'short cut'), *bordear* 'to skirt, go along the edge of' (*borde* 'edge'), *fondear* 'move at the bottom' (*fondo* 'bottom') and other verbs like *volar* 'fly', which implies that the movement takes place in the air.
- Motion + Figure. When verbs give us information about the moving entity: *aletear* 'flap', *cabecear* 'move one's head', *codear* 'nudge', *cocear* 'kick' (a horse or a donkey as the Figure).
- Motion + Result. These are verbs like *chocar(se)*, *estrellar(se)* '(cause to) crash' and *colisionar* 'crash'.

There are several types of Motion + 2 components:
- Motion + Path + Manner. They provide information about the direction of the movement and how it is produced. For instance *abalanzarse* 'dash to', *escaparse* 'run away' and *trepar* 'climb up'.
- Motion + Path + Ground. For example *desembarcar* 'disembark', *aterrizar* 'land', *sumergirse* '(cause to) go down into water' and *expatriar* 'exile'. They indicate the direction of the movement and they are also related with different types of Ground (*barco* 'ship', *tierra* 'land', *agua* 'water', *patria* 'homeland').
- Motion + Manner + Ground. As in the previous example they are in relation to the Ground but they do not indicate the direction but the manner of motion. *Callejear* 'walk around the streets', *ladear* 'move on the hillside', *planear* 'glide (a plane or bird)', *nadar* 'swim'.
- Motion + Figure + Manner. Some examples would be *pisar* 'step' or *patalear* 'kick'. They imply that the feet as a Figure are moving in a given manner.
- Motion + Cause + Manner. These verbs denote a movement with a specific purpose: *patrullar* 'patrol', *merodear* 'walk around', *rondar* 'be on patrol, prowl about'
- Motion + Figure + Co-Motion. This latter component involves taking something or someone from one place to another as in *acompañar* 'accompany', *guiar* 'guide' or *escoltar* 'escort'.
- Motion + Manner + Result. For example, *atropellar* 'run over'.

Motion + 3 components is also a possibility. Cifuentes-Férez (2009) only finds two verbs with this conflation pattern in Spanish. These are *capuzar(se)* '(cause to) dive in' and *zambullir(se)* '(cause to) go down into water in a violent way'. The components they encode are Motion + Path + Ground + Manner, as the Figure descends (Path) into the water (Ground) in a sudden and energetic Manner.

Cifuentes-Férez (2009) states that there seems to be a tendency in Spanish to encode Ground in the verbs. This is not the most common pattern but it does not seem to be as infrequent and exceptional as considered by Talmy (1985). Cifuentes-Férez (2009) finds different types of Path verbs, the more frequent being those indicating 'moving away from the Ground' such as *alejarse* 'move away', *marcharse* 'depart', *partir* 'leave', *irse* 'go away'. In terms of quantity it does not seem that substantial differences between both languages are present regarding the Path lexicon. Cifuentes-Férez also analyzes Manner verbs in Spanish and concludes that its lexicon of Manner verbs is more reduced than in English, with the exception only of Posture verbs.

Crucially, not all comparisons of Spanish motion verbs have been made with English. Cuartero Otal (2016a, 2016b) contrasts motion verbs in Spanish and German and classifies them into directional displacement verbs and manner displacement verbs. He claims that in Spanish there are four types of intransitive motion verbs: (i) those without combination restrictions, i.e. directional displacement verbs e.g. *bajar* 'descend', (ii) verbs that can combine with goal and medium, i.e. non directional displacement verbs, e.g. *andar* 'walk', (iii) those that are only compatible with medium, i.e. displacement without trajectory, e.g. *pasear* 'stroll' and (iv) those encoding manner such as *cojear* 'limb'. In the case of transitive verbs he distinguishes between verbs that can be combined with five arguments, namely origin, medium, goal, subject and localization, e.g. *recorrer* 'go through', and verbs that can be combined with only four arguments, i.e. that can combine either origin or goal but not both at the same time, e.g. *alcanzar* 'reach'.

Using a different methodological approach, Hijazo-Gascón, Ibarretxe-Antuñano, and Guelbenzu-Espada (2013) provide a study in which native speakers of Spanish are asked to classify motion verbs according to semantic criteria: Manner, Manner and Direction, Directional, Posture, Neuter, Other, Not a motion verb. This study aimed at solving one of the main methodological issues in the literature, as the motion verb classifications are not homogeneous. This experiment was inspired by the *interrater reliability tests* that are common in gesture research to avoid subjectivity in the encoding process (see Gullberg 2009b). Two groups of 50 speakers took part in two surveys consisting of 50 motion verbs each. Verbs were classified as prototypical (more than a 75% of speakers coincided), semi-prototypical (50–75% of speakers coincided) or diffused (less than 50% coincidence). The novelty of this study is that it complements previous research on motion verbs, adding the native intuition to previous studies, which elicited data from dictionaries and the introspection of linguists. The results shed some light onto how native speakers see these verbs. In some cases, native speakers' intuitions coincided with the main researchers' classifications. For example deictic verbs, *ir* 'go' was considered a neuter verb by 72% of speakers, but *irse* 'go away' was considered neuter only by 44% of speakers, a finding in line with differences between these two forms that scholars have put forward. By contrast, *venir* 'come' is classified as Path verb by a 75% of speakers. The classification of *caer* 'fall', whose equivalent classifications in other languages have been controversial (see Zlatev and Yangklang (2004) on the Thai equivalent as a Manner+Path verb), seems to be equally controversial for native speakers, who consider it only Directional (40%) and Manner and Directional (38%). Other cases show discrepancies with some scholars' classifications. For example, *esconderse* 'hide' is classified as a Posture verb by native speakers, which echoes Cadierno and Ruiz (2006) but not Sebastián and Slobin (1994) who labelled it as directional. It is also interesting to find discrepancies among native speakers in the classification of *saltar* 'jump', with a clear Manner component, but with native speakers being divided as to whether it should be classified only as a only Manner verb, or as a Manner and Direction verb (both options received the support of a 32% of speakers). However, it is important to note that all the verbs that present a divergent classification from previous studies are among the diffused verbs, i.e. verbs with less than 50% coincidence among native speakers.

During this section the main focus was on Spanish as a prototypical verb framed language. Differences from French and Italian are established in other aspects of motion, starting with the differences in Manner verbs, which are explained below.

2.2 Manner in Romance languages

2.2.1 Manner of motion verbs

The lexical and syntactic properties of Manner of motion are probably one of the most important differences between Italian on the one hand and Spanish and French on the other. These differences will be presented here following Zubizarreta and E. Oh (2007) and Zubizarreta (2007). We refer to these authors for a more detailed account of the lexical-syntactic features of motion verbs in these three languages. Our main focus in this section is to explain the differences in Manner verbs in order to understand the different degrees of the boundary-crossing constraint that will be further developed in the second part of this section.

Zubizarreta and E. Oh (2007) observe that there is variable behavior among the Manner of motion verbs class in different languages. This class shows systematic behavior in English and Dutch, but their behavior is lexically restricted in Italian and almost non-existent in French and Spanish. In other words, in English any Manner of motion verb can express an activity with the syntactic properties of an unergative verb as in *John walked towards the park for two hours*; and it can also express an accomplishment with the syntactic properties of an unaccusative verb as in *John walked to the park in two hours*.

In Italian this variable behavior is possible for certain Manner of motion verbs, but not for all of them. Let us consider these examples from Zubizarreta and E. Oh (2007: 3):

(70) *Maria a corso (fino a casa)*
Maria has run-PTCP.MASC (to the house)
'Maria has run (to the house)'

(71) *Maria è corsa *(fino a casa)*
Maria is run-PTCP.F *(to the house)
'María has run *(to the house)'

(72) *Maria a camminato (fino a casa)*
Maria has walk-PTCP (to the house)
'Maria has walked to the house'

(73) **Maria è camminata (fino a casa)*
Maria is walk.PTCP.F (to the house)

This is a stark intra-typological contrast. Spanish Manner of motion verbs cannot appear in directed-motion construction, as discussed in relation to English in Talmy (1985) and Aske (1989), and French does not seem to be more flexible than Spanish (Lamiroy 1983). Zubizarreta and E. Oh (2007: 49) draw from Folli's (2001) classification of Manner of motion verbs to show the differences in Italian verbs:

- Directed motion verbs. These are unambiguously unaccusative. Their auxiliary in the past perfect is *essere* 'be' and their participles agree in gender with the subject: *entrare* 'enter', *uscire* 'exit', *arrivare* 'arrive', *atterrare* 'land', *partire* 'depart', and *scappare* 'flee'.
- Manner of motion verbs that denote an activity and are unambiguously unergative. Their auxiliary is *avere* in the past perfect tense and their participle is not in agreement with the subject. Folli considers that the following verbs can appear only in unergative activity structures: *camminare* 'walk', *gallegiare* 'float', *galoppare* 'gallop', *danzare* 'dance', *nuotare* 'swim', *sciare* 'ski', *passeggiare* 'walk around', and *vagabondare* 'wander'.
- Manner of motion verbs that can appear either in unergative activity structures or in unaccusative directed-motion structures: *correre* 'run', *rotolare*

'roll', *rimbalzare* 'bounce', *scivolare* 'slide', *gattonare* 'crawl', *saltare* 'jump', *volare* 'fly', *saltellare* 'hop'.

These subsets are clearly differentiated as the verbs in the third group can take a complement headed by the preposition *a* 'to'. These verbs change the auxiliary verb for the past tense and combine with *essere* 'be' when they appear in the directed-motion construction. This is not shared by Spanish, which only uses *haber* as an auxiliary, nor by French, which does keep *être* 'be' as an auxiliary but does not show restructuring properties and there is not an auxiliary shift like in Italian (see Zubizarreta and E. Oh 2007: 49 for a full account). Zubizarreta and E. Oh also argue that Manner of motion verbs in Spanish are mostly unergative and therefore denote activities. However they point out a few exceptions such as *rodar* 'roll' and *deslizarse* 'slide':

(74) *El barril rodó al pie de la colina/debajo de la mesa*
'The barrel rolled to the foot of the hill/under the table'

(75) *La moneda se deslizó dentro del agujero*
'The coin slid inside of the hole'

These verbs express manner of motion and have unaccusative properties. For example, they can appear in absolutive constructions like in (76) and (77), cited in Zubizarreta and E. Oh (2007: 160):

(76) *Rodado el barril al pie de la colina/debajo de la mesa*
roll.PTCP.M the barrel to the foot of the hill/under the table
'The ball having rolled to the foot of the hill/under the table'

(77) *Una vez deslizada la moneda dentro del agujero . . .*
Once slid.PTCP.F the coin inside the hole
'The coin having slid inside the hole . . .'

These authors consider that this is possible for these verbs because they allow a non-volitional and non-agentive interpretation. They find similar patterns in French *rouler* 'roll' and *glisser* 'slide':

(78) *La balle a roulé dans le trou*
the ball AUX.PRS3SG roll.PTCP in the hole
'The ball rolled in the hole'

(79) La pièce de monnaie a glissé dans le trou
      The coin AUX.PRS3SG slid.PTCP in the hole
      'The coin slid into the hole in a second'

French and Spanish share this lack of variable behavior, which is allowed in Italian. In fact the combination of Manner verbs with the French locative clitic *y* 'there' implies a locative event, as in (78) adapted from Zubizarreta and E. Oh (2007: 162):

(80) Jean   y   a   nagé/gaopé/marché/couru
      Jean   LOC.CL AUX   swim.PTCP/gallop.PTCP/walk.PTCP/run.PTCP
      'Jean has swum/galloped/walked/run there'

The only exception is the verb *sauter* 'jump', which can function both as an unaccusative (81) and as a unergative verb (82). This possibility leads to ambiguity when it is combined with *y* 'there, to there', as in (83) (Zubizarreta and E. Oh 2007: 162):

(81) Pierre a sauté dans la piscine
      'Pierre jumps in(to) the pool'

(82) Pierre saute dans la cours
      'Pierre is jumping in the yard'

(83) Pierre y a sauté
      Pierre loc.CL AUX jump.PTCP.M

The last example is ambiguous and could be translated as 'Pierre jumps in there' or 'Pierre jumps into there'. Other authors have also noted differences between Manner of motion verbs in Spanish and French. As mentioned above, Morimoto (2001) differentiates between internal and external manner of motion for Spanish. Fábregas (2007) distinguishes in Spanish between directional manner verbs, such as *volar* 'fly' and *correr* 'run' and non-directional manner verbs such as *flotar* 'float' and *bailar* 'dance'. Kopecka (2009) also differentiates between change of location verbs like *nager* 'swim' and verbs denoting both change of location and motion activity, with some of them leaning more towards activities in a prolonged process (*marcher* 'walk', *courir* 'run') and others leaning more towards a change of location, evoking the result of a process (*grimper* 'climb', *sauter* 'jump'). Other elements in the construction should be also noticed. Stošić

(2001) compares the uses of the French *par* and *à travers* and concludes that the use of these prepositions is conditioned by different conceptualizations of the event. He claims that *par* expresses a connection between an initial and a final location and *à travers* needs a complement expressing the location that the Figure has to make their way through. Since *à travers* is not relational, it can describe non-telic processes (in combination with Manner verbs), such as *Les soldats courent/marchent à travers la ville* 'The soldiers run/march their way through the town'.

However, the differences these authors note do not seem to have the same implications as Italian Manner of motion verbs (Folli 2001; Zubizarreta 2007; Zubizarreta and E. Oh 2007). The accomplishment reading of Manner verb and directional complement is not possible in French and Spanish but it is with certain Italian verbs.

2.2.2 The boundary-crossing constraint in verb-framed languages

The boundary-crossing constraint refers to the impossibility of combining a Manner of motion verb with a directional complement that implies a change of state. This concept was introduced in Chapter 2 in relation to verb-framed languages in general and its implications for the rhetorical style of speakers of these languages. Several scholars have shown that the boundary-crossing constraint is not equally followed across languages. In this section the focus will be on explaining the degree to which this constraint is followed in French, Italian and Spanish. As explained throughout the section, Italian is less rigid with regard to this constraint, which challenges previous assumptions about verb-framed languages.

The debate on the (im)possibility of combining Manner verbs with trajectories was present at the very formulation of the semantic typology. Talmy (1985: 112–113) compares complex motion events in English and its counterparts in Spanish and notes that a translation into Spanish requires either the removal of the Manner component or its segmentation into several events. For example, if someone translates into Spanish a sentence like *She ran from the living-room into the kitchen*, they would need to either substitute the Manner verb run by a Path verb and formulate something like *Entró (corriendo) del comedor a la cocina* 'She entered (running) from the living-room to the kitchen', or segment the event: *Atravesó (corriendo) el comedor y entró a la cocina* 'He crossed the living-room (running) and entered into the kitchen'.

Aske (1989) was the first author to challenge the sharp distinctions envisaged within the typology by claiming that Manner verbs can be used with trajectories in Spanish. An example would be (84):

(84) *El avión voló sobre los Pirineos hacia Francia*
the plane fly.PST.3SG over the Pyrenees towards France
'The plane flew over the Pyrenees towards France'

Aske (1989) considers that the restriction is related to the telicity of the event. Path can be expressed in Spanish outside of the main verb and combined with a Manner verb only if a final location is not predicated (or implied in the context). Therefore, when the utterance is atelic the restriction does not apply: *Daniel corrió hasta el hospital* 'Daniel ran up to the hospital', nor when the utterance is locative, like *Sara bailó en el salón* 'Sara danced in the living-room'. The agrammaticality is only produced with telic utterances: **Manuel bailó a la cocina* 'Manuel danced to the kitchen'.

Aske (1989: 6) considers that there is a general restriction against non-verbal resultative predicates in Spanish. For example, this language does not allow resultative constructions like the English *Pat kicked the door open*. However, there are similar constructions that indicate a change of state in the main verb which are acceptable, as in these examples in Spanish, French and Turkish pointed out by Slobin and Hoiting (1994: 497):

(85) *El hombre abrió la puerta de una patada*
the man open.PST.3SG the door of a kick
'The man opened the door with a kick'

(86) *L'homme a ouvert la porte avec le pied*
the.man have.AUX.PRS.3SG open.PTCP the door with the foot
'The man has opened the door with the foot'

(87) *Adam kapı-yı tekmekiyerek açtı*
man door-ACC kick.GER open.PTCP
'The man opened the door by kicking'

Slobin and Hoiting conclude that this is due to a general preference towards verb-framing patterns, that is, a preference to use a verb before any other form to express a change of state. This tendency seems to be present in other domains and not only in motion, in line with the application of Talmy's (1991, 2000b) typology to other kind of events. Slobin and Hoiting (1994) coin the term *boundary-crossing constraint* because they find these utterances with verbs like *entrar* 'enter', *salir* 'exit', *cruzar* 'cross' share the meaning of crossing a boundary.

From Jackendoff's perspective (1983, 1987), Displacement verbs are headed by the eventive function of GO: [$_{Event}$ GO ([$_{Object}$],[$_{Trajectory}$])], whilst Manner of motion verbs are headed by the eventive function of MOVE: [$_{Event}$MOVE ([$_{Object}$])]. Jackendoff (1990) considers that the restriction noticed by Talmy (1985) and Aske (1989) has an idiomatic solution. This would be the *GO-Adjunct Rule*, which is only applicable in some languages, like English, but not in Spanish. This rule gives Manner of motion verbs the interpretation of GO instead of their assigned interpretation of MOVE.

Morimoto (2001) claims that Jackendoff's proposal is only applicable to Spanish inner Manner of motion verbs, because external Manner of motion verbs can imply a displacement of the Object-theme and they can combine with trajectory complements, fulfilling certain restrictions. These are cases like these taken from Morimoto (2001): *El herido se arrastró por el pasillo* 'The wounded man crawled through the corridor', *Juan nadó hacia la bahía* 'Juan swam towards the bay' but not **Juan caminó fuera del pueblo*, which can only be accepted in Spanish with a locative interpretation 'Juan walked outside of the town', but not with a boundary-crossing interpretation 'Juan walked out of the town'.

Morimoto (2001: 125) classifies the types of trajectory according to their telicity:

Table 3: Types of Trajectories according to telicity (translated from Morimoto 2001: 121).

Telic trajectories	Atelic trajectories
– Destination [A 'to' ([$_{Object/Location}$])]	– Transit [VÍA 'through' ([$_{Object/Location}$])]
– Origin [DE 'from' ([$_{Object/Location}$])]	– Extension [POR 'by' ([$_{Object/Location}$])]
	– Extensive with final boundary [HASTA 'up to' ([$_{Object/Location}$])]
	– Extensive with initial boundary [DESDE 'FROM' ([$_{Object/Location}$])]

Morimoto modifies the rule, adding the specification in italics:

> If the V corresponds to [MOVE ([$_{Object}$])] *and the PP corresponds to a telic trajectory* [$_{VP}$V ... PP] can correspond to [GO([$_{Object}$ α], [$_{Trajectory}$]) WITH/BY MEANS OF (MOVE [α], [MANNER X])].

This allows us to account for the difference between Spanish and English. Morimoto recognizes, however, that there is a small set of verbs that can be in combination of telic trajectory, such as *correr* 'run' and *volar* 'fly', for example *Correr a la farmacia* 'run to the pharmacy', and *Volar a Barcelona* 'fly to Barcelona'. She considers that these exceptions can occur due to restricted applications of the GO-Adjunct Rule. Other authors consider that the difference between English and Spanish lies in the fact that English allows reconceptualization of movement verbs as displacement verbs, e.g. *spin, tumble*, whereas this is not possible in Spanish (Cuartero Otal 2006).

The boundary-crossing constraint has been generalized to all verb-framed languages and what is true for Spanish has been expanded to the other languages in the family. However, it is still a debated issue for scholars working in Romance languages and several scholars have identified exceptions. For example, Baciu (2006) explains that Romanian, despite being a verb-framed language that follows the boundary-crossing constraint, has two verbs for 'run': *a alerga* and *a fugi*. These verbs are used in different contexts: *a alerga* expresses an activity and is impossible to combine with telic constructions, while *a fugi* can be used in directed motion accomplishment constructions.

In some cases the debate has involved the prepositions and not just the semantic nature of the manner of motion verbs. For example, it has been shown that there are some cases in which boundary-crossing is possible in punctual events in Spanish, when the Path is short and the crossing of the boundary is not on purpose, as in *tirarse a la piscina* 'launch oneself to the swimming-pool' (Naigles and Terrazas 1998) and the possible explanation may lie in the preposition. Martínez-Vázquez (2013) explains that Spanish lacks prepositions with an inherent goal meaning, but *a* and *hasta* may introduce an endpoint complement in combination with a manner of motion verb in an appropriate context. In fact, in American Spanish *a* is used for goals in contexts in which *en* is used in Peninsular Spanish: *Entró a la casa* 'S/he entered into the house'. Martínez Vázquez (2001) thinks that in some cases the preposition *hasta* 'up to' (vs. *hacia* 'towards') suggests that the endpoint has been reached as in (88):

(88) *Nadó hasta la roca y se vistió*
 'The girl swam up to the rock and got dressed'

She agrees with Beavers' (2008) consideration of Spanish *hasta*, French *jusque* and Japanese *–made* as delimiters, offering different types of delimitation: temporal, spatial and propositional. In Spanish *hasta* 'up to', borrowed from Arabic *hattá,* is also used to mark inclusiveness: *Canta hasta cuando come* 'He sings even when he eats' and it seems that this could impact its spatial meaning in the following examples from the corpus CREA which Martínez-Vázquez (2013: 148) considers to be an emphatic substitute for *a* 'even up to':

(89) *Niomi, que solo había viajado fuera del Reino Unido en excursiones veraniegas, voló hasta Jamaica, Suecia, Miami o Nueva York*
'Niomi who had only travelled outside the UK in summer trips, flew even up to Jamaica, Sweden, Miami or New York'

(90) *Voló hasta Argentina, para inaugurar esta clínica*
'S/he flew up to Argentina, to inaugurate this clinic'

Martínez Vazquez (2013) claims that English and Spanish are not that different in the restrictions they face. English speakers can choose between satellite- and verb-framed patterns (e.g. constructions with *enter, exit, ascend,* etc.). When using verb-framed patterns, manner complements are not normally admitted, as demonstrated by the following examples from Croft et al. (2010: 13):

(91) *?The bottle entered the cave floating

(92) *?He approached the door crawling

(93) ??She crossed the street running

She explains that, exactly like in English verb-framed patterns, it is not always possible to force Manner into a Spanish verb-framed construction. For example, adding a gerund can be as unacceptable as in English, like (94). Therefore the addition of a gerund seems to be acceptable only when it introduces new information.

(94) *?El año pasado fui a Hawai volando*
?'Last year I went to Hawaii flying'

The use of Manner verbs as the main verb of the event is not that rare in Spanish and in fact it tends to be preferred when Manner is salient, as in these examples from the CREA corpus (Martínez Vázquez 2013):

(95) *La gata saltó a su regazo*
'The cat jumped onto her lap'

(96) *Saltó al piso del balcón vecino*
'She jumped to the floor of the neighboring balcony'

(97) *El marinero saltó del barco y nadó a la orilla*
'The sailor jumped from the boat and swam to the shore'

(98) *Si quisiéramos bucear al fondo deberíamos bajar 5 km*
    'If we wanted to dive to the bottom we should go down around 5 km'

Martínez-Vázquez thinks that it would not make sense to choose a different encoding of those examples and highlight Manner information by using a directional verb and a manner adjunct like *ir saltando* 'go jumping', *ir nadando* 'go swimming' or *ir buceando* 'went diving'.

She also claims that the metonymic uses of Manner verbs in Spanish compensate for the poor Manner repertoire. This is possible because in the non-salient verbal slot a Manner verb loses semantic prominence, which gives easy access to figurative uses of the verb, like (99) which are not possible in the adjunct slot as in (100):

(99) *Era un reloj de plata de dos tapas, que voló al suelo*
    'It was a twin lidded silver watch, which flew to the floor'

(100) ?*El reloj cayó al suelo volando*
    ?'The watch fell to the floor flying'

Metonymic uses explain the suitability of some Manner of motion verbs in directed motion events. Martínez-Vázquez (2013: 153) shows that *flotar* 'float' in (101) is only activating the notion of light displacement and in (102) *escurrirse* 'slip' is losing non-intentionality nuances to express furtive motion. In both cases some of their Manner elements are lost in the metonymy, which allows a directional reading:

(101) *La mulatica flotó hasta el refrigerador y abrió la puerta*
    'The little mixed-raced woman flew to the refrigerator and opened it'

(102) *Cuando los vio desaparecer, se escurrió a la cocina, que le pareció el sitio más seguro*
    'When she saw them disappear, she slipped away into the kitchen, which seemed to her the safest place'.

Pedersen (2014) also looks at the possibility of inserting Manner verbs in constructions of directed motion in a corpus study. He claims that this is accepted when the lexical meaning of the verb implies an element of directed motion. For example, *correr* 'run' has an implicit directional meaning in the sense that when we run we normally take some direction. This allows for telic complements such as *Pedro corrió al baño* 'He ran into the bathroom'. This is not possible with all Manner verbs, *bailar* 'dance', for example, lacks this implicit directionality. His corpus analysis shows clearly that Spanish Manner verbs can be classified into two types. The first type includes those verbs that do not show associated directionality in the lexical meaning of the verb and which are not possible to combine with telic constructions. These are *danzar* 'dance', *flotar* 'float', *conducir* 'drive', *deslizarse* 'slip', *nadar* 'swim', *arrastrarse* 'drag oneself', *cojear* 'limp', *gatear* 'crawl', etc. On the other hand, the second type includes verbs with directionality in their lexical semantics. These verbs can be used in directed motion constructions. These are verbs like *caminar* 'walk', *andar* 'walk', *correr* 'run', *navegar* 'sail', *volar* 'fly', *saltar* 'jump' and *rodar* 'roll'. Pedersen (2014) considers that this is a relatively infrequent but regular pattern in Spanish, and concludes that the constraints are not around the telicity of the Path phrase but on the element of directional meaning associated with the lexical meaning of the verb. Therefore, it seems that even in Spanish the situation is more complex than has been described in the first stages of the typology.

The possibility of using Manner verbs in boundary-crossing situations is also present in Molés-Cases (2016). In her Spanish corpus analysis, she finds three types of Manner verbs used in boundary-crossing situations: (i) cases with force dynamics, e.g. *arrojarse* 'throw oneself', *irrumpir* 'burst in', (ii) punctual and immediate actions with vertical movement, e.g. *lanzarse* 'pounce on', *zambullirse* 'plunge', and (iii) soft and furtive movements, e.g. *deslizarse* 'slide', *escabullirse* 'slip away'. The picture in Spanish seems then to be much more complex than initially thought, and it seems that the restriction cannot be generalized to all Manner verbs.

Similarly, some cases of Manner verbs expressing a boundary-crossing situation have been noted in French. N. Asher and Sablayrolles (1996: 198) show examples with the use of Manner verbs in clear boundary-crossing situations, with a clear change of location, such as *Jean a couru dans le jardin. Il a vu le chat à travers de la fenêtre et a voulu l'attraper* 'John ran into the garden. He saw the cat through the window and wanted to cath it'. In this occasion the combination of a Manner verb with *dans* 'in' does not express a locative meaning. Examples like this show that the typological predictions are not always fulfilled. Berthele (2006: 205) gives some examples of boundary-crossing with *courir* 'run' and *sauter* 'jump' in French, such as *Ils ont sauté hors du lit* 'They jumped out of the bed' or *J'ai couru dans la chambre* 'I ran into the room'. He takes these as possible evidence of more flexibility regarding the constraint in French. This coincides with the exception noted by Zubizarreta and E. Oh (2007) regarding the verb *sauter* 'jump'. Beavers, Levin and Tham (2010: 23) also point out the possibility of boundary-crossing interpretations of *courir dans* and in other examples similar to (103) and (104), taken respectively from Pourcel and Kopecka (2006a: 35) and Stringer (2003: 46):

(103) *Il court dans le jardin*
'He runs in(to) the garden'

(104) a. *Allez, courons dans la maison!*
go.2PL, run.1PL in the house
'Come on, let's run in(to) the house!'
b. ?*Allez, entrons dans la maison en courant!*
go.2PL, enter-1PL in the house in running
?'Come on, let's enter the house running!'

Hendriks and Hickmann (2015) explore further the boundary-crossing constraint in French and confirm that in voluntary motion French speakers tend to encode Path in the main verb, only with the exceptions of *slide*-events. They also see how this impacts on the acquisition of French by English learners, with similar results to the previously reported studies for L2 Spanish by English speakers (Larrañaga et al. 2011; Muñoz-Carrasco 2015). It seems thus that both French and Spanish allow for certain exceptions to the boundary-crossing constraint. It must be noted though that all these authors agree in marking the exceptionality of these cases. Therefore it seems that there are several exceptions and it is possible to use a Manner verb for a boundary-crossing situation under certain circumstances, but this does not mean that this is a general pattern in French nor Spanish.

The use of boundary-crossing constructions in French and Spanish contrasts with the flexibility of this constraint in Italian. Baicchi (2005: 514) explains that Romance languages can replicate the English pattern in "BEYOND events" if one of these features of FORCE is present: immediacy, intensity or resistance (counterforce). When the event describes a sudden act, rather than an ongoing activity, highlighting the force dynamics pattern, Manner verbs can be also used in verb-framed languages. She also notices that the English conflation pattern is more frequent in Italian than in Spanish.

Iacobini and Fagard (2011) contradict Slobin's claim (2004) that Manner verbs are used in verb-framed languages only if Manner is foregrounded, excepting verbs that encode a particular force dynamics that are more instantaneous acts. The boundary-crossing constraint does not seem to be followed in Italian regardless of how punctual the act is. This can be seen in (105) and (106) from Iacobini (2015: 637) in which slow or careful motion crossing a boundary is expressed with a Manner verb.

(105) *Provo a inserire la prima pallottola. Scivola dentro senza attrito*
'I try to insert the first bullet. It slides in without friction'

(106) *La ragazza si inginocchiò a fatica e strisciò fuori*
'The girl knelt down with difficulty and crawled out'

Another factor that favors goal readings of constructions with Manner verbs is the use of complex prepositions, as in these examples adapted from Folli (2008 in Iacobini and Fagard 2011). In (107) the use of *dentro* 'inside' allows for a locative and a directional reading, but in (108) the complex preposition *dentro a* 'inside to, into' renders more unlikely the locative interpretation.

(107) *Gianni corse dentro il parco* [locative / directional]
'Gianni ran inside the park'

(108) *Gianni corse dentro al parco* [directional / (locative)]
'Gianni ran inside (to.the) park'

These authors provide a hierarchy for the degree of relevance of constructions with manner verbs in verb-framed languages, reproduced in Table 4:

Table 4: Manner verbs and boundary-crossing in a Verb-Framed Language (Iacobini and Fagard 2011: 163).

1	2	3	4	5
Giovanni corre sul prato 'John runs on the lawn'	*Giovanni corre verso casa* 'John runs towards home'	*Giovanni è corso a casa (a preparare la cena)* 'John ran home (to cook dinner)'	*Giovanni irrompe in casa* 'John bursts into the house'	*Giovanni striscia a letto* 'John crawls onto his bed'
Motion at location	Motion towards a goal (no attainment of goal)	Attaintment of goal	Boundary-crossing + high force dynamic verb	Boundary-crossing – high force dynamic verb

Another factor concerning the use of manner verbs with the boundary-crossing constraint in Italian is related to pragmatics. Romance languages do not use Manner in an adjunct phrase when the information is implicitly provided. However, Italian allows the use of Manner verbs in boundary-crossing situations even when the verb expresses the habitual default Manner of motion in the Figure, as in their example (109):

(109) *Appena lascio la gabbietta aperta il mio coniglio saltella fuori e viene a curiosare*
'As soon as I leave the small cage open my rabbit hops out and comes to look around'

Iacobini and Fagard (2011) provide a tentative ordering of different possibilities of expressing boundary-crossing situation in verb-framed and satellite-framed languages, the left columns being typical of verb-framed languages and the right columns prototypical of satellite-framed languages. Although cases like (109) are possible, they consider that these should be regarded as exceptions. It remains to be seen how these five possibilities are exploited by Romance languages and whether the restrictions in Manner verbs in French and Spanish translate into a less frequent use of Manner verbs in boundary-crossing situations.

Table 5: Different possible expressions of boundary-crossing events in VF and SF languages (Iacobini and Fagard 2011: 167).

1	2	3	4	5
L'uccello esce dal nido 'the bird exits from the nest'	*L'uccello esce dal nido saltellando* 'the bird exits from the nest hopping'	*L'uccello saltella uscendo dal nido* 'the bird hops exiting from the nest'	*L'uccello saltella fuori dal nido* 'the bird hops out of the nest'	*L'uccello vola fuori dal nido* 'the bird flies out of the nest'
Path Verb No Manner	Path Verb + No default Manner Verb	No default Manner V + Path Verb	No default Manner V + Path Satellite	Default Manner Verb + Path Satellite

The actual frequencies of use of Manner verbs with telic complements in Italian have been tested through experimental designs and through the study of translations from English into Italian. Cardini (2012) tests the interpretation of Manner verbs with telic complements as boundary-crossing or locative events. He combines two different methodologies, an interpretation task and a grammatical judgment task. In the first task participants had to choose whether sentences like *Il gatto corre dentro della stanza* 'the cat runs in the room' were more similar to *Il gatto entrò nella stanza di corsa* 'The cat ran into the room' (directional) or *Il gatto passò del tempo a correre nella stanza* 'the cat spent some time running in the room' (locative). He tested different combinations with *correre* 'run' and *camminare* 'walk' in past and progressive tenses, each of which verbs belongs to one of the subcategories of Manner explained above. These verb forms were combined with *dentro* 'in' and *fuori da* 'out of'. There were also some examples with *a* 'to', in this case in combination with *correre* 'run', *volare* 'fly', *camminare* 'walk' and *zoppicare* 'limp'. The results showed that in general the two types of Manner verbs received similar interpretations. In fact, the *correre*-class only received two more interpretations of directed motion. This is not in line with the semantic classification explained above. However, the results of the grammaticality judgement task shed some light on this issue. Participants evaluated the boundary-crossing combinations with *camminare*-type verbs as having low grammaticality, so they are probably not used in conversation. He concludes that the combinations of manner verb with *dentro*, *fuori da* and *a* can express boundary-crossing if there is an element of directionality either by means of the verb (which is not always possible in Italian) or by pragmatic inferences. This is similar to the proposed concept of directionality for Spanish constructions by Pedersen (2014).

These results are confirmed by Iacobini and Vergaro (2014) who analyze translations from English into Italian. In their study, Manner of motion was kept in the main verb in 42.6% of cases. This percentage did not decrease in boundary-crossing situations, as Manner was kept in the main verb in 38.5% of the boundary-crossing units of translation. Iacobini and Vergaro (2014: 17) propose a scalar arrangement of manner verbs that are more or less compatible with the encoding of motion events in the absence of particles or other directional elements. Those verbs that are most compatible encode an orientation from a source or towards a goal (*scappare* 'flee', *irrompere* 'burst into') or a quick movement (*saltare* 'jump'). On the other hand, the least compatible verbs would be those that are durative and that express aimless motion (e.g. *passeggiare* 'stroll') or that encode fine-grained manner (e.g. *piroettare* 'pirouette'). They conclude that Italian seems to pay some degree of attention to the encoding of Manner in the motion verb in the sentence. However, further evidence would be needed to change the established position of Italian as a low-manner salient language (Cardini 2008, Hijazo-Gascón and Ibarretxe-Antuñano 2013a, 2013b). This high presence of Manner in translations could be due to genre conventions and not to the habitual encoding of speakers in conversation.

To conclude, Italian does not seem to follow the boundary-crossing constraint as much as Spanish and French do. It has more leeway to express Manner than its sister languages and this could be due to the different types of Manner verbs in this language. These verbs show semantic differences that also impact their syntactic behavior by shifting the auxiliary depending on the type of situation they express. This is probably one of the major differences in the encoding of motion events in the three languages. However, it is not clear to what extent these differences have repercussions in the rhetorical style of the speakers. It remains to be seen whether the possibility of using Manner verbs in boundary-crossing events is actually used by speakers of Italian. To my knowledge this has not been tested in speech production experiments. This will constitute one of the novelties of the study presented in this book.

2.3 Path in Romance languages

Manner is not the only semantic component in which Romance languages show contrasts. There are relevant cross-linguistic differences in the encoding of Path, which will be explored in this section. The first part of the section analyzes the potential elements that could be regarded as satellites and delves into the debate regarding the potential existence of satellites in Romance languages. The best candidates to be included in this category are particles in verb-particle constructions, prefixes, adverbial and reflective pronouns. The term pseudo-satellite (Hijazo-Gascón and Ibarretxe-Antuñano 2013a, 2013b) is coined to reflect the specificities of these elements with regard to satellite-framed languages. The last section is devoted to Deixis, a subcomponent of Path according to Talmy (2000) that shows important differences between Spanish on the one hand and French and Italian on the other.

2.3.1 Verb-particle constructions in Romance languages

The inclusion of Italian in the verb-framed languages has been controversial due to the presence in Italian of specific Path encoding constructions that are not present in other languages. Several scholars (Schwarze 1985; Masini 2005; Iacobini and Masini 2007a, 2007b; Spreafico 2008a; Cardini 2008; Cini 2008; Hijazo-Gascón and Ibarretxe-Antuñano 2013) have suggested that the existence of these specific Path encoding constructions allows for some (pseudo-)satellite-framed patterns, which lead to a higher description of Path in this language than in other verb-framed languages. These constructions are analytic or syntagmatic verbs (in Italian *verbi analitici* or *sintagmatici*), also called verb-particle constructions. These consist of a verb and a particle or adverb and are similar to English phrasal verbs. For example, *andare via* 'go away'.

According to Iacobini and Masini (2007b: 161) the primary function of the particles in these constructions is to add directional meanings to the verb root. Therefore, the role of these particles seems very close to that of satellites. However, their existence does not imply that Italian lacks the prototypical Romance lexicalization pattern. It seems that the Path component can be encoded in different elements in Italian, as illustrated in Table 6:

Table 6: Verb-particle constructions in English and Italian (Iacobini and Masini 2007b: 161).

English: *to go*	Italian: *andare* 'go'	
ROOT + SATELLITE	VERB ROOT	ROOT + SATELLITE
to go after	*seguire* 'follow'	*andare/correre dietro* 'go/run after'
to go ahead	*procedere/continuare* 'continue'	*andare avanti* 'go ahead'
to go away	*andarsene* 'go away'	*andare via* 'go away'
to go back	*(ri)tornare* 'go back'	*andare/tornare indietro* 'go back'
to go down	*scendere* 'descend'	*andare giù* 'go down'
to go for	*avventarsi* 'throw oneself'	*andare/lanciarsi contro* 'go for'
to go in	*entrare* 'enter'	*andare dentro* 'go in'
to go on	*continuare* 'continue'	*andare avanti* 'go on'
to go out	*uscire* 'exit'	*andare fuori* 'go out'
to go around	*girare* 'spin'	*andare attorno* 'go around'
to go up	*salire* 'ascend'	*andare su* 'go up'

Schwarze (1985) is the first author who considers the relevance of these constructions and establishes three types of lexical conflation in motion in Italian: (i) Romance type: Path is encoded in the verb: *partire* 'leave', *uscire* 'exit', *entrare* 'enter'; (ii) Motion and Prospective (Deixis) in the verb: including deictic motion verbs such as *andare* 'go' and *venire* 'come'; and (iii) Germanic type: Manner and Motion are lexicalized in the main verb in both intransitive verbs like *saltare* 'jump', *cadere* 'fall', *scivolare* 'slip' and intransitive like *buttare* 'throw' and *portare* 'bring/take'. A number of local adverbs would be in close relation with the Romance type, e.g. *partire via* 'leave away', *uscire fuori* 'exit out', *entrare dentro* 'enter in', *scendere giù* 'descend down', *salire su* 'ascend up'. However these particles are not semantically equivalent to these verbs, as they do not encode the component of Motion. These adverbs can be combined with other types of motion verbs:

(110) *Lui va via / dentro*
       he go.PRS.3SG away / in
       'He goes down / in'

(111) *Lei salta fuori*
       she jump.PRS.3SG out
       'She jumps out'

(112)   *Lui esce fuori*
        he exit.PRS.3SG out
        'He goes out'

(113)   *Lei scende giù*
        she descend.PRS.3SG down
        'She goes down'

The examples (110) and (111) show that Path is encoded in the adverb similarly to satellite-framed languages. In the case of (112) and (113) a reiteration of Path in a pleonastic construction is present, which is quite frequent in Italian. These pleonastic constructions are also frequent in French and Spanish, but only in oral and informal language. However, in Italian these pleonastic constructions can even appear in written literary texts. For example, Schwarze (1985: 369) gives an example of *Pinocchio*:

(114)   *I burattini riconoscono il loro fratello Pinocchio e gli fanno una grandissima festa: ma sul più bello esce fuori il burattino Mangiafuoco, e Pinocchio corre il pericolo di fare una brutta fine.*
        'The puppets recognized their brother Pinocchio and they prepared a great party for him: but the puppet Mangiafuoco *exits out* at the best part, and Pinocchio runs the danger of having a bad end'. [My translation]

Schwarze (1985) notices that French has also local adverbs like *au dehors* 'out', *dedans* 'inside', *en bas* 'down', *en haut* 'up', and he compares the degree of typological restriction in Italian and French. His conclusions are that: (i) French does not have an equivalent to the Italian *via* 'away'; (ii) French forms are all compound; (iii) the use of the construction 'motion verb + local adverb' in French is more restricted, it is stylistically marked or it turns into a semantic specialization (e.g. *aller dedans* 'fit'); (iv) pleonastic constructions like *uscire fuori* 'exit out' are unacceptable in French. Similar conclusions would be reached when comparing Italian and Spanish. Spanish forms are similar to Italian in that they are not all compound (*dentro* 'inside', *fuera* 'outside') but their use is more restricted than in Italian, and there is no Spanish equivalent to the Italian *via* 'away'. Pleonastic constructions are not acceptable in normative Spanish, although they are relatively frequent in informal and oral contexts, mainly in European Spanish. It seems that in this respect Italian seems "less verb-framed" than French and Spanish. However, it is also important to relativize the "Germanic-ness" of Italian constructions. As Schwarze (1985) himself points out, when comparing with German it is important to take into account that Italian constructions are not fully equivalent to the German ones. First, the conflation "Motion + Manner" is less frequent in Italian. Second, local adverbs in German are morphologically derived and they change if they are used to describe movement or static location: e.g. *(her)auf* 'up (there)' / *oben* 'above'.

In a more detailed comparison between Italian and Germanic languages, Masini (2008) examines how they differ in terms of word order and degrees of separation. For instance, in Germanic languages a *particle shift* is produced when the verb and the particle can be separated by a direct object. This seems to be a feature that varies from one Germanic language to another. In German and Dutch verb and particle are separated in main sentences but they come together in subordinate clauses, while in English, in Norwegian and in Icelandic both possibilities are accepted, as in *He called up his friend* and *She called her friend up*.

Other Germanic languages keep a single order in all syntactic contexts: Danish prefers a discontinuous order and Swedish opts for the non-discontinuous order. Masini (2008) explains that Italian syntagmatic verbs tend to follow a continuous order, but the discontinuous order is also possible in some cases For example, it is possible in constructions with *via* (115), in conventionalized expressions (116) and in cases with direct object and a prepositional object introduced by *dalla* 'from.the' (117) and (118):

(115) *Aveva portato le chiavi via*
 have.AUX.3SG portare.PTCP the keys ADV
 'She had taken the keys away'

(116) *Fare un paso avanti*
 make.INF a step forward
 'Step forward'

(117) *Tirare fuori gli occhiali dalla borsa*
 take.INF out the glasses from.the bag
 'Take the glasses out of the bag'

(118) *Tirare gli occhiali fuori dalla borsa*
 take.INF the glasses out from.the bag
 'Take the glasses out of the bag'

Masini admits that (118) presents an ambiguous structure because *fuori da* can be considered as a unit. In her study, Masini searches for corpus data according to the factors that affect particle shift in English, namely the semantics of the phrasal verb (motion or not), length and complexity of the Object, types of object (pronoun or phrase) and whether the Object is a new element in discourse or not (in English the tendency is to express defined noun phrases within the constructions and indefinite noun phrases outside the construction). Nearly all these factors seem to apply to Italian verb-particle constructions too. First, more degree of separation is allowed with locative verbs:

(119) *Questi butterano la porta giù*
       these throw.FUT.3PL the door down
       'They will throw the door down'

This is also the case for shorter and pronoun Objects. However, the definiteness of the noun phrase does not seem to be an influential factor in Italian. Masini (2008: 96) argues that the separation of the components of the syntagmatic verb can be interpreted as a strategy to focus on the event and to defocus the object when the information is already present in discourse, as in (120):

(120) *già l'anno scorso hanno portato fuori 18 miliardi di lire [. . .]*
       already the.year before have.AUX.PRS.3PL take.PTCP out 18 billion of lire [. . .]
       è sul telefono (per mandare le lire fuori)
       be.PRS.3SG on.the phone (to send.INF the lire out)
       'They had taken out 18 billions? Of lire last year already [. . .] it is on the phone (to send the lire out/away)'

In contrast with English, in Italian the discontinuous order is never necessary. It can appear occasionally according to the factors mentioned, but it can never be used when the object is focalized. When the object is presented as new information, the verb and the particle need to be together. This special union of verb and adverb constitutes a strong argument for considering these adverbs to be similar to a satellite. Even though these Italian particles are still very different from those from satellite-framed languages, its morpho-syntactic and semantic characteristics give them more unity, and thus differentiate them from the mere combination of verb and adverb that is present in French or Spanish.

French allows for a type of construction that is comparable to that of Italian syntagmatic verbs, that is, a combination of a motion verb with a spatial particle, as in (121) and (122) taken from Porquier (2001: 124):

(121) *Il m'a sauté dessus*
He me.DAT'AUX jump.PTCP on.top.of
'He has jumped on top of me'

(122) *Je lui ai couru après*
I he.DAT AUX run.PTCP after
'I ran after him'

Porquier (2001, 2003) explains that these are very frequent constructions in oral French, but they do not correspond to the normative syntax of this language. The adverbs that can take part in this constructions are mainly those derived from the prepositions *à* 'in' and *de* 'from', whilst the verbs that can occur in this construction are mostly motion verbs, with few exceptions as 'vocal' verbs such as *crier* 'cry'. Porquier (2003) establishes a contrastive analysis of these structures in French and Italian. He believes that these differ from the English phrasal verb, even though French constructions can be considered a lexical unit from a semantic and syntactic point of view. He also notices that Italian presents some structures that are impossible in French:

(123) Italian: *Si guarda intorno*
French: **Il se regarde autour*
'He looks around'

These Italian constructions also seem impossible, or at least doubtful, in Spanish (?*Se mira alrededor*). This confirms the unity of Italian verb-particle constructions, with constructions equivalent to the ones Porquier noted for French, e.g. *gli corro dietro* 'I run after him', and other constructions which are closer to English phrasal verbs. Porquier also comments on similar structures in Spanish such as *Se me echó encima* 'He threw himself on top of me' and *Me viene detrás* 'He comes after me'. Porquier acknowledges that the role of these adverbs in French is far from that of the English particles in phrasal verbs, which makes it difficult to classify them as satellites. Apart from this, it does not seem that the lexical unit of these constructions is as strong as the Italian syntagmatic verbs. Therefore, the presence of these particles does not seem to invalidate the presence of French in the verb-frame group.

Iacobini (2015) explains thoroughly the role and distribution of verb-particle constructions in Romance languages. In Spanish, Portuguese and Catalan its presence is almost limited to pleonastic uses, i.e. repetitions of the Path encoded in the verb (e.g. *bajar abajo* 'descend down'). These constructions seem to be absent in French, with the exception of the varieties in contact with Germanic languages, namely Canadian and Belgian French (see Section 4). It seems that Romanian does have a large repertoire of particles but the frequency of their use by Romanian speakers remains to be established. Therefore, the languages that have more presence and use of these constructions are Rhaeto-Romance and Italian. Iacobini (2015) explains that the use of these particles is particularly frequent in North-Eastern Italian dialects but its use is widespread in Standard Italian and in other dialects. In the following sections a deeper explanation of Italian verb-particle construction is provided. We will focus first on their origin and we will explore further its current morpho-syntactic and semantic properties.

2.3.1.1 The origin of verb-particle constructions in Italian

The existence of syntagmatic verbs in Italian was rejected in the Italian academic tradition (see Iacobini and Masini 2007b), as it was considered a foreign feature, more characteristic of Germanic languages than of Romance languages. After the seminal works of Schwarze (1985) and Simone (1996) for Italian, and Vicario (1997) for Friulan, debate increased as to the nature and origin of verb-particle constructions. These authors considered that verb-particle constructions were alien to the Tuscan tradition, that they were characteristic of oral language and that they had their origin in the Northern dialects that were in contact with German. For example, Jansen (2004 in Masini 2005) considers that the fact that Italian was standardized late late makes Italian varieties play an important role in its creation and development. Masini (2005) clusters these proposals as the *contact hypothesis*.

However, several studies on syntagmatic verbs have been carried out to test whether this hypothesis should be confirmed or rejected. From a diachronic angle, the occurrence of verb-particle constructions goes back to texts by Dante (13th and 14th Century) and Boccaccio (14th Century). The constructions in these texts are very similar to the current forms and they even present idiomatic meanings (Masini 2005), which seems to contradict the contact hypothesis. Amenta (2008) finds verb-particle constructions in Sicilian texts from the 14th and the 15th Century, where the German influence is not very plausible. Iacobini (2009) inquires into the origins of Italian, and finds verb-particle constructions in Tuscan texts dated before 1375. Therefore these constructions have been present in the language since the very origin of Tuscan, the variety that current Italian stems from, and they are hence part of the History of Italian.

From the perspective of dialectology studies, it has been demonstrated that the use of syntagmatic verbs extends throughout the Italian-speaking domain. For example, their use is documented in the Sicilian dialect and in the Sicilian variety of Italian (Amenta 2008). However, it is clear that these constructions are more frequent in Northern varieties such as Trentino (Cordin 2008) or Piedmontese (Cini 2002 in Cordin 2008), but it is not exclusive to these areas. In some dialects the verb-particle construction is the only possible option, as in Bergamasque (Spreafico 2008a, 2008b; Bernini 2008). Iacobini (2009) claims that syntagmatic verbs are the main system in Northern dialects, which have an encoding type closer to satellite-framed languages. Iacobini (2009) refers to Veneto and Lombardo, closer to German, but also to Occitan and the regional Italian in the Valley of Aosta, more in contact with French. He also provides evidence for the existence of verb-particle constructions in the south of the imaginary line La Spezia-Rimini, which is the traditional border between Western and Eastern Romance languages. He finds evidence of these constructions in central dialects (in Tuscany, Umbria, Le Marche and Lazio). In southern Italian dialects, excepting the above-mentioned presence in Sicilian, their occurrence seems to be weaker. As Iacobini (2009) points out, the role of dialects is fundamental in the case of Italian, which for centuries was only a written language. In some cases the Italian speaker can handle as many as four different levels: standard Italian, regional Italian, the regional dialect and even the local dialect. This makes relatively easy the transfer of features from one level to another. Iacobini (2009) considers that speakers of dialects tend to use fewer syntagmatic verbs when they speak Italian, and when they do they use them in informal contexts. Interestingly enough, speakers of regional Italian, whose first language is not the dialect but have a passive knowledge of it, are found to extend the use of syntagmatic verbs to general Italian in practically all contexts.

Iacobini and Masini (2007a) also reject the contact hypothesis on a morphosyntactic basis. They consider that syntactic calques from Germanic languages to Romance languages are scarce and when they happen they tend to occur in formal written contexts and hardly ever in colloquial style. Another argument against verb-particle constructions in Italian having Germanic origin is the their presence in French (Iacobini and Masini 2007a; Iacobini 2009) and even to some extent in languages that are geographically farther from German like Romanian and Spanish (Vicario 1997). They are also present in other minority languages such as Friulan (Vicario 1997) and Romansch (Berthele 2006). As seen above, other minority languages such as Catalan and Aragonese could be added to this list (Hijazo-Gascón and Ibarretxe-Antuñano 2010; Ibarretxe-Antuñano, Hijazo-Gascón, and Moret-Oliver 2017).

The alternative to the contact hypothesis is the *typological-structural hypothesis* (Masini 2005), which suggests that verb-particle constructions are inherent to the very evolutionary stages of the Italian language. This is mainly due to two types of factors. The first of these are typological factors in relation to the evolution from Latin to Romance languages, as explained above. The evolution of the Latin word order from SOV to SVO entails the change from Modifier-Head to Head-Modifier in Romance languages. Another important step in the evolution from Latin into Romance is the loss of the case system, which evolved into a system based in prepositional phrases, which favors analytic structures. Second, structural factors affect the progressive loss of verbal prefixes with a loss of transparency in their meanings. Therefore, these spatial and locative relations need to be expressed by different means in Romance languages. Iacobini and Masini (2007a) explain that locative meanings previously encoded in prefixes can be expressed by particles. They consider that only half of the locative meanings in Latin can be expressed productively in Italian by means of prefixes, and only one third of prefixes can be considered productive in Italian. These authors consider three key factors in the restriction of use of prefixes: First, Italian motion verbs already have a Latin prefix in their root (e.g. *entrare* 'enter'), which although it is not transparent, makes difficult the addition of another one. Particles are easier to combine with those verbs. Second, particles are more productive because they form a more systematic and open system of expressing spatial relations. Finally, particle constructions are more informal and differ from prefixed verbs because they have developed non-literal meanings. For example, *introdurre* 'introduce' means in Italian 'to initiate, to do something for the first time', and could be used with the original meaning of 'introduce, insert' but it is much more stylistically marked than the construction *mettere dentro* 'put in, introduced', so its frequency of use is lower.

Iacobini (2009) argues against the hypothesis of the Germanic origin of these constructions by highlighting the differences between the Italian constructions and the German separable verbs. These include their different morpho-syntactic behavior and differences in the expression of Path components (Vector, Conformation and Deixis). He also claims that *andare via*, a construction that does not seem to have an equivalent in most Romance languages, does have an antecedent in Latin (in Priscian, AD centuries 5th–6th): *andare viam*, which in turn has an antecedent in Ancient Greek: ἐλθεῖν ὁδοῖ, literally 'go on the way'. He also claims that the cases of calques in bilingual areas mainly focus on idiomatic expressions, like Ladin *morì forà* 'extinguish', literally 'die out' (from German *austerben* 'extinguish') or Belgian French *couper en bas* 'cut in slices' (from Dutch *afsnijden* 'cut in pieces') but these cases are found only in Raetho-Romance variants in Italy (Dolomitic Ladin and Friulan) and not in Italian.

In a later contrastive study, Iacobini (2015) claims that verb-particle constructions are present even in Late Latin, and that their use expanded in Early Romance, although they suffered from a loss of productivity and became marginal in some Romance languages during the second half of the 15th Century.

They however remain alive in Italian, especially in the North-Eastern dialects. In an earlier study, Iacobini (2009) notes that one possible factor that can contribute to this is the sociolinguistic situation of Italy, with its constant interaction between dialects and standard language. Another important factor is that standard Italian was mainly a written language for centuries and that its oral use was not widespread in the majority of the country until the second half of the 20th century. According to Iacobini (2015) the migration from Southern to Northern Italy fostered the prestige of Northern varieties, since verb-particle constructions are frequent in those varieties that increased their frequency of use. They are now a lexical resource of standard Italian in every region, as shown by Mosca (2010). In fact, verb-particle constructions seem to be present already in Classical Latin, like *ire intro* 'go in', *ire foras* 'go out' (see Iacobini 2009 and Mosca 2017). As pointed out by Mosca (2017) these particles convey more precise Path information and in some cases reinforce the Path which is expressed in the satellite, e.g. *exire foras*, literally 'out-go out'.

Therefore, following Masini (2005), Iacobini and Masini (2007a, 2007b), Iacobini (2009) and accepted by other scholars like Schwarze (2008), the general conclusion is that these constructions originated as a consequence of the crisis of the system to express motion in Late Latin. This evolutionary change involved a restructuration of the loss of prefixes and cases and a change in the prepositional and adverbial system of Romance languages. The appearance of these constructions is present in the first stages of Romance languages: *pujar sus* 'go up' (Old Catalan), *venir foras* (Old Provençal), for example. This is consistent with other typological changes in the evolution from Latin, like the change in word order. In this evolution some of the monomorphematic verbs remained, such as *venire* 'come', while some prefixed verbs were perceived as monomorphematic. Examples of the latter include *ex-ire* 'go out' in Latin, which evolved to *exir* (Old Spanish), *uscire* (Italian) and *bessire* (Sardinian).

It is important to note that during this change, denominal verbs were created from elements with an intrinsic directionality: from *montis* 'mountain', verbs meaning 'go up' like *montare* in Italian, and from *altius* 'tall' verbs meaning 'raise' like *alzare* in Italian, *arziare* in Sardinian, etc. It is crucial to bear in mind that the evolution from Latin to Romance languages did not coincide with the change from satellite-framed to verb-framed, because "satellite-like" constructions were still present in Romance languages until the 15th century.

With regard to the influence of German on Italian, Schwarze (1985) considered that it could have favored the dissemination and presence of verb-particle constructions in the Northern and Central Italian dialects. As Iacobini and Masini (2007a) point out, an important German migration took place to North and Central Italy during the Middle Ages, which could explain the higher presence of these constructions in those areas. However, later studies on the use of these particles in different geographical varieties of Italian show that there are no substantial differences in their use (Mosca 2007, 2010; Iacobini 2008). Mosca's data (2007, 2010) consist of dialogues of people giving directions in the street. Data were collected in Vercelli (Piedmont), Pisa (Tuscany), Naples (Campania) and Cagliari (Sardinia) without finding statistically significant differences. Iacobini (2008) analyzes texts in an Oral Italian corpus but cannot find significant differences between speakers from Milan, Rome, Florence and Naples. He does find significant differences according to the register variants, with a higher frequency of verb-particle constructions in informal oral conversations than in formal oral texts, such as radio and television broadcasting. Cerruti (2008), in a study of oral Italian in Turin, finds that these forms are more frequent independently of education levels. Those with more transparent meanings are used more widely. Young participants used more general Italian syntagmatic verbs, whereas older participants preferred Piedmontese dialectal forms.

2.3.1.2 Morpho-syntactic behavior of Italian verb-particle constructions

The focus of this section will be on the morphological and syntactic tests that Masini (2005) and Iacobini and Masini (2007a) use to argue for the unity of verb-particle constructions as a syntagmatic verb. There are different factors that are relevant for deciding their status as constructions, like the length of the element to be inserted, the possibility of topicalization and the feasibility of coordination. According to Iacobini and Masini, the possibilities of separation are quite limited and therefore these constructions seem to be very cohesive and united.

If we start by considering the combinations with a noun phrase as the inserted element, like *Metti su la borsa* 'Put up the bag', the verb and particle cannot be separated: **Metti la borsa su*. A similar verb-adverb combination in Spanish would allow for changes in the word order (both *Pon la bolsa arriba* and *Pon arriba la bolsa* are acceptable), which suggests a less cohesive relation between verbs and adverbs in Spanish.

Topicalization is another factor that illustrates the unity of verb-particle constructions. It is difficult to topicalize them by placing the particle at the beginning of the sentence. The topicalized sentences (124) and (125) (Masini 2005: 150) include the verb-particle constructions *andare dentro* 'go in(side)' and *mettere su* 'put up/on' and their acceptability is debatable.

(124) ?*È dentro che è andato*
 be.3SG inside be.3SG go.PTCP
 'It is inside that he went'

(125) ?*È su che l'abbiamo messo il caffè*
 be.3SG up/on that pron'.AUX.3PL put.PTCP the coffee
 'It is on that we have put the coffee'

Coordination is another relevant factor. Prepositional phrases and noun phrases are easy to coordinate, but syntagmatic verbs do not allow coordination easily. According to Masini (2005: 152), an acceptability cline could be considered, but normally they cannot be coordinated, as in (126):

(126) **Sara ha portato fuori la bici e poi su la spesa*
 Sara have.3SG take.PTCP out the bike and then the shopping
 'Sara took out the bicycle and then up the shopping'

Another characteristic of verb-particle constructions is that they cannot be nominalized. While a verb in a non verb-particle construction can be easily nominalized, this is not possible in verb-particle constructions. For example the nominalization of *Gianni è corso via subito* 'Gianni has run away immediately' is not grammatical: **La corsa via di Gianni subito*. In non-verb particle constructions, however: *Valeria corre da Parma a Reggio* 'Valeria runs from Parma to Reggio' can turn into *La corsa di Valeria de Parma a Reggio* 'Valeria's run from Parma to Reggio'. Masini notes that a nominalization could be permitted in verb-particle constructions only with an infinitive and with the particle following the verb, i.e. *Il correre via di Gianni*, but not **Il correre di Gianni via*.

The argument structure of the verb can also change when the verb is in a syntagmatic construction. For example, the particle *su* 'up' in (127) equates the locative expressed in (128) with a prepositional phrase. However it is not possible to use the verb-particle construction and the prepositional phrase simultaneously (129), examples from Iacobini and Masini (2007b: 158).

(127) *Metti su il caffè*
 put.IMP up/on the coffè
 'Put on the coffee'

(128) *Metti il caffè sul fuoco*
 put.IMP the coffee on.the fire
 'Put the coffee on the fire'

(129) **Metti su il caffè sul fuoco*
 put.IMP on the coffee on.the fire
 'Put on the coffe on the fire'

The final feature of morpho-syntactic behavior of Italian verb-particle constructions is that some of the verbs become unaccusative and form the present perfect with the auxiliary *essere* instead of *avere* (Iacobini and Masini 2007a: 158):

(130) *Il piccione ha volato da Roma a Pisa*
the pigeon have.3SG fly.PTCP from Rome to Pisa
'The pigeon has flown from Rome to Pisa'

(131) *Il piccione è volato via*
'The pigeon be.3SG fly.PTCP away
'The pigeon has flown away'

As previously explained, inaccusative verbs form the perfect perfect tense with *essere* 'be' while transitive verbs do it with *avere* 'have'. All the morpho-syntactic behaviours presented here lead Masini (2005) and Iacobini and Masini (2007a) to conclude that these verb-particle constructions present a high degree of cohesion and that their behavior differs from the mere combination of an adverb and a verb. These features also support the classification of these combinations as a pseudo-satellite device. This is very different from the use of locative adverbs in other Romance languages such as French and Spanish

2.3.1.3 Semantic behavior of Italian verb-particle constructions

From a semantic perspective, Masini (2005) argues that verb-particle constructions belong to three semantic classes. The first semantic class is Intensification, when the verb-particle construction emphasizes a piece of information already encoded in the verb, e.g. *uscire fuori* 'exit out' or *entrare dentro* 'enter into'. These are the pleonastic constructions seen above. The second class is that of Direction markers, when the particle indicates the direction of the movement and complements a Manner or a general verb, e.g. *mettere giù* 'put down' or *saltare dentro* 'jump into'. Finally, she includes a third semantic class for Metaphorical meanings. This class consists of verb-particle constructions that have developed a figurative meaning. These figurative meanings ranges from transparent metaphors like *buttare via*, literally 'throw away' but also 'waste', to more opaque metaphors like *portare avanti* 'take ahead, run a business'. In some cases this figurative meaning evolved into idioms like *fare fuori* 'kill, murder', literally 'make out'. According to Iacobini and Masini (2007a), the constructions with idiomatic meanings tend to preserve the original locative meanings. They give as an example *buttare giù*, a polysemic construction, with a number of meanings that can range from more literal to more abstract: 'throw down', 'knock down', 'swallow', 'undergo', 'write down', 'get down', 'blow upon' and 'weaken'. From a quantitative point of view, it is important to note that the most frequent combinations are not those consisting of intensifications (or pleonasms), as would be the case with locative adverbs and verb combinations in French or Spanish. Iacobini (2008) shows in a corpus study that the ten more frequent combinations are: *andare avanti* 'go ahead', *andare via* 'go away', *venire fuori* 'come out', *tirare fuori* 'pull out', *portare avanti* 'carry on', *mettere dentro* 'put in', *portare via* 'take away', *uscire fuori* 'exit out', *mandare via* 'send away' and *mettere insieme* 'put together'. Only *uscire fuori* is pleonastic.

Several authors (see Masini 2005; Iacobini and Masini 2007a, 2007b; Iacobini 2008, 2009 and also Cordin 2008 for the Trentino dialect) have also claimed that some particles have developed aspectual meanings, as exemplified by Masini (2005: 156) in (132) and (133):

(132) *Luca ha lavato via la macchia*
Luca AUX wash.PTCP away the stain
'Luca has washed the stain off'

(133) *Luca ha lavato la macchia*
Luca AUX wash.PTCP the stain
'Luca has washed the stain'

The particle *via* 'away' marks in (132) the focus on the result (the stain is not there anymore), whilst in (133) it is impossible to know if Luca succeeded in removing the stain. The use of these syntagmatic verbs, as opposed to the use of the verbs without particles, has been associated with telicity and duration (see also Iacobini and Fagard 2011; Iacobini 2015). This is a common phenomenon in satellite-framed languages, but not in Romance languages. Italian constructions with *via* 'away', *fuori* 'out' and *giù* 'down' have developed this additional function and express telicity:

(134) *tirare* 'pull' > *tirare fuori* 'pull out'
volare 'fly' > *volare via* 'fly away'

The verbs on the left in (134) are not telic, but in combination with particles they express telicity. Iacobini and Masini (2007b) deal with this topic extensively, concluding that most verb-particle constructions do not change the *aktionsart* or lexical aspect with regard to plain verbs, so it is inaccurate to consider them aspect markers. However, they note some changes in telicity and suggest that some of these particles could be considered telic particles.

Apart from these morphosyntactic and semantic behaviours, phonological issues contribute to the consideration of these constructions as units. Bernini (2008) and Schwarze (2008) give evidence of how the intonation of a particle is different when it works as part of a prepositional phrase and when it is part of a syntagmatic verb. Therefore, these authors consider verb-particle constructions as important, cohesive and frequent in current Italian. This has implications for the thinking for speaking of Italian speakers, as will be shown in later sections.

Finally, Iacobini and Fagard (2011) propose an implication scale of verb-particle expressions expressing displacement in verb-framed languages, reproduced in Table 7.

Table 7: Implication scale of verb-particle expressions expressing displacement in verb-framed languages (Iacobini and Fagard 2011: 165).

1	2	3	4	5	6	7
Uscire fuori 'exit out'	*Andare fuori* 'go out'	*Spingere fuori* 'push out'	*Precipitarsi fuori* 'bolt out'	*Correre fuori* 'run out'	*Camminare fuori* 'walk out'	*Danzare fuori* 'dance out'
Path	Deixis	Caused Motion	Manner + Orientation + Force Dynamics	Manner + Force Dynamics	Manner ± Force Dynamics – Specific	Manner – Force dynamics + Specific

Iacobini and Fagard consider that Manner verbs differ in their availability, as previously discussed in Section 2.2.2. They claim that Italian does not use combinations of the kind shown in column number 7, and also argue that the type in column 6 is uncommon. They also conclude that this can be generalized to other Romance languages, although Italian shows more combinability and frequency of verb-particle construction. This claim is supported by the results presented in the following chapters.

2.3.2 Prefixes as satellites

It seems clear that the verb-particle constructions in French are not strong enough to be considered either satellite or pseudo-satellite constructions, but are there other type of satellites? Researchers on French have placed the main focus on the existence of of Latin-like satellite-prefixes in French. Kopecka (2004, 2006a, 2006b, 2009, 2013) looks at these intra-typological differences from a diachronic perspective and compares these prefixes with those of satellite-framed languages, such as Polish. An example would be (135):

(135) *Les abeilles se sont envolées de la ruche*
 the bees REFL be.3PL.PRS.AUX out.fly.PTCP from the beehive
 'The bees flew out of the beehive'

Kopecka (2004: 187) suggests that French is closer to satellite-framed languages:

> Cet examen conduit ainsi à la conclusion que, contrairement à la place que la typologie proposée par Talmy lui a accordée en le définissant comme une langue à cadre verbal, le français atteste un certain nombre de préfixes qui encodent une varieté de nuances sémantiques relatives à la notion de trajectoire, spécificité d'une langue à satellite.
>
> [This examination leads to the conclusion that, French, in contrast to the place that the typology proposed by Talmy as a verb-framed language, presents a number of prefixes that codify a variety of semantic nuances relative to the notion of trajectory, which is specific to a satellite-framed language] [My translation].

In Kopecka (2006a: 87) she lists eleven French prefixes that express Path, reproduced here in Table 8. She considers that the prefixation process in French also permits the encoding in the verb of the Figure and the Ground, in cases such as *écrémer* 'skim' or *embouteiller* 'put in bottles'.

Table 8: Path prefixes in French (Kopecka 2006a: 87).

Prefix	Meaning	Examples
a(d)-	'to, toward'	*ac-courir* 'run to', *at-terir* 'land, touch down'
dé(s)-/dis-	'from, off, apart'	*dé-crocher* 'take off, unhook', *décoller* 'soak off'
é-/ex-	'out of'	*s'é-couler* 'flow out', *ex-traire* 'extract'
em-/en- (Lat. *inde*)	'away, off'	*s'en-voler* 'fly away', *s'en-fuir* 'run away'
em-/en- (Lat. *in*)	'in, into'	*en-fouir* 'bury in', *en-fermer* 'enclose'
entre-/inter-	'between, among'	*entre-poser* 'put in / between', *inter-caler* 'insert'
par-	'by, all over'	*par-courir* 'go all over', *par-semer* 'sprinkle all over'
ré-/r(e)-	'back, backwards'	*re-tourner* 'return, turn over', *re-venir* 'come back'
sou(s)-	'under'	*sou-tirer* 'extract, decant'
sur-	'on, over'	*sur-voler* 'fly over'
tra-/trans-/tre-	'across, through'	*trans-porter* 'transport', *trans-percer* 'pierce, go through'

However, Kopecka (2004: 194) herself admits that the morphological productivity of this process is weak, especially in comparison with a Slavonic language, such as Polish, in which prefixes clearly function as satellites. In fact, in Polish the prefixation process is regular and all prefixes can be combined with a displacement verb and all displacement verbs can be combined with prefixes (excepting *wz-* 'up'). She also states that there are different degrees of opacity in the semantic transparence of French prefixes. Importantly, Kopecka (2006a) acknowledges that their productivity in language history has considerably diminished. In fact, most of these prefixes are not productive and only *dé(s)-* encoding a change of state and *re-* with an iterative meaning remain as productive prefixes. Kopecka (2006a: 13) states that prefixed verbs still exist in current forms and combinations between prefixes and verbal roots are not freely formed. This seems to contradict her conclusion that French is a typologically hybrid system in which motion events are distributed along a continuum between the satellite-framed and the verb-framed pattern (Kopecka 2006a: 22).

Kopecka (2006b) performs a very detailed analysis of this satellite conflation pattern in Medieval French and Classic French. In similar vein to diachronic studies on Italian, the process of verb prefixation was in use in French until 15th century. Some of these uses remain in current French, such as *courir* 'run' vs. *accourir* 'run towards something', *tirer* 'pull, draw' vs. *attirer* 'draw to/towards'. The existence of pairs like these was frequent in Old French but its use has considerably decreased in Modern French: only some of these prefixes like *en-* and *ex-/é-* kept their productivity until the beginning of the 20th century.

In an analysis of translations from Old French to Modern French, Kopecka (2013) shows that Path verbs are the most diverse and the most frequently used class of motion verb. Path satellites are frequent, not only taking into account prefixes like (*par-* 'through') but also particles like *dedans* 'into, inside' and *fors* 'out of, outside'. These elements can perform different roles: as adverbs, particles, prefixes or prepositions. She finds that the combination of motion verb and Path particle is not pervasive in Old French, but is still quite common. By contrast, she observes a loss of productivity of these elements and an incorporation of Path in the verb root in Modern French. The Path satellites that are most used are *re-* 'again' and *en*, both as prefix as in *s'enfuir* 'flee' or as a separated element as in *s'en aller* 'go away' (see next section for the uses of *en* in more detail). Other particles found are *dehors* 'outside', *en* 'from', *y* 'there', *par-* 'through' and *re-* 'backward'. Kopecka considers that their variation and productivity are weaker in Modern French. They combine with a limited number of verbs and they are rarely used to create new combinations is low, which results in the loss of elaboration of Path in Modern French. For example, the notion to 'move away' changed from *s'en departir,* which includes three Path elements: *partir* 'leave', *de-* 'off' and *en* 'from here' to *s'éloigner* 'go far, leave' in which the elaboration of Path is lower and the deictic component is lost. She also shows how the typological shift affects the rhetorical style of the speakers. While Old French speakers tended to be more explicit in the trajectory with examples such as *issir fors* 'go out.of' or *entrer + en + en* PP 'enter + from there + into PP', these complex constructions have been substituted by *quitter* 'leave' and *se rentrer* 'go in', which render the trajectory as inferred information. Interestingly she also notices a change in the focus of attention on the portions of Path. While in Old French more attention is paid to the source of motion thanks to the frequent presence of *en*, the French translations tend to change the focus to the goal of motion.

Similarly to Italian, the evolution from Late Latin to Romance languages was accompanied with a typological shift, due to the loss of transparency of these prefixes, which led to the loss of their morpho-syntactic autonomy. The creation of new verbs from nouns (e.g. *arriver* 'arrive' from *ad* + *ripa* 'to' + 'bank/shore') also contributed to this loss. However this process does not seem to be very different to the rest of the family of Romance languages. Bartra and Mateu (2005) find similar processes in Old Catalan, and the very same prefixes identified by Kopecka can be also found in Spanish verbs: *aterrizar* 'land', *despegar* 'take off', *encerrar* 'lock', *intercalar* 'intercalate', *retornar* 'return', *sobrevolar* 'fly over', *transportar* 'transport', etc. Romance languages differ in the number of prefixes that they preserve, in their productivity and in the existence of pairs that contrast prefixed verb and non-prefixed verb. However, it does not seem justified to consider Romance prefixes as satellites, at least not at this diachronic stage. The low frequency of use and the scarce productivity of these prefixes discounts the categorization of French as a hybrid language as suggested by Pourcel and Kopecka (2005). In fact, studies that have contrasted frequency data of Romance languages show that French speakers rarely use prefixes to express Path (Hijazo-Gascón and Ibarretxe-Antuñano 2013a, 2013b; this volume). Therefore, the presence of these prefixes is not a differential factor from other Romance languages (Spanish and Italian should also be considered hybrid then, and probably Catalan, Portuguese and all the other Romance languages). In this sense, the main tenet of the typology would be unjustifiably neglected, since prefixed encoding is not the most characteristic and frequent pattern in French.

2.3.3 Adverbial and reflexive pronouns

Another feature that differentiates French and Italian on the one hand from Spanish on the other is the existence of adverbial pronouns derived from Latin *inde* 'thence' and *ibi* 'there'. Their reflexes in modern Romance languages are used to substitute for the source of the movement complements (*en* in French, *ne* in Italian) and for the goal of the movement complements (*y* in French, *ci* in Italian). The equivalent pronouns in Spanish were lost in the 15th Century (Badia Margarit 1947). They are however frequent in other Romance languages (e.g. in Aragonese and in Catalan their use is frequent, which impacts on a more detailed expression of Path with more cases of Complete Path construction (see Ibarretxe-Antuñano, Hijazo-Gascón, and Moret-Oliver 2017)). Stolova (2015) explains that these adverbial pronouns are part of a new type of word formation. In some cases the pronoun has ended up as a prefix united with the verb in compound tenses. This often happens in French, e.g. *enfuir* 'flee away', with the exception of *s'en aller* 'go away' whose union with the verb is prescribed by normative grammar. Other combinations with the adverbial pronoun are present in Italian *andarsene*, Catalan *anar-se'n* and Romansch *s'inir* 'go away'.

Stolova (2015) explains how a new pattern emerged in the evolution from Latin into Romance. Instead of relying on Classic Latin pattern (spatial preposition + verb), the new pattern consisted of the combination of a verb with the reflexive pronoun *se* and the deictic adverb *inde* 'thence'. The original functions of Latin *se* were the reflective and the reciprocal usage, so this is clearly an innovation in the evolution process. Stolova (2015) claims that according to the literature, the functions of *se* expanded over time, covering the middle *se* and the passive *se*, with occasional occurrences in Classical Latin and a wider use in Late Latin. The neutralization of the difference between the accusative *se* and the dative *sibi* took place in the 4th century. The development of motion verbs with *se* was intensified with the expansion of usage of *se* from Latin to Romance. The pronouns derived from *inde* were incorporated in some cases, in a similar way to the incorporation of the reflexes of *ibi* for existential meanings: French *Il y a*, Spanish *hay*, Catalan *hi ha* 'there is'.

Stolova (2015) puts forward the idea that Spanish *-se*, French *s'en* and Italian *-sene* should be considered as satellites. She gives three main arguments for this. First, because they are constituents of the verbal complex and at the same time they are not part of the verb root. Second, because they do not belong to any of the categories excluded by Talmy as satellites, as they are not Noun or Prepositional Phrases, auxiliaries or inflections. Finally, because they encode Path. She contrasts cases of *ir* and *aller* 'go' vs. *irse* and *s'en aller* 'go away'. In fact, according to Stolova, the isolated occurrence of *voy* 'I go' or *van* 'they go' does not include path information and is not grammatical on its own, whereas utterances including only forms of the paradigm of *irse* 'go away', e.g. *te vas* 'you go away' or *se va* 's/he goes away' do encode Path information and are grammatical. The only possible grammatical utterances containing exclusively a form of *ir* are ¡*voy*! as an answer to the speech act 'Come here!', which according to Stolova is an anaphorical reference. ¡*Vamos*! is also acceptable but only as a discourse marker, similar to 'Come on!' in English. This is an original theoretical proposal and will be further discussed under the next subsection, which explores the notion of pseudo-satellite.

2.3.4 The notion of pseudo-satellite

As explained in the previous chapter, the notion of satellite is not free from debate and controversy, especially among scholars working on satellite-framed languages (see Filipović and Ibarretxe-Antuñano 2015 for an overview). Its boundaries as a category are not always clear and there are different suggestions regarding what should and should not be considered a satellite. As explained in the previous chapter, in some cases authors have proposed new typologies and have avoided the term (Matsumoto 2003; Bohnemeyer et al. 2007; Slobin 2008; Grinevald 2011). This is not the case with verb-framed languages, whose encoding is apparently clear-cut. However, as seen in previous sections, they present some constructions that are similar to those of satellite-framed languages. The fact that they present some satellite-framed characteristics can be a result of previous typological stages. In contrast to other authors (Kopecka 2004, 2009; Simone 2008), the approach adopted here does not attempt to define these languages as mixed or to demote them from the group of verb-framed languages. Talmy establishes this typology on the bases of *the most frequent* lexicalization pattern and not of the *only* one, which allows for variation within the typological groups and the presence of other lexicalization patterns.

But do verb-framed languages really have satellites? It is useful to come back to the original definition of satellite to decide if the non-verb-framed patterns observed in verb-framed languages fit with this definition:

> Satellites are certain immediate constituents of a verb root other than inflections, auxiliaries, or nominal arguments. They relate to the verb root as periphery (or modifiers) to head. A verb root together with its satellites forms a constituent in its own right, the 'verb complex', also not generally recognized. It is this constituent as a whole that relates to such other constituents as an inflectional affix-set, an auxiliary, or a direct object noun phrase. In some cases, elements that are encountered acting as satellites to a verb root otherwise belong to particular recognizable grammatical categories; therefore, it seems better to consider the satellite role not as a grammatical category in its own right but as a new kind of grammatical relation. (Talmy 1985: 102).

The debate about the nature of satellites has led a number of scholars (Filipović 2007a; Beavers et al. 2010; Croft et al. 2010) to question this notion and to propose including other elements that lexicalize Path into this category, mostly prepositions. It has been claimed that this *extended notion of satellite* gives a better account of Latin and Italian lexicalization patterns (Mosca 2017). However, as has been pointed out by Ibarretxe-Antuñano (2017b), the risk of expanding the notion of satellite to these elements is that the category becomes so wide that there would be no difference in lexicalization patterns between verb- and satellite-framed languages, and the typology would not be useful for the classification of languages.

How then should we consider the above-mentioned linguistic elements that lexicalize Path outside the verb in Romance languages? Are they satellites *strictu sensu*? This consideration would involve Italian particles in verb-particle construction, French prefixes, the reflective pronoun *se/si* in the three languages and the adverbial pronouns derived from *inde* and *ibi*. They all encode Path information and they are not auxiliaries or prepositions. They also form a verb complex. As argued by Stolova (2015), derivates from *se*, *inde* and *ibi* do not conflict with Talmy's definition of satellite. However, if we contrast them with satellites in satellite-framed languages there are important differences in two main aspects: transparency and combinability. One of the main problems of considering these elements in Romance languages as satellites is the fact that they are at different stages of the process of lexicalization. The existing prefixes in French (also to a lesser extent in Italian and Spanish) do not have the same degree of transparency to their speakers as *out*, *in* or *up* in English. In some cases they could be even considered as part of the verb root, which automatically renders them unable to act as a satellite. Similar arguments could be used for the reflective pronoun *se* in Spanish. It is true that it encodes some information of Path, especially in contrasting *ir* 'go' and *irse* 'go away'. However, this is not transparent to the speakers and they cannot freely combine it with different verbs. It has also amalgamated so many different meanings that this renders its identification as a Path element rather unclear and limited to very few contrasts. To some extent *irse* 'go away' could be considered as an independent verb to *ir* 'go', rather than as a complex verb. Although Stolova's point in considering *se* a satellite is coherent from a diachronic point of view, in the current state of the language *se* is quite lexicalized and far from the transparency and combinability showed by satellites in other languages. This differs from Italian *ne* and French *en*. Despite their lexicalized use with reflexive verbs and decreasing frequency of use, the fact that *ne* and *en* can be used independently in those languages and that they can be used to substitute for an element with information about the source of the movement makes a clear difference. This morphological behavior brings them closer to the category of satellites. Italian particles like *fuori* 'out' are even more different in this respect. They are relatively easy to combine, their meaning is transparent and they create a verb complex. However, if compared with the satellites of English, German or Russian they are less much less complex and combinable (for example with Manner verbs).

This difficulty in ascribing these elements to the category of satellites justifies the use of a special category for these elements that resemble satellites in some aspects but not in all their features. This encourages a refined definition of *pseudo-satellite*, which has been used in previous analyses of Romance languages (Hijazo-

Gascón and Ibarretxe-Antuñano 2013a, 2013b; Ibarretxe-Antuñano, Hijazo-Gascón, and Moret-Oliver 2017; Hijazo-Gascón 2017). Pseudo-satellites are linguistic elements that encode Path in verb-framed languages and form a verb complex with the verb. They still hold a certain degree of lexical transparency in their encoding of Path information but their combinability and frequency is much lower than in the case of real satellites. This is especially noticeable in their combination with Manner verbs. The notion of pseudo-satellite would comprise several elements: Italian particles like *via* 'away', *su* 'up', *fuori* 'out', etc.; the reflexes of *inde* in Romance languages, e.g. Italian *ne* and French, Catalan and Aragonese *en*, excepting its partitive use; the reflexes of *ibi* (Italian *ci*, Catalan *hi*, French *y* and its variants in Aragonese varieties: *i*, *bi*, etc.) when they encode motion towards the goal, i.e. excepting their existential uses (e.g. *Il y a* in French, *Hi ha* in Catalan). This category is not necessarily exclusive to Romance languages. As pointed out in Hijazo-Gascón and Ibarretxe-Antuñano (2103a: 486), other verb-framed languages present similar elements, such as Turkish *disariya* 'out' and Basque *behera* 'below. ALL'. The concept of pseudo-satellite enables us to distinguish the specific value of these elements within verb-framed language typology. They are transition elements from the previous states of early Romance and intermediate phases of the typological shift, and the distinct features from other elements that have lost this status (e.g. prefixes).

The category of pseudo-satellite also enables us to distinguish a clear distinction from satellites of satellite-framed languages. There are of course variations in the frequency and combinability of satellites (see for example Filipović 2007a for semantic constraints in the use of Serbo-Croatian satellites). However, their use and combinability is still much broader in comparison with verb-framed pseudo-satellites. I acknowledge that adding a new term to the already complex terminology of this framework may be seen as overcomplicating the field. However, I believe that considering these particles as satellites gives rise to potential claims of mixed-type languages or hybrid languages, which is not accurate and creates more problems for the typology.

The use of pseudo-satellite constructions differs in frequency and acceptability across languages and has an impact on the position of the languages in the typological Path salience cline proposed by Ibarretxe-Antuñano (2009), as shown in Figure 5.

Most Romance languages are verb-framed languages and the pseudo-satellite constructions are not used or are not grammatical. This is clearly the case with Spanish and French, wherein several authors have claimed that pseudo-satellite constructions are not frequent and their use is not normative. In a further step along the cline lie Catalan and Aragonese, in which these constructions are present but less than in Italian (Ibarretxe-Antuñano, Hijazo-Gascón, and Moret-Oliver 2017).

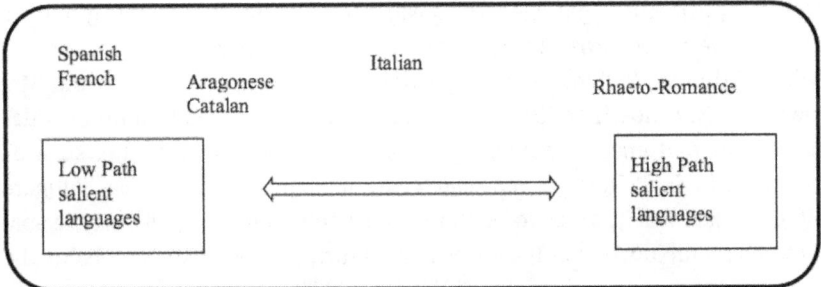

Figure 5: Romance languages in the Path salience cline.

Halfway along the cline we can find Italian in which verb-framed lexicalization is the most frequent, but in which pseudo-satellites are also very frequent. In this case Italian is not a proto-typical verb-framed language, and, as we will see in Chapter 4, it is a high-Path salient language. Finally, Rhaeto-Romance seems to be a satellite-framed language, according to the literature on Romansh (Berthele 2006) and Friulan and Dolomitic Ladin (Vicario 1997). Pseudo-satellite constructions have been identified in the literature on other languages, such as Portuguese, Romanian and Galician but their frequency of use remains to be explored.

The presence of pseudo-satellites entails a higher possibility for the encoding of Path by Italian speakers and an intra-typological variation, but not the consideration of Italian as a satellite-framed language or a mixed language. Other cross-linguistic differences in the encoding of Deixis and Cause are discussed in the following sections.

2.4 Deixis

One of the main linguistic features in which Spanish differs from other Romance languages is that of deictic motion verbs. One of the key points in understanding this concept is that of the deictic centre, which is the person (normally the speaker) at the goal of motion at the time of the utterance. This concept stems from the classical notion of *origo* (Bühler 1934; see also Levinson 1983). Lyons (1977) points out that there are more possibilities and deictic projections in some languages, which enable the addressee to be the deictic centre, such as in *You will come to the party tomorrow, right?*

Different languages show different patterns in the encoding of deictic information. Y. Huang (2006) groups deictic directional elements in two groups: deictic affixes and deictic motion verbs. The first group consists of deictic motion

affixes, morphemes and particles that mean 'hither' or 'thither'. In this group we could include Serbo-Croatian prefixes *od-* 'from the speaker' and *do-* 'to the speaker' (Filipović 2007a), German particles *hin-* and *her-* (Goschler and Stefanowitsch 2009; Goschler 2013; Liste-Lamas 2015). The second group includes motion verbs that encode motion to or away from the deictic centre, such as *come* and *go* in English, *ir* 'go' and *venir* 'come' in Spanish. In this sense, Fillmore (1977) considers deictic verbs to be those whose interpretation relies on the spatial and temporal location of the speech act participants. English is probably the most studied language in this respect. Fillmore (1977) establishes the main conditions for the use of *come* in English:
1. Movement towards the speaker's location at coding time
2. Movement towards the speaker's location at arrival time
3. Movement towards the addressee's location at coding time
4. Movement towards the addressee's location at arrival time
5. Movement towards the home-based maintained at coding time

The concept of *home based* is defined by Fillmore as a situation where the destination is not the participants' actual location but their nominative location, such as their home or workplace at the time of speaking. This is what would allow someone to say in English *I will come to the restaurant next week*, if the restaurant is her current workplace.

Even though COME and GO have been regarded as semantic universals (Miller and Johnson Laird 1976), it has been considered that more language-specific analysis of deictic motion verbs is needed before generalising and making claims about their universality (Fillmore 1983; Goddard 1997). In fact several authors (Sinha 1972; Annamalai 1975; Gathercole 1977) show variation between COME and GO in different languages according to who can be the deictic centre, whether the deictic centre can include other places and what semantic extensions are possible. According to Wilkins and Hill (1995) these are variations in the pragmatic dimension of those verbs, but not in the semantic meaning. This semantic meaning tends to be associated to "motion-towards-speaker" and "motion-towards-non-speaker". In fact, Wilkins and Hill (1995) challenge the notion of the universality of deictic verb with their analysis of Arrente and Longgu, two Australian languages. Some of their main conclusions are that GO is not deictic in all languages and that COME and GO are not strict deictic lexical universals.

The cross-linguistic comparison by Gathercole (1977, 1978) is useful when examining the different cross-linguistic patterns with regard to the deictic centre shift. According to this author, there are two types of deixis. First, immediate deixis when the deictic centre is at the goal of motion at the time of the utterance.

In this case there are three main groups of languages, depending on the possible entities that can act as the deictic centre:
1. Languages that can use *come* with the speaker and the addressee at the goal of motion at time utterance. This is the case with English, Greek, German, Turkish, Nepali, French, Serbo-Croatian, Catalan, among others.
2. Languages in which *come* can be used only with the speaker at the goal of motion at the time of the utterance. This is the case with Spanish, Portuguese, Japanese, Chinese, Thai, among others.
3. Languages in which there is no presuppositional content, like Indonesian

The second type of deixis is that of *extended deixis*, i.e. the situations in which a deictic verb is used but the deictic centre is not at the goal of motion at the time of the utterance. Gathercole provides several examples in different languages of some specific conditions that can exist for COME verbs to be used. In the case of Spanish, for example, she shows that home base is possible in this language when the deictic centre identifies with the place. In *¿Viene Juan a la fiesta esta noche?* 'Does Juan come to the party tonight?' it is implied that the party is happening at a familiar place for the speaker (e.g. in her house/home) or that the speaker is coming to the party too. She also claims that *come* can be used in cases of accompaniment, such as *¿Quieres venir a una fiesta (conmigo)?* 'Do you want to come to a party (with me)?', in which the use of *ir* 'go' is possible but marks distance or lack of intimacy. It is worth noting that languages that belong to the same language family can exhibit different behaviours in relation to deixis. Spanish and Portuguese only allow the speaker to be the deictic centre, while Catalan, French and Italian also allow the addressee to take this role (Ricca 1993; Hijazo-Gascón 2017). It has also been shown that minority languages can present different patterns in different dialects. For example Hijazo-Gascón and Ibarretxe-Antuñano (2010) show that in Aragonese the varieties in contact with Catalan allow the addressee to be the deictic centre but the other varieties do not, probably due to language contact with Spanish.

Other differences have been noted, for example with regard to specificities of other languages. Antonopoulou & Nikiforidou (2002) claim that in Greek it is not possible to make implicit the physical presence of the speaker and the addresse and *erxome* 'come' necessarily implies the presence of one of them: Θα πας στο πάρτυ 'Are you going to the party?' In this example it is implied that the speaker will not be there, whereas in Θα έρθεις στο πάρτυ 'Are you coming to the party?' It is implied that the speaker will definitely be there. In concomitative utterances COME is the only possible use in Greek. In the case of Serbo-Croatian, Filipović (2007a: 113–122) shows how deixis is a prominent feature in the narratives of the speakers thanks to the combinability of the deictic prefixes *od-* 'from the speaker' and *do-* 'to the speaker'. These prefixes can be combined with all prepositions and can accumulate directional phrases onto a single verb.

Deixis has been also considered within Talmy's framework. In his early works Talmy (1985) considered Deixis as "direction" related to Path. Aske (1989) also considered Deixis as a kind of Path. Talmy (2000a, 2000b) establishes that Deixis is a subcomponent of the semantic domain of Path, along with Vector and Conformation, without having the status of a component *per se*.

However, several authors have argued for its importance and claim that deictic meaning has a more prominent role. For example, Choi and Bowerman (1992: 86) place Deixis at the same level as other semantic components like Manner and Cause. They argue that deixis often patterns differently from other kinds of Paths in the way it is lexicalized. In Korean the main verb is usually *kata* 'go' or *ota* 'come', thus conflating motion with deixis. However deictic verbs can be preceded by a Manner and a Path verb, in cases like (134) from Choi and Bowerman (1992: 88), which shows how Deixis clearly stands out in the most frequent motion lexicalization pattern:

(136)   *John-I pang-ey (ttwui-e) tul-e o-ass-ta*
        John-SBJ room-LOC (run-CONN) enter-CONN come-PST-DECL
        [Figure] [Ground] ([Manner]) [Path] [Motion + Deixis]
        'John came in(to) the room (running)'

Similarly, Matsumoto (1996, 2013) argues that Deixis has a prominent role in some languages, particularly in Japanese. As in the case of Korean, German or Jacaltek, Japanese has a specific 'slot' for Deixis independent of Path. Matsumoto, Akita and Takahashi (2017) challenge Talmy's (2000) consideration of Deixis as a subcomponent of Path. They propose two main reasons for establishing Deixis as an independent semantic component. First, Deixis has its own morpho-syntactic slots in a number of languages. These slots are specific to convey deixis and are different from non-deictic Path information. Second, deictic verbs exist independently of the richness of path verbs in a given language (e.g. English and German). Matusmoto, Akita, and Takahashi (2017) consider that the semantics of venitive verbs involve functional properties, including an interactional relationship between the speaker and the moving person. Their use involves a perspective shift between the speaker and the hearer. The location of the speaker should be understood in terms of engagement area, and is influenced by accessibility and visibility. These authors claim that it is necessary to redefine the traditional conception of the semantics of venitive verbs. This is because their meaning not only involves the motion towards the deictic centre, as claimed by Fillmore (1977), but also considers their interactional space and their interactional behaviour. In other words, the semantics of the venitive verb are enhanced by the coexistence of the speaker and the mover at the end of motion in a shared space. The goal should be understood as the space for the speaker's potential interaction with the moving person, and not just the location of the speaker. The use of deictic verbs is sensitive to the speaker's location or space at the time of the uttreance. The location of the speaker is exactly where an interaction can take place, including the current location. According to Matsumoto, Akita, and Takahashi (2017) the goal of venitive verbs is the location where the speaker can interact with the moving person in reality or potentially.

2.4.1 Deixis in Spanish

As noted by several authors (Gathercole 1977, 1978; Ricca 1993; Lewandowski 2014; Hijazo-Gascón 2017), Spanish differs even from other Romance languages in its use of deixis . The speaker is the only possible deictic centre and only *venir* 'come' and *traer* 'bring' can be used to describe motion towards the addressee. Stolova (2015) notes this difference and explains that despite Latin *venire* having reflexes in all Romance languages, the deictic range of the Spanish and Portuguese verbs does not match that of the Latin original verb. She examines this issue further and shows that Corominas and Pascual (1980–1991 V: 770) also note that Latin *venire* did not imply motion towards the speaker, but rather a movement towards any place, regardless of the position of the speaker. It is interesting to see that Old and Classical Spanish still retained the Latin usage, while Old Catalan had the use that is present today in modern Spanish (Badía Margarit 1952). Modern Catalan patterns align today with French and Italian (and Latin) in the use of *venir* for motion towards both the speaker and the addressee, with the exception of the variety spoken in the region of Valencia. Similarly, another dialectal continuum is found in Aragonese, where western varieties share the deictic pattern with Spanish while eastern varieties share it with Catalan. It does not seem clear why the deictic pattern has changed in Iberian languages. Influence from Arabic would seem to be a plausible explanation, as that language shares the same pattern as Spanish and Portuguese. However, the fact that Old and Classical Spanish did not share the Arabic pattern during historical periods when both languages were in more contact challenges this potential explanation. Having no evidence to support these speculations, the origin of these intratypological difference seems an open question for future diachronic research.

Cross-linguistic synchronic research is more fruitful in providing us with a clear understanding of how deixis works in Spanish. Lewandowski (2014) finds differences in the use of deictic verbs between Spanish and Polish. In Spanish *venir* 'come' and *traer* 'bring' imply the presence of the speaker at the goal of movement (e.g. *traelo aquí/*allí* 'bring it here/*there' in contrast with other motion verbs: *entra aquí/allí* 'enter here/there'). However, in Polish, as in most Slavonic languages (Ricca 1993), the use of COME and GO is related to other non-deictic factors. Lewandowski (2014) explains that COME is preferred when the speaker wishes to adopt an arrival-oriented perspective and GO when the event is conceptualised from a source-oriented perspective. He summarises previous research on cross-linguistic variation (Gathercole 1977; Ricca 1993) in Table 9:

Table 9: Hierarchy of Grounds Lexicalised in COME (adapted from Lewandowski 2014: 46).

Goal	Languages
1. The speaker's location at the time of communication act (coding time)	Portuguese, Shibe . . .
2. The speaker's location at the time of the spatial event (reference time)	Jacatlec, Spanish . . .
3. The addressee's location	Catalan, English . . .
4. Another goal of movement	Polish, Russian . . .

In this classification, the encoding of the last category implies the previous ones too. For example, Polish COME lexicalizes the context of 4 but also the previous goals (speaker and addressee). Lewandowski explains that, generally speaking, Polish speakers tend to use COME when the speaker identifies with the goal of motion and GO when the speaker focuses on the departure point of the event. In the case of Spanish, *venir* 'come' lexicalizes only the speaker but at both the coding time and the reference time. Lewandowski (2014) claims that the second possibility in Spanish, motion towards the speaker's location at reference time, allows for both COME and GO to be used but speakers prefer GO when the speaker is absent from the goal of motion. For example (Lewandowski (2014: 49):

(137) *Llegué a la biblioteca y vi que también había ido/?venido mi hermano*
arrive.1SG.PST to the library and see.1SG.PST that also AUX.3SG.PST go.PTCP/?come.PTCP my brother
'When I arrived at the library, I realized that my brother had gone/?come there too?

(138) *He telefoneado desde el aeropuerto y me han dicho que venían/?iban a buscarme*
AUX.1SG called from the airport and me AUX.3PL told that come.3PL.PST/?go.3PL.PST to pick.up.INF.PRON.1SG
'I called from the airport and they told me that they were coming?going to pick me up'

Deixis is still an under researched area in the typology of motion events, having mainly been studied in comparison with Manner and other aspects of Path. Even its classification as a sub-component of Path is controversial. In this study some remarks on deixis will be provided although it will not be the main focus of the research. However, it merited some attention as a relevant intra-typological difference between Spanish on the one hand and French and Italian on the other.

The divergence in the deictic use of Spanish and English deictic venitive verbs has been explored in bilingualism research. It is interesting that early and late bilinguals in both languages seem to accept the usage of English deictic motion verbs in the same way as monolingual English speakers do (Verde 2014). However, the task seems more challenging in the more restrictive deictic system of Spanish, both for late bilinguals and early bilinguals who are heritage speakers. Chui (2016) shows how L2 learners (after two years studying Spanish) produce pragmatic transfer from English to the use of Spanish deictic verbs. Interestingly enough, the verbal deictic system of heritage speakers' seems to be in between those of native and L2 speakers. Although heritage speakers' results are closer to those of native speakers, their use of venitive verbs still differs significantly from them.

Deixis constitutes a challenge for speakers in a second language (L2). A number of studies have been carried out involving different language pairs and all of them concur regarding the difficulty of re-conceptualizing deictic motion verbs in a second language. Lewandowski (2014) shows that the above-mentioned contrasts have implications for the use of Spanish as an L2 by L1 Polish speakers. In a judgement test, they accepted uses of venir 'come' that are not idiomatic in Spanish. He concludes that the L1 thinking for speaking pattern seems difficult to restructure, even in advanced learners. They accepted cases like (139):

(139) - *Hola Natalia, esta noche hago una fiesta en mi casa ¿Te quieres pasar?*
- 'Hello, Natalia, there is a party at my place tonight. Would you like to pop in?'
- *¿En tu casa? Claro que sí, pero vendré sobre las doce*
- 'At your place? Sure, but I will come about twelve'

The speaker is accepting the use of *venir* 'come' with a goal of motion that does not correspond with the location of the deictic centre or a place related to her. Other studies involving Spanish as the target language have shown that this type of difficulty is not exclusive to typologically different languages. Hijazo-Gascón (2017) shows in a production study that advanced learners of Spanish, native speakers of French, German and Italian, face the same challenge in re-shaping the category of deictic verbs. For example (140) is produced by an Italian speaker:

(140) *Me arreglé, salí y vine a tu casa [. . .] Sí, traje el vino a tu casa*
'I got ready, went out and came to your house [. . .] Yes, I brought the wine to your house'

The verbs *venir* 'come' and *traer* 'bring' are not used appropriately here, as the speaker is not in the goal of motion at the time of the utterance. In the case of deixis, the genetic closeness between the three Romance languages and the fact that they belong to the same group in the motion typology does not help Italian and French learners who still find difficult the restrictions in Spanish. As expected, like in the case of the Polish learners, German learners of Spanish also show difficulties in the restructuring of the use of deictic verbs. However, some studies are testing the benefits of explicit instruction of deixis. Colasacco (2019) has designed an intervention study in which students presented with the forms improve their performance in the use of deictic verbs in Spanish as a second language.

2.5 Cause

The contrast between Manner and Path has received most of the attention in the literature, but it is worth remembering that Manner is not the only Co-Event. In his seminal works Talmy (1985, 1991) includes Cause as another Co-Event, in cases like (141), and it should not be disregarded.

(141) *The pencil blew off the table*

Most of the attention on Caused motion has come from researchers focusing on French first language acquisition in contrast with English (see among others Hendriks, Hickmann, and Demagny 2008; Hickmann and Hendriks 2006; Hendriks and Hickmann 2015). Cause can be encoded in causative verbs, like (142), and in intransitive verbs that are used as transitive, like (143):

(142) *Il pousse la valise*
he push.3SG the suitcase
'He pushes the suitcase'

(143) *Jean roule la balle*
    Jean roll.3SG the ball
    'Jean rolls the ball'

Complex causative constructions are also possible. They consist of the combination of the verb *faire* 'make' and a Path or a Manner verb:

(144) *Jean fait monter la valise*
    Jean make.3SG ascend.INF the suitcase
    'Jean puts the suitcase up (on the shelf)'

(145) *Marie fait rouler la balle*
    Marie make.3SG roll.INF the ball
    'Marie makes the ball roll'

This type of constructions is of special interest for this study because it constitutes an intra-typological difference. While other Romance languages can express caused motion with similar structures, e.g. Italian *Piero fa rotolare la palla* 'Piero makes the ball roll', in Spanish these constructions are not commonly used and do not sound idiomatic. This intra-typological difference has consequences in second language acquisition, as we will see in Chapter 5. Hendriks and Hickmann (2015) show that most deviations from the canonical verb-framed typology in French occur in caused motion. In their study, French speakers expressed Cause and agent action (e.g. *pousser* 'push') or Cause and manner (e.g. *rouler* 'roll') and they did it more when encoding *into*-events than *across*-events.

Kopecka and Narasimhan (2012) gather a number of studies which show cross-linguistic variation in the encoding of a special subset of these caused motion events. These studies focus on placement and removal events. The authors of these studies show how the lexical semantics of caused motion verbs is different from those of voluntary motion, and how placement events differ cross-linguistically. On some occasions, the semantic distribution is presented in a range of constructions. Ibarretxe-Antuñano (2012) points out that in the case of Spanish, two semantic components are particularly relevant in the encoding of placement events. These are force dynamics and intentionality. Ibarretxe-Antuñano (2012: 138–139) proposes this continuum, which combines both factors:

(146) a. *Se cae el libro*
        CL fall.3SG the book
        'The book falls'

b. *Se le cae el libro*
   CL DAT.3SG falls the book
   Lit. 'The book falls to him'
   'He drops the book unintentionally'
c. *Deja caer el libro*
   allow.3SG fall the book
   Lit. 'He allows the book to fall'
   'He drops the book unintentionally but softly'
d. *Tira el libro*
   throw.3SG the book
   'She throws the book (intentionally)'
e. *Lanza el libro*
   throw.3SG.away the book
   'He throws the book away'
f. *Arroja el libro*
   throw.3SG.away.violently the book
   'She throws the book away violently'

In (146a) there is no external agent that causes the fall. The agent in (146b) does not show intentionality but she does in all the other cases. Force dynamics is weaker in (146c) and progressively increases into more violent from (146d) to (146e) and (146f). This is a stark contrast with the encoding of these events in Germanic languages. Gullberg (2009b) shows how French and Dutch speakers differ in the way they gesture in the encoding of these events, since in most Germanic languages there is a different verb to encode the placement of horizontal or vertical Figures (Dutch *leggen* vs. *zetten*, Danish *lægge* vs. *sætte*, etc.). Gullberg (2009b) shows that this distinction is so entrenched in speakers that even those Dutch speakers who had a good command of French showed cross-linguistic influence not in speech but in gesture. In a bidirectional study Cadierno, Ibarretxe-Antuñano, and Hijazo-Gascón (2016), Ibarretxe-Antuñano, Cadierno, and Hijazo-Gascón (2016) show how Spanish and Danish differ in the encoding of these events, and demonstrate that it is a difficult domain for reconceptualization in the second language or re-thinking for speaking. For example, Danish learners of Spanish overgeneralised the verb *poner* 'put' in contexts in which the Figure is placed in a container, while native speakers preferred *meter* 'put in' or in some cases *tirar dentro* 'throw inside'.

These differences are not to be underestimated. Filipović (2007b, 2013) shows how these can have crucial repercussions in forensic contexts. In an example from a police interview in California, Filipović (2007b: 262) shows how this can be crucial:

(147) Question: *Okay, You said before that she fell or you dropped her on the stairs?*
Interpreter: *¿Usted les dijo antes de que ella se cayó o la botó en las gradas?*
'You them said before that she REFL.fall-PFV.3SG or her throw.PFV.3SG on the stairs?'
Suspect: *Sí, sí, se me cayó*
'yes, yes, to-me-it-happened-that-she-fell'
Interpreter: *Yes, I dropped her*

The construction *se me cayó* 'it fell to me' is used several times in the transcription. It is usually translated into English with the verb *drop*, which is ambiguous in terms of intentionality. A sentence like *I dropped it* could encode actions of 'dropping' on purpose or not. However, in Spanish this is a clear-cut distinction. If the action is done on purpose the construction chosen is non agentive, like *se me cayó*, which indicates in this case that the suspect did not have the intention of dropping the victim. In fact, in the example this is translated as a clearly agentive construction with *botar* 'throw'. In the transcription the suspect is asked nine times about this fact and at the end it is not clear in English if the suspect performed this action on purpose or not. The importance of intentionality for the encoding of Spanish is shown clearly in in a later experiment, in which Filipović (2013) shows how Spanish speakers remembered better whether or not speakers of the videos shown performed the actions on purpose, and they made it explicit even while they were speaking English. Caused motion is, therefore, another area of motion in which Romance languages exhibit particular characteristics (as showed with studies by Hickmann, Hendriks and colleagues on French and Cadierno, Ibarretxe-Antuñano and colleagues on Spanish). However, to our knowledge not many studies have contrasted how Romance languages resemble each other or differ with regard to caused motion (but see Hijazo-Gascón 2017, 2018; Chapter 4 of this volume, for MAKE + INFINITIVE constructions).

2.6 The position of French, Italian and Spanish in the typology

2.6.1 Spanish as the prototypical verb-framed language

Spanish is probably the second most studied language from the Talmy-Slobin perspective, English being the language that has received most of the attention. This allows us to establish comparisons with previous findings and utilise previous literature to interpret our data. Spanish has been traditionally viewed as the prototype for verb-framed languages. This chapter has explained motion event lexicalization in Spanish. Although I do not reject the classification of

Spanish as the prototypical verb-framed language, it has been shown that some of the intra-typological differences claimed for other languages are also possible in Spanish, e.g. the remains of Latin prefixes. This would make them, thus, equally prototypically verb-framed.

The idea of Spanish as the prototypical verb-framed language stems from Talmy's work and from his choice of Spanish to illustrate his semantic typologies. In the first semantic typology, which classifies languages according to event conflation in the verb, Spanish tends to codify Motion and Path, for instance in verbs like *subir* 'go up', *bajar* 'go down', *salir* 'go out', etc. It is worth recalling that Talmy (1985) does not consider that this is the only lexicalization pattern in verb-framed languages. Spanish also presents verbs lexicalizing Motion and Manner: *saltar* 'jump', *correr* 'run'. In the case of the second typology, which classifies languages according to the encoding of Path, Spanish is clearly a verb-framed language, as this component tends to be encoded in the main verb of the event (Talmy 1991). Manner and Cause components, if expressed, are encoded in more peripheral elements such as gerunds, prepositional phrases or adverbs. Spanish has also raised some interesting questions regarding motion verbs that have helped the typology to move forward, like the boundary-crossing constraint.

Spanish is also a prototypical language from the angle of Slobin's (1991, 1996, 1997) thinking for speaking. It is one of the languages used by Slobin to illustrate his hypothesis. It is in fact one of the five languages included in the seminal study by Berman and Slobin (1994) together with German, Hebrew, English and Turkish. In the chapter on Spanish, Sebastián and Slobin (1994) develop some of the main hypotheses that inspired the literature on thinking for speaking in Spanish. They notice that the set of motion verbs is small in comparison with other languages. Similarly, the amount of locative prepositions is scarce too. This contrasts with its rich distinctions regarding tense and aspect. Manner of motion is not normally expressed and speakers, regardless of their age, do not give much information about this component. These authors identify a U-shaped curve in development at the age of 5 in which speakers tend to give more information than needed. Children at this age reinforce the expression of Path with directional adverbs, creating redundant constructions like *salir fuera* 'exit out', *subir arriba* 'ascend up'. Interestingly this does not happen with younger children, nor with older children or adult speakers. This addition of Path information is also present in the acquisition of Spanish as a second language (Cadierno 2004; Cadierno and Ruiz 2006).

Sebastián and Slobin (1994) claim that in their data none of the speakers specifies origin and goal of motion in complements which are dependent on the same main verb. The tendency is to use only one of them with the verb. This happens at all ages and is not a grammar restriction of the language, but a discourse pattern of speakers. An example would be (148):

(148) *Olga fue en tren de Teruel a Zaragoza*
Olga go.PST.3SG in train from Teruel to Zaragoza
'Olga went from Teruel to Zaragoza by train'

This example is perfectly grammatical but native speakers do not normally use it, although it might be reserved for higher levels of register. According to Sebastián and Slobin (1994), Spanish speakers use other means to describe Path. They do not encode each segment of this component, but leave it to be inferred from the descriptions of the scene and the use of Path verbs that imply a change of location. These descriptions are performed thanks to relative sentences, as in the following example from *La casa de los espíritus* by Isabel Allende, cited in Slobin (1996a: 209):

(149) *Tomó sus maletas y echo a andar por el barrial y las piedras de un sendero que conducía al pueblo*
'He took his suitcases and started to walk through the mud and stones of a path that led to the town'

Slobin (1996a) considers that this pattern is characteristic in Spanish. The English pattern with more than one dependent element of the verb, as in *she walked along a path to the town*, is not frequent in Spanish. Slobin claims that the Manner of motion of the character can be inferred in Spanish from the characteristics of Path (*el barrial, las piedras* 'the mud, the stones'), but that it is not explicitly expressed.

This combination of static and dynamic information, that is, scene description and the use of Path verbs allow the listeners to infer the trajectories of movement too. The thinking for speaking patterns in each language entails the adjustment of certain elements. In other words, the presence or absence of certain linguistic elements can favor the easy encoding of semantic information. Slobin (1991: 12) suggests that when acquiring a language, the child learns a particular way of thinking for speaking. This explains the U-Shape developmental curve mentioned above. Spanish-speaking children tend to elaborate redundant Path structures, but only temporarily. In later stages of the language acquisition process this redundancy disappears (Berman and Slobin 1994: 622). For instance, as in the case of speakers of other verb-framed languages such as Hebrew, Spanish children use relative sentences much more frequently and earlier than speakers of other languages like English and German. Berman and Slobin (1994: 624) believe that the development of a linguistic form can occur earlier and faster if it is very accessible in the mother tongue.

Spanish rhetorical style is characterized by a highly developed aspect-temporal system, but shows less attention towards motion in space. Manner receives less attention and is mentioned only if necessary, while Path information tends to be static. It is noticeable how speakers adjust to the linguistic options available in their language, and that they do not compensate for the semantic components that their linguistic system does not cover. In the case of Spanish, this has been widely tested with different types of data: *Frog Story* narratives (Sebastián and Slobin 1994), the *Canary Row* (McNeill 1992, 2005, McNeill and Duncan 2000), analysis of novels (Slobin 1996a), translations into Spanish (Slobin 1997), to name just a few.

The effect of this lack of compensation for certain semantic components has inspired a number of psycholinguistic experiments. Naigles and Terrazas (1998) study how English and Spanish native speakers react to novel motion verbs, which are presented in syntactic structures that are characteristic of Manner or Path verbs. Their results conclude that English speakers tended to interpret new motion verbs as Manner and Spanish speakers as Path verbs. Other studies have showed linguistic effects in memory (Filipović 2010a, 2010b; Filipović and Geva 2012). These effects are not present in normal conditions, but occur only when speakers are exposed to complex events involving a heavy memory load. In these cases English speakers remember and identify better the Manner of motion of the events. In the case of bilinguals, they remember Manner better than monolingual Spanish speakers but worse than English monolingual speakers (Filipović 2011). This also suggests that there is an interdependence of languages in bilingual processing and memory. A shared pattern for both languages is preferred.

Therefore, the Spanish position in the typology follows the prototypicity of verb-framed languages, from both Talmy and Slobin's perspectives on lexicalization patterns, thinking for speaking and rhetorical style. This is confirmed by evidence from different data such as child language acquisition, second language acquisition, translation studies and experimental studies. Following the typological clines proposed by Slobin (2004) and Ibarretxe-Antuñano (2009), Spanish can be considered a low-salient Manner language and low-salient Path language. Spanish will be used throughout this volume as a point of comparison for inter-typological differences with German and intra-typological differences with French and Italian. It will be the target language of the acquisition study presented in Chapter 5 and as such is core to this research.

2.6.2 The controversial position of Italian in the typology

Having reviewed all the characteristics of Italian, mainly its verb-particle constructions, it does not seem appropriate to consider it as a prototypical verb-framed language. Some authors like Mosca (2007, 2009, 2010) go further and consider that Italian does not seem to show a preference for either the satellite-framed or the verb-framed lexicalization pattern. Baicchi (2005) also states that English lexicalization pattern is possible in Romance languages, and suggests that it is more frequent in Italian than in Spanish. I agree with Iacobini and Masini (2007a, 2007b) who consider that Italian is closer to English than Spanish, but note that it still has a strong tendency to encode Path in the verb root. It is worth remembering that when Talmy established his classification, he did not claim that the type of lexicalization (namely verb-framed or satellite-framed) needs to be the only one that exists in the language. Instead, he highlights that he is referring to the most frequent or the most prototypical. Therefore, I also agree with Simone (2008) that these differences do not mean that Italian should be considered part of the family of satellite-framed languages. Rather, Italian will be considered here as a verb-framed language, although its specificities will be taken into account.

In the case of thinking for speaking (Slobin 1991, 1996), Baicchi (2005) places Italian at an intermediate point on the Manner salience cline. The main reason for this position is that the frequent use of the Germanic conflation pattern would allow Italian speakers to describe Manner easily and more frequently. However, later studies (Cardini 2008; Hijazo-Gascón and Ibarretxe-Antuñano 2013a, 2013b and chapter 4 of this volume) show that Italian does not have a repertoire of Manner of motion verbs which is comparable to satellite-framed languages. Therefore, Italian would be a low-Manner salient language, closer to Spanish and French.

With regard to Path, Italian presents a higher detail of description of Path, as will be presented in the following chapters. This would locate Italian closer to other verb-framed languages which have a higher position on the Path salience cline, such as Basque (Ibarretxe-Antuñano 2004a, 2004b), and Korean and Japanese (Wienold and Schwarze 2002). There are, however, some open questions for research into Italian. One of them regards the boundary-crossing constraint, as this has mainly been studied with regard to the possibility of encoding (Iacobini and Fagard 2011) and with regard to comprehension (Cardini 2012), but not with oral narratives. Another area that has received little attention in Italian is caused motion. This volume will attempt to shed some light on these less-studied aspects of motion in Italian.

2.6.3 The position of French in the typology

French is a verb-framed language and has been considered as such in most studies on French motion events. As already mentioned in the previous chapter, the French academic tradition noticed the difference between French and German motion verbs, and Tesnière (1959) distinguishes between (intrinsic) movement verbs, like *marcher* 'walk' and (extrinsic) displacement verbs, like *entrer* 'enter'. Lamiroy (1983) also considers different types of motion: directional motion (*partir* 'partir'), displacement (*marcher* 'walk') and body movement (*se pencher* 'lean forward'). She claims that direction movements form the present perfect with *être* 'be', whilst displacement verbs use *avoir* 'have'.

French has been also regarded as a hybrid system (Pourcel and Kopecka 2005). However, the so-called hybrid conflation with Manner+Path in the verb, e.g. *grimper* 'climb up', *tomber* 'fall', is also present in other Romance languages, like Italian and Spanish. The acceptance of French as a hybrid system would thus imply that all Romance languages be considered as hybrid, which would mean the typology loses relevance. The other particular feature of French, i.e. the selection of different auxiliaries, is lost in modern Spanish but present in Italian and other Romance languages (and in Old Spanish). Therefore, neither hybrid conflation nor auxiliary verb selection seem strong enough to classify French as a hybrid language in Talmy's typology. Other specific features of French, like the potential existence of satellite-constructions, have been singled out as signs of closeness to satellite-framed languages (Kopecka 2004, 2006a, 2006b, 2009, 2013; Pourcel and Kopecka 2005; Porquier 2001, 2003). These satellite-framed constructions fall into two categories. The first category involves verb and locative adverb combinations similar to the Italian verb-particle constructions, e.g. *Il court dehor* 'He runs out'. The second consists of French prefixes in combination with motion verbs as explained in 2.3.2. However, these patterns have been shown to be insufficiently characteristic and frequent to challenge the position of French as a canonical verb-framed language.

In fact, most scholars of French have identified French as a verb-framed language (see among others Gullberg, Hendriks, and Hickmann 2008; Harr 2012; Berthele 2013; Hendriks et al. 2008; Hendriks and Hickmann 2015; Hickmann 2007; Hickmann and Hendriks 2006, 2010; Hickmann, Hendriks, and Gullberg 2009; Hijazo-Gascón and Ibarretxe-Antuñano 2013a, 2013b; Harr 2012; and Woerfel 2018). Khalifa (2001) contrasts English and French in the area of translation and explains that French lexicalization patterns are very close to those described in classical studies for Spanish: the trajectory is encoded in the main verb, Manner is inferred from context and the boundary-crossing restriction is applied. Berthele (2004, 2006) also compares the data elicited with the Frog story in French, standard German, Swiss German and Romansh. His data show

French as a prototypical verb-framed language, with a small lexicon of Manner verbs, low tendency to express Manner, little description of Path, and static descriptions in comparison to the dynamism of satellite-framed languages. In fact, in a later study Berthele (2013) finds that the use of complex Path is very rare in French. This is supported by more Frog story data which contrasts French with Italian, Spanish and German (Hijazo-Gascón and Ibarretxe-Antuñano 2013a, 2013b, this volume).

Hickmann, Hendriks and Gullberg (2009) also argue in favor of classifying French as a verb-framed language. They claim that Manner verbs in French are used for general location but are not normally used to express changes of location. They also consider that the prefixes noted by Kopecka are a very reduced satellite sub-system that remains from a previous stage of the language. In this vein, Harr (2012) shows how French speakers tend to encode only one semantic element per motion event at all ages (4, 6, 8 and 10 years old). When speakers increase in age they tend to encode more Path and less Manner. Woerfel (2018) also shows that his group of French minimal bilinguals shows a clear preference for bare motion verbs. He finds intra-typological differences in the expression of motion between Turkish and French speakers. A wider use of Manner verb repertoire was displayed in Turkish in comparison with French. Even in cases when Manner of motion was foregrounded, the use of Path verbs was prevalent in French. The similarities between verb-framed languages lead to very similar motion descriptions in French by Turkish-French and French minimal bilinguals, the only significant differences being in the lower frequency with which bilinguals express Manner. However, French seems to influence the Turkish speech of bilinguals, as when compared with Turkish-German bilinguals, they produced more cases of motion being encoded without Path elements.

Experimental studies using different techniques also support the view that French is verb-framed (Carroll et al. 2012; Engemann et al. 2015; Soroli and Hickmann 2012; Hickmann et al. 2017; to name a few). For example, Soroli (2012) shows that even in non-verbal categorization tasks French speakers focused on Path while speakers of Greek and English focused more on Manner. French shows, then, a clear verb-framed pattern for both Manner and Path components. This is also confirmed by the data presented in this volume, and therefore for all the above-mentioned reasons French will be considered here as a clearly established verb-framed language.

3 Motion events in German

German has been one of the languages at the heart of the semantic typology of motion since this field of study was established. As explained above, French traditional scholars such as Tesnière and Bally had noticed the differences between French and German much before Talmy's proposals. German prefixes had already received the attention of linguists from different perspectives. In Talmy's typology, German separate prefixes are classified as satellites, together with English particles and Russian and Latin prefixes. German is thus considered a satellite-framed language. It is rich in morpho-syntactic elements, which encode Path, as it presents several types of prefixation, with different degrees of separability with respect to the verb. It also uses a case system that is used to encode motion Grounds (e.g. directional complements in the accusative vs. locative complements in the dative). It also includes a broad lexicon of Manner verbs. In the following sections we will see how these linguistic devices are used to encode motion, what the characteristics are of German thinking for speaking, and the position of German in motion typology with regard to the Manner and Path clines.

3.1 German lexicalization patterns

As a satellite-framed language, German tends to encode Path outside the main verb. German satellites have been traditionally studied as verb particles and present some differences with regard to English satellites. The grammar of German, Duden, (2006: 677) defines *Verbpartikeln* 'verb particles' as the stressed members of complex verbs, which are linked to the second member only in certain contexts. Traditional grammars divide them into separable and non-separable prefixes, as the first occur in final position in certain syntactic contexts. The members of both categories present syntactic, semantic and phonological differences. On the one hand, separable prefixes, also called prefixoids (*Präfixoid*) or half-prefixes (*Halbpräfix*) are stressed and their position is at the end of the sentence. That is, they are separated from the verb like (150), except in subordinate constructions taking the infinitive form.

(150) *Der Hund bremst zu spät ab*
the.NOM.M dog brake.PRS.3SG too late PRE
'The dog stops too late' [03DE]

(151) Wie der Junge in das Wasser hineinfällt
       as the.NOM.M boy in the.ACC water towards.there-into.PRE.fall.PRS.3SG
       'As the boy falls into the water' [03DE]

Other examples of separable prefixes are *an* 'to'[2] in *ankommen* 'arrive' or *auf* 'up' in *aufstehen* 'get up'. Some adverbs can also work as separable prefixes as in the cases of *fort-* 'away', *her-* 'hither', *hin-* 'thither', *weg-* 'away', *nieder-* 'down', *zusammen-* 'together' and *zurück-* 'back'. It is even possible for some adjectives to work as separable prefixes, like *los-* 'away/off'. Of special interest is the use of *hin-* 'thither' and *her-* 'hither', as these are deictic prefixes, are very frequently used, and are easy to combine with other prefixes to create complex satellites: *hinunter-* 'towards down there', *heraus-* 'towards here out', *herauf-* 'towards here out'. We can see its use in these examples taken from Bamberg (1994: 220):

(152) *Da fiel der Hund zur Erde heraus*
       'There the dog fell hither-out to the ground'

(153) *Als er sich auf die Fensterbank setzte und hinunterfiel, zerbrach das Glas in tausend Stücke*
       'When he got onto the windowsill and thither.down.fell, the glass broke into a thousand pieces'

In (152) the point of view taken, outside the house, is marked by the prefix *her-* 'hither', while in (153) the same verb, *fallen* 'fall', is used, but the perspective is taken from the window. It is difficult to translate all this information into other languages that do not have these resources available (for its difficulty for second language learners see Liste-Lamas 2015, 2016a, 2016b). Bamberg (1994: 219) shows how combinable German satellites are. For example *raus-* 'out' is combined with 12 different verbs in his corpus: *-fallen* 'fall out', *-fliegen* 'fly out', *-gehen* 'go out', *-gleiten* 'slide out', *-hüpfen* 'hop out', *-klettern* 'climb out', *-kommen* 'come out', *-laufen* 'run away', *-rennen* 'run out', *-schlüpfen* 'slip out', *-springen* 'jump out', *-steigen* 'climb out'.

On the other hand, German has also non-separable prefixes. These prefixes are not stressed and combine with verbs that do not follow the regular rule to form the participle with *ge-*. Some of these prefixes are *be-*, *ent-*, *er-*, *ge-*, *ver-*, and *zer-*, with several meanings. Some examples of their (motion and non-motion) compounds are *bezahlen* 'pay', *entkommen* 'get away', *erziehen* 'educate', *gefallen* 'like',

---

2 Please note that the translation of prefixes is approximate.

verbieten 'forbid' or *zerbrechen* 'destroy'. Prefixes with a foreign origin also belong to this group, e.g. *delegieren* 'delegate', *desorganisieren* 'disorganize', *diskriminieren* 'discriminate' and *rekonstruiren* 'reconstruct'. Moreover, the stressed prefixes *lang-* and *recht-* are also non-separable, as in cases like *langweilen* 'bore' and *rechtfertigen* 'justify'. This is also the case with *miss-*, which despite being non-separable appears stressed in some contexts (e.g. *missverstehen* 'misinterpret') but unstressed in others (e.g. *missfallen* 'dislike'). Non-separable prefixes are not considered satellites because they are completely lexicalized.

There is a third type of prefix that is more problematic for the typology. These prefixes can be separable or non-separable depending on the verb they are combined with. For example *durchfallen* 'fail' is separable but *durchqueren* 'cross' is non-separable. They are therefore conjugated in different ways:

(154) *Er fällt immer in Mathe durch*
 he fall.PRS.3SG always in Maths through.PRE
 'He always fails Maths'

(155) *Sie durchquert das große Tor*
 she cross.PRS.3SG the.ACC.N big door
 'She crosses the big door'

Other prefixes with similar combinations are *über-* 'over', *um-* 'around', *unter-* 'down', and *wieder-* 'again'. These can also function as prepositions. German prefixes are used in different semantic domains, but are especially productive in the motion domain, in which they are used to encode different aspects of Path. As previously mentioned, only separable prefixes are regarded as satellites, whilst non-separable prefixes are considered part of a Path verb (Talmy 1985, 2000; Berthele 2004, 2006).

Goschler and Stefanowitsch (2009) find statistically significant associations between some verbs and particles. They use a colloconstructional analysis (Stefanowitsch and Gries 2003, 2005) based on corpus linguistics. They conclude that the degree to which German prefixes can be separated is not a continuum but rather a stage of the lexicalization process. Some of these associations combine Manner verbs with Path particles. This is the case with *klettern* 'climb', with *hoch-* 'high' and *(d)rauf-* 'up'. The same happens with *fallen* 'fall' and *(her)unter-* 'down(here)'. Not surprisingly, the particle *her-* 'hither' is strongly associated with *kommen* 'come', but it seems that both deictic particles (*hin-* and *her-*) are associated with verbs of quick motion like *eilen* 'hurry', *hetzen* 'rush', *rasen* 'speed', and *rennen* 'run'. The particle *rum-* 'around' is significantly associated with *laufen* 'walk, run', *turnen* 'do gymnastics', *krabbeln* 'crawl' and *irren* 'wander'. In this case, the association is semantically coherent as *rum-* does not imply an end point of the movement, and as these verbs denote activities. However, not all the associations can be explained by their having clear semantic motivations. For example, *hin-* 'thither' has a significant association with *gehen* 'go (on foot)' and *fahren* 'go in a vehicle', but not with *laufen* 'walk, run'.

Goschler and Stefanowitsch claim that the relationship between satellite and verb is closer in German than in English, and they consider that the diachronic development of Path lexicalization would be as illustrated in Figure 6.

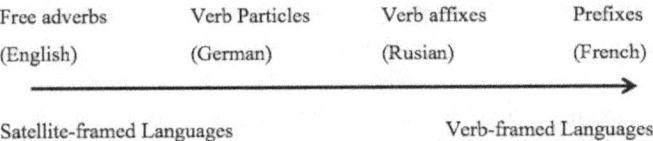

Figure 6: Evolution of Path lexicalization from satellite- to verb-framed languages. (Adapted and translated from Goschler and Stefanowitsch 2009: 113).

Therefore, Goschler and Stefanowitsch think that the difference between verb-framed and satellite framed languages should not be understood as a discreet parameter but as a continuous trend. Even within a language, different verb-particle associations which have a different semantic motivation can present different degrees of union.

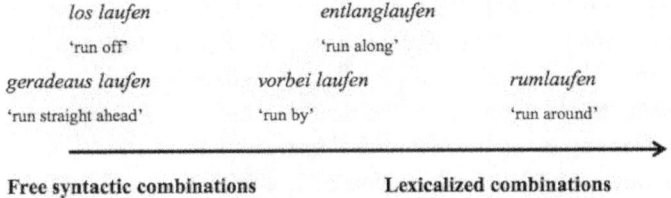

Figure 7: Evolution of Path Lexicalization in German. (Adapted and translated from Goschler and Stefanowitsch 2009: 114).

Having seen the importance of particles in German, let us shift our attention to German motion verbs. Cuartero Otal (2016a, 2016b) compares Spanish and German motion verbs and finds commonalities such as the fact that in both languages the expression of motion combines the same elements: a predicative core element, a subject which refers to the moving entity, and locative information encoded in prepositional or adverbial complements, manner complements (gerunds, adjectives, prepositional phrases, etc.). However, there are three areas in which these languages differ, which Cuartero Otal classifies by order of difficulty. First, they differ in how systematic they are in their possibilities for combination. Germanic languages tend to be systematic whereas Spanish presents more restrictions, e.g. the boundary-crossing constraint. Second, there is a difference in the frequency of usage of those common devices encoding motion. In German there are fewer directional displacement verbs, and they are used less frequently than in Spanish. In fact there are very few simple directional verbs in German: *kommen* 'come', *gehen* 'go' in the case of the intransitive and a few directional transitive verbs: *befahren* 'drive along', *durchqueren* 'cross', *erreichen* 'reach', *verlassen* 'leave', etc. (Cuartero Otal 2016a: 335). Cuartero Otal claims that there are few verbs that do not encode explicitly Manner of motion in German (Cuartero Otal 2016b: 172). Finally and more importantly, there is a difference in the meaning of the constructions in which these verbs occur. Germanic motion constructions can include verbs from other semantic domains such as sound (Meliss 2012 in Cuartero Otal 2016a). These constructions combine the sound verb with a locative complement and describe the special way in which displacement is produced. For example constructions with *stampfen* 'stomp' and *knattern* 'clatter' can indicate motion and are very difficult to render in Romance languages with the same degree of expressivity. Non-separable prefixes make the verb transitive, e.g. *besteigen* 'climb', *verlassen* 'leave', *durchqueren* 'cross'.

Cuartero Otal (2016b: 170) also points out that some satellites can add nuances related to displacement, e.g. *ab-* adds the notion of 'perform a separation displacement', as in *abfahren* 'leave a place by car', *ablaufen* 'leave a place running, start running'. In other cases they indicate an explicit trajectory. This is the case with *herum-/umher-* 'with ambiguous trajectory'. Finally, they can also add deictic information by combining with the deictic prefixes *her-/hin-*. For example, *herein-/hinein-* 'from the outside to the inside to me/away from me', *herauf-/hinauf-* 'from down up to me/away from me' (see also Berthele 2004, 2006; Goschler and Stefanowitsch 2010; Liste-Lamas 2015, 2016a, 2016b; Harr 2012). Cuartero Otal (2016b) finds only two combinatory restrictions in German. First, *herum-* and *umher-* block the combination of locative complements that indicate goal or origin: *Anton läuft *nach Hause/*aus dem Garten herum* '*Anton runs to the house/from the garden around'. Second, transitive displacement verbs show incompatibilities, e.g. if the direct object indicates goal (e.g. *erreichen* 'reach') can only be combined with medium, and verbs whose direct object encodes origin (e.g. *verlassen* 'leave') are only combined with medium and goal.

Verbs and particles are not the only important encoding devices in German. An interesting feature of this language is the fact that it is so rich in morphosyntactic devices that motion can be expressed even without a motion verb (Berthele 2006; de Knop 2017). Berthele (2006) finds some of these cases in some Swiss dialects, which combine *sein* 'to be' with directional complements. He also notes another possibility, which is the use of modal verbs when the motion verb is absent. This is illustrated with (156) and (157), taken from de Knop and Gallez (2011: 10):

(156) *Mein Bruder will in die Schule (gehen)*
'My brother wants (to go) to school'

(157) *Er darf über die Straße (gehen)*
'He may (go) over the street'

In other cases a non-motion verb is used, for example, in the caused motion construction (Gallez 2015: 1):

(158) *Ronaldo köpft Portugal ins Halbfinale*
Ronaldo head.3SG.PRS Portugal in.the.ACC.N semifinal
'Ronaldo brings Portugal into the semifinal with a header'

In other cases there are structures without a verb (Jacobs 2008 in de Knop 2017) such as *Ab ins Bett!* literally 'Off into the bed!'. De Knop (2017) studies this verbless motion construction and finds that semantically they tend to encode the start of the motion Path with elements such as *ab, los, her, zurück*, etc. The motion Paths are conveyed in prepositions (e.g. *in, auf, mit* . . .). And the goal of motion is expressed in a noun in the accusative case. These non-verb constructions are pragmatically dependent on context and are used to express orders, instructions and recommendations. This shows how rich German is in linguistic devices for encoding different semantic components of motion. In the next section we will see how these devices are used to develop a typical satellite-framed thinking for speaking.

3.2 Thinking for speaking in German

German was one of the first five languages analyzed from Berman and Slobin's (1994) perspective, as part of their cross-linguistic comparison in first language acquisition. In that volume, Bamberg (1994) focuses on the acquisition of German thinking for speaking. He highlights the satellite-framed nature of German, in which the same verb, e.g. *kommen* 'come', can be combined with a number of Path satellites, such as *an-* 'towards', *raus-* 'out', *rein-* 'in' and *zu-* 'towards'. Similarly, a satellite like *raus-* 'out' can be combined with a series of Manner verbs: *rausfallen* 'fall out', *rausfliegen* 'fly out', *rausgehen* 'go out', *raushüpfen* 'jump out', etc. Bamberg (1994) concludes that German children use deictic adverbs more frequently than temporal and aspectual adverbs. He also claims that Path prefixes are used from an early age as a general way to encode Path. In fact, the specification of the origin and the goal of the movement become more frequent at the end of the pre-school period. The quantity of Manner verbs in combination with Path satellites and deictic particles is high. This creates a complex system, typically satellite-framed, which children have practically mastered by the age of three.

Further studies contrasting German with other languages reaffirm the position of German as a satellite-framed language and its rhetorical style as such, which follows the characteristics noted by Slobin (1996a, 2000, 2005) for languages in this typological group. For example, following Slobin's methodology of the *Frog story* Bethele (2006) contrasts standard and Swiss German with French and Romansch. He finds a more frequent use and greater diversity of Manner verbs in German, and also more detailed descriptions of Path. In this sense, German speakers tend to include more combinations of verbs with Ground complements. He also finds complex Paths with two or more Grounds associated with the same verb. Manner tends to be used in the description of the owl scene. Finally, German speakers also tend to present more dynamic descriptions of motion. Manner tends to be favored in the expression of these events in German, as studied in de Knop and Gallez (2011). These authors explain how German speakers need to specify manner of motion in certain events whilst the same events would not be specified in other languages like French. For example *aller* 'go' in French needs to be specified in German as *fahren* 'drive a car or ship', *gehen* 'go on foot' or *fliegen* 'fly'. They also explain that in German there is also a 'Manner of location', which is not present in French, for example. This involves the use of verbs like *stehen* 'be standing' and *liegen* 'be lying'.

The development of spatial language is analyzed in Madlener, Skoruppa, and Behrens (2017). These authors re-examine the narratives elicited by Bamberg (1994) with the Frog story (with children aged 3, 5, 9 and adults) and compare them with two longitudinal corpora of the spontaneous speech of German children (from two and a half years to four years and eleven months). The emergence of information density and complexity is analyzed at the utterance level. The analysis focuses on the local and on the global complexity. An interesting novelty of this study is that Madlener, Skoruppa and Behrens looked at how the slots of Figure, verb and Path/Ground were filled at different stages. They find that younger children use fewer complex paths, but that they do not use complex combinations. For example, when they use a complex noun phrase for the Figure, the verb slot will be filled with a lighter verb and a less complex Ground element (e.g. the deictic adverb *da* 'there'). Likewise, if the verb slot is more complex (e.g. a Manner verb) the Figure and the Ground slots tend to be lighter. Complex combinations are used increasingly with age. In other words, the preferences for lighter slot-fillers and the initial restrictions in terms of global complexity decrease over time.

Other studies have also pointed out the importance of Manner in German rhetorical style, mainly in relation to translation. Lübke and Vázquez Rozas (2011) focus on the difficulty of finding accurate translations into German of the Spanish verbs *entrar* 'enter' and *salir* 'exit'. They compare the equivalents used in translations and find that most of these translations do not encode trajectory in German and do not include verbal lexemes equivalent to those of *entrar* and *salir*. They find a great morphological and semantic diversity in the verbs and verb-particle combinations used to translate these two Spanish verbs. German translations tended to present more detailed descriptions of trajectory (via adpositions, adverbs, verbal prefixes and preverbs), and more Manner information. The incorporation of deictic information was also present in cases where they were not present in Spanish (both due to the use of *kommen* 'come' and *gehen* 'go' to translate these verbs and to the use of *her-* and *hin-*). However, Spanish texts presented more descriptions of spatial relations, which were simplified in the German translations.

Molés-Cases (2016) focuses on translation techniques from German into Spanish but she first compares two corpora consisting of novels in German and Spanish. As expected, she finds a high frequency of Manner encoding in the main verb, 87.6% of Manner verbs and 6.51% of Manner+Path verbs. The presence of Manner is also frequent in peripheral elements in more than 60% of the events in the corpus. She also notices the frequent use of metaphors to express Manner information. She finds cases of A GROUP OF PEOPLE IS A RIVER with the verb *stömten* 'come down in torrents', A PERSON IS AN ANIMAL with verbs such as *wieseln* 'scurry (like a weasel)', *galoppieren* 'gallop (like a horse)', *hoppeln* 'hop (like a hare)', *watscheln* 'waddle (like a duck)' and *robben* 'crawl like a seal' and A PERSON IS A GHOST with the verb *geistern* 'wandern around (like a ghost)'. In Spanish there is only one case of metaphor expressing motion: A PERSON IS A BULLET with *Salió disparado*, 'he went out like a shot'.

From the perspective of first language acquisition, Ochsenbauer and Hickmann (2010) show that children and adult German speakers use the same lexicalization patterns. From the age of three onwards, they encode Manner in the main verb and Path outside it. Both components are expressed in compact utterances and are equally salient, as expected in speakers of a satellite-framed language. In Ochsenbauer and Hickmann's study, Manner is widely used in all age groups and in fact it is increasingly encoded in the main verb, following developmental progression. Consequently, Path verbs decrease in use from the age of 10. All age groups used particles to encode Path, with a decrease in the use of prepositional phrases to encode Path from the age of 6. Finally, Ochsenbauer and Hickmann also find a preference for auxiliary constructions, such as *Er geht hoch* 'He goes up'. This frequent use of *gehen* 'go' decreases from the age of 10. These findings are confirmed in Harr's (2012) comparison of French and German first language acquisition. The author shows that the speakers of these languages follow respectively the characteristics of verb-framed and satellite-framed languages. German speakers present a wider variety and use of Manner verbs, etc. showing the typical package of satellite-framed languages at all ages, with Manner and Path in one sentence. She also highlights the fact that it is possible to find both lexicalization patterns in both languages, which leads her to consider the typology as a continuum rather than as a rigid dichotomy. She also raises a few interesting questions in relation to language acquisition. For example, German children use many light verbs to describe voluntary motion, e.g. *gehen* 'go', but not many with caused motion, e.g. *tun* 'make'. A special use is the use of *tun* with dynamic verbs, such as *Er tut laufen* 'he makes run' which seems to be frequent in children's language. Moreover, German children tend to use motion verbs in a creative way. Harr thinks that this may be due to the fact that they make an effort to describe the motion event with the appropriate verb. This is in line with Slobin's premises that speakers of satellite-framed languages focus on Manner and continue to develop their lexicon of Manner verbs. In this sense, they include neologisms which incorporate Manner. She concludes that German children present similar lexicalization patterns to those of adult speakers. These patterns are closer to those of the adult speakers of their own language than they are to those of children of the same age who speak another language, but who are at the same stage of the acquisition process.

German lexicalization patterns have also been studied from the perspective of bilingualism studies. These results confirm the main trend observed in monolinguals. Goschler (2013) analyzes different studies involving varieties of German-Turkish bilinguals and finds blended patterns in bilinguals. One of the features that she notes is the fact that although there is transfer from Turkish, its specific patterns are not directly transferred. This is probably because of internal variation in Turkish but also because German does not offer a similar pattern to verb-framed languages (as English does, for example). She also finds that data elicitations are more prototypical in the verb- or satellite-framed languages when data are collected in written form, whereas oral elicitation favors the use of generic motion verbs and semantically less complex elements. In the same vein, Woerfel (2018) compares the acquisition of Turkish-German and Turkish-

French bilinguals and finds that Turkish-German bilinguals used fewer Manner and Manner+Path verbs than German minimal bilinguals. They also showed a higher usage of two Path elements, more use of generic verbs in locative events and fewer Manner verbs in boundary-crossing situations.

The lexicalization patterns that are shown by monolingual speakers prevail in bilingual speakers with some degree of variation, but depend on a number of factors. Berthele and Stocker (2017) show how the activation of bilingual mode can have an influence in the description of motion in French-German bilingual speakers. The activation of French leads bilinguals to use a lower quantity of Manner verbs and a higher quantity of Path verbs when they are speaking in German. Another factor to take into account is bilingual dominance. Berthele (2017) shows how dominance affects participants' response patterns in some aspects of motion. He tested German-French bilinguals and found that the probability of using Manner verbs in German correlates with German dominance. However, the more dominant French is, the less frequently of Manner verbs are used in German. This effect is not found in French though. In the case of boundary-crossing, he finds an increased likelihood of avoiding Manner verbs when the speaker has stronger dominance in French. In German the boundary-crossing constraint is systematically disambiguated due to its richer morpho-syntactic resources, as it can show crossing in combination with accusative and locative complements in combination with dative complements. These findings on bilingual research confirm the prototypicity of German as a satellite-framed language in contrast with verb-framed languages such as Turkish and French.

3.3 The position of German in the typology

The position of German as a satellite-framed language has not been questioned in previous literature. It seems clear that its linguistic resources allow Path and Manner to be described such that German can be categorised as a prototypical satellite-framed language. The array of linguistic resources with which German speakers tend to describe Manner and Path has been made clear in the previous sections, in which we have reviewed inter-typological comparisons made between German and several verb-framed languages (mainly French, Spanish and Turkish). The prototypical position of German is even clearer when German is compared with other languages that belong to the group of satellite-framed languages. Intra-typological variation involving German has been studied mainly in contrast with Danish (Cadierno and Jessen 2013; Jessen 2014) and Polish (Lewandowski and Mateu 2016). These intra-typological contrasts confirm the establishment of German as a high-Path and high-Manner salient language.

The comparisons between German, Danish and Turkish carried out by Jessen and Cadierno (2013) shed light on intratypological differences in semantic categories of motion events. These studies present data elicited with the stimuli of Vulchanova, Martínez, and Vulchanov (2012), which consists of film clips in which human and animal motion is depicted. Cluster analysis shows that German presents the highest degree of variation with regard to more fine-grained distinctions. Danish speakers mainly clustered the events in four categories (*kravle* 'crawl', *løbe* 'run', *gå* 'go' and *bevæge sig* 'move'), but included only a few variants of specific movements. In contrast, German data show a more complex picture with some categories clearly defined by a single verb across speakers: *krabbeln* 'crawl', *klettern* 'climb', *gehen* 'go', *schlängeln* 'slither' and *laufen* 'run' and other categories where there was some variation between the speakers describing the videoclips: *laufen* 'run' vs. *gehen* 'walk'; *bewegen* 'move', *krabbeln* 'crawl' vs. *kriechen* 'creep' and *laufen* 'run' vs. *rennen* 'spurt'. It seems that categories in German were based on movement on the vertical axis vs. horizontal movement and close contact with the ground with legs/limbs vs. movement with lack of space between ground and Figure. Other less frequent finer-grained verbs also occurred, such as *flitzen*, *sausen* 'dash', *schlendern* 'amble', etc. As an example of how speakers of both satellite-framed languages differed, German speakers mentioned 69 different verbs while Danish speakers used only 41, which is more in line with speakers of Turkish, a verb-framed language, who used 36. This shows a clear salience of German in the Manner cline, since it seems to have a wider lexicon of Manner verbs and a wider use of second-tier Manner verbs.

Lewandowski and Mateu (2016) compare translations from Chapter 6 of *The Hobbit* into German and Polish. In both cases the amount of Manner verb tokens is similar, but German translations present more types, whereas Polish translators provide fewer detailed Manner descriptions. Translators in both languages use translation strategies with different frequency. German translators tend to keep the same Manner information encoded in English in the main verb, while Polish translators use this strategy less frequently and tend to encode less specific Manner information. In the case of Path, German translations showed more diverse Path descriptions than Polish translations.

These trends are confirmed in Lewandowski (2018) with oral data gathered using Charles Chaplin's *City Lights* stimuli from monolingual speakers of German, Polish and Spanish (stimuli used in Pourcel 2005). Polish speakers used more Manner verb tokens to describe Chaplin's movements but they used many fewer Manner verb types, with a quantity closer to Spanish speakers. German speakers used more Manner verb types. Lewandowski considers that this could be due to two factors. First, German particles are morpho-syntactically more flexible than Polish prefixes. This allows for a wider use of Manner verb + satellite combinations. Second, high-Manner verbs in German do not have an equivalent in Polish (nor in Spanish), e.g. *watscheln* 'waddle', *hüpfen* 'hop', which are expressed in the other languages either with a periphrastic expression like 'walk in a hesitant way', 'walk like a duck' or with more general Manner verbs like the equivalents of 'jump'. In the case of Path description, German speakers provide more quantity and more detailed descriptions of Path. This may be due to two factors. On the one hand, German has a wider inventory of satellites and it displays complex satellites (e.g. *heraus* 'out of towards the speaker') that in combination with a Ground element allow for the integration of three Path elements with a single verb. On the other hand, bounded events do not need to be encoded in German in a specific construction pattern, which they do in Polish. In the Slavonic language, prefixes present some semantic restrictions related to aspect that impact on the combination possibilities of prefixed verbs. This leads to fewer dynamic descriptions in Polish than in German.

These results regarding thinking for translating and thinking for speaking show that the rhetorical style of German corresponds strongly with the prototypical features of a satellite-framed language (more Manner lexicon, more descriptions of Manner and Path and more dynamic descriptions). They confirm German as a prototypical satellite-framed language, i.e. it is high-Manner and high-Path salient in terms of the clines proposed by Slobin (2004) and Ibarretxe-Antuñano (2009). The available data from previous studies predict this pattern for most Germanic languages when compared with Slavonic languages (see Filipović 2007a for a Serbo-Croatian vs. English comparison, and Kopecka 2010 for a Polish vs. English comparison). It is also relevant that German seems to be a more prototypical satellite-framed language in comparison with English. As is the case with other Germanic languages (see Ragnasdóttir and Strömqvist 2004), it lacks the Path encoding verbs borrowed from Latin that are present in English, like *ascend*, *descend*, etc. (see Huber 2017 for a historical overview of these borrowings in English). This justifies the choice of German for this study, as the intra-typological analysis of Romance languages will be contrasted with data from a prototypical satellite-framed language. However, before delving into the data analysis, it is important to emphasise that intra-lingual variation should not be overlooked. Even though typology needs to focus on the general tendencies of languages, the study of different varieties within the main languages can provide an interesting insight into the study of motion events. In order to avoid disregarding these details when looking into the bigger picture, diatopic variation in the four languages of the study is presented in the next section.

4 Diatopic variation in the expression of motion

As seen in the previous chapter, the differences between how different varieties describe motion have received increasing attention in the field and have been recognized as one of the challenges for the typology. To a certain extent, it is logical that typologists do not look into dialectological differences in detail. After all, their main aim is to look for common patterns across languages. However, the study of geographical varieties helps to redefine and improve typological classifications. The main contributions towards this goal have been made in precisely the four languages that are present in the study, but mainly with regard to standard and Swiss German. Geographical variation turned out to be an unexpected finding in the present study. Therefore, it is important to look more closely into previous studies that have shown the importance of taking into account dialectal variation in the typology of motion events.

The pioneering work by Berthele (2004, 2006) on standard and Swiss German has paved the way to other authors who have dealt with similar cases of variation within languages. Berthele's works are seminal in bringing dialectology together with Talmy's typology (1991, 2000) and Slobin's thinking for speaking (1991, 1996, 1997). He compares standard and Swiss German; with French (Berthele 2004); and with French and Romansch (Berthele 2004, 2006, 2013). He finds examples of dialectal variation in the expression of motion in German. For example, the Moutathal variant shows statistically significant differences in Path description when compared with standard German. This Swiss variant presents more cases of complex Paths. In fact, the proto-typical use of standard German contains only one Path element. Another feature of Moutathal is the more frequent use of light verbs, like the equivalents of BE or MAKE to indicate movement.

Berthele (2013) highlights the contributions that dialectology can make to typology. While there is a common assumption that encoding Path in the satellite involves a frequent encoding of Manner in the verb slot, Berthele's analysis of Swiss German dialects shows that this assumption is not necessarily true for all languages and variants. This challenges the common conclusion that there is an automatic correlation between high positions in Manner salience and satellite-framed patterns. His studies show that there is considerable variance between speakers and that there are several factors that typology should take account of. For example, the notions of orality and literacy already mentioned in relation to minority languages are also relevant for standard and non-standard variants of the language. Similarly, whether speech communities are small, medium or large seems to be relevant for the typology. The larger the speech community is, the more Manner and Path verbs and Ground elements occur in the description. However in larger speech communities the elaboration of Path seems to be less complex.

This appears to be a feature of languages that have been preserved mainly in oral contexts, such as Romansch (Berthele 2006), Basque (Ibarretxe-Antuñano 2004b, 2009) and Aragonese (Hijazo-Gascón and Ibarretxe-Antuñano 2010; Ibarretxe-Antuñano, Hijazo-Gascón, and Moret-Oliver 2017). Berthele's results are crucial for the Talmy-Slobin framework, as they show that there is also variability within varieties of the same language. This reinforces the idea of the typology as a cline and it allows us to avoid overgeneralizations.

Spanish also presents some degree of variation. Although Sebastián and Slobin (1994) do not find any type of dialectal variation among speakers in Argentina, Chile and Spain, some scholars have found intralingual variation in some varieties. Ibarretxe-Antuñano and Hijazo-Gascón (2011, 2012) find subtle differences among varieties of Northern Peninsular Spanish. In the case of Path they have found cases in the Spanish spoken in the Basque Country (159) and in Aragón (160) where more than one Path element is expressed with the main verb:

(159) *Se queda totalmente sorprendido, tan sorprendido que se cae del árbol al suelo porque del agujero aparece una lechuza*
'He remains totally surprised, so surprised that he falls from the tree to the ground because an owl appears from the hole'

(160) *Pero en un descuido, pues, resulta que el perro se cae de la ventana al suelo*
'But in an oversight, so, it turns out that the dog falls from the window to the ground'

These examples modify Sebastián and Slobin's (1994) conclusions that Spanish speakers do not codify more than one Path element per verb, as in both cases the verb is accompanied by a complement expressing the origin of the movement: *del árbol* 'from the tree' in (159) and *de la ventana* 'from the window' in (160), and by a complement expressing the goal of the movement *al suelo* 'to the ground' in both (159) and (160). In fact, Basque and Aragonese speakers show in Spanish a higher tendency to include some information about Path. While Sebastián and Slobin (1994: 264–265) only find two cases of this in a total of 216 narratives (one in Chile and one in Madrid), in a sample of only 6 speakers for each variety, Ibarretxe-Antuñano and Hijazo-Gascón find 2 cases in Spanish from Aragón and 3 cases in Spanish from the Basque Country. While acknowledging the numerical limitations of the comparison, it is quite striking that there are more cases of Path description even with many fewer speakers.

In the case of Manner description, no major differences were found among the five dialectal variables. However, the Spanish variety spoken in Aragón presents some dialectal devices to express this component. For example, *encorrer* 'chase running', *esbarizar* 'slip', *estozolarse* 'fall hitting oneself', etc. See for example (159) taken from Ibarretxe-Antuñano and Hijazo-Gascón (2012: 357):

(161) *Al perro se le cae mientras tanto el panal de abejas que le empiezan a encorrer*
to.the dog REFL he.DAT fall.PRS.3SG meanwhile the beehive of bees that he.DAT start.PRS3PL to run.INF.after
'Meanwhile the dog unintentionally drops the beehive and the bees start chasing him'

The origin of these verbs might relate to Manner expression being more widely present in the Aragonese language, not only in verbs but also in ideophones such as *china chana* 'slowly' (Hijazo-Gascón and Ibarretxe-Antuñano 2010; Ibarretxe-Antuñano and Hijazo-Gascón 2011, 2012; Ibarretxe-Antuñano, Hijazo-Gascón, and Moret-Oliver 2017). The participants in Ibarretxe-Antuñano and Hijazo-Gascón (2012) are monolingual in Spanish, but the substrat of Aragonese (spoken in their area until the 15th century) is still present in this variety of Spanish, particularly in the lexicon. The results presented in this volume involve speakers from this region and this dialectal difference will be shown even among younger speakers than those in Ibarretxe-Antuñano and Hijazo-Gascón (2011, 2012).

In the case of Italian, its sociolinguistic specificities make it obligatory to take dialectal variation into account in any description of the language. The co-existence of dialect and standard language is pervasive in the Italian-speaking domain. Most studies on Italian motion events have focused on the distribution of verb-particle combinations across varieties (see the studies collected in Cini 2008). However, it seems that no significant differences have been found in the case of motion expression. In an oral corpus Iacobini (2008) does not find significant differences in verb-particle constructions among speakers from Milan, Rome, Florence and Naples. Mosca (2010) also studies motion in four different varieties (Piedmont, Tuscany, Campania and Sardinia) with dialogues in which speakers were giving directions, but her data reveal similar patterns across these varieties. She finds that two macro-groups could be formed according to lexicon, with a more balanced group which has a more consistent use of similar constructions in Sardinian and Piedmontese varieties and a more varied group of constructions in Tuscay and Campania. However, no significant differences are found. She considers that diatopic differences are mainly observable with regard to other domains such as length of dialogue and frequency of digression. Iacobini (2015) explains that there is variation in Italian with regard to aspectual information. Verb-particle constructions are not only used to encode spatial information but also to encode aspectual information in the dialects of North-Eastern Italy (also in Rhaeto-Romance). For example, verb-particle constructions can encode telicity: *comedàr fòra* lit. repair out, 'repair' (Trentino). They can also convey durative value *Vardàr for a le carte* lit. look out 'examine the documents' (Trentino, Cordin 2008: 184). Finally, they can also encode inchoative values, as in *I s'è metìt drè a löcià* lit., which started to be put behind 'to cry', 'They started to cry' (Bergamasque, Bernini 2008: 153). These values are not expressed by verb-particle constructions in other Italian dialects.

For French, Treffers-Daller (2012) investigates the origin of grammatical collocations and verb-particle constructions in Brussels French. Her focus is not exclusively on motion: for example, she analyses the use of verb-particle constructions such as *regarder après* 'look after' and *appeller après* 'call after'. The motion constructions that she analyses are *courir après* 'run after', *sortir hors* 'exit out', *tomber hors* 'fall out' and *tomber en bas* 'fall down'. In contrast to Italian, the origin of whose particles stems from internal changes, Treffers-Daller (2012) argues that external factors should be taken into account to explain the use of particles in Brussels French, in particular the influence of Brussels Dutch. She relies on the concept of *contact-induced change*, i.e. the adoption of structural features in a language due to some degree of bilingualism in the history of the speech community (Matras and Sakel 2007). In fact, her results show that the use of verb-particle constructions is much wider in Brussels French speakers than in Parisians, and that they use them even more than Flemish speakers who speak French as a second language. Treffers-Daller discards the possibility of this phenomenon being an internal development, as these patterns are much more frequent in Brussels French than in the historical corpora. She also finds similarities and differences with the Canadian French constructions noted by Chevalier and Long (2005). For example, Canadian French uses *regarder pour*, similarly to English 'look for', while Belgian French uses *regarder après*, coherently with its parallel construction with *na/naar* 'after' in its contact language Dutch.

Therefore, it seems that diatopic variation is present in the expression of motion events. Even if this variation is very localized and does not pose a major threat to the typology, it is important to bear in mind that finer-grained differences can be found within the varieties of a language. As previously observed in the cases of German and Spanish, the study of geographical varieties can help to challenge some theoretical assumptions and to redefine and improve the typology. These variations may originate in how the languages have evolved, influence from other languages, or even a combination of both, as in some cases structures already present in the language can be favored by language contact or bilingualism in a speech community. It is worth noting that these contributions are relevant not only to the semantic typology of motion events but also in the other direction. In other words, the typology of motion events seems to be relevant for Cognitive Sociolinguistics, an applied area of Cognitive Linguistics that has proven to be successfully applied to different contexts (see Kristiansen and Dirven 2008; Geeraerts, Kristiansen, and Peirsman 2010; Pütz, J. Robinson, and Reif 2014). In the following chapter the typological study will be presented and it will show how these cross-linguistic contrasts impact on the thinking for speaking and rhetorical style of their speakers.

Chapter 4
Typological study: Motion events in French, German, Italian and Spanish

1 Introduction

Intra-typological differences research among satellite-framed languages include investigations of the differences between Serbo-Croatian and English (Filipović 2007a, 2017b), Icelandic and Swedish (Ragnasdóttir and Stromqvist 2004), Danish (Jessen and Cadierno 2013) and between the varieties of the same languages, namely standard and Swiss German (Berthele 2004, 2006, 2017). For verb-framed languages, intra-typological differences have been found regarding Tzeltal (P.Brown 2004), Basque (Ibarretxe-Antuñano 2004a, 2004b, 2006a), Turkish (Slobin 2004, Özçalışkan and Slobin 2003), and Romance languages, mainly Italian (Hijazo-Gascón and Ibarretxe-Antuñano 2013a, 2013b) and Old French (Kopecka 2006a, 2009, 2013).

Variation among Romance languages is crucial to this research study. Even though most Romance languages are verb-framed in their current form, it is interesting to see their evolution, as Latin was originally a satellite-framed language (see Stolova 2015). Therefore it is likely that some traces of Latin typology remain in Romance languages, especially in those that lived on orally, such as Rhaeto-Romance (still a satellite-framed language (Vicario 1997; Berthele 2006, see previous chapter)) or Aragonese, with the presence of satellite-like constructions (Ibarretxe-Antuñano, Hijazo-Gascón, and Moret-Oliver 2017).

However, will this be the same for three of the most spoken Romance languages? French, Italian and Spanish will be contrasted in this chapter to find potential intra-typological differences. In addition to this, these three Romance languages will be contrasted with German, a satellite-framed language. This analysis will enable us to reveal inter-typological differences. The German language presents some characteristic elements to encode motion that will be analyzed, such as satellites and deictic particles.

This chapter is structured as follows. First, the research questions of the study will be presented. Second, methodological aspects will be raised. Then, the focus will be on the analysis, which will take several phases. It will start with the contrast of motion verbs in the four languages. After that, Manner expression will be examined in relation to Manner verbs, total Manner expression, the 'owl scene' in the *Frog Story* and boundary-crossing events. Path will be examined next with the analysis of Minus and Plus Ground, in the whole narrative and in the falling scenes, and Deixis. The component of Cause will also receive some attention. Finally, event granularity will be analyzed in the narratives of the four groups.

2 Research questions and hypotheses

The main research questions of this study are the following:
1. Are there differences and similarities in how motion events are expressed by speakers of languages that belong to different typological groups?

Hypothesis 1: There are inter-typological differences in the expression of motion events between German, the satellite-framed language under study, and the three verb-framed languages present in this research (French, Italian and Spanish).

2. Are there differences and similarities in how motion events are expressed by speakers of languages that belong to the same typological group and to the same linguistic family?

Hypothesis 2: There are intra-typological differences in the expression of motion events among the three verb-framed Romance languages (French, Italian and Spanish).

3. Are these differences due to the specific linguistic resources of each of these languages?
3a. Do the specific resources of German, as a satellite-framed language, trigger inter-typological differences with the Romance verb-framed languages?
3b. Does the existence of verb-particle constructions in Italian lead to intra-typological differences among Romance languages?
3c. Do the Old French directional prefixes lead to intra-typological differences among Romance languages?

Hypothesis 3: There are intra-typological differences in the expression of motion events, even in closely related languages such as French, Italian and Spanish.

Hypothesis 4: In the case that Hypothesis 2 is confirmed and intra-typological differences are found in the rhetorical style of Romance speakers, these differences will be in relation to their specific characteristics, as explained in Chapter 3.

Hypothesis 5: The presence of the pseudo-satellite constructions in Italian and French (verb-particle constructions and prefixes) in contrast with Spanish will imply.

5b. A more frequent encoding of Manner in the verb, because Path can be expressed in an element outside the verb (particle or prefix), similar to satellite-framed prototypical constructions.

5a. A greater elaboration of the Path component by Italian and French speakers

3 Methodology

This section focuses on the experimental design and the procedure for data elicitation. A pilot study was carried out with two speakers per group. This pilot was very useful for obtaining preliminary results and for enabling improvements to the procedure for the final study.

3.1 Experimental design

A cross-sectional study (Larsen-Freeman and Long 1991) was the best type of design for this research project. This type of study suits the purpose of studying inter- and intra-typological differences, as it compares different groups of speakers with similar demographic characteristics at a single point in time. This is a quantitative study, designed to validate the hypothesis through objectives, procedures and statistical analysis. Some qualitative remarks are also included in this section, to achieve a better understanding of the contrasts among these four languages.

According to the qualitative-quantitative continuum proposed by Larsen-Freeman and Long (1991: 15) the present study can be considered as experimental because: (i) All factors but one were kept constant. The one that was not kept constant was modified to see how it affected the phenomenon under study. In this case it was be the first language of the learners. This is our independent variable, which will change the dependent variables when it is modified (e.g. the expression of Manner in verbs or in other elements), and (ii) There must be at least two groups for a study to be considered experimental –an experimental and a control group-. There were four groups in this study, one for each language. The individuals in the groups were randomly distributed. This implies that the groups are comparable. In our typological study the population consisted of speakers of French, German, Italian and Spanish. The sampling was casual and non-probabilistic (Bernardo Carrasco and Calderero Hernández 2000). In other words, the criteria for the selection of individuals depended on the possibility of access, in the present case on a voluntary basis.

Data were analysed using descriptive and inferential statistics. The tests used were non-parametric because a normal distribution could not be assumed, since the data were collected using a semi-directed task (*The Frog Story*, see the following section). The narratives produced by the participants varied in word length and some speakers may have used many more motion verbs than others. The languages under study are one satellite-framed, German, and three verb-framed, namely French, Italian and Spanish. The choice of these languages is relevant because these languages have been mainly contrasted with English but not among themselves.

3.2 Material for data elicitation

The elicitation tool used for this study was *The Frog Story*. This experiment consisted of the free narration of what happens in a children's book with 20 scenes. The story shows how a boy has a pet frog, the frog runs away and the boy looks for it, accompanied by his dog. During his search, he finds different animals, including a deer who picks him up and throws the boy into a pond, where he finds the frog and takes it back home.

The original book, by Mercer Mayer (1969), is entitled *Frog, where are you?* and was first used by Bamberg (1987) for a psycholinguistics study. After that, it was used in the studies of the volume *Relating events in narratives* (Berman and Slobin 1994). Since then, *The Frog Story* has been used to collect texts in several languages, some of them included in in the second volume of *Relating events in narratives* (Srömqvist and Verhoeven 2004). The *Frog story* data have been widely used to study lexicalization patterns and thinking for speaking. However, this has not been its only use, see for example Serratrice (2007) on cohesive reference. In fact, some of the authors in Berman and Slobin's (1994) book focus on features such as temporality, aspectual relations, and perspective (word order, cases, passive voice). In Strömqvist and Verhoeven (2004), other areas are also studied, such as coherence and cohesion, social cognition, bilingualism and cultural issues.

The main advantage of using *The Frog Story* as an elicitation tool was that it is a semi-directed procedure. It is not as open as an interview, nor as closed as a questionnaire. The participants' narratives were constrained by a storyline they had to follow, but the description of the story left space for variants and different *foci* of attention. At the same time, as it is a narrative, some complex linguistic constructions were necessary for describing what was happening in the story. Another advantage is that, being so widely used, it was possible to compare the data of this study with previous research.

However, there are some limitations to be noted. One example is the fact that the scenes are static, in contrast to more dynamic stimuli like *The Canary Row* (McNeill 2000, 2005, 2009; McNeill and Duncan 2000), which consists of participants describing what happens in a Tweety cartoon story. Other dynamic stimuli are *Tomato Man* and *Triangle Man,* developed at the Max Planck Institute for Psycholinguistics in Nijmegen (the Netherlands), short video clips showing a tomato and a triangle moving in three phases of movement (Özyürek, Kita, and Allen 2001; Özyürek et al. 2005). Another disadvantage to using *The Frog Story* is that the story presents a Western bias. This may be problematic when collecting data in non-Western cultures (without pets) or in specifc areas without frogs, e.g. Eastern Isle, where speakers interpreted the frog as a lizard (Ibarretxe-Antuñano 2010). However, despite these dificulties, *The Frog Story* was considered a useful tool for this study, mainly because it provides unified criteria to enable our data to be compared with a range of previous studies both in typology and in second language acquisition.

3.3 Procedure

The procedure for data elicitation with *The Frog Story* was as follows. Each participant completed a linguistic background questionnaire, including some personal data (age, place of birth) and linguistic information (languages spoken and level of proficency). They were given *The Frog Story* and invited to spend a few minutes to look at the book and become familiar with the story. The experiment started when the participant was ready to tell the story. It is important to note that this was not a memory experiment: participants had the booklet in their hands and could look at it whenever they felt it necessary. The instructions were simple: "Describe what is happening in *The Frog Story*".

This study followed the original procedure and oral data were collected. The participants told the story to the researcher for as long as necessary. Each participant was alone in the room with the researcher. A videocamera was located behind the researcher, in order to record the participants' narrative. This is a change from the original procedure, which only used audio recording (see Berman and Slobin (1994) for a detailed account of the original methodology).

3.4 Participants

A total of 53 participants took place in the study, but five of them were excluded. The excluded participants were either early bilinguals (one participant in French and Spanish) or had a different level of Spanish as a second language (four of them had a lower level than B2, two of them were French, one Italian and one German). This latter condition was not relevant for this study but for the study presented in Chapter 5, which involves the same participants. As previously explained, the sampling was casual, and participants were recruited according to the possibility of finding the participants. In any case, all of them shared similar characteristics, as explained in the following sections. All of them were living in Zaragoza, Spain, when the data were collected.

3.4.1 The L1 Spanish group

This group included 12 native speakers of Spanish. We consider this group to be the control group as Spanish is the target language of the acquisition study (Chapter 5). In order to avoid dialectal variation, all the participants came from Aragón, in North-East Spain. Nine of them were originally from the city of Zaragoza, two of them from villages in the same province (Farasdués and Boquiñeni) and one from the city of Huesca. All of them come from Spanish monolingual areas. They share the same diatopic variant, Spanish from Aragón. This variety presents some specific characteristics (Martín Zorraquino and Enguita Utrilla 2000; Enguita Utrilla 2000, 2008; Martín Zorraquino 2004; Porroche Ballesteros 2004). For example, the ascending intonation with the lengthening of the last vowel of the word (*Vamos a Zaragozaaa* 'Let's go to Zaragoza'), the change of stress from the antepenultimate syllable to the penultimate (*pajáro* instead of *pájaro* 'bird'), use of the diminutive *–ico* instead of the standard *–ito*, use of the suffix *–era* for tree names (*olivera* instead of *olivo* 'olive tree'), formation of superlatives with *mucho* instead of *muy* before the modified word, and the overuse of *pues* 'well'. The main difference between Spanish from Aragón and standard Spanish lies in vocabulary, with a frequent presence of *aragonesismos*, i.e. words specifically from Aragón, in many cases rooted in the old Aragonese language, which is now a minority language. Some examples are *laminero* 'sweet-toothed', *embolicar* 'cajole', *esbarizar* 'slip' and *encorrer* 'run after'.

All our participants lived in the city of Zaragoza at the time of the data collection. They were 7 men and 5 women. Their average age was 21.58, with a range of 18 to 28. All of them were native speakers of Spanish and had some knowledge of English, although they reported not using it on a daily basis. They can be therefore considered functional monolinguals because the language used in their daily lives was exclusively Spanish (A.Brown and Gullberg 2012). Five of them reported some knowledge of French and one of them of basic Basque. Three of them had a university degree, six were university students and three had completed vocational training.

3.4.2 The L1 Italian Group

The L1 Italian group contained 12 speakers from different Italian regions. Six were from Veneto, two from Sicily, one from Friuli-Venezia Giulia, one from Emilia-Romagna, one from Sardinia and one from Lazio. They were nine women and three men. Their mean age was 21.58. They had studied Spanish for between 2 and 7 years and at the time of the experiment they had been in Spain between 2 and 9 months. It is important to point out that three of them considered their L1 to be the Venetian dialect. Two of them also spoke this dialect but did not consider it to be their mother tongue. Two of them were speakers of other Italian minority languages: Friulan and Sardinian, but did not consider them to be their first language. They all spoke English, five also French, two German and one of them Portuguese. Eight of them were taking part in a special course at the University of Zaragoza, specifically for students of the degree in Translation at the University Ca' Foscari in Venice. The rest were Erasmus students at the time of data collection.

3.4.3 The L1 French group

The L1 French group included 12 women, all from different areas of France: four are from Auvergne-Rhône-Alpes, two from the Pays de la Loire, one from Provence-Alps-Côte d'Azur, one from Nouvelle-Aquitaine, one from Normandy, one from Île-de-France, one from Grand East and one from Brittany. Their mean age was 21.67, with a range between 20 and 24. They had been studying Spanish for 8, 9 or 10 years. They had been living in Spain for between 3 months and 3 years. Nine of them also spoke English, three Italian and two Portuguese. Two had a university degree and the rest were Erasmus students at the time of data collection.

3.4.4 The L1 German group

The 12 native speakers of German came from different regions of Germany. Most of them, seven, were from North Rhine-Westphalia, two from Baden-Württemberg, one from Saxony and one from Hesse. They were 4 men and 8 women. Their ages ranged from 21 to 37, with a mean of 23.91 years old. They all spoke Spanish and English. They had been studying Spanish for a mean of 4.6 years, ranging from 9 months to 6 years. Nine of them also spoke French and one of those nine also spoke Italian. Eight of them reported knowledge of Latin, one of these eight also of Ancient Greek. One of the participants reported speaking Platt, the dialect of some German regions, such as North Rhine-Westphalia. However, she did not consider it to be her mother tongue. One of them had a university degree, the other was a professional without university degree and the rest were visiting Erasmus students at the time of data collection.

4 Transcription and coding

4.1 Transcription

Once data were collected, the oral narratives were transcribed, thus constituting a corpus for the analysis. To avoid inaccuracies, native speakers of German, French and Italian were asked to revise the transcriptions in those languages. The corpus was developed using CHILDES (MacWhinney 1991), a transcription system used for studies of first, second and third language acquisition, available at http://childes.psy.cmu.edu. The use of this Corpus Linguistics tool is particularly useful, as it is possible to search for words or tagged elements for frequency lists or conduct specific searches including the specific speaker and the context.

CHILDES (*Child Language Data Exchange System*) is the name of a whole system developed by MacWhinney, including the program CLAN and the transcription norms CHAT. Its main purpose is to exchange data on language acquisition in different languages, and researchers can share their data in the database TalkBank, a project from the University Carnegie Mellon, the University of Pennsylvania and the University of Stanford, and coordinated by MacWhinney since 1999. TalkBank has expanded with corpus data from different languages and with different stimuli. Some of these corpora include audio and video. Its original focus on L1 acquisition has expanded to L2 acquisition, bilingualism, Conversation Analysis, phonetics and phonology and language data from patients with aphasia. A number of studies using *The Frog Story* are part of CHILDES too. This system was used to search, speed up the data analysis and develop a digital corpus.

4.2 Classifying motion verbs

One of the main challenges for the study is the fact that there is no unified classification of motion verbs for the languages under scrutiny (nor for others). Each scholar working on the typology of motion events has interpreted differently how verbs encode motion elements in each language. There is clear agreement with regard to the encoding of the verbs which could be considered prototypical (e.g. *bajar* 'descend' clearly encodes Path (downwards direction)), while other verbs are considered differently by different authors. For example *perseguir* 'chase' in

Spanish, is regarded as a Path verb by some authors, as a Manner verb by others and as a Manner+Path verb by others.

As a result of this difficulty, a classification of motion verbs in Spanish was established which follows Slobin's (1996b) methodology, and takes into account other studies that have used *The Frog Story*, such as Sebastián and Slobin (1994) and Cadierno and Ruiz (2006) for Spanish and Ibarretxe-Antuñano (2004a) for Basque, Cifuentes Honrubia (1999) and Cifuentes-Férez (2009) for English and Spanish. I consulted all these studies to see how they classified motion events and based on their categorizations I created my own classification. Some dictionaries were also consulted, such as the *Royal Academy of Spanish Language Dictionary* (RAE 2001) and the *Diccionario de uso del español* by María Moliner (2007). The categories that are defined are:

- Neuter verbs: These only codify the component of motion, such as *ir(se)* 'go', *mover* 'move'.
- Path verbs: *salir* 'exit', *subir* 'go up', *bajar* 'go down', etc.
- Path+Manner verbs: These codify both components in the same verb, e.g. *perseguir* 'chase', *tirar* 'throw'.
- Manner verbs: *correr* 'run', *saltar* 'jump', *pasear* 'stroll', etc.
- Posture verbs: *echarse* 'lie down', *acostarse* 'go to bed'.
- Other motion verbs: these include verbs encoding extension, such as *frenar* 'brake' and *pararse* 'stop'. These verbs encode the end of the temporal and spatial extension of the movement. Other verbs such as *llevar* 'carry', *coger* 'take' o *aparecer* 'turn up' did not fall into the previous categories but are included here.

The subcomponent of Deixis, as part of Path, has been also tagged in the corpus for verbs such as *venir* 'come' (and will be analyzed later in section 9.6.), but is included in the category of Path verbs. It is also relevant to note that some verbs like *volar* 'fly', encode Manner and Ground but are included in the Manner verb category. This methodological decision was made to avoid too many clusters in the analysis, or categories with only one element.

It is also worth commenting on the methodological decision to keep Posture verbs as a separate category. In previous studies, these verbs were considered Manner verbs, but since P. Brown's (2004) work on Mayan languages, in which this feature is prominent, scholars in the field consider them a separate category from Manner to avoid increasing the numbers for Manner verbs.

Another decision made in line with previous studies is to classify *fall* (and its equivalent in other languages) as a Path+Manner verb. This verb used to be considered as a Path verb, but Zlatev and Yangklang (2004) argued that it is part of an intermediate category in Thai, as it normally appears between a Manner and a

Path verb. Following Zlatev and Yangklang's findings, *fall* is considered to encode Path and Manner, as it implies an involuntary movement of the Figure.

The classification present in this study takes into account previous literature to make this data consistent with previous findings. The main studies that were taken into account were Sebastián and Slobin (1994), Cifuentes Honrubia (1999), Ibarretxe-Antuñano (2004a), Cadierno and Ruiz (2006) and Cifuentes-Férez (2009) for Spanish; Kopecka (2004, 2006a) for French Bamberg (1994) and Berthele (2004, 2006) for German; and Mosca (2007) for Italian. It was crucial to establish a classification that was consistent for the four languages so that the data were comparable. The classification needed to have some coherence with previous studies to enable a comparison of the results of the study with those reported in previous literature.

The establishment of this classification involved some introspection, mainly in the case of Spanish data, and consultation with native speakers and linguists of each of the four languages under study. It also involved the scrutiny of definitions of monolingual and bilingual dictionaries. In the case of Spanish, native speakers judgments were also taken into account. In Hijazo-Gascón, Ibarretxe-Antuñano, and Guelbenzu-Espada (2013) a categorization experiment was designed and more than a hundred native speakers of Spanish were asked to classify motion verbs. The results of this study enabled us to contrast native intuition in certain cases and adjust the classification of this study accordingly.

4.3 Methodological challenges and potential solutions

The creation of an accurate classification of motion events involved a number of challenges for the researcher. Probably the most difficult decision to be made concerned how Italian directional adverbs should be classified. As discussed in Chapter 3, these adverbs form phrasal verbs in combination with neutral verbs (e.g. *andare* 'go'), similar to the English or German satellite constructions. However, their status does not seem to be comparable to satellites of German languages in terms of frequency and morpho-syntactic properties. Since one of the main aims of the study is precisely to identify intra-typological differences, the best solution seemed to be to follow the traditional analysis of these particles as directional adverbs and not as satellites. This analysis is more in line with the status of similar linguistic elements in French and Spanish and avoids biases in the interpretation of these elements.

In coherence with this decision, Spanish directional adverbs such as *arriba* 'up', *abajo* 'down', *dentro* 'inside', are not considered as satellites. Cadierno (2004, 2008) and Cadierno and Ruiz (2006) consider that the use of these adverbs by learners of Spanish in combination with *ir* 'go' is a sort of "satellization", transferred from their L1 Danish. In the present study, directional adverbs of Romance languages are always counted as Ground complements and never as satellites. This methodological decision facilitates the comparison of the three Romance language data. It is acknowledged, however, that "satellizations" are the closest constructions for learners of Spanish whose L1 is satellite-framed, as will be further explained in Chapter 5.

Another methodological decision was necessary with regard to pronominal (e.g. *irse* 'go', *caerse* 'fall') and non-pronominal verbs (e.g. *ir* 'go', *caer* 'fall'). Most of the studies in Romance languages count these verbs as the same, normally expressed as *ir(se)* and *caer(se)*. The difference between these two types of verbs is not among the main aims of the present volume and would require another study. However, it was considered relevant to note the difference and count them both as separate verbs and as the same verb. In the case of French and Italian, pronominal verbs posed an additional challenge, as in some cases the presence of an adverbial pronoun, e.g. *en* in French and *ne* in Italian 'from here', requires the pronominalization of the verb: French *s'en aller*, Italian *andarsene*.

These adverbial pronouns are still used in French and Italian, but their equivalents have been lost in Spanish. Adverbial pronouns are mainly used in lexicalized constructions or with other functions, such as partitive (*Ne vengono cinque (= di loro)* 'Five are coming (= of them)') or as prepositional complement (*Ci penserò dopo (= su quello)* 'I will think it later (= about that)'). These pronouns come from Latin *inde* > *en* in French, *ne* in Italian and mark the origin of motion, while the pronouns marking the goal come from Latin *ibi* > *y* in French, *ci* in Italian (see Stolova 2015 on the origin of these pronouns). The spatial use of these pronouns is not very frequent today but it can be still heard. The following examples were found in the corpus of the present study:

(162) *mais là c´est une autre animal qui en sort.* [05FR][3]
      But over.there this.is a other animal that ADVP exit.PRS.3SG
      'but over there there is another animal coming out (from there)'

(163) *però durante la notte la rana se ne scappa.* [05IT]
      But during the night the frog REFL ADVP flee.PRS.3SG
      'but during the night the frog runs away (from there)'

---

[3] The code corresponding to the speaker that utters the example is included in brackets. This code is made of a randomly assigned number and the language code for her first language: ES for *español* 'Spanish', IT for *italiano* 'Italian', FR for *français* 'French' and DE for *Deutsch* 'German'.

The verbs *s'en aller* and *andarsene* are considered Path verbs for two reasons: (i) The existing possibility of marking Path through these adverbial pronouns, and (ii) the fact that these verbs cannot be pronominalized without the adverbial pronoun (only with *se* in French or *si* in Italian). This is an intra-typological difference from Spanish, since *irse* does not have a clear difference with the non-pronominal counterpart *ir*, so in Spanish both are considered as neuter.

Another methodological decision regards the stative positional verbs in German. Talmy (1985, 1991, 2000a, 2000b) considers stative situations to be part of motion events, but they are not included in the analysis of motion events in Slobin's tradition (Berman and Slobin 1994; Strömqvist and Verhoeven 2004). In the present study, static events have not been considered for any language. German speakers use static position verbs, such as *sitzen* 'sit, be sitting', *liegen* 'be lying', *stehen* 'be in a vertical position', opposed to dynamic position verbs such as *setzen* 'sit down', *legen* 'lay' and *stellen* 'put in a vertical position'. These verbs should be considered as posture verbs. However, given the characteristics of this study, static position verbs have not been included in the analysis. The equivalent in the Romance languages *essere/stare seduto* (Italian), *être assis* (French) and *estar sentado* (Spanish) were not included in the study of Italian, French and Spanish. If German static verbs had been included, the data could be biased, as the languages would have been treated differently.

I am aware that the classification of one verb in one group or another might be debatable, as some verbs are more prototypically Manner or Path-oriented than others. However, effort has been made to maintain coherence within the study and in relation to the semantics of the four languages. To make our data comparable, the classification of previous studies has been followed as far as possible. When this has not been possible due to discrepancies between different authors, various dictionaries and native speakers have been consulted.

5 Analysis

The analysis for both studies presented in this book, follows the methodology established by Slobin and collaborators in *Relating Events in Narrative* (Berman and Slobin 1994; Strömqvist and Verhoeven 2004). Some additional remarks are made in relation to other areas that are not analysed in Slobin's tradition: the analysis of boundary-crossing events, deictic motion events and causative constructions. These analyses provide insight into other areas that present inter- and intra-typological differences among the languages of the study. The data will be analyzed as follows.

First, the analysis will focus on motion verbs and how different groups produce types and tokens of motion verbs. The list of types and tokens is provided in relation to the six categories of motion events explained above. However, unlike other studies, the type-token ratio is not calculated here, since it has been shown that this measure is not completely reliable if it is not calculated in relation to the length of utterances. Since the types of verbs are very similar in the four language groups, it does not seem particularly relevant to calculate the ratio between types and tokens.

The next step is the analysis of Manner in these languages. First, the proportion of Manner verbs in relation to all the motion verbs is studied. After that, I analyze the Total Expression of Manner, taking into account all the motion events that encode Manner (in the verb and/or in other elements). The *owl scene* is also analyzed, to check whether speakers of these languages pay attention to Manner in the expression of the motion event of the owl flying out of a tree. The use of Manner-encoding verbs in boundary-crossing situations are also part of the analysis, with a particular focus on the *jar scene*.

The component of Path is examined with the Minus and Plus Ground analysis. The general trend is that verb-framed languages prefer Minus Ground events (e.g. *The dog fell*) and satellite-framed languages tend to have more Plus Ground (e.g. *The dog fell from the window*). This analysis is conducted across the whole narrative as well as being focused on the so-called falling scenes. These scenes are particularly important because they show motion events in which Figures fall: the fall of the dog from the window, the fall of the beehive from the tree, the fall of the boy from the tree and the boy and the dog falling from the cliff. Instances in which more than two Ground elements are included in the motion event will be also looked at (e.g. *The dog fell from the window to the ground*).

Given the cross-linguistic differences among the four languages in relation to deixis, I will also examine the use of deictic motion verbs (e.g. *come* and *bring*) and German deictic particles. Additionally, a specific causative construction, MAKE + motion verb, seems to be productive in French and Italian but not in Spanish (nor German). This construction is also included in the analysis.

Finally, Slobin coins the term "journey" for cases of complex Path. In particular, journeys are frequent in the deer scene. Slobin (1996a) divides this scene into six narrative segments (changed later to four in Slobin (1997b)). This analysis consists of checking how many of these segments are mentioned by participants. Normally verb-framed language speakers do not mention as many segments as satellite-framed language speakers. The results of this analysis are reported, considering both the six and the four segments.

6 Statistical methods

The data in this study were analyzed through descriptive statistics, including information about mean, range and standard deviation. Since our experiment was a free task, high standard deviations were expected. It was expected, for example, that speakers would differ in the length of their narratives, the number of verbs used, etc. The data included percentages of use of the different variables (Manner verbs, Total Manner Expression, Plus Ground, Plus Ground with more than two elements, etc.). The arcsine formula was applied because proportion data tend to be skewed when the distribution is not normal. The values were then transformed into angle values or radians.

Given the nature of the free task, a normal distribution could not be assumed. Therefore, non-parametric tests were used. When comparing independent samples, i.e. speakers of different languages, two tests were used: the Kruskal-Wallis test was used when the four groups are compared, while the Mann-Whitney test was used to compare pairs of groups. The α level to consider a significant difference was $p < .050$ for the Kruskal-Wallis test (and Wilcoxon) and $p < .025$ for the Mann-Whitney test, as it is the second test in the same data. When outliers were found, the inferential statistical tests were repeated. Only the final results, without outliers, are presented in the results sections and the boxplots.

7 Results of the typological study: Motion verbs

The first step in Slobin's methodology is to examine the quantity of motion verbs used in the narratives of *The Frog Story*. Both types and tokens of motion verbs are considered and it is expected that satellite-framed language speakers will present a higher number of both motion verb types and tokens. This difference is due to the fact that in satellite-framed languages Manner is easily encoded in the verb and that there is a larger lexicon of Manner verbs in these languages.

The motion verbs found in the narratives are classified into the following categories: neutral motion verbs, Path verbs, Manner+Path verbs, Manner verbs, Posture verbs and other motion verbs. The full classification of motion verbs in all the narratives for the four groups is reproduced in Appendix I. However, as explained above, the affiliation of some of these verbs into one category or another might not be as easy as may be expected. For example, the verbs meaning 'hide' *esconderse* (Spanish), *nascondersi* (Italian), *se cacher* (French) and *verstecken* (German) have been included as Path motion verbs, because it is considered that a trajectory towards the place to be hidden is implied in their meaning in all four languages. Likewise, there are other problematic verbs, specific to each language, which will be further discussed in the following sections.

7.1 Spanish motion verbs

The Spanish-speaking participants used 41 motion verbs and 193 tokens. It is worth remembering that this figure shows a distinction between pronominal verbs with *se* and the corresponding non-pronominal verbs, e.g. *caer* and *caerse* 'fall'. This distinction may be relevant for the study of Romance languages, although it will be taken into consideration only occasionally in this study. If we consider pronominal verbs as their counterparts without *se* as variants of the same verb, i.e. the same verb type, the total number of types is reduced to 35 motion verbs. These are the Spanish motion verbs in alphabetical order:

Acercarse 'approach', *acabar* 'end up', *acostarse* 'lie down (in bed)', *aparecer* 'turn up', *apoyarse* 'lean on', *bajar* 'go down', *caer* 'fall', *caerse* 'fall', *correr* 'run', *coger* 'take', *empujar* 'push', *dejar* 'leave', *echarse* 'lie down', *encorrer* 'chase (running)', *escaparse* 'escape', *esconder* 'hide', *esconderse* 'hide oneself', *frenar* 'brake', *huir* 'flee', *introducirse* 'insert oneself', *ir* 'go', *irse* 'go', *lanzar* 'throw (away)', *lanzarse* 'throw oneself', *llegar* 'arrive', *llevar* 'carry', *llevarse* 'carry', *marcharse* 'go away', *meterse* 'get into', *mover* 'move', *pasear* 'stroll', *pegar un salto* 'jump', *perseguir* 'chase', *salir* 'exit', *saltar* 'jump', *subir* 'go up', *subirse* 'go up', *tirar* 'throw', *tropezarse* 'trip', *volver* 'come back', *volverse* 'come back'.

It is worth noting the occurence of a dialectally marked verb, *encorrer* 'chase running', which has been marked as Manner+Path verb. This is a verb widely used in the area of Aragón, where the participants come from. It comes from Latin *incurrere* 'run towards' (Arnal Purroy and Lagüéns Gracia 2014) and it is used in Aragonese and in the variety of Spanish spoken in Aragón.

7.2 Italian motion verbs

The Italian speakers used 60 types of motion verbs, or 53 types if we consider pronominal verbs with *si* as the same type as their non-pronominal counterparts. The sample includes 210 tokens. The Italian motion verbs used are the following:

Accucciarsi 'curl up (e.g. a dog)', *afferrare* 'snatch', *aggrapparsi* 'grab', *allontanare* 'walk away', *allontanarsi* 'walk away', *alzare* 'raise', *alzarsi* 'stand up', *andare* 'go', *andarsene* 'go away', *appoggiare* 'lean', *appoggiarsi* 'lean on', *arrampicare* 'climb', *arrampicarsi* 'climb (up)', *arrivare* 'arrive', *attraversare* 'cross', *avvicinarsi* 'move closer', *buttarsi* 'throw oneself', *cadere* 'fall', *camminare* 'walk', *cascare* 'fall', *correre* 'run', *dirigersi* 'head', *fare un volo* 'make a flight', *fermarsi* 'stop', *frenare il suo andare* 'stop, lit. brake his pace', *finire* 'end', *fuggire* 'flee', *gettare* 'throw', *incastrare* 'wedge in', *incastrarsi* 'wedge oneself in', *inginocchiarsi* 'kneel', *intrappolare* 'trap', *inseguire* 'chase', *nascondersi* 'hide', *perlustrare* 'go searching', *portare* 'bring/take', *portarsi* 'bring/take', *posarsi* 'lie on', *prendere* 'take', *rincorrere* 'chase running', *ripassare* 'pass again', *ritornare* 'come back', *ritrovarsi* 'meet again', *salire* 'ascend', *saltare* 'jump', *saltellare* 'hop', *scappare* 'escape', *scavalcare* 'climb over', *scomparire* 'disappear', *sedersi* 'sit down', *sollevare* 'lift', *spostarsi* 'move over, change place', *spuntare* 'appear (showing one part of the body)', *trascinare* 'drag', *trasportare* 'transport', *travolgere* 'drag violently', *tornarsene* 'come back', *usire* 'exit', *venire* 'come', *volare* 'fly'.

It is interesting to see how very specific verbs are used, such as *accucciarsi* 'curl up (e.g. a dog)' encoding Path+Ground, stemming from *cuccia* 'dog basket'. This is an interesting verb as it belongs to the lexicalization type that includes Ground, like, for example, *alunizar* 'land on the moon' in Spanish, which is considered by Talmy as a minority lexicalization pattern. It is also possible to find differences with Spanish in pronominalization possibilities such as *arrampicar(si)* 'climb up', and the presence of verbs with an adverbial pronoun *ne* such as *andarsene* 'go away'.

7.3 French motion verbs

The French speakers used 53 types of motion verbs (50 if pronominal verbs are considered the same type as non pronominal counterparts). The total number of tokens is 225. The motion verbs found in French were:

Aller 'go', *accrocher* 'hook', *amener* 'bring/take', *apparaître* 'appear', *arriver* 'arrive', *atterrir* 'land', *bouger* 'move', *chasser* 'chase away', *courir* 'run', *décrocher* 'unhook', *descendre* 'go down', *disparaître* 'disappear', *échapper* 'escape', *emmener* 'bring/take', *filer* 'nip', *freiner* 'brake', *grimper* 'climb (up)', *jeter* 'throw', *lâcher* 'throw away', *laisser* 'leave', *monter* 'go up', *parcourir* 'go all over', *partir* 'depart', *porter* 'brig/take', *poursuivre* 'chase', *prendre* 'take', *ramasser* 'pick', *repartir* 'depart again', *retourner* 'come back', *revenir* 'come back', *s'accrocher* 'cling to', *s'approcher* 'approach', *s'appuyer* 'lean', *s'arrêter* 'stop', *s'echapper* 'escape', *secouer* 'shake', *s'éloigner* 'walk away', *s'en aller* 'go away', *s'enfuir* 'flee', *se cacher* 'hide', *se coucher* 'go to bed', *se diriger* 'head', *se mettre* 'get into', *se pencher* 'tilt', *se rapprocher* 'approach', *se redresser* 'stand back up', *se relever* 'pick yourself up', *se retrouver* 'find oneself in', *se tenir* 'stand', *sortir* 'exit', *soulever* 'raise', *suivre* 'follow', *tomber* 'fall'.

It is interesting to find the adverbial pronoun *en* in combination with certain verbs, such as *s'en aller* 'go away', as explained above. It is also worth noting the case of *s'enfuir* 'huir'. In both cases it is necesary to add *en* to make the verb pronominal, i.e. compatible with *se*. The verb *s'enfuir* has been classified here as a Manner+Path verb, since it gives more information than *fuir* 'huir', as it implies that the person flees from a place. There are pseudo-satellite prefixes noted by Kopecka (2004, 2006b) such as *repartir* 'depart again' and *emmener* 'bring/take', which will be explained in more detail in Section 9.6.

7.4 German motion verbs

The German speakers used 67 types of motion verbs, 65 if we consider verbs with *sich* as the same type as non-pronominal counterparts. The total number of tokens is 213.

Abhauen 'clear off', *abladen* 'unload', *anhalten* 'stop', *ankommen* 'arrive', *aufhalten* 'find oneself in', *aufstehen* 'stand up', *auftauchen* 'appear', *beeilen* 'hurry', *bremsen* 'brake', *bringen* 'bring/take', *buckeln* 'arch one's back', *eilen* 'hurry', *eindringen* 'penetrate into', *entfliehen* 'escape', *entwischen* 'escape', *fallen* 'fall', *festhalten* 'take', *fliehen* 'flee', *fliegen* 'fly', *flüchten* 'flee', *folgen* 'follow', *führen* 'guide', *gabeln* 'pick up, lit. fork up', *gehen* 'go (on foot)', *gelangen* 'reach', *das Gleichgewicht halten* 'keep one's balance', *hängen* 'hang', *holen* 'grasp', *klettern* 'climb', *kommen* 'come', *landen* 'land', *lassen* 'leave', *nehmen* 'take', *platschen* 'splash', *plumpsen* 'plop', *reiten* 'ride', *rennen* 'run', *schieben* 'push', *schleichen* 'creep', *schleppen* 'drag', *schmeißen* 'throw', *sich aufmachen* 'hurry', *sich befinden* 'find oneself', *sich ducken* 'duck', *sich festhalten* 'hold', *sich legen* 'lie down', *sich machen* 'move', *sich nähern* 'get closer', *sich knien* 'kneel', *sich schleichen* 'creep', *sich setzen* 'sit down', *spießen* 'spear', *springen* 'jump', *stecken* 'get into', *steigen* 'climb', *steuern* 'drive', *stupsen* 'push', *stürzen* 'fall', *tragen* 'take', *treten* 'step', *verfolgen* 'chase', *das Gleichgewicht verlieren* 'lose balance', *verlassen* 'leave', *verschwinden* 'disappear', *verstecken* 'hide', *wackeln* 'shake', *werfen* 'throw'.

There are other methodological decisions taken with respect to German. For example, separable verbs that change their meaning (e.g. *ankommen* 'arrive' vs. *kommen* 'come') have been considered as independent verbs, while the separable verbs in which the satellite does not modify the meaning of the verb are considered to be the same type of verb, for example *sich nähern* and *sich annähern* 'get closer'. Whenever possible Berthele's (2006) analysis has been followed to interpret the German data of this study.

It is worth remarking on the classification of *gehen* 'go, walk' as a Manner verb whilst the Romance verbs *ir*, *aller* and *andare* 'go' are considered neutral verbs. German *gehen* indicates Manner, since its meaning is 'movement on foot', as can be observed in the definitions of dictionaries. The German verb therefore includes a Manner component that is not present in similar Romance verbs.

Another interesting German motion verb is *sich machen*, literally 'make' with the reflexive pronoun, but used here with the meaning of 'move'. As explained in Chapter 3, it is frequent in some languages to use non-motion verbs such as MAKE as the main verb of the motion event. It has been classified here as a neutral verb. It has also been challenging to classify the separable verb *abhauen* 'clear off'. It was decided to include it in the group Manner+Path due to the way it is defined in monolingual dictionaries *heimlich und plotzlich weggehen*, i.e. leave a place secretly and suddenly.

The related verbs *verfolgen* 'chase' and *folgen* 'follow' have been classified into different groups. The verb *folgen* is clearly a Path verb, whereas *verfolgen* is included as a Manner+Path verb, in line with all the verbs meaning 'chase' in the other languages. The problem is that *verfolgen* can occasionally mean 'follow', as reflected in monolingual dictionaries. This verb is included as Manner+Path for two reasons. First, the first definition included in the dictionary entries for this verb is 'chase', which is therefore considered to be the prototypical meaning. Second, native speakers consulted emphasised the importance of the difference between both verbs and do not consider them synonyms.

A similar problem is found with the verb *verschwinden*. Bilingual dictionaries give translations similar to 'disappear', and so to be coherent with the other three languages it would make sense to include this verb in the category of other motion verbs. However, Berthele (2006) classifies this verb as a Path verb. This apparent contradiction is due to the double meaning of this verb: 'disappear' and 'go away', as a synonym for *weggehen* and *weglaufen* 'go away'. It was decided, therefore, to be consistent with previous studies on German, and include *verschwinden* within Path verbs.

7.5 Motion verb comparison

The languages of the study are compared with regard to their lexicon of motion verb, as shown in Table 10.

As expected, satellite-framed language speakers use more types of motion verbs, which is consistent with previous literature that follows Slobin's framework and methodology. Of the Romance languages, Italian presents more types of motion verbs and interestingly its 60 types is not far short of the number

Table 10: Types and tokens of motion verbs.

	Spanish	Italian	French	German
Types	41	60	53	67
Tokens	193	210	225	213
Types (without pronominal distinction)	35	53	50	65

presented in German. Spanish and French, on the other hand, seem to meet the expectations for prototypical verb-framed languages and show fewer types and fewer tokens. Table 11 shows the distribution of types (and tokens between brackets) for each verb category:

Table 11: Types (and tokes) of motion verbs in L1s.

	L1 Spanish	L1 Italian	L1 French	L1 German
Neutral verbs	3 (22)	2 (5)	2 (8)	1 (3)
Path verbs	14 (64)	20 (69)	18 (68)	11 (47)
Manner+Path verbs	8 (70)	13 (84)	10 (87)	11 (57)
Manner verbs	7 (11)	10 (16)	3 (14)	23 (62)
Posture verbs	3 (6)	6 (12)	8 (16)	8 (9)
Other motion verbs	6 (20)	9 (20)	12 (30)	13 (35)
Total	41 (193)	60 (210)	53 (225)	67 (213)

A large difference is found in the use of Manner verbs. As expected, German presents a wider variety of Manner verb types. It is also interesting to see the difference between Path verbs, between the satellite-framed language on the one hand and the three verb-framed languages on the other. In the following sections the differences in encoding meaning will be explained in detail.

8 Results of the typological study: Manner

Manner expression in French, German, Italian and Spanish is examined through four different analyses. First, the proportion of Manner verbs in comparison with the total number of motion verbs is analyzed. Second, all the linguistic elements encoding Manner will be studied. This analysis therefore includes Manner verbs and other elements that encode Manner, such as adverbs, gerunds and prepositional phrases. The third analysis focuses on how Manner is expressed in the owl scene, following the traditional methodology by Berman and Slobin (1994) and other studies on motion using *The Frog Story* (among others, the studies collected in Strömqvist and Verhoeven 2004). The final analysis deals with the expression of Manner in boundary-crossing situations, which is not included in the traditional analysis.

8.1 Manner verbs

Table 12 shows the types and tokens of Manner verbs[4] along with the mean and percentage in each of the languages.

Table 12: Manner verbs for the four language groups.

	Motion Verb Types	Manner Verb Types	Manner Verb Tokens	Mean (Manner verbs per speaker)	% Manner verbs
Spanish	41	8	11	0,92	5,88%
Italian	60	10	16	1,34	7,62%
French	53	3	14	1,17	6,23%
German	67	23	62	5,16	29,11%

The proportion of Manner verbs used varies according to the language of the speakers. The satellite-framed language under study, German, presents a total of 23 types of Manner verbs, with 62 occurrences. This corresponds to a 29.11% of the total number of Motion verbs. German speakers used a mean of 5.16 Manner verbs. These results are consistent with previous studies on satellite-framed languages. As expected, Romance language speakers show fewer types of Manner verbs, without striking differences among them. Italian speakers used 10 types of Manner verbs, Spanish speakers used 8 types, whilst French speakers used only 3. Manner verbs were 7.62% of the motion verbs used by Italian

---

[4] The verbs that encode both Manner+Path are not included here, nor in the analysis of total Manner expression. This is a methodological decision, as in previous studies this type of verb were not taken into account when analyzing Manner (e.g. *fall*).

speakers, 6.23% in the case of French speakers and 5.88% in the case of Spanish speakers.

The Spanish Manner verbs used are the following: *correr* 'run' (5), *lanzarse* 'leap on' (1), *empujar* 'push' (1), *pasear* 'stroll' (1), *pegar un salto* 'make a jump' (1), *saltar* 'jump' (1) and *tropezarse* 'stumble' (1). Only three Manner verbs are found in French: *courir* 'run' (11), *secouer* 'shake' (2) and *filer* 'dash' (1). The Manner verb types in Italian are: *correre* 'run' (6), *saltare* 'jump' (2), *camminare* 'walk' (2), *fare un volo* 'fly, lit. make a flight' (1), *posarsi* 'place oneself' (1), *saltellare* 'hop' (1), *trascinare* 'drag' (1), *travolgere* 'crush' (1), *volare* 'fly' (1) and *afferrare* 'grasp' (1). Some of these Italian verbs are more specific than those used by French and Spanish speakers and could be considered as second-tier, according to Slobin's (1997b) classification, whereas Spanish and French speakers used general first-tier Manner verbs.

In contrast to the Romance languages, German presents more types of Manner verbs, some of them very specific. The complete list of Manner verbs is as follows: *gehen* 'go, walk' (14), *klettern* 'climb' (10), *rennen* 'run' (8), *springen* 'jump' (8), *fliegen* 'fly' (3), *gabeln* 'pick up, lit. fork up' (2), *beeilen* 'hurry' (1), *buckeln* 'bow and scrape' (1), *eilen* 'hurry' (1), *holen* 'grab' (1), *platschen* 'splash' (1), *plumpsen* 'plop'(1), *reiten* 'ride' (1), *schieben* 'push' (1), *stupsen* 'nudge' (1), *sich schleichen* 'creep' (1), *schleichen* 'creep' (1), *schleppen* 'lug' (1), *sich aufmachen* 'hurry' (1), *spießen* 'stick' (1), *steurern* 'steer' (1), *treten* 'step' (1), *wackeln* 'wobble' (1). It is interesting to note how specific some of these verbs are. The use of *gabeln*, literally 'fork up', is used in the scene in which the deer gets up and picks the child up with his horns. It would be very difficult to translate this verb into Romance languages as a single verb. It would be necessary to use a periphrasis to say something like *coger como un tenedor* 'pick up like a fork'. Similarly it would be difficult to replace the verb *buckeln* 'bow and scrape' with a single word when trying to describe this action in a verb-framed language. The Royal Academy of Spanish language includes in its dictionary the verb *corcovear* or *dar corcovos*, that is, 'make jumps like certain animals that bow the back'. However, this verb is not frequent in Spanish and it would be hardly ever used in a context like this. Therefore, these data support the idea that satellite-framed language studies present more and more specific Manner verbs than verb-framed languages. The descriptive statistics of Manner verbs is as shown in Table 13.

The result for Manner verbs revealed a significant difference among the four groups ($p = .000$) in the Kruskal-Wallis test. As expected, a significant difference is found between the German and the Spanish groups, German and the French groups, and the German and the Italian groups with a value of $p = .000$.

Table 13: Descriptive statistics Manner verbs.

Language	Mean	N	SD	Range
Spanish	.1667	12	.15453	.42
Italian	.2450	12	.13814	.50
French	.1742	12	.15991	.36
German	.5958	12	.11123	.33
Total	.2954	48	.22497	.75

Romance groups do not show significant differences between them when contrasted with the ManWhitnney test (Spanish-Italian p = .582; Spanish-French p = .843; Italian-French p = .539). Therefore, it is clear that German speakers differ from Romance speakers in their use of Manner verbs. This can be seen very clearly in Figure 8.

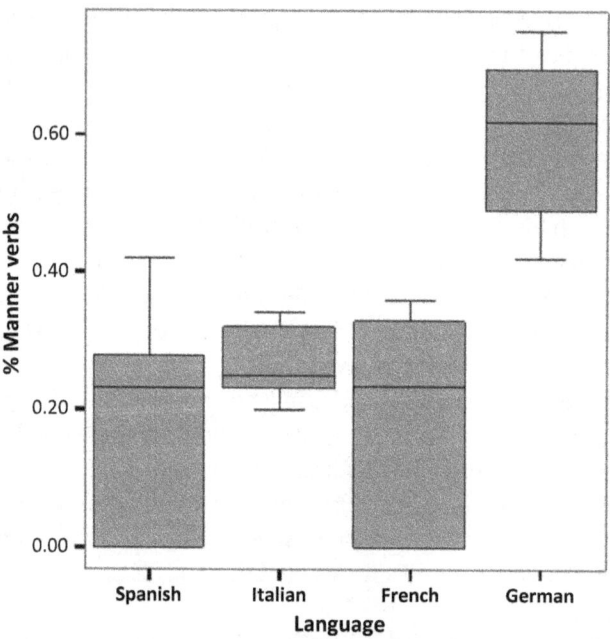

Figure 8: Percentage of Manner verbs in L1.

8.2 Total manner expression

The aim of this analysis is to find whether Romance language speakers compensate for the fact that they do not tend to encode Manner in the main verb, by encoding this information in other linguistic elements, such as adverbs, gerunds and prepositional phrases. Therefore, all the motion events in which Manner of motion is expressed are included here.

The linguistic elements encoding Manner used by the Spanish speakers are as follows: adjective phrases *asustado* 'scared' (3), *cabreado* 'angry' (1), *camuflado* 'camouflaged' (1), *grande* 'big' (1), *muy asustado* 'very scared' (1), *preocupado* 'worried' (1), *todo contento* 'very happy' (1); adverbial phrases such as *perfectamente* 'perfectly' (1), prepositional phrases *de cabeza* 'head first' (1), *de repente* 'suddenly' (1); participles *enganchado* 'hooked' (1), *montado* 'mounted' (1) and gerunds *corriendo* (3) 'running', *correteando* 'running around' (3) and *volando* 'flying' (1).

Adjective phrases are also found in Italian: *felice* 'happy' (3), *spaventato* 'scared' (2) *contento* 'glad' (1), *terrorizato* 'horrified' (1). Similarly, adverbial phrases are also found: *bene* 'well' (1), *così* 'like this' (1), *disgraziatamente* 'unfortunately' (1); and prepositional phrases too: *con il muso* 'with the nose' (1), *con la coda tra le gambe* 'with the tail between the legs' (1), *con la testa* 'with the head' (1), *con la testa sott'acqua* 'with the head under water' (1), *di un metro e mezzo* 'of a metre and a half'. Interestingly, in the narratives of the Italian speakers there is not a single case of a gerund encoding Manner of motion. There are however gerunds used in the Italian data that encode other semantic components, such as Path (*salendo* 'going up' (1), Manner+Path: *cadendo* 'falling' (2) and *scappando* 'running away' (1)) and other types of motion events (*depositando* 'placing' (1) and *portando* 'bringing'). Gerunds have been considered as the prototypical way to encode Manner in verb-framed languages, but this does not seem to be the case with Italian gerunds.

French speakers also used adjective phrases, in cases such as *blessé* 'hurt' (1) and *tout content* 'very happy' (1), *tout net* 'suddenly' (1). Adverbial phrases were also used: *brusquement* 'brusquely' (1), *discrètement* 'discreetly' (1), *gentilement* 'gently' (1), *tout d'un coup* (1) 'all of a sudden', *tout à coup* 'all of a sudden' (1). Prepositional phrases were also present in the data, such as *du coup* 'all of a sudden' (3) and *à califourchon* 'on shoulders' (1). There are also nominal phrases introduced by a partitive: *des quatre fers* 'all of a sudden (brake)'; participles: *accroché* 'hooked' (1) and gerunds introduced by prepositions: *en courant* 'running' (3).

Finally, adjective phrases were also found in German data: *etwas ungeschickt* 'a bit clumsy' (1), *ganz arg* 'very angry' (1), *ganz aufgeregt* 'very nervous' (1), *ganz schnell* 'very quickly' (1), *sicher* 'sure' (1); adverbs like *freiwillig* 'freely' (1), *heimlich* 'secretly' (1), *irgendwie* 'somehow' (1), *plötzlich* 'suddenly' (5), *rechtzeitig* 'in time' (1), *unabsichtlich* 'unintentionally' (1). The satellite *mit* 'with' is also considered to express Manner, since it occurs with *gehen* 'walk' with the meaning of 'accompany, walk with someone'. The use of *mit* adds a nuance, more than a complete change of meaning.

The non-parametric tests for Total Manner Expression show a significant difference among the four groups ($p = .000$) in the Kruskal-Wallis test. The Mann-Whitney test shows that the German group differs again from the Romance languages groups ($p = .000$ for the three comparisons). No significant differences are shown among the Romance languages (Spanish-Italian $p = .880$; Spanish-French $p = .651$; Italian-French $p = .847$). This is represented in Figure 9.

Table 14: Descriptive statistics Total Manner Expression.

Language	Mean	N	SD	Range
Spanish	.3392	12	.22809	.64
Italian	.3542	12	.14419	.56
French	.3208	12	.16467	.48
German	.7192	12	.13655	.44
Total	.4333	48	.23603	.98

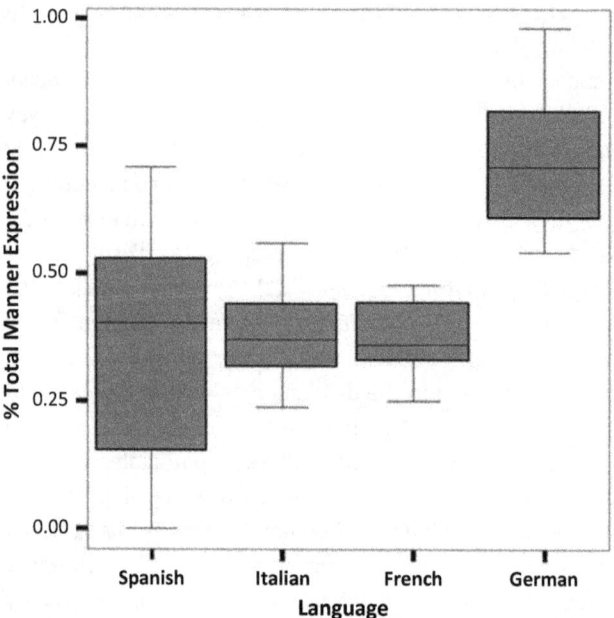

Figure 9: Percentage of Total Manner Expression in the L1s.

Therefore, these data support Slobin's claim that satellite-framed language speakers pay more attention to Manner of motion and encode it more often in their narratives. This is also the case in the encoding in the main verb and in the total encoding of Manner in different elements in the event. In other words, verb-framed language speakers do not compensate for the lack of Manner verbs with the encoding of Manner in other linguistic elements. These findings are consistent with previous literature, as discussed in Section 2.2. of Chapter 3.

8.3 The owl scene

The analysis of the owl scene (represented here in Figure 10) is classic in the field of motion events typology. The analysis is very straightforward, just focusing on the participants' description of how the owl exits from the tree. While satellite-framed language speakers tend to encode Manner to describe such event, e.g. *The owl flies out of the tree*, verb-framed language speakers tend to omit Manner and leave it to be inferred, e.g. *El búho sale del árbol* 'The owl comes out of the tree'.

Figure 10: The owl scene.

Since *The Frog Story* is a free task, participants do not necessarily mention this event. Table 15 shows the type of verb used by the speakers who did describe how the owl flew out of the tree. All the Spanish, French and Italian speakers who describe this event used a Path verb. In the case of German speakers only a Manner verb is found. This is 16.67% of the total:

Table 15: Owl scene description in the L1s.

	Manner verbs	Path verbs
Spanish	0%	100%
Italian	0%	100%
French	0%	100%
German	16,67%	83,33%

The verbs used for this particular motion event are: in Spanish *salir* 'exit' (5); in Italian *uscire* 'exit' (6) and *venire (fuori)* 'come (out)' (1); and in French *sortir* 'exit' (8). In German the most frequent verb is *kommen* 'come' (5) in combination with two satellites *raus-* (2) 'out' and *heraus-* 'out (to here)'. The Manner verb used is *fliegen* 'fly' (1), but there were few occurrences so no statistical tests were carried out. However, the general trend described in the literature is present in the data, with a clear inter-typological contrast. These data do not reveal intra-typological contrasts among Romance language speakers. In the case of German, the use of Manner is lower than in other satellite-framed languages, which may indicate an intra-typological difference on the other side of the typology.

8.4 The boundary-crossing constraint

The boundary-crossing constraint (Aske 1989; Slobin and Hoiting 1994) consists of the semantic blocking of Manner verbs when describing a motion event that implies the crossing of a boundary (see Chapter 3, Section 4.1.). It was expected that the data from this research would reveal inter-typological differences between German and Romance languages. *The Frog Story* is not specifically designed to examine boundary-crossing events, but it can give us a general idea about how these particular events are expressed in the four languages of the study. There were two steps to the analysis: first, Manner verbs used by the speakers were checked for whether they were used in boundary-crossing situations; second, the analysis focuses on one particular scene, the jar scene. In this scene, there is a clear boundary-crossing boundary as the frog gets out of the jar in order to escape. The analysis focused on how each speaker described this event and what type of verb and ground was used to describe it.

As expected, the German speakers frequently used Manner verbs as the main verb for boundary-crossing motion events. This happened in eight cases with the following verbs: *springen* 'jump' (3 occurrences), *klettern* 'climb' (2), *fliehen* 'flee, run' (2) and *flüchten* 'run' (1). A good example would be (164):

(164) *Als er nachts schlief, sprang der Frosch aus dem Glas* [11DE]
when he at.night sleep.PRS.3SG, jump.PST.3SG the.NOM frog out the.DAT glass
'When he sleeps at night, the frog jumped out of the glass'

In two of these cases, two events (the frog getting out of the jar and the frog leaving the house) are conflated into the same event, as in (165):

(165) [. . .] *flieht der Frosch aus seinem Glas durch das offene Fenster* [05DE]
flee.PRS.3SG the.NOM.M frog out the.DAT.N glass through the.ACC.N open window
[. . .] 'the frog jumped out of the glass through the open window'

The Romance language speakers respected the boundary-crossing constraint and showed only two cases of Manner verbs being used to express the crossing of a boundary. Both cases refer to the moment when the boy jumps out of the window:

(166) *entonces el chico salta por la ventana* [09ES]
then the boy jump.PRS.3SG through the window
'Then the boy jumps out of the window'

(167) *per il bambino per saltare fuori dalla finestra* [07IT]
for the child for jump.INF out of.the window
'for the child to jump out of the window'

These results are coherent with previous studies on boundary-crossing. Slobin and Hoiting (1994) claim that this constraint is only possible in verb-framed languages when there is a sudden, quick movement. In any case, inter-typological differences are clearly shown in these data, with a clear difference between German and Romance speakers in the use of Manner verbs in these events.

A further analysis was carried out in order to reveal intra-typological differences in our data. The focus is on the "jar scene", i.e. the scene where the frog gets out of the jar (Figure 11):

Figure 11: The jar scene.

The jar scene was selected because it shows a clear boundary-crossing event, which participants in the experiment are likely to describe. Other scenes with clear boundary-crossing events are the owl scene and the dog scene, where the boy gets out of the window. However, the motion depicted in the latter scene might be ambiguous, as it can be also considered that the boy falls from the window to the ground (without crossing any boundary). The jar scene was thus considered a suitable stimulus to see how speakers describe a boundary-crossing event. The following types of motion events were considered: Manner verb + Ground, Manner verb, Manner+Path verb + Ground, Manner+Path verb + Manner complement, Manner+Path verb, Path verb + Ground, Path verb + Manner complement, Path verb, and other verb. Table 16 shows the occurrences and Table 17 shows the percentages of the types of motion event used for the boundary-crossing situations:

Table 16: Expression of Boundary-crossing events for the jar scene.

Expression of boundary-crossing	Spanish	Italian	French	German
Manner verb + Ground	0	0	0	7
Manner verb	0	0	0	0
Manner+Path verb + Ground	3	6	3	3
Manner+Path verb + Manner	0	0	1	0
Manner+Path verb	7	1	4	0
Path verb + Ground	1	4	1	1
Path verb + Manner	0	0	1	0
Path verb	0	0	1	0
Other	0	1	1	1

Table 17: Percentages of Boundary-crossing events for the jar scene.

Expression of boundary-crossing in Percentages	Spanish	Italian	French	German
Manner verb + Ground	0.00%	0.00%	0.00%	58.33%
Manner verb	0.00%	0.00%	0.00%	0.00%
Manner+Path verb + Ground	25.00%	50.00%	25%	25%
Manner+Path verb + Manner	0.00%	0.00%	8.33%	0.00%
Manner+Path verb	58.33%	8.33%	33.33%	0.00%
Path verb+ Ground	8.33%	33.33%	8.33%	8.33%
Path verb + Manner	0.00%	0.00%	8.33%	0.00%
Path verb	0.00%	0.00%	8.33%	0.00%
Other	0.00%	8.33%	8.33%	8.33%

The inter-typological differences are clearly marked in this analysis. The German speakers preferred to use a Manner verb with a ground complement, as in examples (164) and (165). This is the encoding used by 7 of the 12 German participants (a 58.33%). None of the Romance-language speakers chose this option, showing a clear boundary-crossing constraint. There is a in interesting case with regard to Italian, half the speakers of which (6 occurrences, 50%) preferred to use a Manner+Path verb with a ground complement, as in (168):

(168) *Però durante la notte questa rana scappa dal barattolo* [10IT]
    but during the night this frog escape.PRS.3SG from.the jar
    'But this frog escapes from the jar during the night'

In one case, this ground complement is an adverbial pronoun, which refers to the jar:

(169) *Decise di metterla in un vaso e tenerla con se, però durante la notte*
    decide.PST.3SG of put.her in a jar and have.her with REFL, but during the night
    la rana se ne scappa [05IT]
    the frog REFL ADVP escape.PRS.3SG
    'He decided to leave her in a jar and keep her with him, but at night the frog escapes (from the glass)'

This option is only used by a 25% of the French and the Spanish participants, who preferred simply to use a Manner+Path verb without any ground, as in (170) and (171):

(170) *La rana se escapa* [10ES]
    the frog REFL escape.PRS.3SG
    'The frog escapes'

(171) *La grenouille s'est échappée* [08FR]
    the frog REF.be.PRS.3SG escape.PTCP.FEM
    'The frog has escaped'

Unlike the option preferred by the Italians, encoding the verb without a ground leaves implicit the information about the crossing of the boundary. In a way, this can be considered a more prototypically verb-framed encoding, as the information about the trajectory is inferred. A potential intra-typological difference might be present here, although further research is needed, with more specific stimuli for the expression of boundary-crossing. These data partially support the findings from the previous studies, which claim that Italian has a looser position with regard to the boundary-crossing constraint. It is also interesting to note that, contrary to what might have been expected, the Romance speakers' do not prefer to use exclusively Path verbs. There were just 4 cases of this by Italian speakers (*uscire* 'go out'), 3 cases by French speakers (*sortir* 'go out') and 1 by a Spanish participant (*salir* 'go out'). Further research is needed to explore intra-typological differences in boundary-crossing motion events.

9 Results of the typological study: Path

Inter-typological differences are expected in the expression of Path. According to previous literature, German speakers explicitly encode Path in satellites and other elements and elaborate Path trajectories with different Ground complements, while Romance speakers encode Path in the main verb of the event and leave other details of the trajectory to be inferred. Intra-typological differences are also expected. According to previous literature, Romance language speakers present different linguistic devices to encode Path, such as Italian verb-particle constructions or French prefixes. Intra-typological differences are then bound to Path and not to Manner.

The next section of this chapter deals with the satellites found in the German data and their combinations with motion verbs. Some attention will be given to the directional adverbs of Romance languages, to decide whether they can be considered pseudo-satellites. In particular, the Italian particles employed in the verb-particle constructions were closely examined. Second, the data are analyzed following Slobin's foundational comparison of Plus and Minus Ground in the full narratives and the falling scenes. The only traditional element of Slobin's analysis that was not replicated here was that involving bare verb and verb with complements, since this analysis is more relevant for satellite-framed languages, and therefore not so appropriate for the purpose of this study.

Unexpectedly, more Path elements were used by the Spanish speakers of the study than what is normally reported in standard Spanish. Due to this geographical variation, the analysis was repeated with speakers from Madrid and Argentina. The use of deictic motion events was also examined to explore inter and intra-typological differences. This is an additional analysis to previous studies that have not looked into deictic motion verbs in *The Frog Story*.

9.1 Satellites and pseudo-satellites

Talmy (1991, 2000a, 2000b) considers that satellites are one of the most common encoding devices for Path. As explained in Section 4.2 of Chapter 2, the notion of satellite is not exempt from criticism and limitations, and has been the origin of heated debates within this framework. However, the main aim of this section is to show how Path is encoded in this linguistic device in German and how it can be compared to its closest equivalent in Romance languages, namely Italian pseudo-satellites.

These are the Path satellites found in German: *ab* 'from' (6), *an* 'to' (5), *auf* 'up' (3), *hoch* 'up' (3), *los* 'off' (3), *nieder* 'down' (1), *raus* 'out' (7), *rein* 'inward'

(2), *runter* 'down' (6), *vorbei* 'by, past' (1), *weg* 'out' (4), *zu* 'towards' (3), *zurück* 'back' (1).[5] Some of these satellites are combined with the deictic prefixes *hin-* 'thither' and *her-* 'hither': *heran* (1), *heraus* (5), *herunter* (3), *hinauf* (1), *hinein* (3), *hinterher* (2), *hinunter* (2).

The combinations with a satellite found in the data are: *abbremsen* 'brake' (2), *abhauen* 'run away' (2), *abladen* 'unload' (1), *abwerfen* 'throw off' (1), *ankommen* 'arrive' (1), *anhalten* 'stop' (2), *sich annähern* 'approach' (1), *sich anschleichen* 'sneak' (1), *aufgabeln* 'pick up' (1), *aufspießen* 'spear' (1), *sich aufstehen* 'stand up' (1), *hochspringen* 'jump up' (3), *losrennen* 'run off' (2), *losreiten* 'ride off', *sich niederknien* 'kneel down' (1), *rausklettern* 'climb out' (1), *rauskommen* 'come out' (4), *rausspringen* 'jump out' (1), *raussteigen* 'climb out' (1), *reinschmeißen* 'throw inside' (1), *reinfallen* 'fall inside' (1), *runterfallen* 'fall down' (4), *runterschmeißen* 'throw down' (1), *runterwerfen* 'throw down' (1), *vorbeifliegen* 'fly past' (1), *weglaufen* 'run away', *wegrennen* 'run away', *wegschleppen* 'drag away' (1), *wegtragen* 'carry away', *zugehen* 'approach', *zusteuern* (1) 'head for', *zuspringen* (1) 'jump towards', and *zurückgehen* (1) 'go back'.

In some cases, the satellite not only encodes Path but also changes the verb meaning. The following verbs are classified as different verb types from the same verbs without satellites: *abhauen* 'run away', *abladen* 'unload', *ankommen* 'arrive', *anhalten* 'stop' and *sich aufstehen* 'stand up'. These are good examples of how lexicalization of Path in German can be interpreted as a cline (see Chapter 3, Section 3).

Romance languages are not considered to have satellites, with the exception of Romansch. However, as already seen in Chapter 3, Italian does present a number of particles that are elements in verb-particle constructions. Several authors have considered them similar to satellites (see Chapter 3, Section 2.3.1). The following are found in our corpus: *via* 'away' (7), *fuori* 'out' (6), *giù* 'down' (4) and *dietro* 'after' (1). The verb-particle combinations found are: *andare via* 'go away' (1), *andarsene via* 'go away' (1), *portare via* 'take away' (2), *portarsi via* 'take away' (1), *trascinare via* 'drag away' (1), *uscire fuori* 'go out' (3), *venire fuori* 'come out' (2), *saltare fuori* 'jump out' (3), *buttarsi giù* 'throw oneself down' (1), *cadere giù* 'fall down' (1), *fare cadere giù* 'throw, lit. make (someone/somebody) fall down' (1), *correre dietro* 'run after' (1). These particles are not as frequent as German satellites, but they are frequent in the data and are easy to combine. In fact only *uscire fuori* 'go out', *cadere giù* 'fall down' and to some

---

5 Please note that the translation of these particles as satellites is approximate and that they might not coincide with the prototypical meaning of these linguistic elements, which can also be used as prepositions, adjectives or adverbs.

extent *andarsene via* 'go away (from a place)' are pleonastic. This is the reason why the term pseudo-satellite has been coined.

This combinability and frequency of Italian particles differs from similar linguistic elements in Spanish and French. Three directional adverbs occur in the Spanish data: *abajo* 'down' (2), *afuera* 'out' (1) and *fuera* 'out' (1), but they are all pleonastic, that is, they reiterate the Path component already encoded in the verb: *caer(se) abajo* 'fall down' *salir (a)fuera* 'go out'. French data only pesent the use of a directional adverb: *après* 'after', in combination with *courir* 'run'. These cases are not considered pseudo-satellites, as Italian particles permit a greater combinability and more frequency than do Spanish particles. This is probably the greatest intra-typological difference among Romance languages in the expression of Path. The analysis of Minus vs. Plus Ground will reveal whether the presence of these items impacts on the expression of Path in the narratives.

9.2 Minus Ground vs. Plus Ground

Slobin's analysis of Minus Ground vs. Plus Ground in *The Frog Story* was used to determine whether the inter- and intra-typological differences identified in the literature occur in the data. Slobin considers Minus Gound events to be those that lack a linguistic element that encodes the semantic component of Ground, as in (172):

(172) *Et le chien, il tombe* [01FR]
 and the dog, he fall.PRS.3SG
 'And the dog, he falls'

In this case, the French speaker used the verb *tomber* 'fall', which encodes Path in the verb. The direction of the movement –downwards- can be easily inferred. On the other hand, Plus Ground motion events do define some type of Ground, as in (173). Verb-framed languages frequently encode only one Ground element per verb:

(173) *[el niño] cae de un barranco* [11ES]
 the child fall.PRS.3SG from a cliff
 '[The child] falls from a cliff'

The speaker in (173) used a prepositional phrase to codify the Ground, in this case the source of the movement, as *caer* 'fall' implies a previous higher position.

It is however possible that the verb encodes more than one Ground element. This is more frequent in satellite-framed languages, such as German:

(174) [. . .] *fällt dieses von dem Ast herunter. . . auf den Boden* [12DE]
fall.PRS.3SG this from the.DAT.M branch hither.down. . . on the.ACC.M ground
[. . .]'it falls down from the branch here down. . . to the ground'

The German speaker in (174) gave a very rich description of Path. The compound satellite *herunter* is made of the deictic prefix *her-* 'hither' and the satellite *unter* 'down'. The source of the movement is encoded in *von dem Ast* 'from the branch' and the goal of the movement in *auf dem Boden* 'to the ground'. Romance languages permit the encoding of two Ground elements in the verb, as explained below. However, this is not frequent and does not seem to be part of the rhetorical style of these languages. None of the French and Spanish speakers in the study encoded two Ground elements in combination with the same verb, even though this is a grammatically acceptable option in both languages. A few examples were found in Italian, though, such as (175):

(175) *fa cadere il bambino e il cane giù da un dirupo su un lago* [03IT]
make.PRS.3SG fall.INF the child and the dog down from a cliff over a lake
'[He] makes the child and the dog fall off a cliff into a lake'

In (175), a Ground element corresponds to the source of the movement –*da un dirupo* 'from a cliff'- and the other corresponds to the goal of the movement –*su un lago* 'to a lake', similarly to the German example in (174).

The analysis of Plus Ground and Minus Ground motion events is presented in the following sections. I applied this analysis to all the motion events present in all the narratives in 9.3. and for the falling scenes in 9.4. This second analysis is pertinent as it focuses on the parts of the story where the trajectory of the movement is more relevant. The final section will deal with cases in which more than one Ground element is used.

9.3 Minus Ground vs. Plus Ground in the narratives

The aim of this analysis in the complete narratives is crucial because it reveals how speakers encode Path in the whole story, in contrast with the second analysis that reveals how speakers encode Path in the scenes that lead them to express Path. The total results for the whole narratives are represented in Table 18:

Table 18: Plus Ground and Minus Ground in L1s.

	Motion verbs	Minus Ground	Mean Minus Ground	% Minus Ground	Plus Ground	Mean Plus Ground	% Plus Ground
Spanish	193	94	7,92	48,78%	99	8,33	51,28%
Italian	210	69	5,75	32,86%	141	11,75	67,14%
French	225	126	10,5	56%%	99	8,25	44%
German	213	83	6,92	38,97%	130	10,83	61,03%

The fact that the Italian speakers produce more occurrences and a higher percentage of Plus Ground than the German speakers could be due to the fact that in this analysis German satellites were not counted as Plus Ground elements, while Italian pseudo-satellites were counted as Grounds. Previous studies do not include satellites as Grounds because this would bias the data towards satellite-framed languages. In the case of Italian pseudo-satellites, I decided to include them in this Plus Ground analysis to be consistent with previous literature on Romance motion events, which considers these particles only as locative adverbs.

The Kruskal-Wallis test shows a significant difference ($p = .004$) among the groups. The Mann-Whitney test enables us to identify where this significant difference lies. German presents a statistical trend with regard to Spanish ($p = .069$) and ($p = .100$). This is expected as the speakers of Romance languages produce fewer Plus Ground elements. Italian shows a trend with German ($p = .068$), with a higher production of Plus Ground cases. There are no significant differences between Spanish and French ($p = .651$). The most surprising result in this analysis is the fact that Italian speakers present a significant difference from Spanish speakers ($p = .000$) and from French speakers ($p = .008$). Therefore, an important intra-typological difference is found: Italian seems to behave differently in relation to the expression of Path from the other Romance languages. Italian does in fact present data closer to that of satellite-framed languages. Indeed, the Italian speakers produced more occurrences of Path expression than the German speakers.

It is also worth examining the type of Plus Ground events found. The main tendency in verb-framed languages is to express –if at all- only one Ground element. In fact, in all the data collected by Sebastián and Slobin (1994) and Slobin (1996a), from speakers at all ages in Madrid, Argentina and Chile (a corpus of 216 narratives), the speakers only produced 2 cases of Plus Ground with 2 elements with the same verb. Some dialectal differences were found, however

Table 19: Descriptive statistics % Plus Ground.

language	Mean	N	SD	Range
Spanish	.7908	12	.11603	.45
Italian	1.0033	12	.13317	.44
French	.7658	12	.20843	.59
German	.9083	12	.13790	.49
Total	.8671	48	.17662	.77

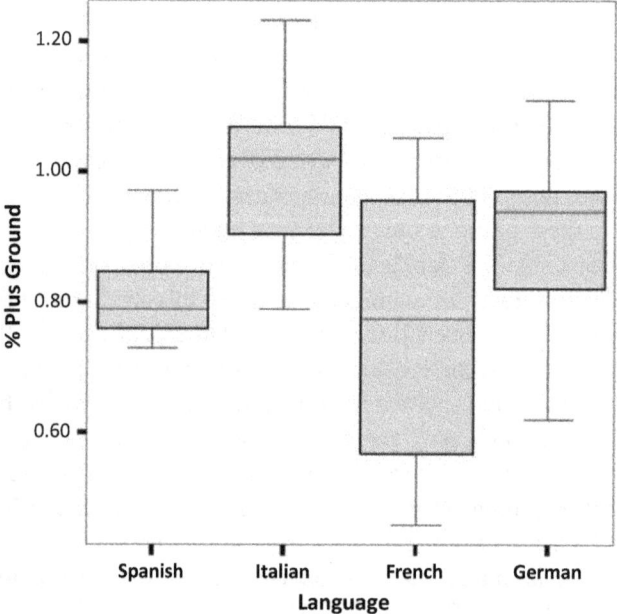

Figure 12: Plus Ground Percentage in L1s.

(Ibarretxe-Antuñano and Hijazo-Gascón 2011, 2012), in the varieties of Spanish spoken in the Basque Country and Aragón.

The fact that Spanish speakers rarely encode two Ground elements in the same event has been generalized as a feature of all verb-framed languages. In fact, however, this does not apply to all of them. Ibarretxe-Antuñano (2004b, 2009) shows that Basque tends to detail Path expression and its speakers use several Path components in the same event. This shows that there can be intra-typological variation within verb-framed languages. It is much more frequent to find events with more than two Ground elements in satellite-framed languages. In fact, in this study we find 8 occurrences of Plus Ground events with more than one element produced by German speakers, as in (176):

(176) [...] *flieht der Frosch aus seinem Glas durch das offene Fenster*
flee.PRS.3SG the.NOM.M frog out its.DAT.N glass through the.ACC.N open window
[...] 'the frog flees from out of its glass through the open window' [05DE]

In some cases the Ground complements are pleonastic, i.e. they repeat the same information about the trajectory, as in (177):

(177) [...] *und die beiden nach unten fielen. . . den Abgrund hinunter in einen Teich*
and the.PL both towards down fall.PST.3PL. . . the.ACC.M cliff thither.down into a.ACC.M pond
[. . .] 'and both fell down. . . the cliff down (there) into a pond' [08DE]

All the complements and satellites in (177) reinforce the downwards direction of the movement, which is also present in the verb *fallen* 'fall'. These events with more than one Ground are one of the main inter-typological differences between satellite and verb-framed languages. None of the speakers of French and Spanish describe any movement with more than two Ground elements in the way it is done by German speakers in (176) and (177).

Italian data again reveal unexpected results. The transalpine language seems closer to satellite-framed languages with regard to the use of Plus Ground events with more than one Ground element. There are 12 cases of Plus Ground motion events with two or even three Ground elements. In some cases, these are events with a Ground element and a directional adverb, as in (178) and (179):

(178) *Però cade giù dalla finestra* [05IT]
however fall.PRS.3SG down from.the window
'However, [he] falls down from the window'

(179) *E si buttano giù da un dirupo* [05IT]
and refl throw.PRS.3.PL down from a cliff
'And they throw themselves off a cliff'

In these examples *giù* 'down' marks the goal of the movement. In (178) this meaning is pleonastic with the verb, whilst it is not in (179). This directional adverb is combined in these examples with elements that encode the source of the movement, which helps to describe the complete trajectory of the Figure.

Directional adverbs are not exclusive to Italian, but are also present in the other Romance languages. However, directional adverbs in French or Spanish present important differences in use with their Italian counterparts. First, they do not appear in combination with another element that shows the Ground, as in (178) and (179). Secondly, they are pleonastic as in (180) and (181):

(180) *Y el perro cae abajo* [03ES]
and the dog fall.PRS.3SG down
'And the dog falls down'

(181) *Y salen afuera para buscarla* [05ES]
and exit.PRS.3PL out to search.INF.it
'And they exit out to search it [the frog]'

In other cases, Italian speakers use two Ground elements without a directional adverb, as in (182):

(182) *da una parte un po' più alta cade in basso* [04IT]
from a part a bit more high fall.PRS.3.SG in down
'[He] falls down from a slightly higher part'

This example also encodes source and goal of the movement in the same event. There are other cases, very similar to satellite-framed language constructions, in which Path is expressed by means of a source complement, a goal complement and a directional adverb, as in (183) and (184):

(183) *fa cadere il bambino e il cane giù da un dirupo su un lago* [03IT]
make.PRS.3SG fall.INF the boy and the dog down from a cliff over a lake
'[he] makes fall the boy and the dog from a cliff into a lake'

(184) *e l'ha fatto cadere giù da un piccolo dirupo fino dentro all'acqua* [08IT]
and it.have.PRS.3SG make.PTCP fall.INF down from a small cliff until inside to.the.water
'and [he] has thrown it off a small cliff into the water'

It seems that there is a clear intra-typological difference between Italian and the other Romance languages with regard to Plus Ground encoding. This intra-typological difference is supported by statistical analysis, as shown in Table 20.

Table 20: Statistical descriptions Plus Ground 2 or more elements.

Language	Mean	N	SD	Range
Spanish	.0000	12	.00000	.00
Italian	.1600	12	.18844	.46
French	.0000	12	.00000	.00
German	.1458	12	.13688	.34
Total	.0765	48	.13672	.46

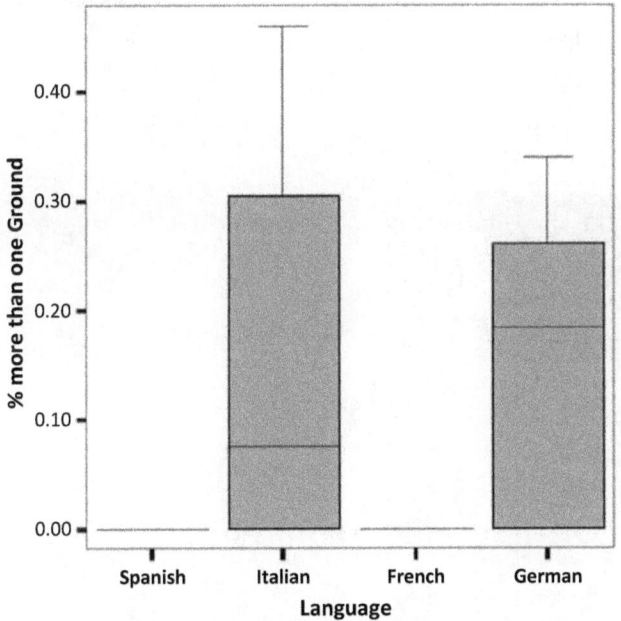

Figure 13: Percentages Plus Ground with 2 or more elements in L1s.

The Kruskal-Wallis test shows a significant difference among the four groups ($p = .001$). The Mann-Whitney test shows a significant difference between German and Spanish ($p = .014$) and also between German and French (same p-value). Interestingly, there is no significant difference between German and Italian ($p = .932$). When Romance languages were contrasted, a trend was found between Italian on the one hand and French and Spanish on the other. This trend is very close to the α level ($p = .039$).

9.4 Minus Ground vs. Plus Ground in the falling scenes

Most of the studies that have used *The Frog Story* as the elicitation tool have analysed the Minus and Plus Ground elements in the so-called *falling scenes*. The motion event is considered particularly salient in these scenes, and therefore speakers are more likely to describe it. There are four of these scenes, called in the literature *the dog scene*, *the beehive scene*, *the boy scene* and *the deer scene*. The results for each of the scenes and the total findings for all of them are presented in this section.

9.4.1 The dog scene

In this scene, the dog is looking through the (open) window, and falls out. This scene is represented in Figure 14:

Figure 14: Dog scene.

The results for this scene are as follows:

Table 21: Dog scene in L1s.

	Total	Minus Ground	Plus Ground	1 Ground	More than 1 Ground	%Minus Ground	% Plus Ground
Spanish	9	2	7	7	0	22.22%	77.78%
Italian	12	2	10	9	1	16.67%	83.33%
French	10	4	6	6	0	40%	60%
German	13	3	10	9	1	23.08%	76.92%

Italian and German have a higher elaboration of Path, with more Plus Ground elements, which is consistent with the results of Path expression in the whole narrative seen in the previous section.

9.4.2 The beehive scene

In this scene, participants need to describe the movement of the beehive that falls from the tree, as depicted in Figure 15:

Figure 15: The beehive scene.

These are the results for this scene:

Table 22: The beehive scene in the L1s.

	Total	Minus Ground	Plus Ground	1 Ground	More than 1 Ground	%Minus Ground	% Plus Ground
Spanish	5	4	1	1	0	80%	20%
Italian	5	4	1	1	0	80%	20%
French	9	9	0	0	0	100%	0%
German	5	3	2	1	1	60%	40%

In this case, speakers seem to use Minus Grounds, using only the motion verb without any specifications regarding the trajectory of the movement. There are however differences, as French speakers do not present any Plus Ground event, whereas in German Minus and Plus Ground uses are more balanced.

9.4.3 The boy scene

This scene is the same as the owl scene, and is used for the analysis of Manner. However in this analysis the focus is not on the owl coming out of the tree but on how speakers describe the fact that the boy falls.

Figure 16: Boy scene.

The results for this scene are represented in Table 23. As we see, in Italian and in German all the descriptions of this event are produced with a Ground element, but in French and Spanish these proportions are reduced to 40% of Plus Ground.

Table 23: The boy scene in the L1s.

	Total	Minus Ground	Plus Ground	1 Ground	More than 1 Ground	%Minus Ground	% Plus Ground
Spanish	5	3	2	2	0	60%	40%
Italian	6	0	6	6	0	0%	100%
French	5	3	2	2	0	60%	40%
German	3	0	3	3	0	0%	100%

9.4.4 The deer scene

The deer scene is the most complex, and the scene that tends to receive most attention from the participants. This scene is represented in Figure 17:

Figure 17: Deer scene.

More motion events are used to describe this scene than the previous ones. In this case speakers use at least a Ground element. Consistent with previous results, the Italian and German speakers produced more events with two or more elements, as shown in Table 24:

Table 24: Deer scene in the L1s.

	Total	Minus Ground	Plus Ground	1 Ground	More than 1 Ground	% Minus Ground	% Plus Ground
Spanish	21	0	21	21	0	0%	100%
Italian	19	3	16	12	4	15.79%	84.21%
French	24	7	17	17	0	29.17%	70.84%
German	22	1	21	17	4	4.55%	95.45%

9.4.5 Overall analysis of the falling scenes

A global analysis of Minus and Plus Ground in the falling scenes produced the results shown in Table 25:

Table 25: Total results from the falling scenes in L1s.

	Total	Minus Ground	Plus Ground	1 Ground	More than 1 Ground	% Minus Ground	% Plus Ground
Spanish	40	9	31	31	0	22.5%	77.5%
Italian	42	9	33	28	5	21.43%	78.56%
French	48	23	25	25	0	47.92%	52.08%
German	43	7	36	30	6	16.28%	83.72%

In general, speakers tend to present similar results of Minus and Plus Ground in the analysis of the falling scenes to those they present for the whole narrative. However, there is here a higher number of Plus Ground in the falling scenes, as represented in Table 26 in which Plus Ground percentages in the whole narratives and in the falling scenes is compared.

The statistical analysis of the falling scenes results reveals a significant difference (Kruskal-Wallis, $p = .000$). When contrasting group pairs, a significant difference is found between French and Spanish ($p = .001$), French and German ($p = .000$) and French and Italian ($p = .000$). There are no significant differences

Table 26: Comparison % Plus Ground whole narrative vs. falling scenes.

	% Plus Ground Whole Narrative	% Plus Ground Falling Scenes
Spanish	51.28%	77.5%
Italian	67.14%	78.56%
French	44%	52.08%
German	61.03%	83.72%

between Spanish and German ($p = .932$), Spanish and Italian ($p = .932$) or Italian and German ($p = 1.000$).

Table 27: Descriptive statistics % Plus Ground in falling scenes.

Language	Mean	N	SD	Range
Spanish	1.3417	12	.35143	.89
Italian	1.3667	12	.31552	.84
French	.8658	12	.26664	.95
German	1.3658	12	.32511	.95
Total	1.2062	60	.36716	.95

Again, in the proportion of motion events with more than one Ground, Italian has more similarities with German than it does with French and Spanish. Kruskal-Wallis shows a p-value of .013. The significant difference lies in German vs. Spanish (Mann-Whitney, $p = .025$) and French (Mann-Whitney, $p = .015$). There is a trend between Italian vs. Spanish and French (Mann-Whitney, $p = .033$). There are no significant differences between Spanish and French ($p = 1.000$)

The falling scenes seem, therefore, to confirm previous results obtained from the Plus Ground analysis of the whole narratives. Only one aspect differs from previous results, which is particularly interesting. This is that the Spanish speakers did not present significant differences in the falling scenes with regard to either German or Italian, with which it had a trend in the whole narrative, but with French. These results do not seem to be consistent with previous studies on Spanish that have placed this language as the prototypical verb-framed language, with more tendency to Minus Ground events.

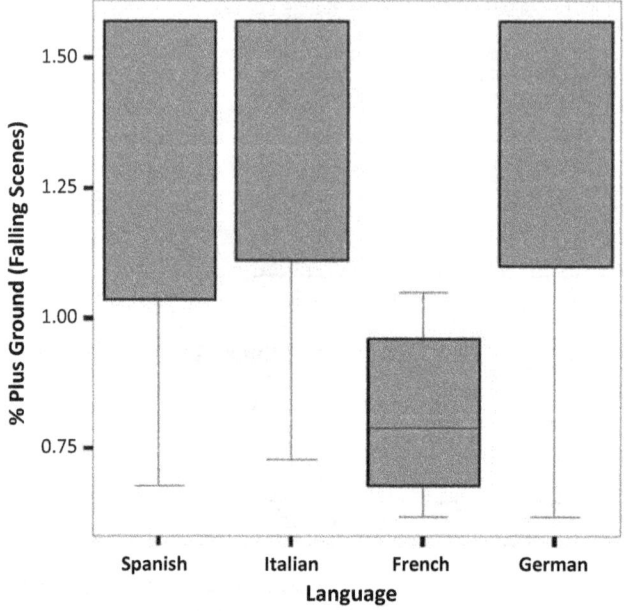

Figure 18: Percentage of Plus Ground in the falling scenes in L1s.

Table 28: Descriptive statistics % Plus Ground 2 or more elements in the falling scenes.

Language	Mean	N	SD	Range
Spanish	.0000	12	.00000	.00
Italian	.2917	12	.49754	1.57
French	.0000	12	.00000	.00
German	.3108	12	.47649	1.57
Total	.1215	60	.33239	1.57

This greater number of presentations of Path information may be due to the geographical variety of the language spoken by the Spanish participants in this study. Previous studies (Ibarretxe-Antuñano and Hijazo-Gascón 2012) have shown the tendency to describe Path in more detail by speakers of the Spanish variety spoken in Aragón. It was thus decided to repeat the analysis, substituting the data

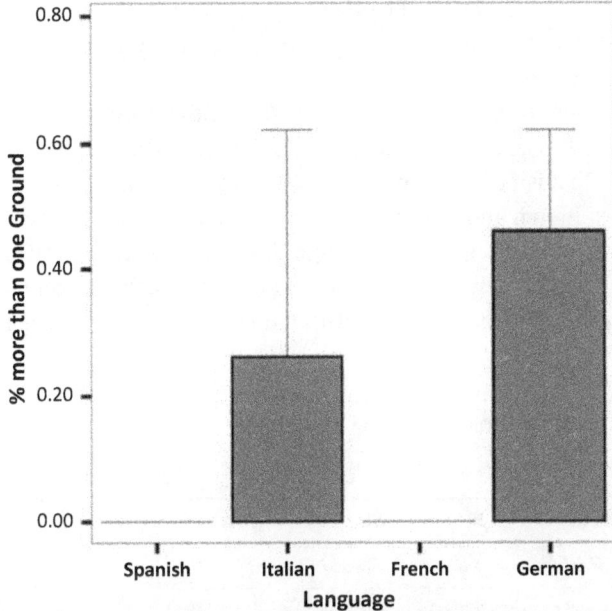

Figure 19: Percentage Plus Ground with two or more elements in the falling scenes in L1s.

from our group of Spanish speakers with the data gathered by Slobin and his colleagues from other varieties of Spanish.[6]

9.5 Falling scenes with Slobin's Spanish data

The main differences between Slobin's Spanish data and the Spanish data collected for this research lies in the geographical varieties used and in the number of participants. As the participants were all adult university students, both datasets are similar in terms of age and stage of study, and are therefore comparable with the French, Italian and German data.

As explained above, our participants spoke the Spanish variety spoken in Aragón, in northern Spain. They were all functional monolinguals, with some knowledge of other languages, mainly English. Slobin's data are mixed with regard to their origin. They were 18 participants, six from Madrid, six from Argentina and six

---

[6] I would like to thank Dan I. Slobin for allowing me to use his data for the purpose of this analysis.

from Chile. In order to be consistent with the other language groups, I decided to use only 12 of these participants, hence only the data from Madrid and Argentina were used for the analysis presented here.

The statistical tests were repeated with the new data and a significant difference was found in the Kruskal-Wallis test (p = .000). Mann-Whitney test revealed a trend between Spanish and Italian (p = .078) and Spanish and German (p = .060). In both cases, Italian and German speakers presented higher percentages of Plus Ground in the falling scenes. A significant difference was also found between Spanish and French (p = .023), although in this case the French speakers presented a lower percentage of Plus Ground cases. This can be seen in Figure 20:

Table 29: Descriptive statistics % Plus Ground in Falling Scenes with Slobin's data.

Language	Mean	N	SD	Range
Italian	1.3667	12	.31552	.84
French	.8658	12	.26664	.95
German	1.3658	12	.32511	.95
Spanish (Slobin)	1.0908	12	.32618	.95
Total	1.2062	60	.36716	.95

The statistical analysis was carried out only in relation to Minus and Plus Ground. It was not performed with Plus Ground with two or more elements because there is only one case among Slobin's data. This result is so minimal that it was not considered worthwhile repeating the statistical analysis of more than two Grounds with the new dataset.

The analysis of the falling scenes shows some interesting results. First, it is interesting that although French and Spanish had similar results in the overall narrative, in the falling scenes, the Spanish speakers tended to produce significantly more Plus Ground than do the French. In these scenes, the speakers of all the languages increased their Plus Ground percentage because this information is cognitively more salient. However, it seems that this happens to a lesser degree in French.

A second point of interest is that the data support the findings of previous studies on geographical varieties of Spanish and motion events (Ibarretxe-Antuñano and Hijazo-Gascón 2011, 2012) that point to a higher degree of Path elaboration in northern varieties of Spanish. This reminds typologists that

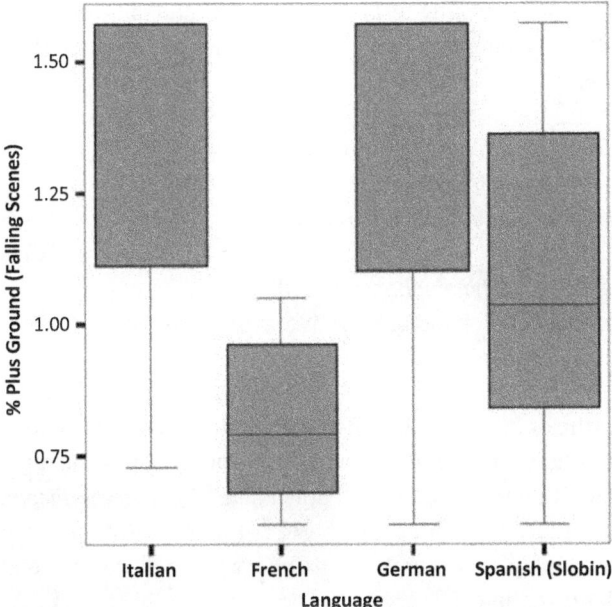

Figure 20: Percentage Plus Ground in falling scenes in L1s (Slobin's data).

social and geographical variation can also play a role in the study of language contrasts.

9.6 Deixis

Following Talmy's (2000a, 2000b) typological framework, Deixis is one of the subcomponents of Path. As seen in Section 2.4 of Chapter 3, deictic information is considered a relevant issue for both inter- and intra-typological variation, both with regard to how it can be encoded (in the main verb, in an additional verb, in prefixes or particles) and to who can act as the deictic centre, i.e. the Figure where the movement encoded by venitive verbs (i.e. *come*) ends. The *Frog Story* is not specifically designed to test the use of deixis, so high frequencies of deictic motion verbs or particles are not expected. However, as this elicitation tool involves some degree of free production, it was considered interesting to observe how our participants used these deictic elements in this task.

The main inter-typological difference between the languages of this study with regard to deixis, is the fact that German encodes deixis not only in the main verb of the event (e.g. *kommen* 'come') but also in the particles *hin-* 'to there' and *her-* 'to here'. It is interesting to note that the German speakers used *hin-* 6 times and *her-* 9 times. Examples of how these particles are used are (185) and (186):

(185) *und der Junge fällt den Baum herunter* [06DE]
and the.NOM.M boy fall.PRS.3SG the.ACC.M tree to-here.down
'and the boy falls down (here) from the tree'

(186) *bis er in einen kleinen Teich hineinplumste* [09DE]
until he.NOM in a.ACC.M small pond to.there-into.splash.PST.3SG
'Until he splashes into a small pond'

Satellites and deictic particles are found in different combinations: *sich heranschleichen* 'sneak towards here' (1), *herauskommen* 'come out here' (4), *herausflüchtern* 'flee out to here' (1), *herunterfallen* 'fall down here' (3), *hinterherfliegen* 'fly here behind' (1), *hinaufsteigen* 'climb up there' (1), *hineinfallen* 'fall into there' (1), *hineinplumpsen* 'plop into there' (1), *hinunterfallen* 'fall down there' (2), *hinunterstürzen* 'fall down there' (1).

These data reveal that these particles are productive in German, and are very frequently used by German speakers, even in narratives where deictic information does not seem particularly salient. The fact that German speakers have a specific linguistic resource to encode Deixis, and that they use it, lead to their narratives showing more deictic information than do those produced by speakers of Romance languages, which do not have these deictic particles. Speakers of Romance languages (and of other languages too) would need an adverb or a prepositional phrase to express the same information and would do it only if particularly salient. A search of the data of deictic adverbs shows that our Romance-speaking participants do not use deictic adverbs to describe motion events. The Spanish speakers only used *allí* 'there' twice, the Italian Speakers only used *lì* 'there' once, and the French speakers only used *là* 'there' once. The corresponding adverbs for 'here' were not used for motion contexts. This inter-typological pattern is in line with Slobin's (1991, 1996a) thinking for speaking hypothesis. Similar to what happens with Manner, therefore German speakers tend describe deictic motion frequently, whereas Romance language speakers do so only when it is very salient.

In the case of deictic motion verbs and their use, it should be noted that Gathercole's (1977, 1978) typology of deictic verbs overlaps and crosscuts Talmy's (1991, 2000a, 2000b) typology. Gathercole focuses on the deictic centre, which determine the use of venitive or COME verbs. Some languages such as Spanish only permit one deictic centre, i.e. the Speaker, whereas others such as English permit both addressee and speaker to be the deictic centre. Therefore *come* in English can mean motion towards the person who speaks or towards the addressee, whereas in Spanish *venir* come can be used only towards the addressee or places identifiable with him or her (Gathercole 1977, 1978 and Chapter 3, Section 2.4). Interestingly, most of the languages that only permit the main speaker to be the addressee seem to be verb-framed languages (Spanish, Japanese, Portuguese, Turkish), but there are both verb- and satellite-framed languages who permit the addressee to be the deictic centre (English, German, Dutch, French, Italian, Catalan). In the case of our study, the use of COME verbs is therefore both an inter-typological difference (German vs. Spanish) and an intra-typological difference (French/Italian vs. Spanish). As shown in Table 30, the Spanish speakers did not present any instances of venitive verbs:

Table 30: Deictic motion verbs in *The Frog Story*.

	Itive (GO verbs)	Venitive (COME verbs)	Causative Itive (TAKE verbs)	Causative Venitive (BRING verbs)
Spanish	*ir* (7), *irse* (12)	*venir* (0)	*llevar* (7)	*traer* (0)
Italian	*andare* (4), *andarsene* (2)	*venire* (2)	*Portare* (9), *portarsi* (1)	
French	*aller* (6), *s'en aller* (2)	*revenir* (2)	*porter* (1)	
			emmener (4)	*amener* (1)
German	*gehen* (14)	*kommen* (19)	*tragen* (5)	*bringen* (2)

These results show that the narrators of *The Frog Story* are not likely to report any event ending motion in the speaker, as this is not part of the story. Consequently, Spanish speakers do not use any venitive verbs, whether for spontaneous motion like *venir* 'come', or for causative motion like *traer* 'bring'. Venitive verbs can be used in the other languages in this study, regardless of whether they are satellite or verb-framed, as they are not exclusively used to express motion towards the speaker. Interestingly, German speakers used the venitive verb much more than Romance speakers, as *kommen* was used 19 times, whereas *venire* and *revenir* were used only twice in each group.

It is also worth noting that German speakers used a venitive (*bringen* 'bring') and an itive causative verb (*tragen* 'take') whereas French and Italian speakers used only one causative deictic verb (*porter* and *portare(si)*), which could be interpreted as being used for itive or venitive contexts. It is also important to note that the French participants used the general verb *porter* 'take/bring', which can have both itive and venitive meanings, and *emmener* 'take' and *amener* 'bring'.

These are very interesting verbs in French. Whereas *amener* 'bring' can be used with direction to the deictic centre (to the addressee or the speaker), *emmener* 'take' is used for different locations and includes an additional dimension, namely that it is used for taking/carrying animate objects, in contrast to *emporter* 'take', which is only used with inanimate objects. The *Dictionnaire de l'Academie Française* explains in a note that:

> Contrairement à *Emporter*, qui le plus souvent s'emploie avec des noms d'êtres inanimés, *Emmener* s'emploie uniquement avec des noms d'êtres animés. *On emmène ses enfants en vacances,* mais *on emporte ses livres. On emmène son chien,* mais *on emporte son parapluie.*
>
> [*Emmener* is exclusively used with animate nouns, in contrast to *emporter*, which is most often used with inanimate nouns. We take the children on holiday [with *emmener*], but we take their books [with *emporter*]. We take his dog [with *emmener*], but we take his umbrella [with *emporter*]].[7]

This difference between animate and inanimate objects should translate to *amener* vs. *apporter* 'bring', although in this case the *Dictionnaire de l'Academie Française* recognises they are sometimes used interchangeably (and recommends maintaining the distinction in language use).[8] This seems to be an additional intra-typological difference in Deixis, in this case between French and the other Romance languages. In this case, these prefixes could be considered former pseudo-satellites, as studied by Kopecka (2006a), although they are almost lexicalised and their frequency and combinability seem to be low in Modern French in comparison with previous stages of the language. In any case, more data on the use of these different verbs is needed.

In conclusion, even though *The Frog Story* is not specifically designed to see how speakers use deictic motion, it shows interesting trends with regard to deixis. A clear inter-typological difference is found, with the use of German particles and a frequent use of German venitive verbs in contrast with Romance languages. It seems that deixis is relevant information that is encoded in German even when it is not particularly salient, in contrast with what happens in Romance languages.

An intra-typological distinction is also found with regard to the use of venitive verbs. Given that the speaker exclusively acts as the deictic centre in Spanish, no cases of venitive verbs were present in the Spanish narratives. This restriction does not apply to French and Italian and their speakers did use some

---

7 My translation. Original note in French can be found at https://www.dictionnaire-academie.fr/article/A9E1066 (accessed 06/04/2021)
8 See https://www.dictionnaire-academie.fr/article/DNP0012 (accessed 06/04/2021)

venitive verbs, albeit infrequently in comparison with the German participants. The French participants used a more varied set of causative verbs than the Spanish and Italian speakers, in this case taking into account whether the Figure is animated or not. This seems a promising area for future research on intra-typological differences. Different factors come into play in terms of deixis, which remains complex topic that merits further investigation.

9.7 Specific aspects of Path in the four languages of the study

The explanation of the characteristics of the four languages of the study concludes with the analysis of Path. In terms of inter-typological differences, German results corroborate the characteristics expected according to previous literature and its position in the typology. Namely, it does detail Path components, with a higher presence of Plus Ground events. German also seems to pay special attention to deixis. This particular subcomponent of Path was frequently encoded in the narratives, both in deictic motion verbs (for spontaneous and caused motion) and in the particles *hin-* 'to there' and *her-* 'to here'.

Romance languages differ in their characteristics with regard to Path descriptions. This is particularly interesting, taking into account the expected similarities in Manner descriptions. In the case of Spanish expression of Path, native speakers of this language behave as expected, with a lower use of Ground elements than satellite-framed languages such as German. However, it was interesting to notice a geographical variation in the analysis of the falling scenes, as the speakers from Aragón presented more cases of Manner than did speakers from Argentina and Madrid. This result has interesting implications for typology, including the role that geographical variation can play in the typology. Further research on typology should thus go beyond inter- and intra-typological differences and explore the role of dialectal and sociolinguistic factors. In the case of Deixis, Spanish shows an intra-typological difference, as venitive verbs such as *venir* 'come' and *traer* 'bring' can only be used in movements towards the speaker. This restriction has an impact in our data, which show no cases of venitive verbs by native speakers of Spanish. French and Italian do permit the addressee to be the deictic centre, and therefore venitive verbs can be used with more flexibility. A few cases of such verbs are found in the narratives of participants from Italy and France, although with a much lower frequency than in those of German speakers.

The data also show that French is a prototypical verb-framed language, both with regard to Manner and Path. French speakers express fewer Grounds than all the other languages in the study. Indeed, it is important to mention that the pseudo-satellite prefixes described by Kopecka (2004, 2006a) are not frequent in these data. Only a few such cases were found: *amener* 'bring' and *emmener* 'take'; and *décrocher* 'unhook' and *accrocher* 'hook'. An occurrence of *s'enfuir* 'flee (away)' was found, but none of *fuir* 'flee'. There were several cases of verbs formed by the iterative prefix *re-* 'again', such as *repartir* 'leave again', *retourner* 'come back' and *revenir* 'come again', but only one opposition was found: *partir* 'leave'. There were other verbs that have a prefix, but we consider that these are very lexicalised, as in Italian or Spanish, *parcourir* 'go all over' and *descendre* 'go down'. The frequency of these verbs is very low, as can be seen in Appendix I. Therefore, it does not seem that prefixes in current French are comparable with satellites in languages such as German or English, in contrast with Kopecka's (2004, 2006a) claims about French being a mixed pattern language.

Italian shows a very different picture. It can clearly be confirmed that Italian shows similar Path descriptions to those of a satellite-framed language. The Italian speakers do not present a significant difference from the German speakers in their descriptions of Plus Ground events, but they do show a trend with the French and Spanish speakers. The Italian speakers even differ significantly from the French speakers in the description of Path in the falling scenes. The reason for this intra-typological difference seems to be the productivity and frequency of use of verb-particle constructions in Italian. The particles present in these constructions, traditionally considered as directional adverbs, have more frequency and combinability than directional adverbs in French or Spanish and less than German satellites, and have been considered as pseudo-satellites in the literature (see Hijazo-Gascón 2011a, 2017; Ibarretxe-Antuñano and Hijazo-Gascón 2012; Ibarretxe-Antuñano, Hijazo-Gascón, and Moret-Oliver 2017). For example, *via* 'away' can be combined with neutral verbs such as *andarsene* 'go away': *e se ne va via* [02IT] 'and he goes away'; with Manner+Path verbs like *scappare* 'escape': *che scappa via* [04IT] 'that escapes (away)'; and even with *pure* Manner verbs such as *trascinare* 'drag': *e lo trascina via insieme al cagnolino* [12IT] 'and he drags him away close to the little dog'. Overall, it seems clear that there are intra-typological differences among Romance languages in the expression of Path.

10 Results: Causative constructions in Romance languages

Cause is a semantic component that is not normally analyzed in *The Frog Story* data. However, an intra-typological difference was found among the three Romance languages. The construction "MAKE + motion verb" is frequently used by Italian and French speakers, whilst it is not used at all by Spanish speakers.

Examples (187) to (190) show how this construction is productive in Italian and French.

(187) *Fa cadere il bambino e il cane giù da un dirupo su un lago* [03IT]
    make.PRS.3SG fall.INF the boy and the dog down from a cliff over a lake
    'Makes fall (throws) the boy and the dog down from a cliff to a lake'

(188) *E fa uscire delle api* [09IT]
    and make.PRS.3SG exit of.the bees
    'and makes that the bees go out'

(189) *Le cerf fait tomber le petit garçon dans l'eau* [06FR]
    the deer make.PRS.3SG the small boy in the.water
    'The deer makes fall (throw) the little boy to the water'

(190) *Le petit garçon se fait jeter par la fenêtre* [06FR]
    the small boy REFL make.PRS.3SG throw.INF through the window
    'The little boy gets himself thrown out of the window'

This construction is very productive in both Italian and French. However, it is not part of the rhetorical style of Spanish speakers, who express this movement with causative motion verbs such as *tirar* 'throw' (6 occurences), *lanzar* 'throw away' (2) and *dejar* 'leave' (1). Similarly, this construction is not present in German, and its speakers expressed caused motion with verbs such as *werfen* 'throw' (3), *schmeissen* 'throw' (3) and *lassen* 'leave' (1).

A closer look into Italian and French constructions shows how they are used in addition to cause motion verbs. Italian speakers use verbs such as *gettare* 'throw' (3) and *buttarsi* 'throw oneself' (1). They also used the construction with *fare* 'make' and motion verb in 8 cases, 7 as the combination *fare cadere* 'make fall' and 1 with *fare uscire* 'make exit'. French speakers use causative verbs like *jeter* 'throw' (4), *lâcher* 'throw away' (1) and *laisser* 'leave' (1). The causative construction with *faire* 'make' is used 14 times, 11 times in the combination *faire tomber* 'make fall', 1 with *faire bouger* 'make move' and in two cases, it is used with se: *se fait jeter* 'get oneself thrown' (1) and *se fait poursuivre* 'get oneself be chased' (1).

The use of these constructions shows an intra-typological difference among verb-framed Romance languages. This difference occurs in an unexpected aspect of motion, the expression of Cause, where Spanish shows a difference with the other two Romance languages.

11 Results: Event granularity

The analysis of event granularity analysis aims to examine complex events. Slobin designs this analysis using the *deer scene*, because it represents a journey or complex Path. This complex Path can be described by means of one or several sentences. With this analysis, Slobin aims to determine whether speakers of different types of languages mention the same number of segments (6 in Slobin 1997a, 4 in Slobin 1997b, both replicated here). In Slobin (1997a) a 75% of Spanish speakers mention three or more segments, whereas 100% of English speakers mention more than three.

Slobin segments the deer scene as follows: (a) the deer starts running; (b) the deer runs carrying the child; (c) the deer stops on the edge of the cliff; (d) the deer throws the child; (e) the child and the dog fall down; (f) the child and the dog land in water. These are the data obtained in this study:

Table 31: Event granularity. Deer scene in 6 segments in L1s.

	Speakers mention 3 or more	Percentage
Spanish	3	25%
Italian	3	25%
French	6	50%
German	7	58,33%

These data support previous findings in Slobin's research. Satellite-framed language speakers describe the complex event more, including more phases in their description. It is surprising though, that French does not follow the prototypical tendency of verb-framed languages: half the French participants mentioned three phases or more.

The other analysis consists of 4 segments instead of 6. These are: (a) change of location: the deer moves, runs, arrives at the cliff; (b) negative change of location: the deer stops at the cliff; (c) causative change of location: the deer throws boy (down); and (d) change of location: the boy and the dog fall to the ground. Slobin (1997b) performs the analysis with several languages on both sides of the typology and finds that satellite framed languages mention a mean of three segments, whilst verb-framed language speakers mention a mean of two. He concludes that speaking a satellite-framed language could predispose speakers to pay more attention to the different phases of the motion event. In the current research the results are as follows:

Table 32: Event granularity. Deer scene in 4 segments in L1s.

	Mean by speakers	Percentage
Spanish	2	41,67%
Italian	2,17	30%
French	2,33	50%
German	2,5	58,34%

These results are numerically lower than Slobin (1997b) in relation to the mean of segments mentioned. However, our data are consistent with Slobin's claims, as German has a higher mean and a higher proportion of speakers mentioning three or more segments of the journey. Half of French speakers mention three segments or more. In this sense it seems that the French speakers tend to segment more complex Paths, mentioning several segments. Finally, the Italian and Spanish speakers present the expected results for verb-framed languages.

12 Conclusions on the typological study

Both inter- and intra-typological differences were examined, revealing interesting results in both cases. This is particularly relevant for the intra-typological differences, as the languages in the studies are also genetically related, with Romance languages stemming from Latin. In the case of the Manner component of motion, the analysis has considered the proportion of Manner verbs used in relation to the total of motion verbs. There has also been an examination of the total Manner expression, namely the proportion of motion events that included any kind of Manner information, regardless of whether it was encoded within or without the verb, in a different element such as adverbs, adjectives or gerunds. The owl scene has been particularly scrutinized in order to see how speakers describe Manner in a scene in which this component is clear. Finally, the boundary-crossing constraint has been considered in the analysis.

The results obtained in relation to Manner enabled us to examine inter-typological differences, both in its encoding in the verb and in other elements. The German speakers presented significant differences from the other languages in the study, with a higher proportion of Manner in their narratives. This study thus supports previous research which indicates that speakers of satellite-framed languages pay more attention to Manner details and tend to encode this semantic component in their narratives. No intra-typological differences were found among Romance languages, which all tend to express Manner with less elaboration, which is also consistent with previous literature.

The analysis of Path description, however, revealed both inter- and intra-typological differences in the languages under study. First, the focus was on German satellites and its combinability with motion verbs, and on the use and combinability of Romance directional adverbs, particularly so for Italian. The frequent use of verb-particle constructions in Italian goes together with the greater detail in its description of Path. It is surprising to find this intra-typological difference, since the Italian participants not only presented more Plus Ground events, but even aligned with the German participants, with similar scores and no significant differences with the satellite-framed language neither in the analysis of the whole narrative, nor in the analysis of the falling scenes. By contrast, the Italian speakers did present statistical trends with Spanish and French in the data for the whole narrative, and even a significant difference with French in the falling scenes. This greater description of Path was also reflected in the use in Italian of several cases of motion events with more than one Ground. This was very different from the other two Romance languages in the study, which do not present a single occurrence of this type.

Therefore, the existence of verb-particle constructions in Italian seems to trigger differences with respect to French and Spanish in the elaboration of Path. Italians may encode more Manner when using these constructions, as Path is encoded in the particle, leading to intra-typological contrasts in relation to Manner. However, the intra-typological differences resulting from these verb-particle constructions seem to be limited to Path, not to Manner.

Previous literature considers French as a mixed-patterned language, due to the existence of Path prefixes. However, the results of the present study show that these prefixes do not seem to trigger any differences in relation to Spanish and Italian. Rather, the narratives of the French speakers seem to be prototypically verb-framed. The linguistic resources available to French speakers, namely directional adverbs or satellite prefixes (Kopecka 2004, 2006a) do not imply a greater description of Path. The existence of these linguistic resources in French (and which also exist in other Romance languages), is not questioned here, but their use does not seem to be frequent enough to consider the rhetorical style of French to be different to that of verb-framed languages. This is somewhat unexpected, as the presence of remains of Old French does not seem to have an impact on current states of the language, at least in relation to motion description. The traditional form of Slobin's analysis carried out in this study rejects the hypothesis that the French language is a hybrid system between verb-framed and satellite-framed languages. According to our results, French is clearly a verb-framed language.

Furthermore, this study has examined two aspects of *The Frog Story* that are not traditionally analyzed, namely Deixis and Cause. Deixis, a subcomponent of Path, seems to be a very relevant notion in the rhetorical style of German speakers. The German group showed high frequencies of use of deictic verbs and deictic particles *hin-* 'to there' and *her-* 'to here' in different satellital combinations. This might be an interesting intra-typological difference with other satellite-framed languages that is worth exploring in future research. In the case of Romance languages, Gathercole's (1977, 1978) classification of languages according to their deictic center has been useful in identifying an intra-typological difference between Spanish and the other two Romance languages. The speaker can be the only deictic centre in Spanish, and consequently venitive verbs were not used in *The Frog Story*, whilst they were used in Italian and French.

In the case of Cause, a specific construction has been identified as specific to French and Italian. This is the construction with *faire/fare* 'make' + motion verb that was not used by German and Spanish speakers. The relatively frequent use of this construction, mainly in combination with *cadere/tomber* 'fall' to indicate 'throw', reveals an unexpected intra-typological difference between Romance languages in the expression of Cause.

Unexpected results were also found in relation to Spanish geographical varieties, which revealed differences in relation to Path in the falling scenes. Although our participants from Aragón (Spain) had a prototypical description of Path in the whole narrative, in the falling scenes these speakers described Path prominently, with a very high proportion of Plus Ground events, to the extent that there was even a significant difference from the number of Path descriptions from the French speakers. In order to mitigate any bias in the data, the analysis of the falling scenes was repeated with data from other varieties of Spanish (Madrid and Argentina). In this second analysis the Spanish speakers aligned with the French speakers, with fewer cases of Plus Ground events. On the other hand, the German and the Italian speakers had more cases of Plus Ground. These results concerning geographical variation are consistent with those of previous studies (Ibarretxe-Antuñano and Hijazo-Gascón 2011, 2012), which found that speakers of northern dialects of Spanish, at least from Aragón and the Basque Country tended to describe Path in more detail, potentially due to current or historical contact with other languages, such as Basque and Aragonese.

Finally, the event granularity was also studied, through the deer scene, which enabled us to observe how speakers break down the event into different segments. German, as expected, segments the event most: each speaker mentions more segments than do speakers of the other languages, and a greater proportion of speakers mention three or more segments. In the case of verb-framed languages, speakers mention fewer segments. However, there are some differences: French speakers are more likely to express event granularity, which differs from how the speakers of Italian and Spanish describe this scene.

There are, therefore, important intra-typological differences that should not be overlooked in motion events typology. Italian showed a higher presence of Plus Ground events, with one and with several elements of Ground in the same event. Spanish presents geographical differences in relation to the expression of Path, and French shows a higher predisposition to describe different segments in complex Paths or journeys. These differences are even more surprising in the light of the fact that these languages also belong to the same linguistic family. The Italian intra-typological difference is of particular interest, as this may challenge its position in the typology as a high-Path salient language, in line with the Path cline put forward by Ibarretxe-Antuñano (2009).

These results are crucial for typology studies, as the general trend among typologists is to consider that two languages will behave in similar ways just because they have the same genetic origin. While this may be true in some cases, it remains very important not to make any overall assumptions and to have a closer look to check potential differences. The present study contributes to the field of motion events and thinking for speaking, in particular to the study of Path. As already seen in previous research (Ibarretxe-Antuñano 2004a, 2004b, 2009), Path is a compulsory component that can be expressed with different degrees. While previous studies placed too much emphasis on Manner when ascribing languages to the typology (e.g. Cardini (2008) on Manner in Italian), the present study demonstrates that focusing on Path is essential for a better understanding of motion in general.

It remains to be seen whether the participants in the study are aware of the extent to which all these inter- and intra-typological differences are the source of cross-linguistic influence. This is the focus of the following chapter.

Chapter 5
Acquisition study of motion events in L2 Spanish

1 Introduction

Most studies in motion event typology focus on the acquisition by verb-framed language speakers of a satellite-framed language. In this study, however, the target language is Spanish, a verb-framed language. Several studies on the acquisition of motion events have Spanish as the target language. However, the L1 of the Spanish learners in these studies tends to be a satellite-framed language, mainly English (e.g. Negueruela et al. 2004; Larrañaga et al. 2011; among others (see Chapter 2)) or Danish (Cadierno 2004; Cadierno and Ruiz 2006). There are no studies, to my knowledge, that focus on motion events by German learners of Spanish. One of the aims of the present study is the examination of intertypological differences between German and Spanish. In other words, the aim is to identify whether German learners produce cross-linguistic influence in their L2 Spanish in relation to how they encode Manner and Path.

Previous research on acquisition of motion events where L1 and the L2 belong to the same typological group is scarce, and has mainly focused on the satellite-framed group (see Chapter 2 for a revision). The study of the acquisition of Spanish by French and Italian speakers is, therefore, a novel and a relevant addition to the literature. By identifying relevant intra-typological differences, principally with regard to the components of Path and Cause, the previous chapter challenged previous assumptions. It was shown that the Romance languages are not completely alike, as Italians used more Path elements and both Italian and French had specific Cause constructions. One of the main aims in this chapter is to examine whether these differences impact on the acquisition of motion events by French and Italian learners with a B2 level of Spanish.

The present study is relevant from an SLA perspective because motion verbs are included in the early stages of the language teaching curriculum. Previous literature on different language pairs has shown mixed results with regard to how motion verbs are acquired, with some studies showing clear cross-linguistic influence from the first language, despite the frequency of motion events in any language. As Jarvis and Pavlenko (2008) suggest, motion is a domain prone to conceptual transfer from the L1 into the L2.

The traditional analysis of motion events with the *Frog story* is complemented with new analyses for boundary-crossing, deixis and caused motion constructions. In the case of Manner, the focus is on Manner verbs, Total Manner expression and the owl scene. The boundary-crossing component is also scrutinized with the analysis of the jar scene. I also study the component of Path with the analysis of Plus vs. Minus Ground in the whole narratives and the falling scenes. Deictic verbs and Causative constructions will be also analyzed. Finally, Slobin's event granularity will be also included.

The analysis of each of these components (e.g. Plus Ground, Manner verbs, etc.) will involve two different comparisons. First, I contrast the performance of groups of French, Italian and Germans in L2 Spanish and the control group. Second, each group's performance in L1 and L2 is compared. This allows us to follow the methodological framework put forward by Jarvis (2000, 2010) to find evidence of cross-linguistic evidence with methodological rigor. This methodology is also coherent with the multilingual turn proposed by Ortega (2013), because the comparisons are not exclusively drawn between learners and native speakers. The additional comparison of the production of three groups of learners with different L1 background is coherent with Ortega's (2013) suggestions for a multilingual approach to Second Language Acquisition.

The chapter will be structured following these different analyses. It is important to note that some of these analyses have been published in Hijazo-Gascón (2018), in particular those in relation to Manner, Plus Ground and Causative constructions. The data are reproduced in this book to show the full picture of the acquisition of L2 Spanish motion events. Some of these published data are explained here more in detail. The rest of the data are published for the first time in this book.

2 Research questions and hypotheses

The Research questions of the Acquisition Study are:
1. Do satellite-framed language speakers' narratives in L2 Spanish show conceptual transfer from their first language? If so, what semantic components will present conceptual transfer?

Hypothesis 1. Satellite-framed language speakers will present cases of conceptual transfer from their L1 into L2 Spanish. A more detailed account of the components of Manner and Path is expected.

2. Do verb-framed language speakers' narratives in L2 Spanish show conceptual transfer from their first language? If so, what semantic components will present conceptual transfer?

Hypothesis 2. Verb-framed language learners of Spanish will present conceptual transfer from their L1 into L2 Spanish. It is expected that the component of Path will present more conceptual transfer, given the different linguistic resources to encode Path in Spanish, Italian and French

3 Methodology

3.1 Methodology to identify cross-linguistic influence

One of the isues in cross-linguistic influence's methodology was the lack of unified criteria for researchers to apply. Before the work of Jarvis (2000, 2007, 2010), there was a lack of agreement on how to research transfer. As a consequence, the results of transfer studies were not always comparable, which made it very difficult to have a good understanding of this phenomenon. A consistent methodology was needed to consolidate studies on cross-linguistic influence as a research field. This situation has changed in recent years thanks to Jarvis' proposals (2000, 2007, 2010), which have prepared the basis for a rigorous methodology that has been widely accepted in the field.

Jarvis showed the incongruence that when revising literature on transfer, one could find contradictory conclusions regarding the effects of transfer in the acquisition process. He claimed that this is due to the lack of consistency in methodology, which makes these studies lack coherence among themselves and thus means their results are not comparable. While some authors focus on the interlanguage comparisons of groups of different L1s, others do on the comparison between interlanguage and L1 of the same group of speakers. These two types of comparisons should be taken into account when comparing studies and drawing conclusions. Jarvis also highlights the importance of carrying out empirical studies supported by statistical analysis. Jarvis (2000, 2010) claims that there are three possible effects of cross-linguistic influence and all three should be analysed to achieve rigour in research on this area:

Intragroup Homogeneity (within-group similarities). This effect is found when speakers of the same L1 behave in a uniform manner when using the L2. In other words, speakers with the same L1 under study should behave as a group with respect to the L2. It is important to note that similarities within a group of speakers who share the L1 can be provoked by general cognitive processes of acquisition or even by the characteristics of the second language. The occurrence of intra-group homogeneity per se does not rule out the possibility that the interlanguage performance is common to all learners of this L2 regardless of their L1.

Intergroup heterogeneity (between-group differences). In this case the effect is produced when comparing speakers who have the L2 in common but whose L1s are different. Evidence of transfer of the L1 can be proved when the outcome of the comparison is a divergence in the performance of both groups in the L2. Finding inter-group heterogeneity is a stronger argument for cross-linguistic evidence, as it rules out the possibility that the interlanguage behaviour is common to all learners. However, in some cases its presence may not be due to transfer, for example when the effects of the L1 coincide to produce the same behaviour in the interlanguage.

Cross-language congruity (between-language similarities). In this case the uses of speakers in the L2 are parallel. This comparison is important because it determines the relationship between the origin and the effects of cross-linguistic influence. It shows the phenomenon in the L1 that triggers the behaviour in the interlanguage. This effect is the most trustable proof of evidence but in some cases can also produce inaccurate interpretations. The performance in the L1 and the L2 may differ because learners tend to use the most prototypical and more general elements, but not necessarily because of transfer. It can also be the case that L1 and L2 discourse are perfectly congruent, but the behaviour in the interlanguage is not necessarily motivated by the L1.

Jarvis (2010: 175) adds a fourth type of effect that should be researched to improve the empirical rigor of his model. This is referred to as *intralingual contrast* (within language differences), i.e. the features of the target language used by learners. This emphasizes the differences in the learner's performance of features of the target language that vary with respect to how they correspond to features of the source language. Table 33 is included to clarify differences between the different types of evidence, the comparisons that they entail and their premises:

Table 33: The four types of evidence for cross-linguistic influence (Jarvis 2010: 182).

Evidence	Comparison	Premise	Combined premise
intragroup homogeneity	within-group	group-representative behaviour	group-based phenomenon
intergroup heterogeneity	between-group	group-specific behaviour	
cross-language congruity	between-language	source-like behaviour	source-based phenomenon
intralingual contrasts	within-language	source-stratified behaviour	

Jarvis (2000) argues that at least two of these effects should be identified in order to verify that the phenomenon under study is due to cross-linguistic influence. These four types of evidence are part of Jarvis' (2010) comparison-based approach to detect cross-linguistic influence.

This study on the acquisition of motion events on L2 Spanish follows Jarvis' (2000, 2010) methodological framework to identify cross-linguistic effects. Therefore, the analysis of each motion element will be done in two stages. First, the performance of the three groups of learners will be compared with a control group of native speakers of Spanish. This comparison will let us examine the intragroup homogeneity in the L1, i.e. to confirm that speakers of the same L1 group show similar patterns as a group in their performance in the L2. The second effect of cross-linguistic influence according to Jarvis is intergroup heterogeneity, that is, the comparison of the L2 speakers grouped by their L1, as the performance of learners with the same linguistic background tends to be similar. Comparing learners with different L1s supports the attribution of language production to L1 transfer.

The second stage of the analysis will compare the narratives produced by each group in their L1 and their L2. This analysis will allow us to check whether the patterns of performance in the L2 are similar to what the learners of Spanish do in their L1. This is the third factor in Jarvis's framework: cross-language congruity between the L1 and the interlanguage of the group. The last factor included in Jarvis (2010) is intralingual contrasts, which can be seen in this study in the performance of the control group and how this relates to the description of Spanish provided in chapters 2 and 3.

3.2 Experimental design, material for data elicitation and procedure

The experimental design is parallel to the typological study. Four groups of 12 speakers took part in the experiment. Participants were asked to narrate *The Frog story* to the researcher in Spanish, which was the second language for all, with the exception of the control group. The *Frog story*, a wordless picture booklet for children, has been mainly used for typological studies (see Section 4.3.1) but also for L2 acquisition studies (e.g. Cadierno 2004). The participants looked at the story twice, one in their L1 and one in the L2, with the readings taking place on two different days, separated by a completely free day in the middle. The data collection was balanced in order to avoid order effects, that is, half of the participants of each group did the task in L1 first and the other half in their L2 first.

3.3 Participants

The participants in this study were the same participants who took part in the study on typology in Chapter 4 –Section 3.4- for information on their socio-cultural characteristics-. There was some variability among them with regard to their age and sex, but these factors do not seem to be particularly relevant for the acquisition of motion events, with no effect in previous studies. The participants in the Spanish group were considered the control group for the acquisition study. As noted in Chapter 4, none of the Spanish speakers spoke other languages on a daily basis or considered themselves to be bilingual. Therefore, they can be considered functional monolinguals (A. Brown and Gullberg 2012). The participants who spoke Spanish as their L2 were living and studying in Spain at the time of data collection. They were speaking Spanish on a daily basis and it can be thus considered their stronger L2, although, as in most acquisition studies in which English is not the L1 or L2, the role of other languages (mainly English) cannot be completely ruled out. I will use L2 to refer to Spanish, regardless of the order of acquisition (it will be probably the L3 for most participants), assuming that it is the learners' strongest foreign language because of the immersion context.

The participants' proficiency in L2 Spanish is of course a crucial factor to take into account, and this needs to be checked for the validity of the study. All the participants in the experiment needed to have the same level of proficiency in Spanish, so that this factor can be ruled out as the potential cause of any differences between groups. Their proficiency was measured by two official examiners of the DELE exam (*Diploma de Español como Lengua Extranjera*) issued by the Instituto Cervantes.[9] They watched the recordings of the participants narrating *The Frog story* and were asked to assess the oral production skills of the participants. They determined that all of the participants that took part in the experiment had a B2 level of proficiency, according to the CEFRL and the *Plan Curricular del Instituto Cervantes* (PCIC), which maps the CEFRL levels on to the Spanish language.[10] The participants were assessed as being at a B2 level of proficiency in their oral production skills. Although it is not clear what their level was in other skills (like reading comprehension or writing), this is irrelevant to this research since the experiment is based exclusively on oral skills.

---

[9] These examiners were experienced Spanish teachers at the Instituto Cervantes in Warsaw and Moscow.
[10] The participants that had a lower or a higher level were taken out of the Study.

The CEFRL considers that language learners may have different levels in each language skill.

The assessment by two official examiners is particularly important because it allows us to establish a clear homogeneity in the level of Spanish of the learners. Their linguistic questionnaires showed different learning histories, however. For example, most of the French learners had been studying Spanish for a longer period of time, since they started learning Spanish in high school. Most of the German learners had been also studying Spanish for longer periods of time. In contrast, the Italian learners had been studying Spanish for a shorter period of time, but were more specialized, as most of them were studying Translation and Interpreting degrees. There were also individual differences with regard to the time spent in Spanish-speaking countries and/or contact with Spanish-speaking friends.

The B1-B2 levels of the CEFRL identify learners as *independent users*, in contrast with the A1-A2 (basic users) and C1-C2 (competent users). According to the CEFRL, B2 level language users:

> Can understand the main ideas of complex text on both concrete and abstract topics, including technical discussions in his/her field of specialization. Can interact with a degree of fluency and spontaneity that makes regular interaction with native speakers quite possible without strain for either party. Can produce clear, detailed text on a wide range of subjects and explain a viewpoint on a topical issue giving the advantages and disadvantages of various options (Council of Europe 2001: 24)

The CEFRL levels are general and need to be specified for each language. In the case of Spanish, the Instituto Cervantes defines the linguistic criteria to consider that a language user is at each of the levels in its Curricular Plan: *Plan Curricular del Insituto Cervantes* (PCIC) (Instituto Cervantes 2006), which states that B2 language users:

- Have the linguistic resources that are necessary to participate in communicative exchanges with a good degree of fluency, accuracy and naturalness, such that their interlocutors do not need to make a special effort in the exchange.
- Have a level of awareness of the language that enables them to avoid mistakes, and have enough resources to bridge ambiguities and identify the interlocutor's communicative intentions.
- Use a broad linguistic repertoire, enough to express themselves with arguments and nuance, without impeding errors and with clear pronunciation.
- Consider the effect of their interventions and adapt the register and level of formality to the situation and to their interlocutors.

- Have enough linguistic ability to face a problem, make a complaint and solve conflicts, by using their ability to argue in Spanish and use a persuasive language.

Therefore, our participants have a considerable level of proficiency.[11]

4 Transcription and coding

The transcription procedures were the same as specified in Chapter 4 for the study on typology. The CHILDES system (MacWhinney 1991) was used to create a corpus and tag the relevant linguistic elements, using the programme CLAN and the transcription norms CHAT (see Section 4.1. of Chapter 4). The codification for motion events followed the same principles as explained in the previous study, in order to compare the verbs used in the L1 and the L2 and between the L2 of the different learners' groups and the control group. Therefore, motion verbs were classified into six categories: Manner, Path, Manner+Path, Posture, Neutral and Other motion verbs.

In the case of the groups of learners, it is important to clarify the use of verbs that do not exist in the target language. Most of these verbs, such as *cribar* or *arrengarse*, were included under the category of "neutral verbs", to avoid assumptions about the speaker's intention. These verbs encode motion –given the context in which they are used- but it would be hard to attribute specific semantic components to them, as it is not clear what Spanish verb the learners wanted to use. There is only one case in which the meaning seemed clear enough, and this is *estoparse*, which is considered a lexical transfer from the French verb *stopper* 'stop'. This verb was classified into the category "other motion verbs" in order to be coherent with other verbs such as *pararse* 'stop'.

5 Analysis

The analysis follows the tradition of Slobin and colleagues research using *The Frog story* (Berman and Slobin 1994; Slobin 1996a; Strömqvist and Verhoeven 2004; for SLA see Cadierno 2004, among others, and her review of the field in Cadierno 2017). This analysis mainly focuses on the encoding of Manner and Path. The analyses on Manner include Manner verbs, Manner in the whole event and the use of

---

[11] See the CERFL and the PCIC for a detailed account of the descriptors for each level.

Manner in the owl scene. In the case of Path, as in the traditional studies, I examine the use of Minus and Plus Ground in the narratives and in the falling scenes. Slobin's analysis also includes event granularity, by using the deer scene.

To determine whether the cross-linguistic differences found among the four languages lead to cross-linguistic influence in the target language, these analyses are complemented in the current study with the study of boundary-crossing events, in particular in the jar scene, deictic motion verbs, and causative constructions, following the same methodology as in the study on typology in Chapter 4.

As mentioned above, in this study the comparisons are not exclusively drawn among the four groups of participants (control and three L1 language groups) but also within each group between their performance in the L1 and the L2. This will be done for each of the different aspects under study.

6 Statistical methods

The statistical methods used for the first step of the analysis, i.e. the inter-group comparisons, are the same as in the study in Chapter 4: the Kruskal-Wallis test to find significant differences between the four groups, and the Mann-Whitney test for significant differences between two groups. Both tests are non-parametric, due to the nature of the sample. As previously mentioned, the same statistical tests employed in the study on typology are used in this study, with the percentages being turned into angle values (radians).

In the second step of the analysis, for the comparison between L1 and L2 for each group, the Wilcoxon test is used, as we are dealing with related samples. The α levels are $p < .050$ for the Kruskal-Wallis and $p < .025$ for Mann-Whitney. The α level for the Wilcoxon test is $< .050$.

7 Results: Motion verbs

This section focuses on the types and tokens of the motion verbs used in the L2 learners' narratives. Motion verbs fall into different categories: Path, Manner, Manner+Path, Posture and other motion verbs. A full detailed classification of all the motion verbs used by all the groups can be found in Appendix II. The focus in this section is on the L2 Spanish motion verb used by the three groups of learners (see Section 7.1. of Chapter 4 for the motion verbs used by the control group).

A few methodological issues need to be taken into account. As in the case of the study on typology, pronominal verbs with *se* and non-pronominal verbs are counted as different types. The participants also used some incorrect pronominalizations, e.g. *huirse. These pronominalizations do not seem to be transfers from the L1 but overgeneralizations (R. Ellis 1994) of the use of *se* in Spanish, as will be seen below. An additional characteristic of learner language is the use of innovation and neologisms. Our participants used a few new motion verbs, which may have their origins in a lexical transfer from the L1 or from communicative and learning strategies. Most of these verbs have been considered neuter verbs, with the exception of *stopper* 'stop', as explained above. Both incorrect pronominalizations and new motion verbs are marked with an asterisk (*).

7.1 L1 Italian learners of L2 Spanish

The Italian learners of L2 Spanish used 37 types of motion verbs and 172 tokens. If we consider the pronominal verbs as the same verb, the number lowers to 31 types. This is a noticeable decrease from the L1 performance, when they used 60 types. These are the verbs used in Spanish:

Acercarse 'approach', *adelantar* 'overtake', *apoyarse* 'lean on', *caer* 'fall', *caerse* 'fall', *coger* 'take', *correr* 'run', *conducir* 'lead', *colgar* 'hang', *echar* 'throw', *encontrarse* 'find oneself', *escapar* 'escape', *escaparse* 'escape', *esconder* 'hide', *huir* 'flee', *huirse**, *incorporarse* 'sit/get up', *ir* 'go', *irse* 'go', *levantarse* 'get up', *llegar* 'arrive', *llevar* 'carry', *llevarse* 'carry', *pararse* 'stop', *perseguir* 'chase', *salir* 'exit', *salirse**, *saltar* 'jump', *seguir* 'follow', *subir* 'go up', *subirse* 'go up', *tirar* 'throw', *tomar* 'take', *traer* 'bring', *trepar* 'climb up', *volar* 'fly' and *volver* 'come back'.

There are cases of overuse of *se*. For example, *huirse*, a pronominalization of the verb *huir* 'run away', which does not correspond with the L2 nor with the L1 (**fuggirsi*). The sentence with this new pronominalization is (191):

(191) *Pero esa rana durante la noche se huyó* [05IT]
but this frog during the night CL flee.PST.3SG
'But this frog ran away during the night'

The pronominalization of *salirse* implies very specific uses, mainly with liquids with the meaning of 'burst' or 'leak', in cases such as *Se ha salido la leche del tazón*, literally 'he milk burst out of the mug', or in idioms like *salirse con la suya* 'get away with'. However, the pronominalizations in motion events are not correct, as in (192):

(192) *Cuando el búho se sale de su casita* [08IT]
when the owl CL exit.PRS.3SG from its house.DIM
'When the owl gets out of its little house'

This pronominalization is not acceptable in Italian either (*uscirsi). This fact, together with the excessive overgeneralizations in the other groups of learners leads us to conclude that these pronominalizations are not due to cross-linguistic influence from the L1.

7.2 L1 French learners of L2 Spanish

The French learners used a total of 47 types of motion verbs, corresponding to 209 tokens. When counting pronominal verbs as the same types, the number of types is 42. They used 53 types and 225 tokens in their L1. These are the verbs they used in Spanish:

Acercarse 'approach', *agitar* 'shake', *alejarse* 'walk away', *aparecer* 'turn up', *apoyarse* 'lean on', *andar* 'walk', *arrengarse**, *arrodillarse* 'kneel', *bajar* 'go down', *caer* 'fall', *caerse* 'fall', *cargar* 'load', *coger* 'take', *colgar* 'hang', *correr* 'run', *dejar* 'leave', *desaparecer* 'disappear', *echar* 'throw', *encontrarse* 'find oneself', *enderezarse* 'straighten up', *entrar* 'enter', *escaparse* 'escape', *estoparse**, *huir* 'flee', *huirse**, *ir* 'go', *irse* 'go', *lanzar* 'throw', *levantarse* 'get up', *llegar* 'arrive', *llevar* 'carry', *llevarse* 'carry', *marcharse* 'go away', *meterse* 'get into', *pararse* 'stop', *perseguir* 'chase', *ponerse* 'place oneself', *salir* 'exit', *saltar* 'jump', *seguir* 'follow', *sentar* 'sit down', *subir* 'go up', *subirse* 'go up', *tirar* 'throw', *tomar* 'take', *traer* 'bring', *trepar* 'climb up' and *volver* 'come back'.

A case of *huirse* 'flee' is found, exactly as in (191). In French there are two verbs: *fuir* and *s'enfuir*, but not **se fuir*. The example is presented in (193):

(193) *La rana se huye* [03FR]
       the frog CL flee.PRS.3SG
       'The frog runs away'

There are two new verbs coined by French learners, *arrengarse* and *estoparse* as seen in (194) and (195):

(194) *Se arrenga a una parte de un árbol, pero al final no es un árbol. . .* [04FR]
       CL arrengar.PRS.3SG to a part of a tree, but to.the end NEG be.PRS.3SG a tree
       'It *arrenga* to a part of the tree, but it is not a tree in the end'

(195) *[El ciervo] va a correr pero se estopa al extremo de la tierra* [04FR]
       [the deer] go.PRS.3SG to run but CL estopar.PRS.3SG to.the extreme of the ground
       '[The deer] is going to run but it stops at the edge of the land'

It is not completely clear what semantic components the learner would have wanted to include in (194), she could mean *climb, go up, hold*, etc. It was decided to consider this new verb as a neutral motion verb, to avoid biases and misinterpretations of the speakers' intention. In the case of (195) it seemed clear that the verb *estoparse* is a lexical transfer from L1 French verb *stopper* 'stop' (which of course is a borrowing from English *stop*).

7.3 L1 German learners of L2 Spanish

The German learners produced 46 types and 174 tokens of motion verbs in Spanish. If pronominal verbs are not counted apart, the total is 41 types. In the L1 they used 67 types and 213 tokens. These are the verbs used in L2 Spanish:

Acercarse 'approach', *acostarse* 'lie down (on bed)', *andar* 'walk', *aparecer* 'turn up', *arrodillarse* 'kneel', *caer* 'fall', *caerse* 'fall', *correr* 'run', *cribar**, *cambiar su posición* 'change one's position', *perder el equilibrio* 'lose one's balance', *darse un salto** 'make a jump, lit. give oneself a jump', *desaparecer* 'disappear', *dirigirse* 'lead', *encontrarse* 'find oneself', *escapar* 'escape', *escaparse* 'escape', *frenar* 'brake', *huir* 'flee', *huirse**, *ir* 'go', *irse* 'go', *levantarse* 'get up', *llegar* 'arrive', *llevar* 'carry', *llevarse* 'carry', *marcharse* 'go away', *montar* 'ride', *pararse* 'stop', *perseguir* 'chase', *ponerse* 'put oneself', *quitar* 'take from', *regresarse* 'come back', *salir* 'exit', *saltar* 'jump', *seguir* 'follow', *subir* 'go up', *sujetarse* 'hold on', *tirar* 'throw', *tomar* 'take', *traer* 'bring', *venir* 'come' and *volar* 'fly'.

There is an additional case of *huirse*:

(196) *Y que se ha huido* [01DE]
 and that CL have.PRS.3SG.AUX flee.PTCP
 'and that he has run away'

Other pronominalizations include *darse un salto 'jump', the correct use would be *dar un salto*:

(197) *El perro se da un salto de la ventana* [10DE]
 the dog CL give.PRS.3SG a jump from the window
 'The dog jumps from the window

There is also the case of *regresarse*, which is not marked as incorrect because it is a frequent pronominalization in some varieties of Latin American Spanish, but the narrative of this participant does not present any other Latin American features at lexical, pronunciation or syntactic level and she did not report having studied in any Latin American country. It seems plausible that the excessive use of *se* is an overgeneralization by learners of Spanish which might be due to general learning processes and not to cross-linguistic influence.

The word *cribar* is used in the narrative of one participant. Although *cribar* is a verb in Spanish, meaning 'winnow' or 'sieve', it was used as a motion verb. It was used in a context of 'climb' or 'ascend' –see (198)-, but it was considered a neutral verb to avoid bias, as in previous cases.

(198) *Y Lucas que antes había cribado a un árbol* [05DE]
 and Lucas that before have.IMP.3SG.AUX cribar.PTCP to a tree
 'and Lucas, that had *cribado* to a tree before'

Finally, the verb *quitar* 'remove' is used, and included in the category of other motion verb. However, its use does not seem to correspond to its Spanish meaning:

(199) *Y todas las abejas quitan del panal* [12DE]
 and all the bees remove.PRS.3SG from.the beehive
 'And all the bees leave the beehive'

It seems more coherent to interpret *quitar* as 'leave': it could be a case of lateral transfer from the speaker's L3 French *quitter* 'leave'.

7.4 Comparison of motion verbs

Table 34 shows a comparison of types and tokens across the three groups of learners and the Spanish control group, and also between the L1 and L2 of each group of learners. The uses in Spanish are shaded to allow both types of comparison.

Table 34: Types and tokens of motion verbs in L1s and L2 Spanish.

	Spanish (control)	Spanish L2 (IT)	Italian	Spanish L2 (FR)	French	Spanish L2 (DE)	German
Types	41	37	60	47	53	46	67
Tokens	193	172	210	209	225	174	213
Types (without pronominal distinction)	35	31	53	42	50	41	65

Some groups of learners produce even more types of motion verbs in L2 Spanish than native speakers, with the French speakers producing 47 and the Germans 46. The Italian learners produced fewer types of motion verbs in the L2: 37, which was very close to the number produced by the control group. This is unexpected as Italian and Spanish are very closely related languages, so it may have been thought that Italian learners would have a broader lexical range for their narratives. In any case, there were few differences among the groups with regard to verb types.

When comparing the number of motion verbs produced between L1 and L2 of each group, as expected we find fewer types in the L2. The German learners used 67 types in German but only 46 in Spanish. Similarly, the Italian speakers used 60 verb types in their L1 but only 37 in the L2. The results for the French speakers were more similar for both languages, with 53 types in the L1 and 47 in the Spanish L2. These differences between the native speakers and the groups of learners are expected, as the L1 is any speaker's dominant language and therefore lexical competence is higher.

A further comparison was made across the L2 groups, in terms of how motion verbs were classified. German and French learners present more motion verb types than did Italian learners and Spanish native speakers. However the differences in the number of verb types are not large. Types included are shown in Table 35, with occurrences shown in brackets.

Table 35: Types and tokens of motion verbs in L2 Spanish.

	L1 Spanish	L1 Italian	L1 French	L1 German
Neutral verbs	3 (22)	2 (23)	3 (37)	3 (30)
Path verbs	14 (64)	11 (54)	13 (52)	10 (37)
Manner+Path verbs	8 (70)	10 (55)	10 (75)	9 (62)
Manner verbs	7 (11)	4 (9)	5 (10)	8 (14)
Posture verbs	3 (6)	4 (10)	6 (9)	6 (7)
Other motion verbs	6 (19)	6 (21)	10 (26)	11 (24)
Total	41 (193)	37 (172)	47 (209)	46 (174)

8 Results: Manner

This section uses different analyses to focus on the semantic component of Manner. First, I examine Manner verbs and the total expression of Manner, i.e. the expression of Manner within and without the verb, and the owl scene. Finally, I also analyze boundary-crossing events with a particular focus on the jar scene. In all these cases, first, learners' narratives are compared with those of the native speaker control group. Then, each group's narratives are compared in terms of what they produced in their L1 and L2.

8.1 Manner verbs

Table 36 shows the Manner verbs[12] used for the speakers in each of the groups and the percentage with regard to the total number of motion verbs used.

Table 36: Manner verbs in L2 Spanish.

	Manner verbs types	Manner verb tokens	Mean types per speaker	Mean tokens per speaker	Percentage of Manner verbs
L1 Spanish (control)	7	11	0.58	0,92	5.64%
L1 Italian	4	9	0.33	0,75	5.23%
L1 French	5	10	0.42	0,83	4.78%
L1 German	8	14	0.66	1,17	8.05%

The group of German learners presented the highest proportion of Manner verbs in relation to the total of motion verbs, even though they were relaying the narrative in their L2. This is particularly relevant because Spanish does not seem to favor the expression of Manner and has a more restricted Manner verb lexicon than German (see Chapter 3). They also present more types of Manner verbs (8) than the other groups of learners (5 used by French and 4 by Italians), and hence were closer to the Spanish control group, who produced 7 types of motion verbs. This pattern is also shown in the tokens, with the German learners using Manner verbs 14 times in Spanish, followed by the native speakers (11), French learners (10) and Italian learners (9).

---

[12] As in the study on typology, Manner+Path verbs are not included in this analysis nor in the Total Manner Expression. This was a methodological decision, because previous studies have not taken these verbs into account for the analysis of Manner. In any case, the frequencies of Manner+Path verbs among the different groups seem similar, so it is likely that their inclusion in the analysis would not imply major changes in the results.

The participants in the control group used the following verbs (tokens in brackets): *correr* 'run' (5), *lanzarse* 'throw oneself' (1), *empujar* 'push' (1), *pasear* 'stroll' (1), *pegar un salto* 'jump' (1), *saltar* 'jump' (1) and *tropezarse* 'trip' (1). Italian learners used: *correr* 'run' (4), *saltar* 'jump' (2), *volar* 'fly' (2) and *conducir* 'lead' (1). French learners mentioned *correr* 'run' (6), *agitar* 'shake' (1), *andar* 'walk' (1), *cargar* 'load' (1) and *saltar* 'jump' (1). German learners used *correr* 'run' (6), *volar* 'fly' (3), *saltar* 'jump' (2), *andar* 'walk' (1), *darse un salto* 'jump' (1) and *montar* 'ride' (1).

The Kruskal-Wallis test shows no significant differences among the four groups ($p = .649$). Table 37 shows the descriptive statistics and the boxplot in Figure 21 shows clearly that the data are very similar for the four groups.

Table 37: Descriptive statistics for Manner verbs in L2 Spanish.

Group	Mean	N	SD	Range
L1 Spanish	.1667	12	.15453	.42
L1 Italian	.1158	12	.17333	.39
L1 French	.1400	12	.14740	.32
L1 German	.2042	12	.19280	.48
Total	.1567	48	.16584	.48

For the second phase of the analysis, I compared the narratives in the L1 and the L2 for each of the groups of learners. As mentioned, because the comparison is between the production of the same speakers, the Wilcoxon statistical test was used. The Italian participants did not show significant differences in how they expressed Manner in their L1 and L2 ($p = .161$), and nor did the French ($p = .593$). In other words, the proportion of Manner that Romance participants used in their narratives is similar in their L1 and L2. This result is unsurprising, because, in the typological study, none of the Romance languages showed significant differences from Spanish in relation to Manner verbs. However, the data reveal significant differences in the behavior of the German group between their L1 and L2 ($p = .002$). They have adapted to reduce the proportion of Manner verbs in line with the rhetorical style of Romance languages. This result is also consistent with the typological restrictions that Spanish imposes on those learners, as it offers fewer Manner verbs than their L1.

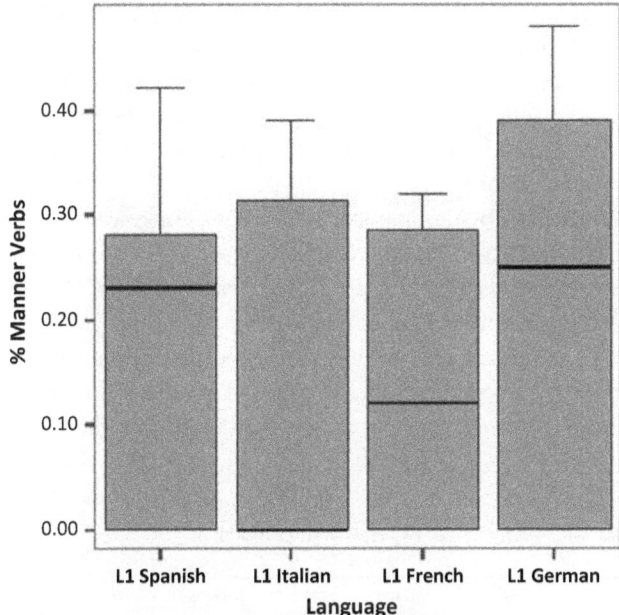

Figure 21: Percentage of Manner verbs in L2 Spanish.

8.2 Total Manner expression

In this analysis, any linguistic element that encodes Manner is included. Therefore, it not only focuses on Manner verbs, as in the previous section, but also on adverbs, gerunds, prepositional phrases and other elements indicating Manner. The purpose of this analysis is to examine whether learners compensate for the scarcity of Manner verbs in Spanish, by expressing Manner with other elements. The German data are of particular interest, since in the typological study they presented significant differences with the other groups in this respect.

The linguistic elements used by the control group to encode Manner outside the verb were the following adjective phrases: *asustado* 'frightened' (3), *cabreado* 'pissed off' (1), *camuflado* 'camouflaged' (1), *grande* 'big' (1), *muy asustado* 'very frightened' (1), *preocupado* 'worried' (1) and *todo contento* 'super happy' (1); the adverbial phrase *perfectamente* 'perfectly' (1); prepositional phrases *de cabeza* 'head first' (1) and *de repente* 'suddenly' (1); participles *enganchado* 'hooked' (1) and *montado* 'ridden' (1) and gerunds such *corriendo* 'running' (3), *correteando* 'running around' (3) and *volando* 'flying' (1).

In the case of Italian speakers, they used the adjectival phrase: *enfadadas* 'angry' (1); the adverbial phrase *boca abajo* 'face down' (2); prepositional phrases *de repente* 'suddenly' (3) and *en brazos* 'in arms' (1); participles *atrapado* 'trapped' (1) and *encerrado* 'enclosed' (1) and gerunds: *corriendo* 'running' (3) and *saltando* 'jumping' (1). French learners expressed Manner with adjective phrases such as *bloqueado* 'blocked' (1) and *quieto* 'still' (1); the prepositional phrase *en brazos* 'in arms' (1); the participle *encerrada* 'enclosed' (1) and gerunds such as *corriendo* 'running' (3) and *enganchando* 'hooked' (1).

The linguistic resources used by German learners of L2 Spanish were adjective phrases such as *muy felices* 'very happy' (1); the adverbial phrase *así* 'so' (1); prepositional phrases *de repente* 'suddenly' (7), *en silencio* 'quitely' (1), *por la cabeza* 'headfirst' (1) and gerunds such as *corriendo* 'running' (3).

The statistical tests reveal that none of the groups of learners produce significantly more Manner than the control group (or than one another). No significant differences were found between the three groups of learners and the group of native speakers ($p = .159$).

Table 38: Descriptive statistics for Total Manner Expression in L2 Spanish.

Group	Mean	N	SD	Range
L1 Spanish	.3392	12	.22809	.64
L1 Italian	.2542	12	.20514	.54
L1 French	.2167	12	.17495	.50
L1 German	.3667	12	.16653	.62
Total	.2942	48	.19870	.64

The Wilcoxon test produces similar results for the within-group comparison in speakers' L1 and L2. The Italian learners did not present significant differences in the use of Manner in either language ($p = .239$), nor did French learners ($p = .147$). However, a significant difference was again found for German learners ($p = .002$), who seem to adapt their thinking for speaking to the L2 and reduce the proportion of Manner elements.

8.3 The owl scene

The owl scene is part of the traditional analysis of *The Frog story* to determine whether participants describe the motion event of the owl flying out of the tree with some encoding of motion. As seen in the previous chapter, verb-framed language speakers do not tend to express Manner in this scene, and prefer Path

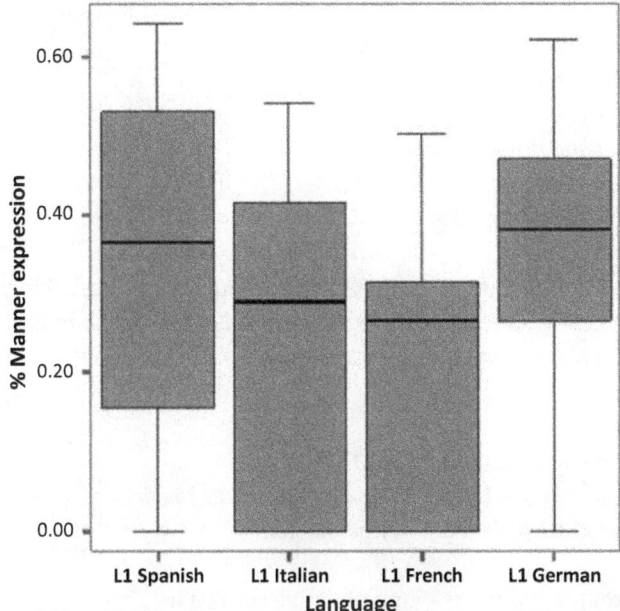

Figure 22: Percentage of Total Manner Expression in L2 Spanish.

verbs such as *exit*. However, satellite-framed languages do express Manner and use *fly* or similar verbs. Since the narrative of *The Frog Story* is a free task, not all the participants describe this event.

None of the L2 Spanish learners used a Manner verb in the description of the scene. The Italian learners used *salir* 'exit' (7), the French learners opted for *salir* 'exit' (6) and *aparecer* 'turn up' (1), and the German learners used *salir* 'exit' (2) and *aparecer* 'turn up' (2). It is worth remembering that native speakers only used *salir* 'exit' (5).

8.4 The boundary-crossing constraint

The boundary-crossing constraint is part of the rhetorical style of verb-framed languages. In the typological study, inter-typological differences were found between German and the Romance languages. The question posed in this section is whether these differences led to cross-linguistic influence. A first look into the use of Manner verbs to express a boundary-crossing in the narratives showed just three cases in which the learners used a Manner verb in combination with a ground. German learners produced two cases:

(200) *Y el perrito salta de la ventana* [03DE]
and the dog.DIM jump.PRS.3SG of the window
'And the little dog jumps out of the window'

(201) *El perro se da un salto de la ventana* [10DE]
the dog CL give.PRS.3SG a jump of the window
'The dog jumps from the window'

However, both cases are ambiguous, since they can be interpreted as describing the event with the movement starting at the window and not inside the house. There was an additional Manner verb used in a boundary-crossing situation by a French learner:

(202) *A ver si la rana no ha saltado dentro* [2001FR]
to see whether the frog NEG have.PRS.3SG.AUX jump.PTCP inside
'Let's see whether the frog has not jumped inside'

This case is similar to that found in the group of native speakers:

(203) *Entonces el chico salta por la ventana* [09ES]
then the boy jump.PRS.3SG by the window
'Then the boy jumps through the window'

These examples are in line with the instances of boundary-crossing that Slobin found in verb-framed languages, namely that boundary-crossing events with a Manner verb potentially occur only when the movement is sudden and fast.

As in the typological study, the "jar scene" was analyzed to see how participants described a motion event that necessarily implies the crossing of a boundary. The event in question shows how the frog gets out of the jar at the beginning of the story. The *Frog story* is a free task, so not every participant described this event; in the case of the learners, some participants described it twice because they adjust their production. This is why the total number of events was not always twelve. The results are presented in Tables 39 and 40.

Comparing the three groups of learners and the control group, it is interesting that there are no cases of Manner verb nor of Manner complements with other types of verb, which seems a clear adjustment to the L2 rhetorical style. Most Spanish and French learners used a Manner+Path verb (like *escapar* 'flee') without Ground, which means that no boundary-crossing event was mentioned. The Italian learners used this option as often as they used the Manner+Path verb with a Ground, while the German learners demonstrated a clear preference

Table 39: Boundary-crossing tokens in the jar scene.

	MN verb + Ground	MN+P verb + Ground	MN+P verb + Mn	MN+P verb	P verb + Ground	N + Ground	N verb
Spanish NS	0	3	0	7	1	0	0
L1 Italian	0	4	0	4	2	1	0
L1 French	0	4	0	5	2	0	2
L1 German	0	4	0	1	4	3	0

Table 40: Percentages Boundary-crossing in the jar scene.

	MN verb + Ground	MN+P verb + Ground	Mn+P + Mn	MN+P verb	P verb + Ground	N + Ground	N verb
Spanish NS	0,00	25,00	0,00	58,33	8,33	0,00	0,00
L1 Italian	0,00	36,36	0,00	36,36	18,18	9,09	0,00
L1 French	0,00	30,77	0,00	38,46	15,38	0,00	15,38
L1 German	0,00	33,33	0,00	8,33	33,33	25,00	0,00

to include a Ground to describe this motion event, either with a Manner+Path verb (33.33%), with just a Path verb (33.33%) or with a neutral verb (25%). Only one German speaker described the event without a Ground. An interesting finding is that all groups of learners included descriptions with a neutral verb, with or without Ground, generally *ir* or *irse* 'go'. This seems to be a general learning or communicative strategy, because these verbs were not used either by Spanish native speakers to describe this motion event, nor in the narratives in L1 French, German and Italian. The high frequency of neutral verbs in the three groups of learners points towards a more general learning or communicative strategy or simplification. In other words, by using neutral verbs, they can communicate the basic meaning without making mistakes at the risk of not being completely accurate. Table 41 with the results of the L1 typological study is reproduced here for comparison of the jar scene description between the L1 and the L2 in each group.

A comparison between the performance of each group in their L1 and L2 shows interesting results. The French learners maintained their L1 lexicalization pattern, as it works for them since it is shared with the L2. The Italian learners showed an increase in the Manner+Path verb without Ground (as did the French learners and the native speakers), but the frequency with which they encoded

Table 41: Percentages of the boundary-crossing in L1s.

	MN verb + Ground	MN+P verb + Ground	MN+P + Mn	MN+P verb	P verb + Ground	P verb + Mn	P verb	Other
Spanish	0,00	25,00	0,00	58,33	8,33	0,00	0,00	0,00
Italian	0,00	50,00	0,00	8,33	33,33	0,00	0,00	8,33
French	0,00	25,00	8,33	33,33	8,33	8,33	8,33	8,33
German	58,33	25,00	0,00	0,00	8,33	0,00	0,00	8,33

Manner+Path verbs with a Ground remained unchanged. It may be thought that the increase of Minus Ground by both French and Italian speakers is a simplification strategy, as a Minus Ground event means a reduction of words in this event. However, this does not seem the case because the German learners did use a ground element in the vast majority of cases. They changed the type of verb to adjust to the rhetorical style of the L2. In their L1 they mainly used Manner verbs, as is prototypical for a satellite-framed language, and they changed to Manner+Path verbs in the L2. Overall it seems that there is some cross-linguistic influence from the L1 in the jar scene, but also some readjustment or re-thinking for speaking. As in other aspects of motion, the French learners' L1 shares many characteristics with Spanish, so they did not need to adjust much. In the case of Italians, they seem to retain some tendency to use the ground with a Manner+Path verb, although they started adapting and changed from the L1 to the L2, using Plus and Minus ground with equal frequency as Manner+Path verbs. Finally, German speakers adapted the type of verb for this event, while none of them used a Manner verb, which is the preferred pattern in the L1. However, they kept their L1 preference for Plus Ground, with the vast majority of the participants using a Plus Ground event.

9 Results: Path

In this section, several aspects about Path will be examined. The first is the finding of satellizations in L2 Spanish. This is followed by analysis of Minus and Plus Ground, for both the whole narratives and for the falling scenes. A final subsection on deixis sheds light on how the different deictic patterns are acquired by learners of L2 Spanish.

9.1 Satellizations in L2 Spanish

Spanish tends to be considered as the prototypical verb-framed language, and as such, it lacks the category of satellites like *out* or *up* (see chapters 2 and 3 on this issue). What is more, Spanish does not even have the pseudo-satellites that were identified in Chapter 4 for Italian, like *via* 'away'. The closest Spanish constructions to pseudo-satellites are the combinations of motion verb with directional adverb, but their uses are pleonastic and infrequent. The results of the study on typology raise the question as to whether German and Italian learners will transfer the satellites and pseudo-satellites from their L1 by using Spanish directional adverbs as satellites. This is a phenomenon identified by Cadierno (2004: 29–30) in Danish learners of Spanish:

(204) *Entonces el perro saltó afuera de la ventana*
then the dog jump.PST.3SG out of the window
'Then the dog jumped out of the window'

(205) *El ciervo mueve al niño y a su perro abajo en un precipicio*
the deer move.PRS.3SG to.the child and to his dog down in a cliff
'The deer moves the child and his dog down in a cliff'

(206) *Cuando el chico intenta irse arriba de algunos árboles*
when the boy try.PRS.3SG go up of some trees
'When the boy tries to go up of some trees'

Cadierno shows more examples in her corpus and considers that Danish learners might be unconsciously transferring their L1 lexicalization pattern from their L1, with the component of Path outside of the verb, as in (204). She also suggests the possibility of communicative transfer (R. Ellis 1994), that is, the use of transfer as communicative strategy to express a word that they do not know and decide consciously to use a directional or neutral motion verb in combination with a directional adverb as in (205) and (206). The semantic and combinatory characteristics of Spanish directional adverbs in (204)-(206) are very different from those of satellites. However, these are the closest elements to satellites one can find in Spanish. This is the reason why Cadierno (2008a: 261) coins the term *satellization* for these constructions in Spanish.

There are very few cases of satellizations in our data in comparison with Cadierno (2004), with just a few constructions consisting of a motion verb and a directional adverb that do not correspond to the target language. A German learner produced the following:

(207) *El ciervo no puede correr más adelante* [12DE]
 the deer NEG can.PRS.3SG run.INF more forward
 'The deer cannot run further'

This could be a satellization, with *adelante* 'forward' as a satellite, but it is not as clear as the cases found in Cadierno (2004). It is unlikely that (207) can be considered a communication transfer because the learner has already found the appropriate verb, and it is also difficult to consider as a satellite an element that is modified with *más* 'more'.

There two cases consisting of just a motion verb and a prepositional phrase (without a directional adverb) like (208) and (209) that could seem similar to satellizations. However, these cannot be considered satellizations because one of the main differences in Talmy's framework is the difference between preposition and satellite.

(208) *Su próxima idea era ir a una piedra* [DE]
 his next idea be.IMP.3SG go.INF to a stone
 'His next idea was to go to a stone'

(209) *E intenta ir sobre la piedra* [08IT]
 and try.PRS.3SG go.INF over the stone
 'And he tries to go on the stone'

There are other constructions produced exclusively by Italian learners that do not adapt to the rhetorical style of the target language, yet which are easy to understand:

(210) *El niño comenzó a ir lejos de su casa* [09IT]
 the child start.PST.3SG to go.INF far from his house
 'The child started to go far from his house'

(211) *Lo deja dentro de un lago* [11IT]
 it leave.PRS.3SG inside of a lake
 '[He] leaves it inside of a lake'

These cases might be considered as satellizations, as they are similar to those of the Danish learners reported in Cadierno (2004), although *lejos* and *dentro* are quite different to satellites like *down* or pseudo-satellites like *via* 'away'. More satellizations were expected but the data do not reveal any more. This result might be due to the speaker's level of proficiency in L2 Spanish or to the psychotypology, i.e. the perceived distance might have prevented learners from transferring these elements to their L2. We will discuss this issue further when the full picture emerges of Path expression in the L2 narratives.

9.2 Minus vs. Plus Ground in the whole narratives

This analysis uses Ground-encoding complements to determine the expression of Path. Slobin considers as Minus Ground those events which lack any Ground element, as in (212):

(212) *Finalmente el panal cae* [07FR]
finally the beehive fall.PRS.3SG
'Finally the beehive falls'

Plus Ground events, on the other hand, include a main verb with some element that encodes Ground. This Ground element can encode the source, the medium or the goal of the movement, as in (213), where *del árbol* 'from the tree' encodes the source of the movement:

(213) *y se cae del árbol* [04FR]
and CL fall.PRS.3SG from.the tree
'and [it] falls from the tree'

First, the proportion of Plus Ground events in the whole narrative will be examined. This analysis sheds light on the expression of Path in the participants' free task:

Table 42: Minus and Plus Ground in L2 Spanish.

	Tokens Minus Ground	Mean Minus Ground per speaker	% Minus Ground	Tokens Plus Ground	Mean Plus Ground per speaker	% Plus Ground
L1 Spanish (control)	94	7.92	48.78%	99	8.33	51.28%
L1 Italian	70	5.92	41.04%	102	8.5	58.96%
L1 French	115	9.58	55.02%	94	7.83	44.98%
L1 German	62	5.17	35.84%	112	9.25	64.16%

The German learners expressed more Plus Ground events, and therefore, more expression of Path, with a 64.16% of motion events including at least one element about Ground. They were followed by the Italian group with a 58.96%, and by the control group with a 51.28%. Native speakers had balanced proportions of Minus and Plus Ground. Finally, the group of French learners showed a 44.98% of Plus Ground. They were therefore the only group that presented a preference for Minus Ground clauses. In the same vein, the mean of Plus Ground events per student was higher in German learners (9.25), and lower in the Romance languages: Italian learners (8.5), native speakers (8.33) and French learners (7.83). The descriptive statistics are presented in Table 43.

The final inferential results –after the removal of outliers- are presented in Figure 23. The Kruskal-Wallis test found a significant difference p = .016 among the four groups. The Mann-Whitney test showed a statistical trend in the expression of Path between the control group of native speakers and the German learners (p = .027), whilst the Italian and French speakers did not show significant differences from the Spanish native speakers (Spanish control-Italian learners p = .260; Spanish control-French learners p = .316). These results point to a cross-linguistic influence of the German speakers in their L2. Interestingly, this is confirmed by the significant difference found between German learners and the French learners (p = .007). It is also very interesting to see that the German learners did not present significant differences (p = .291) with the Italian learners. The results of the Italian learners are especially noteworthy, since they did not present significant differences in the expression of Path either with the Spanish native speakers or with the German learners, but they did with French learners (p = .024).

Table 43: Descriptive statistics Plus Ground.

Group	Mean	N	SD	Range
L1 Spanish (control)	.7908	12	.11603	.45
L1 Italian	.8950	12	.16605	.55
L1 French	.7467	12	.12003	.44
L1 German	.9583	12	.23151	.77
Total	.8477	48	.18069	.77

It can be concluded from the above analysis of the expression of Path that intertypological differences were present in the L2 of the groups of learners. The German learners expressed Path more than the other groups, even when they were speaking in their L2 Spanish. The case of the Italian learners is of particular

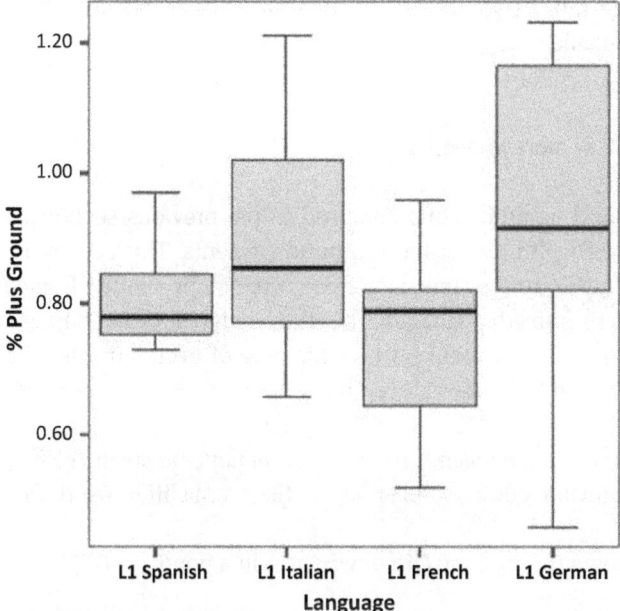

Figure 23: Percentage Plus Ground in L2.

interest, as they presented a significant difference with the French learners but not with the German learners. This means that they retained their L1 tendency to express Path in their L2. They did not present a significant difference with the native speakers group. This can be interpreted as an adjustment to the thinking for speaking of the L2. Evidence of cross-linguistic influence is the fact that there are significant differences in the expression of Path between the Italian and French learners, despite the rhetorical style of their L1s being coherent with that of the Spanish L2. In other words, this is a clear case of inter-group heterogeneity in the learners' Spanish.

The final confirmation of cross-linguistic evidence in the L2 production is found when comparing the L1 and the L2 in the groups of learners. The Wilcoxon tests revealed no significant differences between the narratives of the German and French speakers in the L1 and the L2 (p = .638 for both groups). Therefore, they followed the pattern of their L1 in how they expressed Path when they narrated in the L2, which is why they presented a statistical trend very close to the alpha level with the native speakers. The Italian learners presented a statistical trend (p = .110) between the L1 and L2. It seems that they were in the process of adapting their L2 thinking for speaking to the L2. They showed some features of the L1, such as a higher frequency of Path, but they were adapting to the narrative style in the L2. This shows that their thinking for speaking pattern is dynamic.

9.3 Plus Ground with 2 or more elements

Some of the Plus Ground motion events analyzed in the previous section include a main motion verb with two or more Ground elements. This section focuses on this type of Plus Gournd events, which are common in satellite-framed languages but not in verb-framed languages. The study on typology in Chapter 4 showed that German and Italian speakers use this type of events in their L1, with examples like (212) and (213), reproduced here:

(214) *Und die beiden nach unten fielen. . . den Abrund hinunter in einen Teich*
and the.PL both towards down fall.PST.3PL. . . the.ACC.M cliff down.thither in a.ACC.M pond
'And both fell down through the cliff down there in a pond' [08DE]

(215) *Fa cadere il bambino e il cane giù da un dirupo su un lago* [03IT]
make.PRS.3SG fall.INF the child and the dog down from a cliff over a lake
'[He] makes the boy and the dog fall down from a cliff to a lake'

None of the Spanish native speakers in our data produced any of this type of motion event. It is possible to have motion events with two Plus Ground elements, and some cases have been found in Sebastián and Slobin (1994), Slobin (1996a), Ibarretxe-Antuñano and Hijazo-Gascón (2011, 2012), but they are extremely infrequent. Spanish speakers tend to infer Path trajectories, as this component is mainly encoded in the verb. In the narratives in L2 Spanish there are some cases of Plus Ground with more than one element, produced by German learners:

(216) *Y cae en el suelo de la ventana* [08DE]
and fall.PRS.3SG in the ground from the window
'And [he] falls to the ground from the window'

(217) *Y el perro cayó de la ventana al jardín* [11DE]
and the dog fall.PST.3SG from the window to the garden
'And the dog fell from the window to the garden'

And by Italian learners:

(218) *Y se cae desde una pequeña montaña dentro de un lago* [01IT]
 and CL fall.PRS.3SG from a little mountain inside of a lake
 'And [it] falls from a small mountain inside of a lake'

(219) *Y lo lleva desde la roca a un despeñadero* [02IT]
 and him take.PRS.3SG from the rock to a precipice
 'And [the deer] takes him from the rock to a precipice'

(220) *Y el niño y el perro cayeron del barranco hasta dentro de un río* [09IT]
 and the child and the dog fall.PST.3PL from the cliff until inside of a river
 'And the child and the dog fell from the cliff to inside of a river'

A statistical trend is found among the four groups (Kruskal-Wallis, $p = .116$). There are very few cases so the numerical difference is interesting in itself, mainly because there are no cases produced by Spanish native speakers and French learners. Therefore it is very relevant that although this type of events are not frequent in Spanish, the German and the Italian learners presented 2 and 3 cases respectively in L2 Spanish, which is less than in their L1. The Wilcoxon test does not show significant differences for any group. Italian learners do not show significant differences between the L1 and L2 ($p = .326$) and Germans ($p = .237$). It seems that there is cross-linguistic influence in this aspect of motion.

9.4 Minus vs. Plus Ground in the falling scenes

The analysis of Minus and Plus Ground was also applied to the so-called falling scenes, to examine the expression of Path in specific scenes where this component is particularly salient. These are the scenes of the dog, the beehive, the boy and the deer. In all of them, a Figure falls (see the pictures in section in Chapter 4, Section 9.4). These are particularly relevant motion events and participants tend to describe it, especially the deer scene. However, as was the case with the owl scene these events were not necessarily described by all the speakers and the total numbers are not necessarily twelve events per group.

9.4.1 The dog scene

In this scene, the dog falls from the window to the ground. These are the data in L2 Spanish:

Table 44: The dog scene in L2 Spanish.

	Total	Minus Ground	Plus Ground	1 Ground	More than 1 Ground	% Minus Ground	% Plus Ground
Spanish (control)	9	2	7	7	0	22.22%	77.78%
L1 Italian	6	1	5	5	0	16.67%	83.33%
L1 French	12	5	7	7	0	41.67%	58.33%
L1 German	11	2	9	7	2	18.18%	81.81%

Again, the Italian and the German learners presented more description of Path, as in the analysis of Minus vs. Plus Ground for the complete story.

9.4.2 The beehive scene

These are the data for the scene where the beehive falls to the ground:

Table 45: The beehive scene in L2 Spanish.

	Total	Minus Ground	Plus Ground	1 Ground	More than 1 Ground	% Minus Ground	% Plus Ground
Spanish (control)	5	4	1	1	0	80%	20%
L1 Italian	4	2	2	2	0	50%	50%
L1 French	7	6	1	1	0	85.71%	14.29%
L1 German	6	2	4	4	0	33.33%	66.67%

The German and the Italian learners presented more Plus Ground, although in the case of Italian it is 50%. Both native speakers and French learners showed in this scene more Minus Ground than Plus Ground.

9.4.3 The boy scene

This is the same scene as the owl scene, but the analysis here focuses on how the speakers described the boy falling from the tree to the ground. These are the data:

Table 46: The boy scene in L2 Spanish.

	Total	Minus Ground	Plus Ground	1 Ground	More than 1 Ground	% Minus Ground	% Plus Ground
Spanish (control)	5	3	2	2	0	60%	40%
L1 Italian	3	0	3	3	0	0%	100%
L1 French	5	2	3	3	0	40%	60%
L1 German	7	1	6	6	0	14.29%	85.71%

In all cases, the Italian learners included a Ground element. Together with the German learners, the Italians again presented the highest percentages of Plus Ground.

9.4.4 The deer scene

The last *falling scene* shows how the deer has the boy on his antlers, starts running, stops and the boy and the dog fall into a pond. This is the most complex scene in the booklet and it tends to be described by practically all participants, as it is a crucial motion event in the plot. The results are as follows:

Table 47: The deer scene in L2 Spanish.

	Total	Minus Ground	Plus Ground	1 Ground	More than 1 Ground	% Minus Ground	% Plus Ground
Spanish (control)	21	0	21	21	0	0%	100%
L1 Italian	16	3	13	11	2	18.75%	81.25%
L1 French	26	9	17	17	0	34.62%	65.38%
L1 German	14	0	14	14	0	0%	100%

In this case, all the Spanish native participants presented all motion events with a Ground, and the German learners did the same. The Italians presented a very high percentage of Plus Ground (81.25%), whilst the French learners presented a more moderate percentage of 65.38%. Only the Italian learners produced utterances with more than one Ground element in this scene.

9.4.5 Total falling scenes

To sum up, these are the results for Minus and Plus Ground for all the falling scenes.

Table 48: Total results from the falling scenes in L2 Spanish.

	Total	Minus Ground	Plus Ground	1 Ground	More than 1 Ground	% Minus Ground	% Plus Ground
Spanish (control)	40	9	31	31	0	22.5%	77.5%
L1 Italian	29	6	23	21	2	20.69%	79.31%
L1 French	50	22	28	28	0	44%	56%
L1 German	38	5	33	31	2	13.16%	86.84%

The statistical analysis of the falling scenes in L2 Spanish revealed a significant difference between the groups (Kruskal-Wallis, $p = .021$). The significant difference lied between the French and the German learners (Mann-Whitney, $p = .012$) and between the French and the Italians ($p = .024$). There was even a trend between the French and the control group ($p = .039$). The other groups did not present significant differences with the native speakers (with Italian learners $p = .977$; with German learners $p = .932$). There were no significant differences between Italian and Germans ($p = .843$). These results are represented in Figure 24.

Table 49: Descriptive statistics Plus Ground in the falling scenes in L2 Spanish.

Group	Mean	N	SD	Range
L1 Spanish	1.3417	12	.35143	.89
L1 Italian	1.3267	12	.36069	.78
L1 French	.9683	12	.38169	1.05
L1 German	1.3667	12	.30994	.78
Total	1.2188	60	.37170	1.05

Only 4 cases of Plus Ground with more than one element were found in the falling scenes: two in the Italian group and two in the German group. The numbers were too low for a statistical analysis to be conducted, but in any case, it seems clear enough that this happens only in these two groups of learners, who encoded Path more frequently.

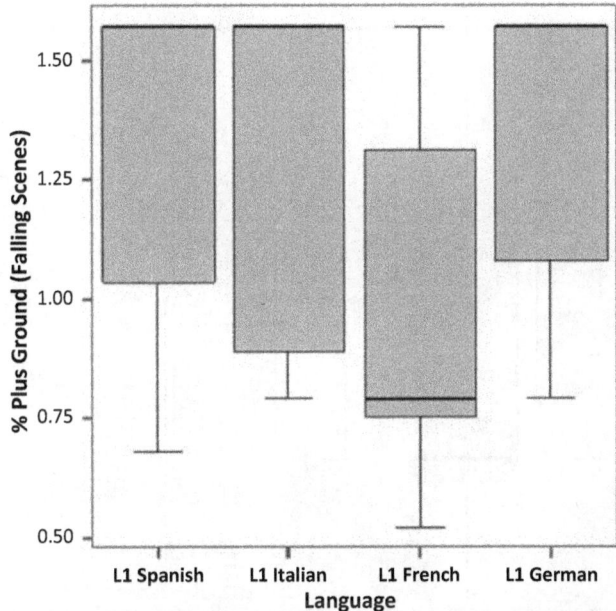

Figure 24: Percentage Plus Ground in the falling scenes in L2 Spanish.

In the study of typology, these data needed to include a different Spanish-speaking group, given that our participants use a variety of Spanish that seems to express Path more than other varieties (Ibarretxe-Antuñano and Hijazo-Gascón 2011, 2012). The same analysis is carried out here with Slobin's data – with speakers from Madrid and Argentina-. These are the results:

Table 50: Descriptive statistics percentages in the falling scenes in L2 Spanish with Slobin's data.

Language	Mean	N	SD	Range
L1 Italian	1.3267	12	.36069	.78
L1 French	.9683	12	.38169	1.05
L1 German	1.3667	12	.30994	.78
L1 Spanish (Slobin)	1.0908	12	.32618	.95
Total	1.2188	60	.37170	1.05

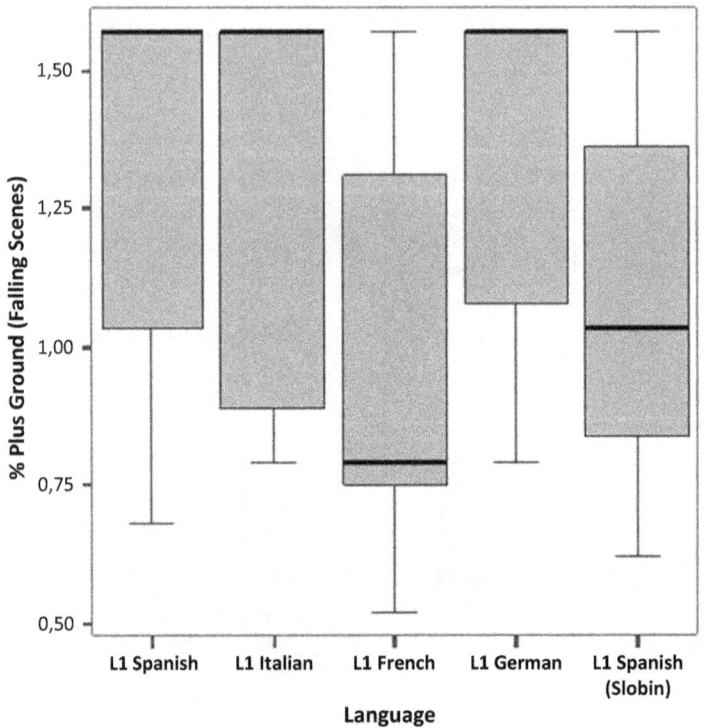

Figure 25: Percentage of Plus Ground in falling scenes with Slobin's data.

There was a significant difference across all the groups (Kruskal-Wallis p = .018). When comparing each of the groups of learners with the new control group (Slobin's participants), the Mann-Whitney test showed that there was a statistical trend between the Spanish speakers and the German learners (p = .078), but no significant differences in relation to either the Italian group (p = .198) or to the French group (p = .198).

Finally, comparing L1 and L2 showed that, as in the typological analysis, the German speakers presented a higher proportion of Plus Ground in the falling scenes in the L2, with 86.84%. They were followed by the Italians with 79.31% and by the native speakers with 77.5%. Finally, the French speakers produced 56% of Plus Ground events. The performance of each group in their L1 and L2 is shown in Table 51.

The statistical analysis of the comparison between L1 and L2 showed no significant differences between the narratives of any of the groups in their L1 and L2 (Italian group p = .686; French group p = .236; German group p = .933). It seems that they did not adapt their thinking for speaking with regard to Path,

Table 51: Plus Ground comparison between L1 and L2.

	Plus Ground in L1	% Plus Ground in L1	Plus Ground in L2	% Plus Ground in L2
Italian group	33	78,56%	23	79,31%
French group	25	52,08%	28	56%
German group	36	83,72%	33	86,84%

which can lead to positive or negative transfer, depending on whether or not their L1 pattern coincides with that of the L2. Overall, the German speakers did show a trend with regard to the native speakers, so they might be in the process of adjusting. The French speakers, however, did not change their pattern from their L1, and did not need to, because it coincides with the L2. The Italian learners did not change between their L1 and L2 but reduced their level of expression of Plus Ground to the point that they did not show significant differences with native speakers. However the Italians did show a significant difference with the French learners, which illustrates an interesting cross-linguistic influence. This highlights the importance of not just comparing the learners' performances with those of native speakers, but also between different types of learners.

9.5 Deixis

The semantic subcomponent of Deixis tends to present a challenge for second language learners. In the previous chapter, we saw how deixis presents a number of differences among the four languages of the study. Talmy's verb-framed and satellite-framed typology is intersected by Gathercole's (1977, 1978) typology based on the deictic centre. In this typology Spanish is different to the other three languages of the study as it only allows the speaker to be the deictic center, and not the addressee. The study of typology revealed that the participants who speak other languages as their L1 used venitive verbs in *The Frog Story*. None of the Spanish speakers used them because there is no situation of motion towards the speaker in the story.

The focus of this subsection is whether L2 speakers are aware of these differences and use venitive verbs in the L2 in cases where the goal of the movement is not the speaker or any place in relation to her. The general results for the L2 narratives are reproduced in Table 52. Table 53 illustrates the uses in the L1s for comparison.

Table 52: Deictic verbs used in L2 Spanish.

	Itive (GO verbs)	Venitive (COME verbs)	Causative Itive (TAKE verbs)	Causative Venitive (BRING verbs)
Spanish	*ir* (7), *irse* (12)	*venir* (0)	*llevar* (7)	*traer* (0)
L1 Italian	*ir* (9), *irse* (14)	*venir* (0)	*llevar* (8), *llevarse* (3)	*traer* (1)
L1 French	*ir* (7), *irse* (29)	*venir* (0)	*llevar* (3), *llevarse* (3)	*traer* (2)
L1 German	*ir* (15), *irse* (14)	*venir* (1)	*llevar* (3), *llevarse* (3)	*traer* (1)

Table 53: Deictic verbs used in L1s.

	Itive (GO verbs)	Venitive (COME verbs)	Causative Itive (TAKE verbs)	Causative Venitive (BRING verbs)
Spanish	*ir* (7), *irse* (12)	*venir* (0)	*llevar* (7)	*traer* (0)
Italian	*andare* (4), *andarsene* (2)	*venire* (2)	*Portare* (9), *portarsi* (1)	
French	*aller* (6), *s'en aller* (2)	*revenir* (2)	*porter* (1)	
			emmener (4)	*amener* (1)
German	*gehen* (14)	*kommen* (19)	*tragen* (5)	*bringen* (2)

Venitive verbs are used across the groups of learners. The numbers are not high, but it is worth remembering that these stimuli are not specifically designed for the elicitation of deictic motion events. There is only one example with *venir* by a German speaker:

(221)   *De repente el panal cayó y muchas... abejas... vinieron... sí* [2011de]
         of sudden, the beehive fall.PST.3SG and many... bees... come.PST.3PL... yes
         'Suddenly the beehive fell and many... bees... came... yes'

There are four examples with *traer*, which were produced by learners of each L1.

(222)   *tomó su rana y la trajo a su casa* [2009IT]
         take.PST.3SG a frog and her bring.PST.3SG to her house
         '[He] took his frog and brought her to his home

(223) *el ciervo lo trae colgado de los cuernos hasta un precipicio* [2002FR]
 the deer it bring.PRS.3SG hold.PTCP of the horns until a cliff
 'the deer brings holding on the horns up to a cliff'

(224) *que le trae hasta un estanco* [2005FR]
 that it.DAT bring.PRS.3SG until a pond
 'that brings it until a cliff'

(225) *porque trae Juan sobre su cabeza* [2011DE]
 because bring.PRS.3SG Juan over his head
 'because Juan brings over his head'

Another interesting finding is the frequent use of *ir* and *irse*. This is coherent with the findings in the boundary-crossing jar scene, where *ir* and *irse* were used by all groups, probably as a general learning strategy. The verbs *ir* and *irse* are very frequent and can be used as a communication and learning strategy when L2 speakers do not want to risk using a more complicated verb. It can be concluded that deictic motion events pose a challenge for L2 learners. It is probably one of the most difficult aspects to readjust in the re-thinking for speaking process. More studies on this aspect are needed with more suitable stimuli. The fact that cross-linguistic influence appears even in a narrative task that is not specifically designed for the testing of this issue shows that it is a difficult item to acquire.

10 Results: Causative constructions in L2 Spanish

As seen in the previous chapter, the Italian and French speakers used a specific caused motion construction that was not present in the Spanish speakers' data. It will be interesting to see whether learners are aware of this intra-typological difference and whether they attempt to use it in their L2. The analysis in this section is qualitative, as it was not one of the areas anticipated by the research questions. However, I consider it is a very interesting case of cross-linguistic influence and therefore worth including in the analysis.

These constructions use the verb MAKE and a motion verb in its infinitive form. These constructions exist in Italian and French, as reproduced in (226) and (227):

(226) *Fa cadere il bambino e il cane giù da un dirupo su un lago* [03IT]
 make.PRS.3SG fall.INF the boy and the dog down from a cliff over a lake
 'Makes fall (throws) the boy and the dog down from a cliff to a lake'

(227) *Le petit garçon se fait jeter par la fenêtre* [06FR]
the small boy CL make.PRS.3SG throw.INF through the window
'The little boy makes himself thrown through the window'

As seen in the study on typology, these constructions are not present in the narratives of the Spanish speakers of the study. These constructions do not pose a communicative problem for the interaction with Spanish native speakers, but they are not used by them, and not part of their rhetorical style. It is interesting that these constructions are quite frequent in the narratives in L2 Spanish by the Italian and the French learners, with 4 and 6 tokens respectively. This can be considered a case of transfer to nowhere (Kellerman 1995), as it consists of the transfer of a linguistic element from the L1 that does not have a correspondent in the L2. Some examples are:

(228) *Pero de repente lo hace caer* [10IT]
but of sudden it.ACC.M make.PRS.3SG.INF fall.INF
'but suddenly [he] makes it fall'

(229) *Y hace caer al niño* [10IT]
and make.PRS.3SG fall.INF to.the child
'And makes the child fall'

(230) *Y el ciervo hace caer al perro y al niño en un estanque* [07FR]
and the deer make.PRS.3SG fall.INF to.the dog and to.the child in a pond
'And the deer makes the dog and the child fall into a pond'

(231) *Y hace caer el nido* [08FR]
and make.PRS.3SG fall.INF the nest
'And [he] makes the nest fall'

It is worth clarifying that these constructions are used by different speakers. Four of the Italian speakers produced 8 cases of these constructions in their L1. In the same vein, six different French learners produced 13 tokens of these constructions in their L1. These speakers were not necessarily those who produced this construction in the L2.

The construction in L2 Spanish was present only with the combination *hacer* 'make' + *caer* 'fall', although in their L1s speakers used it with other verbs too. In L2 Spanish there are other combinations of this construction with non-motion verbs, such as the following:

(232) *Entonces el niño dice al perrito que haga silencio* [10IT]
then the child say.PRS.3SG to.the dog.DIM that make.SBJV.3SG silence
'Then the boy tells the dog to make silence'

(233) *Mientras el perro él se hace picar por las abejas* [02FR]
while the dog he CL make.PRS.3SG sting.INF by the bees
'In the meanwhile, the dog makes himself be stung by the bees'

It is worth examining these constructions, as they are a good example of conceptual transfer from the L1 and indicate an interesting intra-typological difference about the linguistic resources to express motion.

11 Results: Event granularity

The last item in the traditional analysis of *The Frog story* is the event granularity (Slobin 1996a, 1997b). This part of the analysis focuses on complex Paths and is based on the deer scene. Slobin's hypothesis is that speakers of a satellite-framed language tend to mention more segments of this complex Path than verb-framed language speakers. This has been confirmed in a number of studies (see Chapter 2) and replicated with similar results in our study on typology in Chapter 4. We will now examine whether this is transferred to L2 Spanish.

Slobin (1996a) categorises the deer scene into the following phases: (a) the deer starts running; (b) the deer runs carrying the boy; (c) the deer stops at the edge of the cliff; (d) the deer throws the boy; (e) the boy and the dog fall; (f) the boy and the dog land on water. These are the results for L2 Spanish, with a reminder of the results from their L1:

Table 54: Event granularity. Deer scene with 6 segments in L2 Spanish (and L1s).

	Speakers who mention 3 or more in the L2 (and in the L1)	Percentage in L2 Spanish (and in their L1)
Spanish (control)	3	25%
L1 Italian	4 (3)	33,33% (25%)
L1 French	6 (6)	50% (50%)
L1 German	3 (7)	25% (58,33%)

It is interesting to observe that the French learners mention the most segments of complex Path in L2 Spanish, with more than half of them mentioning three or more segments. This number coincides with the results in their L1. Italian speakers show a similar result in the L2 to their L1: four of them mention 3 or more segments, one more than the L1. Finally, German speakers seem to adapt quite well to the L2, with a clear change from their L1 to the L2, from 7 speakers mentioning 3 or more segments in German to only 3 in the L2. It might be that the perceived distance between L1 and L2 –Kellerman's psychotypology- has intervened.

Slobin (1997b) simplifies the complex path into 4 segments: (a) change of location: the deer moves, runs, arrives at the cliff; (b) negative change of location: the deer stops at the edge; (c) causal change of location: the deer throws the boy; and (d) change of location: the boy and the dog fall into the water. Again, Slobin's studies show that verb-framed language speakers mention fewer segments than satellite-framed language speakers.

Table 55: Event granularity. Deer scene in 4 segments in L2 Spanish (and L1s).

	Mean per speaker in the L2 (and in L1)	Percentage of speakers who say 3 or more segments (and in L1)
Spanish (control)	2	41,67%
L1 Italian	2 (2,17)	33,33% (30%)
L1 French	2,25 (2,33)	50% (50%)
L1 German	2 (2,5)	25% (58,34%)

In Table 55, we can see the data obtained in the analysis with four segments. The results are very similar to the test with six segments. The French learners produce a higher number of mentions of different segments, while the other groups correspond with the mean.

12 Conclusions on the L2 acquisition study

This chapter has focused on the acquisition of motion events in L2 Spanish by German, French and Italian learners. With the choice of these language combinations, this research study on L2 acquisition considered the two typological groups in Talmy's theory: a satellite-framed language, namely German and three verb-framed languages: French, Italian and Spanish. Motion is a conceptual domain prone to transfer in second language acquisition (Jarvis and Pavlenko

2008). It is interesting, therefore, to examine whether inter- and intra-typological differences can be the source of this transfer. The methodology put forward by Jarvis (2000, 2010) to study cross-linguistic influence has been carefully used for the experimental study. Our data were analyzed in relation to a control group of native speakers, but the results were also compared among the three groups of learners to enable the consideration of any inter-group heterogeneity. The participants narrated the same story twice, which enables their speech in the L1 and the L2 to be compared. These multiple comparisons allow us to confirm that the differences found in each of the groups are the result of cross-linguistic influence from the L1.

This methodology, apart from being robust to gather evidence of cross-linguistic evidence, is also coherent with the multilingual turn in SLA (Ortega 2013). The comparisons established here are not exclusively made with native speakers but also take into account how other L1 speakers perform, and also what is the difference between their performance in their L1 and L2.

The component of Manner has been examined through different analyses, and shows very similar results among the groups. These analyses consisted of Manner verbs, the total expression of Manner, the owl scene and the boundary-crossing events. In all these cases we can conclude that there is a *re-thinking for speaking* (P. Robinson and N. Ellis 2008) in the sense that learners adjust to the rhetorical style of the second language. In order to achieve this, the German learners needed to reduce the extent to which they use Manner in their L1. In fact, they showed a significant difference in the use of Manner when they told the story in the L1 and the L2. The Italian and French learners, by contrast, performed very similarly in both L1 and L2, as the lexicalization patterns among the three Romance languages are similar with regard to Manner, in that they contain very low levels of Manner expression. The readjustment made by the German learners is also present in the use of Manner in the owl scene and in the boundary-crossing events.

A more complex picture was found in the case of Path. Unlike Manner, this is a compulsory semantic component of motion, which makes Path expression harder to adjust to the L2. Previous studies on L2 Spanish found frequent cases of satellizations (Cadierno 2004; Cadierno and Lund 2004; Cadierno and Ruiz 2006), i.e. constructions with motion verbs and a directional adverb, as transfers from similar patterns in the L1. However, this was not the case in our data and neither German nor Italian learners used satellizations, mirroring their satellite or pseudo-satellite constructions. Therefore, some readjustment to the L2 rhetorical style seems to be made.

In the analysis of Minus and Plus Ground, the German learners showed a statistical trend with native speakers, which was very close to a significant difference. Interestingly, French and Italian learners presented a significant difference in the encoding of Path, with the Italians producing more frequent Path encoding in their L2 Spanish than the French. However, there was no difference between any of these groups and the control group. In other words, all three groups of learners seemed to adapt to the rhetorical style of the L2, although some traces of the L1 can be seen when contrasting different groups of learners.

None of the groups showed significant differences when comparing the L1 and L2 narratives –only a trend in Italian learners- with regard to Plus Ground. It seems that the German learners transfer their Path patterns into their L2 Spanish. Similarly, Romance language speakers seem to follow their L1 patterns. The French learners produced similar lexicalization patterns to those of the native speakers, so they did not need to change their lexicalization pattern. In the case of the Italians, the statistical trend between their L1 and L2 narratives seems to indicate an adjustment to the L2 rhetorical style. However, the fact that they differ significantly from French learners suggests a clear case of cross-linguistic influence. It would be an effect of cross-linguistic influence, as noticed by Jarvis (2000): inter-group heterogeneity in the discourse between learners and inter-group congruency between the L1 and the L2.

These results on the expression of Path in the complete narratives are confirmed by the data from the falling scenes. Again, significant differences are found between the French learners on the one hand and the Italian and German learners on the other. Two different control groups were used for this analysis. First, our participants' data were used, but since it seems that Spanish from Aragón encodes Path in more detail (see Ibarretxe-Antuñano and Hijazo-Gascón 2011, 2012; Chapter 4 of this volume), the analysis was repeated with Slobin's data from Madrid and Argentina. In this second analysis, Slobin participants produced significantly more Path than French learners, and less than German learners with a statistical trend. This is more in line with previous literature on Spanish motion events. The comparison between L1 and L2 for the Plus Ground in falling scenes showed no significant differences.

We can conclude that cross-linguistic influence plays a crucial role in the expression of Path in L2 Spanish. The influence of the L1 lexicalization pattern for Path has a positive outcome in the case of French learners and negative in the case of German learners. The Italian learners, meanwhile, seem to be in the process of readjustment, as their behaviour between the L1 and L2 seems to change -with a statistical trend- and they do not present significant differences from native speakers in how they express Path. It seems that the Italian learners are in the process of re-thinking for speaking. Deictic verbs are also an area of language prone to cross-linguistic influence. This can be surprising as deictic verbs such as *come* and *go* are very frequent in any language and are taught in the second language classroom at the very early stages of the learning process. However, it seems that all the learners of Spanish use them with a clear influence from their L1, even at B2 level. The semantics of deictic verbs is extremely complex form a contrastive point of view, as shown in Talmy's and Gathercole's typologies. As a result, acquiring the lexicalization patterns and use of these verbs in terms of rhetorical style is particularly challenging for learners. However, *The Frog story* is not specifically designed to test Deixis and further research is needed.

A final analysis following Slobin's tradition, the event granularity, was also discussed. Both versions of the test were performed (Slobin 1996a, 1997b). In both cases L2 learners showed similar results both among themselves and with the native speakers, though the German group made an adjustment. The French learners differed more from the rest of the groups in this test. As in their L1 they mentioned more segments of complex Paths.

Finally the analysis considered the component of Cause, since causative constructions are very interesting because they show cross-linguistic influence from the first language. In fact the German group did not present any of these constructions in Spanish. These constructions constitute an intra-typological difference, which is transferred to the L2 narratives. From an acquisition point of view, these causative constructions are a clear case of transfer to nowhere, as explained by Kellerman (1995), because they do not have an equivalent in Spanish and therefore the learners are transferring from their L1s ignoring the input of the L2.

To conclude, in this chapter we have provided enough evidence to show how cross-linguistic influence occurs in the semantic domain of motion. The extent of cross-linguistic influence is different for each semantic component. This evidence has emerged from different points of comparison, including data from the study of typology and comparisons with native speakers, among groups of learners and also within the same group in both L1 and L2. This allows us to observe the effects classified by Jarvis (2000, 2010) as intra-group homogeneity, inter-group heterogeneity, intra-group congruency and intralingual contrasts. It is also clear that cross-linguistic influence is present not only when acquiring a language that belongs to one group of the typology when the L1 belongs to the other, but also when both L1 and L2 belong to the same typological group. Finally, it is worth recalling that our goal is not to determine grammatical errors nor communication problems, but aspects of rhetorical style (Slobin 1996a). In fact, the data presented here support the hypotheses of re-elaboration of thinking for speaking in the L2 (Cadierno 2004) and re-thinking for speaking (N. Ellis and P. Robinson 2008). Examples of these are the case of German learners adapting to the expression of manner in the L2, and Italian learners in the expression of Path. The cross-lingustic influence found here contributes more data about the co-existence of several languages in the mind of a bilingual or multilingual speaker. In contrast with traditional views of language as being rigid and static, we can see how the languages present in the speaker's mind interact and influence each other, not necessarily in a explicit way. In the case of motion these relationships are subtle, as they are at the conceptual level.

Chapter 6
Conclusions and future directions

1 Introduction

This volume has focused on Talmy's typology of motion events and Slobin's thinking for speaking hypothesis in four languages: French, German, Italian and Spanish. It has also examined the acquisition of Spanish as a second language by speakers of these other three languages, mainly in relation to cross-linguistic influence among the languages of the learners. This final chapter gives the conclusions and implications of each of the studies presented in the book, namely on typology and on second language acquisition. It also includes a section on applications of this research, with regard to the potential and benefits of using what we know about semantic typology and second language acquisition in the language class. In this section, previous studies on teaching motion events are discussed, mainly in relation to the *Focus on Form* approach (Long 1991), which has been the main approach to teaching motion events.

Finally, it is also suggested that the acquisition of motion events in a second language –and typological contrasts in general- should benefit from the new role of (pedagogical) translation in second language teaching. Mediation activities and strategies (Council of Europe 2001, 2018) are part of the learning of a second language. It is argued here that Applied Language Typology (Filipović 2017a, 2017b) can be used for the development of mediation activities. The chapter ends by proposing new directions for further research on the acquisition of motion events in second languages.

2 Conclusions in relation to the typology

The main aim of the study on typology was to identify inter- and intra-typological differences among the four languages of the study. Five hypotheses were established in Chapter 4 in relation to the research questions of this study (see Section 2). This section returns to these hypotheses to discuss whether they can be confirmed by this research.

Hypothesis 1: There are inter-typological differences in the expression of motion events between German, the satellite-framed language under study, and the three verb-framed languages present in this research (French, Italian and Spanish).

This hypothesis was confirmed in relation to the component of Manner. The German speakers produced significantly a higher proportion of Manner verbs than the Romance language speakers. They also produced significantly more motion events where this component is encoded in any linguistic element. In addition to this, German speakers used Manner verbs for boundary-crossing motion events, unlike Romance language speakers. However, the hypothesis is only partially confirmed with regard to the component of Path. The German speakers did provide more detailed descriptions of Path. These differences between the German speakers and the French and the Spanish speakers were significant, whereas no significant difference was found in the expression of Path between the German and the Italian speakers. Moreover, in both languages, there were cases of Plus Ground with more than one Ground element.

Hypothesis 2: There are intra-typological differences in the expression of motion events among the three verb-framed Romance languages.

Hypothesis 3: There are intra-typological differences in the expression of motion events, even in closely related languages such as French, Italian and Spanish.

Hypotheses 2 and 3 are closely related and only partially confirmed. There were no significant differences among the three Romance languages with respect to Manner. None of these languages expresses Manner with a high frequency. We could only observe subtle differences in the lexicalization choices for boundary-crossing events, with the Italian speakers using more Manner+Path verbs than the speakers of the other languages for this type of events, in line with previous research that suggests that Italian speakers have more flexibility respect the boundary-crossing constraint. Even so, none of the Romance groups used Manner verbs for boundary-crossing events.

Intra-typological differences were found with regard to Path expression, but with different results. The Italian speakers used Path elements significantly more frequently than the French and the Spanish speakers. In fact, Italian levels of Path expression were similar to those of German speakers. This was confirmed with the results of the analysis of Plus Ground events in the whole narratives and in the falling scenes. One of the subcomponents of Path, Deixis, was shown to be particularly interesting from a contrastive point of view. The languages of the study can be grouped differently, according to Talmy's typology of motion events (German vs. the rest) or to Gathercole's typology on deixis, based on the deictic centre (Spanish vs. the rest), which revealed intra-typological differences. Whereas French and Italian speakers can use venitive verbs towards the addressee, Spanish speakers only use it towards the speaker. This is reflected in the use of venitive verbs in *the Frog Story*: they were only used by speakers of Italian and French.

Another intra-typological difference was found with regard to the semantic component of Cause. The French and the Italian speakers used specific constructions with the verb *make* followed by an infinitive to express Cause (e.g. *faire tomber* 'make fall'), which were not used by Spanish speakers, who preferred to use caused motion verbs, such as *tirar* 'throw'.

Hypothesis 4: In the event that hypothesis 2 is confirmed and intra-typological differences are found in the rhetorical style of Romance speakers, these differences will be in relation to the specific characteristics of French, Italian and Spanish. For example, the use of prefixes in French to encode Path, the use of verb-particle constructions in Italian and the different deictic pattern in Spanish, that only allows the speaker to be the deictic centre.

This hypothesis was confirmed because the intra-typological differences found seem to be in relation to specific characteristics of each of the languages. Path expression is more frequent in Italian because this language contains specific linguistic elements that can encode Path, such as pseudo-satellites. In the case of deictic verbs, these differences between French, Italian and Spanish are coherent with the characteristics of each of these languages, as described in Gathercole's typology on deixis. Finally, the intra-typological differences in relation to Cause are also triggered by the specific constructions present in Italian and French. French prefixes were the only specific feature that did not seem to have a strong influence in the rhetorical style of French learners, as it was not frequently used.

Hypothesis 5: The presence of these pseudo-satellite constructions in Italian and French (verb-particle constructions and prefixes) in contrast with Spanish speakers will imply:

5a. A more frequent encoding of Manner in the verb, because Path can be expressed in an element outside the verb (particle or prefix), similarly to satellite-framed prototypical constructions.
5b. A greater elaboration of the Path component by Italian and French speakers.

Hypothesis 5a was completely refuted. The use of pseudo-satellites in Italian did not lead to a higher presence of Manner in the narratives of the Italian speakers. There were a few cases of combinations of Manner verbs with particles, e.g. *trascinare via* 'drag away'. However, they occurred too infrequently to lead to significant differences in the expression of Manner between the Italian speakers on the one hand and the French and the Spanish speakers on the other. The Romance languages are similar with regard to how they express Manner, but they all present significant differences from German. It is with regard to Manner expression, therefore, where they can be considered as a unified group.

Hypothesis 5b was only confirmed for the expression of Path in Italian because of its use of verb-particle constructions. The hypothesis was not confirmed for French, whose speakers encoded Path with similar frequency to Spanish. The specific resources of Old French that have been found in previous research (Kopecka 2004, 2006a) do not seem to lead to intra-typological differences in the current state of the language, and French thinking for speaking seems to be coherent with the prototypical thinking for speaking patterns of verb-framed languages. Interestingly, the use of prefixes is relevant in relation to deictic caused motion verbs, as *emmerer* 'bring/take' and *amener* 'bring', which were found in the data and show a noteworthy intra-typological difference with Italian and Spanish. Further research is needed on intra-typological and intra-genetic differences in deictic motion verbs with specific stimuli for this purpose.

The presence of prefixes that could be considered as pseudo-satellites in French seems to be marginal and limited to Deixis in very specific cases and reiteration of motion (e.g. *revenir* 'come (again)'). The use of prefixes in other motion verbs seems lexicalized. As Kopecka (2009) suggests, these prefixes are a legacy of a former state of the language. Previous states of other Romance languages also show similar prefix-motion verb constructions, as part of the evolution from Latin to Romance and the typological shift from satellite-framed to verb-framed (see 2015 for a detailed explanation of both evolutionary changes). The results of the study on typology presented in this book reject the classification of French as a hybrid language in terms of Talmy's typology, because the alleged satellite-framed constructions present in the language are very infrequent in the data. The rhetorical style of French speakers in this study is as prototypical as that of Spanish speakers, whose language is considered the most prototypical verb-framed language. No significant differences were found in any of the analysis, with just a statistical trend in the results of the analysis of event granularity, with the French speakers mentioning more segments of complex journeys. There are other intra-typological differences in other aspects of the typology, such as specific constructions for Cause, but none in relation to Path and Manner. These results have methodological implications for the study of motion events, in that the mere existence of a specific construction (e.g. directional prefixes in combination with motion verbs) does not necessarily lead to changes in its typological status. It is important to determine the use of these linguistic elements to conclude whether their presence implies a change in the rhetorical style of the language under study.

2 Conclusions in relation to the typology — 267

The conclusions of the typological study confirm the clear inter-typological differences between German, a satellite-framed language, and three Romance verb-framed languages. However, this study should also raise awareness of the risks of overgeneralizing about languages which belong to the same typological group. The comparisons between French, Spanish and Italian show the existence of intra-typological differences within verb-framed languages. Romance languages are often treated in typology as a monolithic block, but this research shows that they are more diverse than expected. It has been shown that Italian is the Romance language that diverges more from the prototypicality of verb-framed languages, mainly in relation to Path. This supports Ibarretxe-Antuñano's (2009) Path salience cline, and the view that the Talmian typology is a cline rather than a clear-cut dichotomy (Slobin 2004; Ibarretxe-Antuñano 2009). The results shed light on other relatively under-researched components of Motion typology, such as Deixis and Cause. Future research will contribute more on these areas of motion, and thus move beyond the traditional focus on Manner and Path.

A further difference was seen in geographical varieties of Spanish, which were found to have an impact on results in the analysis of falling scenes. The Spanish control group did not present significant differences with the German and the Italian speakers (although they did for the whole narratives). The repetition of this analysis with speakers of other varieties of Spanish showed clearly that speakers from Madrid and Buenos Aires have a more verb-framed prototypical encoding of Path than Spanish speakers from Aragón. This result confirms previous studies that have drawn the attention of typologists to the importance of sociolinguistic and geographical varieties, such as Berthele (2004, 2006) for Standard and Swiss German. The participants of this study were speakers from Aragón, in the North-East of Spain. Together with the Spanish variety spoken in the Basque country their variety, Spanish from Aragón, has been identified, as describing Path more than other varieties (Ibarretxe-Antuñano and Hijazo-Gascón 2011, 2012). Therefore, future research on typology should also take into account potential intra-typological differences –even within the same linguistic family- and geographical and sociological varieties in certain aspects of the typology. Future research taking into account a more integrated perspective would be beneficial for a more holistic analysis of the expression of motion in different languages.

These findings support those in previous studies like that of Fernández, de Souza and Carando (2017: 263), who conclude that the linguistic distance between two languages should not be contrasted based on the overall genetic or typological relationship between the languages in question. According to these authors, the linguistic distance should be examined more in detail: construction by construction. In relation to this, Perek and Hilpert (2014) coin the term *constructional tolerance*, that is, the extent to which a language tolerates or discourages unconventional combinations of lexical items and constructions. This should be also borne in mind in future typological studies.

In the present study, this relevance of examining linguistic distance in detail is perfectly exemplified by the use of different constructions by languages from different groups, regardless of their genetic and typological affiliation. For example, the main typical general predictions from typology were found in motion expressions with Manner (German vs. French-Italian-Spanish, satellite-framed vs. verb-framed languages), but they were not found in the results on motion expressions with Path –Plus Ground- showing intra-typological variation, (German-Italian vs. French-Spanish). Deictic motion constructions showed a different type of grouping regardless of typology and genetic affiliation (Spanish vs. French-German-Italian), and so did the analysis of Caused Motion constructions with MAKE (Italian-French vs. German-Spanish). Future research on this area should acknowledge this variation and take into account the variability within typological groups depending on which constructions are preferred.

3 Conclusions in relation to second language acquisition

The second study in this book focused on the acquisition of Spanish as a second language. The main aim of this study was to determine whether the inter- and intra-typological differences found in the study on typology lead to cross-linguistic influence in the second language. The results of this study are relevant for studies on transfer and second language acquisition in general. First, let us check whether the hypotheses were confirmed.

Hypothesis 1: Satellite-framed language speakers will present cases of conceptual transfer from their L1 into L2 Spanish. A more detailed account of the components of Manner and Path is expected.

This hypothesis was confirmed with regard to Path but not in relation to Manner. The expression of Manner in L2 Spanish by the German learners did not differ significantly from that of the native speakers, nor from that the French and the Italian learners. However, there was a significant difference when comparing the performance of the German speakers in their L1 and the L2. In other words, they adjusted their L1 pattern to express Manner less when they talked in Spanish. There is thus a re-adjustment of the thinking for speaking to the rhetorical style of the L2. This might be due partly to the limited linguistic resources with which to express Manner in Spanish, which is less common and less frequent in that language. The German speakers also seem to adapt to the boundary-crossing constraint, not using Manner verbs in boundary-crossing situations. This differs from the results obtained by Larrañaga et al. (2011) with native English speakers. It might be that being immersed in Spanish has helped the German learners in our study to adapt to the thinking for speaking of L2 Spanish in this respect, or it might be that the task has influenced the results. In any case, more research is needed in this area.

On the other hand, however, the German speakers did present conceptual transfer from the L1 into L2 Spanish with regard to the component of Path. In fact, they presented significantly more descriptions of Path than the French learners and a statistical trend with native speakers. Further evidence of this transfer was the comparison between the narratives of the German learners in their L1 and L2: the extent to which they express Path did not change and they presented similar levels of frequency in both languages. This is in line with previous research on L2 Spanish by speakers of satellite-framed languages (e.g. Cadierno 2004; Cadierno and Ruiz 2006; among others). There is, however, one difference with regard to these previous studies, which is the scarcity of "satellizations" in the data of the current study. There are different possible explanations for this result. It may be a result of differences in how data were collected, namely orally in this study and in written form in those of Cadierno. Another possibility is that while Cadierno's data were collected in Denmark, in the present study the context of immersion may have militated against German learners using satellizations, as they do not hear them in the input that they are exposed to in their daily lives. In any event, however, the hypothesis was confirmed in relation to Path.

Hypothesis 2: Verb-framed language learners of Spanish will present conceptual transfer from their L1 into L2 Spanish. It is expected that the component of Path will present more conceptual transfer, given the different linguistic resources to encode Path in Spanish, Italian and French.

Again, this hypothesis can be only partially supported. It was refuted for the expression of Manner and only partially confirmed for the expression of Path. There were no major intra-typological differences in the expression of Manner among the three Romance languages under study. In other words, when the Italian and the French learners narrated in Spanish, they did not present significant differences in how they expressed Manner either among themselves or with the native speakers of Spanish. Furthermore, no significant differences were shown in the expression of Manner in the Italian and the French learners when comparing the L1 and the L2.

The only difference in Manner expression was found in relation to boundary-crossing events, where the Italians tended to use more Manner+Path verbs in combination with a Ground complement than the other two groups, which was also reflected in L2 Spanish. However, none of the three groups used Manner verbs with boundary-crossing motion events, with the already known exception of sudden and fast movements, (see Chapter 3, Section 2.2.2.)

The component of Path presents a more complex picture. First, it is worth recalling that there is intra-typological variation among the three Romance languages, with Italian speakers describing Path significantly more than French and Spanish speakers. However, in the narratives in L2 Spanish, there were no significant differences between Italian learners and Spanish speakers. This finding shows some readjustment to the patterns of the L2. This readjustment is confirmed when comparing the Italian narratives in their L1 and the L2, which show a statistical trend. However, cross-linguistic influence cannot be ruled out completely as an explanation for this performance, because the Italian learners presented a statistically significant difference from the French learners in how they expressed Path. This shows that the influence of the L1 is still present, albeit in the process of being adapted to the rhetorical style of L2 learners. This result can be identified through Jarvis' (2000) method, which is based on establishing different types of comparison to identify cross-linguistic influence. It also shows the importance of avoiding exclusive comparisons with monolingual native speakers, as some of the information can be missed.

In the case of the French learners and their expression of Path in Spanish, their rhetorical style in the L1 coincided with the rhetorical style of the L2. This means that their task is in principle easier, as they can just keep the same pattern as in their L1. In a way, we can consider that their performance might be an effect of positive transfer, since differences occur only in terms of the granularity of the event, wherein French speakers mention more phases of the journey than they do in their L1.

However, French does not align with Spanish in two areas of motion that require future research, namely deictic motion events and caused motion constructions. In both cases, French and Italian present different characteristics from Spanish –as explained in Chapter 4- and these are transferred to their narratives in the L2. Both groups of learners present inaccurate uses of deictic verbs, with venitive verbs being used to describe motion that is not towards the speaker or a place that is identifiable with the speaker. Similarly, both groups show occurrences of transfer of the construction MAKE + INFINITIVE, which is used to express caused motion in French and Italian but is not used in Spanish (neither in our data, nor in previous studies on Spanish caused motion such as that of Ibarretxe-Antuñano 2012). The case of the caused motion constructions is a clear case of transfer to nowhere (Kellerman 1995), that is, cases in which learners transfer a feature of the L1 to the L2 even though this is not a characteristic feature of the L2. In this sense, Kellerman's psychotypology seems to play a crucial role in the domain of motion events, as previously suggested by Cadierno (2004). The perceived distance that speakers consider between the L1 and L2 may imply positive transfer but also transfer to nowhere, because the similarities between languages are overstated. In other words, learners may not accept meanings and structures in one of their languages even if they are shared with the other language because they assume that their languages differ, as is captured in the notion of psychotypology (Filipović 2019b: 18).

When the two languages are very similar, the correspondences in terms of pronunciation, lexicon, etc. may result in the cost of communication being very low (Filipović 2019b). This means, therefore, that learners continue to use in the L2 similar constructions to the L1 at no cost, because they can be easily understood. The example used by Filipović and Hawkins (2013) is word order in L2 English by speakers of L1 Japanese and L1 Spanish. The communication cost of keeping the L1 word order in the L2 is too high for Japanese learners, as using their SOV pattern would risk the message not being successfully rendered in English. By contrast, Spanish learners have a common basic SVO pattern with the target language (English), and assume that the word order patterns are fully shared. However, in reality Spanish allows more word order flexibility than English, and allows sentences like *Ayer vino mi amigo*, which would be ungrammatical in English **Yesterday came my friend* and which is exactly what Spanish learners produce in their L2 English (Filipović and Hawkins 2013). This seems to be the situation with some of the different patterns in relation to motion events in this study.

There are other phenomena that play a role in the acquisition of motion events. For example, we have seen an overuse of neutral verbs such as *ir* and *irse* 'go' and the creation of new motion verbs. The overuse of general motion verbs seems to be a general feature of L2 learners. For example, Cadierno (2010) found an overuse of general motion verbs such as *gå* 'go' by Spanish, Russian and German learners of L2 Danish and, in the same vein, Römer, O'Donnell, and N. Ellis (2014) found an overuse of *go* –and also *move* and *come*- by Spanish, German and Czech learners of L2 English. All learners in their study relied on general, highly frequent verbs, and produced lower numbers of specific less frequent verbs in verb-argument constructions. Nevertheless, conceptual transfer seems to play a big role in the acquisition of the semantics of motion in an L2. This confirms Jarvis and Pavlenko's (2008) conclusion that movement is a semantic domain prone to conceptual transfer. After all, motion is a basic domain where it is hard to avoid influence from the L1.

Our results can be also interpreted from the perspective of the Complex Adaptive System Principles (CASP) model for bilingualism (Filipović and Hawkins 2019).

This model relies on five key learning and processing principles, namely: (A) minimize learning effort, (B) minimize processing effort, (C) maximize expressive power, (D) maximize efficiency in communication and (E) maximize common ground. The most important principle that underlies the behavior of our learners in this study is (E) maximize common ground (see Filipović and Hawkins 2019 and Filipović 2019b for a detailed explanation of all the principles). Maximizing Common Ground is specific to bilingual communication and operates in synchrony with the other principles. According to Filipović (2019b: 60) bilingual learners seek common grammatical and lexical representations and their processing mechanisms in the L1 and L2. When both languages share an element, this element will be used more in both languages, regardless of their frequency in each individual language itself. For example, the overuse of general motion verbs in the L2 by our participants. When the languages do not share the linguistic elements, common ground is created by introducing entities from one language into the other or by avoiding certain elements, e.g. reducing the number of Manner verbs. According to Filipović (2019b: 65) second language learners can present some attempts to maximize common ground, resulting in detectable departures from the norms of a certain language, such as the overuse or underuse of a particular element (e.g. the overuse of Path elements by Italian learners). In certain cases, these uses can even be atypical or ungrammatical uses –as modulated by the internal-psycholinguistic factor of proficiency (Filipović 2019b)-, such as the use of causative constructions with *make* or the use of incorrect deictic patterns. All these phenomena, the results of seeking common ground, are identified in previous research as cross-linguistic influence (Jarvis and Pavlenko 2008). What CASP for bilingualism does in addition is explain and predict how the competition or collaboration of multiple factors plays out on different occasions and leads to specific outcomes in bilingual production.

From a broader perspective, the findings of the current acquisition study support the notion of the multilingual turn in second language acquisition (Ortega 2013), as some of the main findings are the results of comparisons with different groups of learners. As Ortega (2013) suggests it is important that this type of comparisons are established in SLA research, rather than designing studies exclusively based on the comparison with native speakers. In the same vein, Filipović (2019b: 55) argues, bilingual-specific language use should not invite researchers to focus on constant comparison with monolinguals. In fact, bilingualism should become the form and the focus of investigations related to language and monolingual-like use should be seen as a "departure" from this norm.

The main focus of this book is on semantic contrasts and rhetorical style. The results presented here contribute to current studies that shed light on how different languages coexist in the multilingual mind. The influences between them may also exist at a conceptual level, as demonstrated with the study on second language acquisition in this book.

4 Moving forward: Applications of this research

The investigation presented in this book shows how motion events, and typological contrasts in general, are a crucial area for research on cross-linguistic evidence. They are also valuable for studies on multilingualism to see how speakers maximize common ground without necessarily succeeding in the process. Raising second language learners' awareness of these contrasts would enable them to grasp de different nuances and achieve a better acquisition and rhetorical style in the L2. Including these contrasts in language learning programs would be beneficial for learners. Cadierno (2008b) considers that there are three reasons to teach motion events explicitly in the classroom. First, studies on typology show that the cross-linguistic differences in this area are complex enough to cause difficulties in their acquisition. Second, Slobin's studies show that typological differences have an impact on discourse patterns. Learners tend to establish meaning-form mappings that do not correspond with native uses and sometimes are inadequate. Finally, she considers that teaching motion events is compatible with certain pedagogical approaches to language teaching, such as Focus on Form (Long 1991) as explained below. In this vein, Röme, N. Ellis, and O'Donnell (2014) argue that foreign language teaching should acknowledge the pervasiveness of constructions in the use of language. Of course, it would not be necessary to address every typological contrast, but as a minimum, those that are crucial and relevant for improving understanding of different bilingual memory and rhetorical style should receive more attention. In this sense, those contrasts studied within Applied Language Typology by Filipović (2017a, 2017b) would be a good start.

But when and how should these contrasts be explained and used in the L2 classroom? In my experience teaching Spanish as a second language, I found it difficult to find space for this in the second language curricula, which are organized based on grammatical items, communicative functions, vocabulary, pronunciation, pragmatic aspects and cultural content. Little space is devoted to semantics in the L2 classes, apart from the necessary semantic explanation of grammatical items, such as the three topics *par excellence* in the teaching of Spanish: past tenses, the *ser/estar* 'be' differences and subjunctive/indicative mood contrasts. It seems important that semantics receives at least some attention, especially, when we know from research that constructions and meaning-form associations are pervasive in language, as stated by Römer, O'Donnell, and N. Ellis (2014), among others.

4.1 Pedagogical approaches to teaching typology

A number of authors have proposed different methods for teaching typological contrasts in the classroom. Cadierno (2008b) explains that the Total Physical Response (J. Asher 1977) can be a suitable pedagogical approach for teaching motion events. In this approach, students are encouraged to enact the movements taught by the teacher. Elliott and Yountchi (2009) developed a pedagogical implementation of Total Physical Response to teach Russian motion events, with good but limited results, due to the small sample of the study. They argue for the need for more research on language pedagogy and motion events.

Cadierno (2008a, 2008b) also points to Focus on Form (Long 1991, see Miquel López and Ortega Olivares (2014) for an application to Spanish) as the best pedagogical approach to teach typological contrasts. Focus on Form emphasizes the teaching of grammar within the Communicative Approach. Similarly, de Knop has applied Pedagogical Grammar to the teaching of Cognitive Linguistics, mainly motion events in L2 German (see for example de Knop and Dirven 2008). Cadierno (2008b) includes some practical activities for the teaching of Spanish as a foreign language following this approach, such as giving instructions, drawing maps, using exercises with directions, and using cartoons to create stories. Similarly, Hijazo-Gascón (2018) also suggests some activities based on Focus on Form, such as memory games, tasks of identification of motion verbs in texts, comparison of texts with more and less Manner expression, use of videos to describe how people move, and role-play activities (e.g. as a pilot and co-pilot). In a similar vein, Hijazo-Gascón, Cadierno, and Ibarretxe-Antuñano (2016) include a series of similar activities for placement events with verbs such as *dejar* 'leave', *meter* 'put in', *poner* 'put on', etc. Other authors have developed practical activities for teaching motion events from a different pedagogical perspective. Aguiló-Mora and Negueruela (2015) propose teaching motion events from the perspective of Sociocultural Theory, based on Vygotskian principles. They test how learners present difficulties in restructuring meaning in the L2 when they give addresses.

There are also a few studies which have measured different types of pedagogical intervention on the teaching of motion events. These studies compare the results of different teaching interventions –normally an innovative and a traditional teaching methodology- with different groups, with the aim to establish better practice in second language teaching. R. Evans (2015) combines negative evidence and some aspects of White's (2012) Conceptual Approach with the explicit aim of teaching motion events explicitly in L2 English to low-intermediate L1 Spanish learners. His pedagogical intervention seemed to have a positive effect among the learners, who used more Manner of motion verbs and satellites. In a wider study, Colasacco (2019) designs a different pedagogical intervention to demonstrate the benefits of teaching deictic motion verbs from a Cognitive Linguistics perspective. In her study, German and Italian learners of Spanish showed better command of deictic motion verbs, one of the difficulties observed in the present book (see Chapter 5), when they were taught following a Cognitive Linguistics approach. These are good examples of how research can be applied to the classroom that show the benefit of pedagogical interventions which take into account typological contrasts. Further research is needed on other aspects of motion or other typological contrasts, however, to see the benefits of explicit teaching of typology.

All the above-mentioned pedagogical approaches in this section are an excellent start for raising awareness of typological contrasts. However, most of these activities focus on the practice of form rather than meaning. Whilst recognizing the importance and the benefits of all these pedagogical approaches, therefore, I would like to consider a different approach that can complement the approaches outlined above by increasing focus on the acquisition of semantics. The proposal here is to use pedagogical translation to allow some space for the teaching of semantic contrasts. It is intended as a complement and, by no means as an exclusive pedagogical approach to teaching motion events or other typological contrasts. I argue that pedagogical translation is an excellent method which can complement Focus on Form activities and have more *Focus on Meaning* in the language classroom.

4.2 Focus on meaning: Pedagogical translation and mediation

The relationship between translation and second language teaching has never been an easy one. For a long time, translation has been practically banned from the second language classroom, at least in the Western world, because it has been largely identified with Grammar-Translation traditional methodologies. This methodology originated in the tradition of teaching Latin and Ancient Greek and consisted of the translation of sentences and words out of context. With the development of new methodologies to teach languages, such as the Direct Method – and those that followed it- translation (and the use of the L1 in the classroom) was criticized and excluded from the classes (see Leonardi 2010 for a detailed explanation). González Davies (2004) considers that the Grammar-Translation model is obsolete and she agrees with Hatim and Mason (1990) that translation is now considered a dynamic process of communication. According to González Davies (2004), the teaching of translation should be related to Humanistic teaching principles, the Communicative Approach, Cooperative Learning and Social constructivism. All of these perspectives recognise the importance of learner autonomy.

González Davies (2007) claims that translation has never been properly understood in the teaching of English as a foreign language, and this can be applied to the teaching of any foreign language. However, as she rightly points out, contact between languages has always been of interest in the field, as is illustrated by the central role of the L1 in some of the theories and studies in relation to Error Analysis, Cross-linguistic-influence, Contrastive Analysis, studies on Interlanguage, Psychotypology, etc. González Davies argues that translation has a pivotal role in all these studies but has not been seriously researched in relation to second language acquisition, and that, used in an informed way, translation can be both an effective language learning skill and strategy. She considers that the use of translation as a meaningful communicative procedure adds reality to the classroom because it involves communication with a clear aim. González Davies (2007) also considers that the use of translation in the foreign language classroom makes students improve different aspects of their target language, such as syntax, pragmatics and cultural aspects. I would like to add semantics to that list.

In fact, as pointed out by Leonardi (2011: 18), translation might be a deliberate teaching choice for teachers, but it is at the same time a "naturally occurring and cognitive activity for students learning a foreign language, which cannot be stopped or avoided". Leonardi (2010) explains that the use of translation in the foreign language classroom augments the traditional four skills, reading, writing, speaking and listening. However, Leonardi notes that translation should not only be considered in terms of accuracy. Instead, translation activities can serve different purposes, including the consideration of semantic and pragmatic problems (Leonardi 2010: 81), which is coherent with the teaching of typological contrasts.

According to Sánchez Cuadrado (2019: 301), Pedagogical Translation requires three conditions in order to be an effective approach. First, it is important to define at the outset which aspect of the cross-linguistic dimension of language learning will be the focus. Second, it is important that Pedagogical Translation approaches incorporate developments in language pedagogy such as cooperative learning and task-based learning (see González Davies 2004; Sánchez Cuadrado 2016). Finally, it is important to carry out empirical research to determine the value of pedagogical translation. For example, Sánchez Cuadrado (2019) gives an example of a pedagogical intervention to show how Pedagogical Translation in combination with Focus on Form is effective in the teaching of *ser* and *estar* 'be'.

4 Moving forward: Applications of this research — 277

Similar studies could be conducted which focus on typological contrasts and motion constructions.

In fact, some of the benefits of pedagogical translation can be easily mapped to prevent some of the issues identified in the results of this research from arising, such as transfer and overuse of certain constructions. Sánchez Cuadrado (2016) explains that pedagogical translation helps in the development of reading comprehension, in the contrastive study of the L2 and in familiarizing students with dictionaries. All these activities can help the prevention of cross-linguistic influence. In the same vein, Leonardi (2010: 81) argues that one of the main benefits of using translation activities in L2 classes is the control of L1 transfer over L2 acquisition, while Sánchez Cuadrado (2016) considers that pedagogical translation helps with the understanding of cohesion devices, the understanding of different types of texts and differences in language use and register. All of these advantages of pedagogical translation contribute to the learner acquiring the rhetorical style of the L2. This should not come as a surprise as, after all, data from translations are important evidence underpinning Slobin's thinking for speaking hypothesis. For example, Slobin (1996a) analyses motion events in four novels in Spanish, four novels in English and their corresponding translations into the other language. This project is expanded in Slobin (2005) with the analysis of the translations of *The Hobbit* to eleven languages (see also Ibarretxe-Antuñano and Filipović 2013 and Cifuentes-Férez and Rojo 2017 in relation to motion events and translation).

The need to work on typological contrasts in the classroom meets the incremental need of preparing language learners (or language users) to deal with some degree of non-professional translation competence. Leonardi (2010) considers pedagogical translation as the fifth skill in in second language learning, together with the traditional skills of reading, writing, listening and speaking. In the same vein, Carreres, Noriega and Calduch (2018: 18) discuss the notion of translation competence. These authors consider that despite the professionalization of the field, many of the skills involved in translation competence are not exclusive to professional translators, but are in fact shared by advanced multilingual speakers.

Pedagogical translation is closely related with the notion of *mediation*, which is already present in the *Common European Framework of Reference for Languages* (Council of Europe 2001) and further developed in the *Companion Volume to the CEFRL* (Council of Europe 2018) in relation to plurilingual/pluricultural competences. Mediation is defined as the written or oral activities that make communication possible between persons who are unable to communicate with each other directly (Council of Europe 2001). These activities might involve translation, interpreting, paraphrase, summaries, or reformulation for another person who does not understand the source text. It is worth recalling that:

> The CEFR consists of far more than a set of language proficiency levels. [. . .] the CEFR broadens the perspective of language education in a number of ways, not least by its vision of the user/learner as a social agent, co-constructing meaning in interaction and by the notions of mediation and plurilingual /pluricultural competences.
>
> (Council of Europe 2018: 23).

The CEFR replaces the traditional model of four skills –reading, writing, listening and speaking- with communicative language activities and strategies, which are presented under four modes of communication: reception, production, interaction and mediation. The aim of this change is to reflect how language is used and to capture the complex reality of communication. When the learner is mediating, she acts as a social agent who helps to convey meaning and helps to create bridges and so help others to construct or understand the new meaning in an appropriate form. This can happen in a social, pedagogical, cultural, linguistic or professional context. Understanding typological contrasts between two different languages –or even within variants of the same languages- can help the learner to create these bridges. For example, in professional mediation, typological contrasts can lead to serious misunderstandings in forensic contexts (Filipović 2007a, 2017b, 2019a; Ibarretxe-Antuñano and Filipović 2013; Filipović and Hijazo-Gascón 2018; Hijazo-Gascón 2019, see Chapter 2), when interpreters from Spanish into English add Manner to render the narrative more native-like, or when they disambiguate whether a dropping action was done on purpose or accidentally from English into Spanish. A better understanding of how our languages work in terms of typological contrasts would help learners –at any proficiency level- to have a better awareness of how semantics contrasts work in both languages. Mediation activities such as pedagogical translation are thus ideal opportunities for incorporating semantics and applied typology in the second language classroom.

Some of these mediation activities can be easily linked to typological contrasts. *The Companion Volume* (Council of Europe 2018: 106) includes three types of mediation activities: mediating a text, mediating concepts and mediating communication. Some of the activities which focus on mediating a text can be related to typology, such as translating or interpreting a text, note-taking, processing texts or relying upon specific information. Activities in relation to different expression of Manner, Path or Deixis can be developed to raise students' awareness of how these semantic components are encoded in their own language and the L2. In the case of mediating concepts, the Companion Volume includes activities such as working together in a group and leading group work to facilitate and manage interaction, to collaborate to construct meaning and to encourage conceptual talk. All this can be done taking typological contrasts into account in the mediation activities. For example, students can be asked to discuss different types of translation or what is implied when adding Manner to Manner-neutral originals. For instance, does this render the text more expressive in literary translation? Does this add violence in the interpretation of a witness testimony? They can also reflect on complex notions that are different from their L1, such as different deictic motion patterns. Finally, mediating communication involves the facilitation of pluricultural spaces, acting as an intermediary in informal situations and facilitating communication in delicate situations and disagreements. The discussion of how different languages present typological contrasts and the implications they might have in different contexts can create a plurilingual space, which involves more languages than the L1 and the L2. These contrasts can be also used to illustrate miscommunication when Deixis or Manner of motion is not understood. Overall, practical activities on mediation can benefit from the use of Applied Language Typology (Filipović 2017a, 2017b) and the results of studies such as this book. Future action is therefore needed in the development of teaching materials on mediation and applied typology.

5 What is next? Future research

The two studies presented here are of course not free of limitations that should be addressed in future research. The first relevant issue is the variation in the number of participants in the different studies on motion events. The number of participants in our study is 12 per each group, so future research with larger groups would be beneficial. That being said, 12 speakers per group provided enough material to present robust results: 84 narratives, 48 in the L1s of the participants and 36 in Spanish as a second language. This is a considerable amount of data that would not be easy to collect with comparable participants, although of course larger groups would strengthen its validity.

Another important variable, but one which was beyond the scope of this study, is the number of languages each participant spoke, at what level of proficiency and how it/they might have influenced them. In the world today, it is very likely that English would play some kind of role in the acquisition of another L2-L3. Although the current study has considered Spanish as the strongest L2 of the participants (regardless of the order in which they acquired their languages) as they are in an immersion context, it is not possible to rule out some influence from English. There was also some variability in the length of the participants' stay in Spain. Further research may determine whether to what extent they might play a role in transfer in motion events. We cannot rule out reverse transfer from L2 Spanish into the L1s of our participants, and further research with complete monolinguals is likely to reinforce the results presented in this study.

An important methodological issue that needs to be addressed by researchers in this field is the different types of classification for motion verbs that have been found in previous literature. This study has attempted a classification that is coherent with previous studies by Berthele, Cadierno, Cifuentes Honrubia, Cifuentes-Férez, Ibarretxe-Antuñano and Slobin, as well as with the speakers' own judgements (Hijazo-Gascón, Ibarretxe-Antuñano, and Guelbenzu-Espada 2013). Further research should take into consideration these different methodological decisions in order to classify each motion verb as part of one category or another.

Finally, more stimuli need to be used in further research. These results are robust, but are based on *The Frog story*, with its strengths and limitations. Future research should use other types of stimuli, for example for deictic verbs (see Hijazo-Gascón 2017; Andriá and Hijazo-Gascón 2018) or for caused motion (see Gullberg 2009a, 2009b; Cadierno, Ibarretxe-Antuñano, and Hijazo-Gascón 2016; among others).

This study opens new directions for future research, both on typology and second language acquisition. In the case of typology, the finding that the Italian language presents and frequently uses some satellite-like constructions or pseudo-satellites poses interesting implications that need to be taken into account for future research. Studies on typology should study each language while taking care to avoid generalized assumptions in relation to the belonging to the same typological group and the same linguistic family. The results of the study on typology also show that the focus on Path is particularly interesting and rich in verb-framed languages. The vast majority of studies focus on Manner, but Path should not be overlooked. Finally, from a theoretical point of view, this study reinforces previous claims and consideration of the motion event typology more as a cline than a clearcut dichotomy. Our results can easily be interpreted in terms of the Manner salience cline (Slobin 2004, 2006) and Path salience cline (Ibarretxe-Antuñano 2004b, 2009a). These clines are particularly useful for identifying and interpreting intra-typological differences. It is clear that the three Romance languages studied here are low-salient in Manner, but Italian is high-salient in Path while French and Spanish are low-salient in both components. Further research on other Romance languages would confirm how this cline works, and perhaps integrated with previous research on the evolution of Romance languages, such as that of Stolova (2015). For example, Aragonese and Catalan show some common characteristics (Ibarretxe-Antuñano, Hijazo-Gascón, and Moret-Oliver 2017), and Romansch seems to be a satellite-framed language (Berthele 2006). Further studies with Portuguese, Friulan, Sardinian, Asturian, Galician, Romanian, etc. would be of great interest.

It is also worth remarking that intra-typological differences are found not only in the widely studied semantic components of Manner and Path but also in other less-studied areas within the motion events typology, such as deixis and caused motion constructions. The use of venitive verbs, such as *revenir* and *venire* 'come' was found to be different in French and Italian with respect to Spanish. In this sense, Gathercole's typology on deictic motion events depending on the role of the deictic center plays an important role in defining this intra-typological difference. Further research is needed to complement incipient research on intra-typological motion and deictic verbs (in L2 Spanish: Lewandowski 2014; Hijazo-Gascón 2017; Andriá and Hijazo-Gascón 2018). In the case of construction of caused motion more research is needed on intra-typological differences. The different use of constructions with MAKE + infinitive is particularly significant. Further research on this area would add to the results already found on inter-typological differences (Gullberg 2009b; Cadierno, Ibarretxe-Antuñano, and Hijazo-Gascón 2016). Another area that needs further research is that of the gesture component. This was beyond the scope of this volume, but the intra-typological differences found at the linguistic level in this book can lay the foundation for the study of similar or different gestural patterns between speakers of languages within the same typological group. Finally, the interplay with sociolinguistics and dialectology is another area for future research. The findings presented in Chapter 4 on the diatopic differences between Spanish from Aragón and Spanish from Madrid and Argentina can lead to future research in other varieties. Similarly, the study of conceptual domains other from motion would also expand the field.

In the case of second language acquisition, it would be interesting to see the results presented by L2 learners of Spanish by speakers of other L1 Romance languages, such as Portuguese or Romanian. It would also be interesting to see the extent to which there are similarities and differences to the results found in the present study in the language of L2 learners of French, Italian and German with different levels of proficiency. In the same vein, longitudinal studies similar to those by Stam (2015) would make valuable contribution to our understanding of how the thinking for speaking patterns change and readjust over time.

It would be equally interesting to find reverse studies to this one, that is, studies in which Spanish speakers are learners of French, German and/or Italian, because we could see if Spanish learners of these languages find similar challenges in readjusting their rhetorical style to L2 French, German and/or Italian. Another interesting direction for future research is to focus on comprehension of motion events, since the majority of the studies on motion events are based on production. Finally, the new methodologies on psycholinguistic research (e.g. eye-tracker) offer interesting possibilities in this regard for the design of new experiments that can shed light on the relation between motion event typology and other cognitive abilities such as memory and attention.

The ultimate aim of this research was to contribute to the debate regarding how languages influence one another and interact in a speaker's mind. The results show that the process of acquiring a second language and the readjustments of the thinking for speaking patterns is as complex as it is fascinating. Even in closely genetically and typologically related languages, the influences are noticeable and diverse, and depend on each semantic component and on each construction. This complexity and diversity is a further reason to maintain our interest in how meaning is expressed in different languages and how we reshape and readapt this meaning in all the languages we speak.

Appendix 1: Motion verbs in Spanish, Italian, French and German *Frog Stories*

	Spanish	Italian	French	German
NEUTER VERBS	*irse* (12) 'go' *ir* (9) 'go' *mover* (1) 'move'	*andare* (4) 'go' *spostarsi* (1) 'move over, change place'	*aller* (6) 'go' *bouger* (2) 'move'	*sich machen* (3) 'move'
	tokens: 22 **types: 3**	**tokens: 5** **types: 2**	**tokens: 8** **types: 2**	**tokens: 3** **types: 1**
PATH VERBS	*salir* (31) 'exit' *llegar* (6) 'arrive' *acercarse* (5) 'approach' *acabar* (3) 'end up' *marcharse* (3) 'go away' *subir* (3) 'go up' *subirse* (3) 'go up' *esconderse* (2) 'hide oneself' *volver* (2) 'come back' *volverse* (2) 'come back' *bajar* (1) 'go down' *esconder* (1) 'hide' *meterse* (1) 'get into' *introducirse* (1) 'insert oneself'	*uscire* (28) 'exit' *arrivare* (6) 'arrive' *salire* (5) 'go up' *ritornare* (4) 'come back' *avvicinarsi* (3) 'move closer' *allontarnarsi* (3) 'walk away' *alzare* (2) 'raise' *andarsene* (2) 'go away' *tornarsene* (2) 'come back' *finire* (2) 'end' *incastrarsi* (2) 'wedge oneself in' *sollevare* (2) 'lift' *venire* (2) 'come' *accucciarsi* (1) 'curl up (a dog)' *allontanare* (1) 'walk away' *attraversare* (1) 'cross' *dirigersi* (1) 'head' *intrappolare* (1) 'trap' *nascondersi* (1) 'hide' *ripassare* (1) 'pass again'	*sortir* (20) 'exit' *partir* (10) 'depart' *monter* (9) 'go up' *repartir* (4) 'depart again' *suivre* (4) 'follow' *arriver* (3) 'arrive' *s'éloigner* (3) 'walk away' *revenir* (2) 'come back' *s'approcher* (2) 'approach' *s'en aller* (2) 'go away' *se rapprocher* (2) 'approach' *descendre* (1) 'go down' *parcourir* (1) 'go all over' *se mettre* (1) 'get into' *se cacher* (1) 'hide' *se diriger* (1) 'head' *retourner* (1) 'come back' *soulever* (1) 'raise'	*kommen* (19) 'come' *landen* (6) 'land' *verschwinden* (6) 'disappear' *folgen* (4) 'follow' *verlassen* (4) 'depart' *verstecken* (2) 'hide' *sich nähern* (2) 'get closer' *ankommen* (1) 'arrive' *gelangen* (1) 'reach' *eindrigen* (1) 'perpetrate into' *stecken* (1) 'get into'
	tokens: 64 **types: 14**	**tokens: 69** **types: 20**	**tokens: 68** **types: 18**	**tokens: 47** **types: 11**

(continued)

	Spanish	Italian	French	German
MANNER +PATH VERBS	*caer* (18) 'fall' *caerse* (18) 'fall' *escaparse* (16) 'escape' *tirar* (6) 'throw (away)' *perseguir* (5) 'chase' *encorrer* (3) 'chase (running)' *huir* (2) 'flee' *lanzar* (2) 'throw'	*cadere* (35) 'fall' *scappare* (18) 'escape' *arrampicarsi* (7) 'climb (up)' *inseguire* (8) 'chase' *scavalcare* (3) 'climb over' *cascare* (2) 'fall' *fuggire* (2) 'huir' *rincorrere* (2) 'chase running' *gettare* (3) 'throw' *arrampicare* (1) 'climb' *buttarsi* (1) 'throw oneself' *perlustrare* (1) 'go searching' *spuntare* (1) 'appear (showing one part of the body)'	*tomber* (48) 'fall' *poursuivre* (13) 'chase' *s'échapper* (10) 'escape' *grimper* (4) 'climb (up)' *s'enfuir* (4) 'flee' *jeter* (4) 'throw' *atterrir* (1) 'land' *chasser* (1) 'chase away' *échapper* (1) 'escape' *lâcher* (1) 'throw away'	*fallen* (25) 'fall' *verfolgen* (8) 'chase' *fliehen* (6) 'flee' *steigen* (5) 'climb (up)' *schmeißen* (3) 'throw' *werfen* (3) 'throw' *abhauen* (2) 'largarse' *stürzen* (2) 'clear off' *entfliehen* (1) 'escape' *entwischen* (1) 'escape' *flüchten* (1) 'flee'
	tokens: 70 **types: 8**	**tokens: 84** **types: 13**	**tokens: 87** **types: 10**	**tokens: 57** **types: 11**
MANNER VERBS	*correr* (5) 'run' *lanzarse* (1) 'throw oneself' *empujar* (1) 'push' *pasear* (1) 'stroll'	*correre* (6) 'run' *saltare* (2) 'jump' *camminare* (1) 'walk' *fare un volo* (1) 'make a flight' *posarsi* (1) 'lie on' *saltellare* (1) 'hop' *trascinare* (1) 'drag'	*courir* (11) 'run' *secouer* (2) 'shake' *filer* (1) 'nip'	*gehen* (14) 'go (on foot)' *klettern* (10) 'climb' *rennen* (8) 'run' *springen* (8) 'jump' *fliegen* (3) 'fly' *gabeln* (2) 'pick up, lit. fork up' *beeilen* (1) 'hurry'

Appendix 1: Motion verbs in Spanish, Italian, French and German *Frog Stories* — **285**

(continued)

	Spanish	Italian	French	German
	pegar un salto (1) 'jump' *tropezarse* (1) 'trip'	*travolgere* (1) 'drag violently' *volare* (1) 'fly' *afferrare* (1) 'snatch'		*buckeln* (1) 'arch one's back' *eilen* (1) 'hurry' *holen* (1) 'grasp' *platschen* (1) 'splash' *plumpsen* (1) 'plop' *reiten* (1) 'ride' *schieben* (1) 'push' *stupsen* (1) 'push' *sich schleichen* (1) 'creep' *schleichen* (1) 'creep' *schleppen* (1) 'drag' *sich aufmachen* (1) 'hurry' *spießen* (1) 'spear' *steurern* (1) 'drive' *treten* (1) 'step' *wackeln* (1) 'shake'
	tokens: 11 types: 7	tokens: 16 types: 10	tokens: 14 types: 3	tokens: 62 types: 23
POSTURE VERBS	*echarse* (3) 'lie down' *apoyarse* (2) 'lean on' *acostarse* (1) 'lie down (in bed)'	*sedersi* (4) 'sit down' *apoggiarsi* (3) 'lean on' *agrapparsi* (2) 'grab' *alzarsi* (1) 'stand up' *apopggiare* (1) 'lean' *inginocchiarsi* (1) 'kneel'	*se pencher* (6) 'tilt' *s'accrocher* (2) 'cling to' *se relever* (2) 'pick yourself up' *se tenir* (2) 'stand' *s'appuyer* (1) 'lean'	*hangen* (2) 'colgar' *aufstehen* (1) 'stand up' *sich knien* (1) 'kneel' *sich ducken* (1) 'duck'

(continued)

	Spanish	Italian	French	German
			se coucher (1) 'go to bed' *se redresser* (1) 'stand back up' *décrocher* (1) 'unhook'	*sich legen* (1) 'lie down' *setzen* (1) 'sit down' *das Gleichgewicht verlieren* (1) 'lose balance' *das Gleichgewicht halten* (1) 'keep one's balance'
	tokens: 6 types: 3	tokens: 12 types: 6	tokens: 16 types: 8	tokens: 9 types: 8
OTHER MOTION VERBS	*llevar* (7) 'carry' *coger* (5) 'take' *lleva*r*se* (3) 'carry' *aparecer* (2) 'turn up' *frenar* (2) 'brake' *dejar* (1) 'leave'	*portare* (9) 'bring/take' *prendere* (4) 'take' *ritrovarsi* (1) 'meet again' *scomparire* (1) 'disappear' *fermarsi* (1) 'stop' *frenare il suo andare* (1) 'stop, lit. break his pace' *portarsi* (1) 'bring/take' *trasportare* (1) 'transport' *incastrare* (1) 'wedge in'	*prendre* (7) 'take' *s'arrêter* (5) 'stop' *emmener* (4) 'bring/take' *se retrouver* (4) 'find oneself in' *disparaître* (3) 'disappear' *apparaître* (1) 'appear' *freiner* (1) 'brake' *accrocher* (1) 'hook' *amener* (1) 'bring/take'	*nehmen* (12) 'take' *tragen* (5) 'take' *bremsen* (4) 'brake' *festhalten* (3) 'take' *anhalten* (2) 'stop' *bringen* (2) 'bring/take' *aufhalten* (1) 'find oneself in'

(continued)

	Spanish	Italian	French	German
			laisser (1) 'leave' *porter* (1) 'bring/take' *ramasser* (1) 'pick'	*auftauchen* (1) 'appear' *sich befinden* (1) 'find oneself' *abladen* (1) 'unload' *führen* (1) 'guide' *lassen* (1) 'leave' *sich festhalten* (1) 'hold'
	tokens: 20 types: 6	tokens: 20 types: 9	tokens: 30 types: 12	tokens: 35 types: 13
TOTAL	tokens: 193 types: 41 **SPANISH**	tokens: 210 types: 60 **ITALIAN**	tokens: 225 types: 53 **FRENCH**	tokens: 213 types: 67 **GERMAN**

Appendix 2: Motion verbs in L1 and L2 Spanish

	Spanish (Control group)	L2 Spanish (L1 Italian)	L2 Spanish (L1 French)	L2 Spanish (L1 German)
NEUTER VERBS	*irse* (12) 'go' *ir* (9) 'go' *mover* (1) 'move'	*ir* (9) 'go' *irse* (14) 'go'	*irse* (29) 'go' *ir* (7) 'go' *arrengarse** (1)	*ir* (15) 'go' *irse* (14) 'go' *cribar** (1)
	tokens: 22 **types: 3**	**tokens: 23** **types: 2**	**tokens: 37** **types: 3**	**tokens: 30** **types: 3**
PATH VERBS	*salir* (31) 'exit' *llegar* (6) 'arrive' *acercarse* (5) 'approach' *acabar* (3) 'end up' *marcharse* (3) 'go away' *subir* (3) 'go up' *subirse* (3) 'go up' *esconderse* (2) 'hide oneself' *volver* (2) 'come back' *volverse* (2) 'come back' *bajar* (1) 'go down' *esconder* (1) 'hide' *meterse* (1) 'get into' *introducirse* (1) 'insert oneself'	*salir* (30) 'exit' *llegar* (7) 'arrive' *subir* (7) 'go up' *subirse* (1) 'go up' *acercarse* (2) 'approach' *seguir* (2) 'follow' *adelantar* (1) 'overtake' *esconder* (1) 'hide' *salirse** (1) *traer* (1) 'bring' *volver* (1) 'come back'	*salir* (22) 'exit' *seguir* (6) 'follow' *subir* (5) 'go up' *subirse* (4) 'go up' *acercarse* (3) 'approach' *entrar* (2) 'enter' *llegar* (2) 'arrive' *meterse* (2) 'get into' *alejarse* (1) 'walk away' *bajar* (1) 'go down' *marcharse* (1) 'go away' *traer* (2) 'bring' *volver* (1) 'come back'	*salir* (13) 'exit' *subir* (8) 'go up' *acercarse* (4) 'approach' *seguir* (4) 'follow' *marcharse* (2) 'go away' *llegar* (2) 'arrive' *acercar* (1) 'approach' *dirigirse* (1) 'lead' *venir* (1) 'come' *regresarse* (1) 'come bak'
	tokens: 64 **types: 14**	**tokens: 54** **types: 11**	**tokens: 52** **types: 13**	**tokens: 37** **types: 10**

(continued)

	Spanish (Control group)	L2 Spanish (L1 Italian)	L2 Spanish (L1 French)	L2 Spanish (L1 German)
MANNER+PATH VERBS	*caer* (18) 'fall' *caerse* (18) 'fall' *escaparse* (16) 'escape' *tirar* (6) 'throw (away)' *perseguir* (5) 'chase' *encorrer* (3) 'chase (running)' *huir* (2) 'flee' *lanzar* (2) 'throw'	*caer* (12) 'fall' *caerse* (16) 'fall' *escaparse* (8) 'escape' *escapar* (6) 'escape' *huir* (5) 'flee' *perseguir* (4) 'chase' *huirse**(1) *echar* (1) 'throw' *trepar* (1) 'climb up' *tirar* (1) 'throw'	*caerse* (30) 'fall' *caer* (16) 'fall' *perseguir* (9) 'chase' *huir* (7) 'flee' *escaparse* (6) 'escape' *tirar* (2) 'throw' *echar* (2) 'throw' *huirse** (1) *lanzar* (1) 'throw' *trepar* (1) 'climb up'	*caerse* (19) 'fall' *caer* (17) 'fall' *huir* (8) 'flee' *escapar* (6) 'escape' *perseguir* (5) 'chase' *escaparse* (2) 'escape' *huirse** (2) *tirar* (2) 'throw' *seguir* (1) 'follow'
	tokens: 70 types: 8	tokens: 55 types: 10	tokens: 75 types: 10	tokens: 62 types: 9
MANNER VERBS	*correr* (5) 'run' *lanzarse* (1) 'throw oneself' *empujar* (1) 'push' *pasear* (1) 'stroll' *pegar un salto* (1) 'jump' *saltar* (1) 'jump' *tropezarse* (1) 'trip'	*correr* (4) 'run' *saltar* (2) 'jump' *volar* (2) 'fly' *conducir* (1) 'lead'	*correr* (6) 'run' *agitar* (1) 'jump' *andar* (1) 'walk' *cargar* (1) 'load' *saltar* (1) 'jump'	*correr* (6) 'run' *volar* (3) 'fly' *saltar* (2) 'jump' *andar* (1) 'walk' *darse un salto** (1) *montar* (1) 'ride'
	tokens: 11 types: 7	tokens: 9 types: 4	tokens: 10 types: 5	tokens: 14 types: 8

(continued)

	Spanish (Control group)	L2 Spanish (L1 Italian)	L2 Spanish (L1 French)	L2 Spanish (L1 German)
POSTURE VERBS	echarse (3) 'lie down' apoyarse (2) 'lean on' acostarse (1) 'lie down (in bed)'	levantarse (4) 'get up' apoyarse (3) 'lean on' colgar (2) 'hang' incorporarse (1) 'sit/get up'	levantarse (4) 'get up' apoyarse (1) 'lean on' arrodillarse (1) 'kneel' colgar (1) 'hang' enderezarse (1) 'straigthen up' sentar (1) 'sit down'	levantarse (2) 'get up' acostarse (1) 'lie down (in bed)' arrodillarse (1) 'kneel' sujetarse (1) 'hold on' cambiar su posición (1) 'change one's position' perder el equilibrio (1) 'lose one's balance'
	tokens: 6 types: 3	tokens: 10 types: 4	tokens: 9 types: 6	tokens: 7 types: 6
OTHER MOTION VERBS	llevar (7) 'carry' coger (5) 'take' llevarse (3) 'carry' aparecer (2) 'turn up' frenar (2) 'brake' dejar (1) 'leave'	llevar (8) 'carry' coger (5) 'take' llevarse (3) 'carry' pararse (3) 'stop' encontrarse (1) 'find oneself' tomar (1) 'take'	coger (5) 'take' aparecer (3) 'appear' llevar (3) 'carry' llevarse (3) 'carry' pararse (3) 'stop' tomar (3) 'take' encontrarse (2) 'find oneself' dejar (1) 'leave' desaparecer (1) 'disappear' estoparse* (1) ponerse (1) 'place oneself'	aparecer (8) 'appear' llevarse (3) 'carry' llevar (3) 'carry' pararse (2) 'stop' tomar (2) 'take' desaparecer (1) 'disappear' encontrarse (1) 'find oneself' frenar (1) 'brake' ponerse (1) 'put oneself' quitar (1) 'take from' traer (1)'
	tokens: 19 types: 5	tokens: 21 types: 6	tokens: 26 types: 10	tokens: 24 types: 11
TOTAL	tokens: 193 types: 41 SPANISH (CONTROL GROUP)	tokens: 172 types: 37 L2 SPANISH (L1 ITALIAN)	tokens: 209 types: 47 L2 SPANISH (L1 FRENCH)	tokens: 174 types: 46 L2 SPANISH (L1 GERMAN)

References

Achard, Michel & Susanne Niemeier (eds). 2004. *Cognitive linguistics, second language acquisition, and foreign language teaching*. Berlin & New York: Mouton de Gruyter.

Acquaroni, Rosana. 2008. *La incorporación de la competencia metafórica a la enseñanza-aprendizaje del español como segunda lengua a través de un taller de escritura creativa: estudio experimental*. Madrid: Universidad Complutense de Madrid dissertation.

Aguiló-Mora, Francisca & Eduardo Negueruela. 2015. Motion for the other through motion for the self: the conceptual complexities of giving-directions for advanced Spanish heritage learners. In Kyoko Masuda, Carlee Arnett & Angela Labarca (eds.), *Cognitive linguistics and sociocultural theory*, 73–100. Berlin & New York: Mouton de Gruyter.

Ahlqvist, August. 1875. *Die Kulturwörter der westfinnischen Sprachen*. Helsinki: Warsenius.

Aikhenvald, Alexandra. 2004. *Evidentiality*. Oxford: Oxford University Press.

Akita, Kimi. 2017. The typology of manner expressions: a preliminary look. In Iraide Ibarretxe-Antuñano (ed.), *Motion and space across languages. Theory and applications*, 39–60. Amsterdam & Philadelphia: John Benjamins.

Alcina, Juan & José Manuel Blecua. 1975. *Gramática española*. Barcelona: Ariel.

Alferink, Inge & Marianne Gullberg. 2014. French-Dutch bilinguals do not maintain obligatory semantic distinctions: evidence from placement verbs. *Bilingualism: Language and Cognition* 17(1). 22–37.

Alhmoud, Zeina, Alejandro Castañeda Castro & Teresa Cadierno. 2019. Construcciones comparativas: aproximación descriptiva y didáctica desde la gramática cognitiva. In Iraide Ibarretxe-Antuñano, Teresa Cadierno & Alejandro Castañeda Castro (eds.), *Lingüística cognitiva y español LE/L2*, 198–220. London: Routledge.

Alonso Alonso, Rosa. 2016. Cross-linguistic influence in the interpretation of boundary-crossing events in L2 acquisition. *Review of Cognitive Linguistics* 14(1): 161–182.

Alonso Alonso, Rosa, Teresa Cadierno & Scott Jarvis. 2016. Cross-linguistic influence in the acquisition of spatial prepositions in English as a foreign language. In Rosa Alonso Alonso (ed.), *Cross-linguistic influence in second language acquisition*, 93–121. Bristol: Multilingual Matters.

Alonso Raya, Rosario, Alejandro Castañeda Castro, Pablo Martínez Gila, Lourdes Miquel López, Jenaro Ortega Olivares & José Plácido Ruiz Campillo. 2005. *Gramática básica del estudiante de español*. Barcelona: Difusión.

Alonso-Aparicio, Irene & Reyes Llopis-García. 2019. La didáctica de la oposición imperfecto/perfecto simple desde una perspectiva cognitiva. In Iraide Ibarretxe-Antuñano, Teresa Cadierno & Alejandro Castañeda Castro (eds.), *Lingüística cognitiva y español LE/L2*, 274–299. London: Routledge.

Ameka, Felix K. & James Essegbey. 2013. Serialising languages: Satellite-framed, verb-framed or neither. *Ghana Journal of Linguistics* 2(1), 19–38.

Amenta, Luisa. 2008. Esistono i verbi sintagmatici nel dialetto e nell'italiano regionale di Sicilia? In Monica Cini (ed.), *I verbi sintagmatici in italiano e nelle varietà dialettali. stato dell'arte e prospettive di ricerca*, 159–174. Frankfurt: Peter Lang.

Andersen, Roger. 1983. Transfer to somewhere. In Susan Gass & Larry Selinker (eds.), *Language transfer in language learning*, 177–201. Rowley, MA: Newbury House.

Andriá, Maria & Alberto Hijazo-Gascón. 2018. Deictic motion verbs in Greek as a foreign language by Spanish and Catalan L1 learners: A preliminary approach. *Glossologia* 26. 121–135.

Annamalai, Elay. 1975. The semantics of the verbs *vaa* and *poo* in Tamil. *Indian Linguistics* 36. 212–216.

Antonopoulou, Eleni & Niki Nikiforidou. 2002. Deictic motion and the adoption of perspective in Greek. *Pragmatics* 12(3). 273–295.

Asher, James. 1977. *Learning another language through actions: The complete teacher's guideboock*. Los Gatos, CA: Sky Oaks.

Arnal Purroy, María Luisa & Vicente Lagüens Gracia. 2012. Léxico diferencial e historia: A propósito del diccionario diferencial del español de Aragón (DDAR). In Emilio Montero Cartelle & Carmen Manzano Rovira (eds.), *Actas del VIII congreso internacional de historia de la lengua española. Santiago de Compostela 14–18 de septiembre de 2009*, 1219–1236. Santiago de Compostela: Meubook.

Asher, Nicholas & Pierre Sablayrolles. 1996. A typology and discourse semantics for motion verbs and spatial PPs in French. *Journal of Semantics* 12. 163–209.

Aske, John. 1989. 'Path predicates in English and Spanish: A closer look'. In *Proceedings of the 15th annual meeting of the Berkeley Linguistics Society*, 1–14. Berkeley, CA: Berkeley Linguistics Society.

Athanasopoulos, Panos. 2009. Cognitive representation of color in bilinguals. The case of Greek blues. *Bilingualism: Language and Cognition* 9. 89–96.

Athanasopoulos, Panos & Emanuel Bylund. 2013. The "thinking" in thinking for speaking: where is it? *Language, Interaction and Acquisition* 4. 91–100.

Baciu, Ileana. 2006. Goal of motion constructions in English and Romanian: The case of "a alerga" and "a fugi". *Revue Roumaine de Linguistique* 51(1). 43–54.

Badia Margarit, Antoni. 1947. *Los complementos pronominalo-adverbiales derivados de ibi e inde en la Península Ibérica*. Madrid: CSIC.

Baicchi, Annalisa. 2005. Translating phrasal combinations across the typological divide. In Marcella Bertucelli Papi (ed.), *Studies in the semantics of lexical combinatory patterns*, 487–519. Pisa: Pisa University Press.

Bally, Charles. 1965. *Linguistique Générale et Linguistique Française*. Bern: Francke.

Bamberg, Michael. 1987. *The acquisition of narratives: Learning to use language*. Berlin: Mouton de Gruyter.

Bamberg, Michael. 1994. Development of linguistic forms: German. In Ruth A. Berman & Dan I. Slobin (eds.), *Relating events in narrative. A cross-linguistic development study*, 189–238. Mahwah, NJ: Lawrence Erlbaum.

Bartra, Anna & Jaume Mateu. 2005. Aspecte i prefixació verbal en català antic [Aspect and verbal prefixation in Old Catalan]. *Caplletra* 39. 85–108.

Beavers, John. 2008. On the nature of goal marking and delimitation: Evidence from Japanese. *Journal of Linguistics* 44. 283–316.

Beavers, John, Beth Levin & Shiao-Wei Tham. 2010. The typology of motion expressions revisited. *Journal of Linguistics* 44. 183–216.

Berlin, Brent & Paul Kay. 1969. *Basic color terms: Their universality and evolution*. Berkeley: California University Press.

Berman, Ruth A. & Dan I. Slobin (eds). 1994. *Relating events in narrative: A cross-linguistic developmental study*. Hillsdale, NJ: Lawrence Erlbaum.

Bernardo Carrasco, José & José Fernando Calderero Hernández. 2000. *Aprendo a investigar en educación*. Madrid: Ediciones Rialp.

Bernini, Giuliano. 2008. Per una definizione di verbi sintagmatici. La prospettiva dialettale. In Monica Cini (ed.), *I verbi sintagmatici in italiano e nelle varietà dialettali. Stato dell'arte e prospettive di ricerca*, 141–158. Frankfurt: Peter Lang.

Berthele, Raphael. 2004. The typology of motion and posture verbs: A variationist account. In Bernd Kortmann (ed.), *Dialectology meets typology. Dialect grammar from a cross-linguistic perspective*, 93–126. Berlin & New York: Mouton de Gruyter.

Berthele, Raphael. 2006. *Ort und Weg. Die sprachlichen Raumreferenz in Varietäten des Deutschen, Rätoromanischen und Französischen*. Berlin & New York: Mouton de Gruyter.

Berthele, Raphael. 2013. Disentangling manner and path. Evidence from varieties of German and Romance. In Juliana Goschler & Anatol Stefanowitsch, *Variation and change in the encoding of motion events*, 55–75. Amsterdam & Philadelphia: John Benjamins.

Berthele, Raphael. 2017. When bilinguals forget their manners. Language dominance and motion event description. *VIAL. Vigo International Journal of Applied Linguistics* 14. 39–70.

Berthele, Raphael & Ladina Stocker. 2017. The effect of language mode on motion event descriptions in German-French bilinguals. *Language and Cognition* 9(4). 1–29.

Bialystok, Ellen. 2007. Cognitive effects of bilingualism: How linguistic experience leads to cognitive change. *International Journal of Bilingualism* 10(3). 210–223.

Boers, Frank & Seth Lindstromberg (eds). 2008. *Cognitive linguistics. Approaches to teaching vocabulary and phraseology*. Berlin & New York: Mourton de Gruyter.

Bohnemeyer, Juergen, Nick Enfield, James Essegbey, Iraide Ibarretxe-Antuñano, Sotaro Kita, Friederike Lüpke & Felix Ameka. 2007. Principles of event segmentation in language: the case of motion events. *Language* 83(3). 495–532.

Boroditsky, Lera. 2001. Does language shape thought? English and Mandarin speakers' conceptions of time. *Cognitive Psychology* 43(1). 1–22.

Boroditsky, Lera, Lauren A. Schmidt & Webb Philips. 2003. Sex, syntax and semantics. In Dedre Gentner & Susan Goldin-Meadow (eds.), *Language in mind: Advances in the study of language and thought*, 61–79. Cambridge, MA: MIT Press.

Brown, Amanda & Marianne Gullberg. 2008. Bidirectional cross-linguistic influence in L1-L2 encoding of manner in speech and gesture: A study of Japanese speakers of English. *Studies in Second Language Acquisition* 30(2). 225–251.

Brown, Amanda & Marianne Gullberg. 2010. Changes in encoding of path of motion after acquisition of a second language. *Cognitive Linguistics* 21(2). 263–286.

Brown, Amanda & Marianne Gullberg. 2012. Multicompetence and native speaker variation in clausal packaging in Japanese. *Second Language Research* 28(4). 415–442.

Brown, Penelope. 2004. Position and motion in Tzeltal Frog Stories. The acquisition of narrative style. In Sven Strömqvist & Ludo Verhoeven (eds.), *Relating events in narrative: typological and contextual perspectives*, 37–58. New York: Psychology Press.

Brown, Roger W. & Eric H. Lenneberg. 1954. A study in language and cognition. *The Journal of Abnormal and Social Psychology* 49(3). 454–462.

Bühler, Karl. 1934. *Sprachtheorie. Die Darstellungsfunktion der Sprache*. Jena: Gustav Fisher.

Bylund, Emanuel. 2011a. Language-specific patterns in event conceptualization: Insights from bilingualism. In Aneta Pavlenko (ed.), *Thinking and speaking in two languages*, 108–142. Clevedon: Multilingual matters.

Bylund, Emanuel. 2011b. Segmentation and temporal structuring of events in early Spanish-Swedish bilinguals. *International Journal of Bilingualism* 15. 56–84.
Bylund, Emanuel. 2008. Procesos de conceptualización de eventos en español y en sueco. Diferencias translingüísticas. *Revue Romane* 43(1). 1–24.
Bylund, Emanuel. 2009. *Conceptualización de eventos en español y en sueco. Estudios sobre hablantes monolingües y bilingües.* Stockholm: Stockholm University dissertation.
Bylund, Emanuel & Scott Jarvis. 2011. L2 effects on L1 event conceptualization. *Bilingualism: Language and Cognition* 14(1). 47–59.
Cadierno, Teresa. 2004. Expressing motion events in a second language: A cognitive typological perspective. In Michel Achard & Susanne Neimeier (eds.), *Cognitive linguistics, second language acquisition and foreign language pedagogy*, 13–49. Berlin & New York: Mouton de Gruyter.
Cadierno, Teresa. 2008a. Learning to talk about motion in a foreign language. In Peter Robinson & Nick C. Ellis (eds.), *Handbook of cognitive linguistics and second language acquisition*, 239–275. London: Routledge.
Cadierno, Teresa. 2008b. Motion events in Danish and Spanish: A Focus on Form pedagogical approach. In Sabine de Knop & Teun de Rycker (eds.), *Cognitive approaches to pedagogical grammar*, 259–294. Berlin & New York: Mourton de Gruyter.
Cadierno, Teresa. 2010. Motion in Danish as a second language: Does the learner's L1 make a difference? In ZhaoHong Han & Teresa Cadierno (eds.), *Linguistic relativity in SLA: Thinking for speaking*, 1–33. Bristol: Multilingual matters.
Cadierno, Teresa. 2017. Thinking for speaking about motion in a second language: Looking back and forward. In Iraide Ibarretxe-Antuñano (ed.), *Motion and space across languages: Theory and applications*, 279–300. Amsterdam & Philadelphia: John Benjamins.
Cadierno, Teresa & Alberto Hijazo-Gascón. 2013. Cognitive linguistic approaches to second language Spanish. In Kimberly Geeslin (ed.), *The handbook of Spanish second language acquisition*, 96–110. Hoboken, NJ: Wiley.
Cadierno, Teresa, Iraide Ibarretxe-Antuñano & Alberto Hijazo-Gascón. 2016. Semantic categorization of placement verbs in L1 and L2 Danish and Spanish: Placement verbs in L1 and L2 Danish. *Language learning* 66(1). 191–223.
Cadierno, Teresa & Karen Lund. 2004. Cognitive linguistics and second language acquisition: motion events in a typological framework. In Bill VanPatten, Jessica Williams, Susanne Rott & Mark Overstreet (eds.), *Form-meaning connections in second language acquisition*, 139–154. Hillsdale, NJ: Lawrence Erlbaum.
Cadierno, Teresa & Peter Robinson. 2009. Language typology, task complexity and the development of L2 lexicalization patterns for describing motion events. *Annual Review of Cognitive Linguistics* 7. 245–276.
Cadierno, Teresa & Lucas Ruiz. 2006. Motion events in Spanish L2 acquisition. *Annual Review of Cognitive Linguistics* 4. 183–216.
Cameron, Lynn & Graham Low (eds). 1999. *Researching and applying metaphor*. Cambridge: Cambridge University Press.
Campos, Héctor. 1999. Transitividad e intransitividad. In Ignacio Bosque & Violeta Demonte (eds.), *Gramática descriptiva de la lengua española*, 1519–1575. Madrid: Espasa.
Canale, Michael & Merrill Swain. 1980. Theoretical bases of communicative approaches to second language teaching and testing. *Applied linguistics* 1(1). 1–47.
Cardini, Filippo-Enrico. 2008. Manner of motion saliency: An inquiry into Italian. *Cognitive Linguistics* 19(4). 535–569.

Cardini, Filippo-Enrico. 2012. Grammatical constraints and verb-framed languages: The case of Italian. *Language and Cognition* 4(3). 167–201.
Carreres, Ángeles, María Noriega-Sánchez & Carme Calduch. 2018. *Mundos en palabras: Learning advanced Spanish through translation*. London: Routledge.
Carroll, Mary & Christiane von Stutterheim. 2003. The representation of spatial configurations in English and German and the grammatical structure of locative and anaphoric descriptions. *Linguistics* 31(6). 1011–1044.
Carroll, Mary, Katja Weimar, Monique Flecken, Monique Lambert & Christiane von Stutterheim. 2012. Tracing trajectories: Motion event construal by advanced L2 French-English and L2 French-German speakers. *Language, Interaction and Acquisition* 3(2). 202–230.
Castañeda Castro, Alejandro. 2006. Aspecto, perspectiva y tiempo de procesamiento en la oposición imperfecto/indefinido del español. Ventajas explicativas y aplicaciones pedagógicas. *RAEL: Revista Electrónica de Lingüística Aplicada* 5. 107–140.
Castañeda Castro, Alejandro. 2012. Perspective and meaning in pedagogical descriptions of Spanish as a foreign language. In Guadalupe Ruiz Fajardo (ed.), *Methodological developments in teaching Spanish as a second and foreign language*, 221–272. Newcastle upon Tyne: Cambridge Scholars Publishing.
Castañeda Castro Alejandro (ed.). 2014. *Enseñanza de gramática avanzada de ELE. Criterios y recursos*. Madrid: SGEL.
Castañeda Castro Alejandro & Jenaro Ortega Olivares. 2019. Los usos atributivos de ser y estar desde la gramática cognitiva. In Iraide Ibarretxe-Antuñano, Teresa Cadierno & Alejandro Castañeda Castro (eds.), *Lingüística cognitiva y español LE/L2*, 120–144. London: Routledge.
Cerruti, Massimo. 2008. Verbi sintagmatici e sinonimi monorematici nell'italiano parlato. Dimensione diafasica, diatopica, diastratica. In Monica Cini (ed.), *I verbi sintagmatici in italiano e nelle varietà dialettali. Stato dell'arte e prospettive di ricerca*, 193–208. Frankfurt: Peter Lang.
Chafe, Wallace & Johanna Nichols (eds). 1986. *Evidentiality: The linguistic coding of epistemology*. Norwood, NJ: Ablex.
Chamorro, María Dolores, Gracia Lozano López, Aurelio Ríos Rojas, Francisco Rosales Varo, José Plácido Ruiz Campillo & Guadalupe Ruiz Fajardo. 2006. *El ventilador*. Barcelona: Difusión.
Chen, Liang. 2007. *The acquisition and use of motion event expressions in Chinese*. Munich: Lincom.
Chen, Liang & Jiangsheng Guo. 2009. Motion events in Chinese novels: Evidence for an equipollently-framed language. *Journal of Pragmatics* 41. 1749–1756.
Chevalier, Gisèle & Michael Long. 2005. Finder out pour qu'on les frigge pas up, comment c'qui workont out: Les verbes à particules en chiac. In Patrice Brasseur & Anika Falket (eds.), *Français d'Amérique: Approches morphosyntaxiques. Actes du colloque international grammaire comparée des variétés de français d'Amérique*, 201–212. Paris: L'Harmattan.
Choi, Soojung & Melissa Bowerman. 1991. Learning to express motion events in English and Korean: The influence of language-specific lexicalization patterns. *Cognition* 41(1). 1–33.
Choi, Soojung & Melissa Bowerman. 1992. Learning to express motion events in English and Korean: The influence of language specific lexicalization patterns. In Beth Levin & Stephen Pinker (eds.), *Lexical and conceptual semantics*, 83–121. Oxford: Blackwell.

Choi, Soojung & James Lantolf. 2008. Representation and embodiment of meaning in L2 communication. Motion events in the speech and gesture of advanced L2 Korean and L2 English speakers. *Studies in Second Language Acquisition* 30. 191–224.
Chui, Daniel. 2015. Claro que vengo a tu fiesta: La enseñanza de los verbos deícticos ir/venir y traer/llevar a estudiantes angloparlantes. *Revista de Filología y Lingüística de la Universidad de Costa Rica* 41(1). 53–77.
Cifuentes Honrubia, José Luis. 1999. *Sintaxis y semántica del movimiento: Aspectos de gramática cognitiva*. Valencia: Instituto de Cultural Juan Gil-Albert.
Cifuentes-Férez, Paula. 2009. *A cross-linguistic study on the semantics of motion verbs in English and Spanish*. Munich: Lincom Europa.
Cini, Monica (ed.). 2008. *I verbi sintagmatici in italiano e nelle varietà dialettali. Statto dell'arte e prospettive di ricerca*. Frankfurt: Peter Lang.
Colasacco, Marina Anna. 2019. A cognitive approach to teaching deictic motion verbs to German and Italian students of Spanish. *IRAL. International Review of Applied Linguistics in Language Teaching* 57(1). 71–95.
Cook, Vivian. 1991. The poverty-of-the-stimulus argument and multicompetence. *Second Language Research* 7(2). 103–17.
Cook, Vivian. 1994. The metaphor of access to Universal Grammar. In Nick C. Ellis (ed.), *Implicit learning and language*, 477–502. Cambridge, MA: Academic Press.
Cook, Vivian. 2012. An attempt to isolate, and then differentiate, transfer and interference. *International Journal of Bilingualism* 16(1). 11–21.
Cook, Vivian. 2016. Transfer and the relationships between the languages of multi-competence. In Rosa Alonso Alonso (ed.), *Cross-linguistic influence and second language acquisition*, 24–37. Bristol: Multilingual Matters.
Cook, Vivian & Benedetta Bassetti (eds). 2011. *Language and bilingual cognition*. New York: Psychology Press.
Cordin, Patrizia. 2008. L'espressione di tratti aspettuali nei verbi analitici dei dialetti trentini. In Monica Cini (ed.), *I verbi sintagmattici in italiano e nelle varietà dialettali. Stato dell'arte e prospettive di ricerca*, 175–192. Frankfurt: Peter Lang.
Council of Europe. 2001. *Common European framework of reference for languages: Learning, teaching, assessment*. Cambridge: Press Syndicate of the University of Cambridge.
Council of Europe. 2018. *Common European framework of reference for languages: Learning, teaching, assessment. Companion volume with new descriptors*. Cambridge: Press Syndicate of the University of Cambridge.
Coventry, Kenny & Pedro Guijarro-Fuentes. 2008. Spatial language learning and the functional geometric framework. In Peter Robinson & Nick C. Ellis (eds.), *Handbook of cognitive linguistics and second language acquisition*, 114–138. London: Routledge.
Coventry, Kenny, Berenice Valdés & Pedro Guijarro-Fuentes. 2010. Thinking for speaking and immediate memory for spatial relations. In ZhaoHong Han & Teresa Cadierno (eds.), *Linguistic relativity in SLA. Thinking for speaking*, 154–182. Bristol: Multilingual Matters.
Croft, William A. 2001. *Radical construction grammar: Syntactic theory in typological perspective*. Oxford: Oxford University Press.
Croft, William A., Jóhanna Barðdal, Willem Hollmann, Violeta Sotirova & Chiaki Taoka. 2010. Revising Talmy's typological classification of complex event constructions. In Hans C. Boas (ed.), *Constructional approaches to language*, 201–236. Amsterdam & Philadelphia: John Benjamins.

Cuartero Otal, Juan. 2006. ¿Cuántas clases de verbos de desplazamiento se distinguen en español? *RILCE* 22(1). 13–36.
Cuartero Otal, Juan. 2016a. Estudio contrastivo de la expresión de desplazamiento en español frente al inglés y el alemán. In María José Domínguez Vázquez & Silvia Kutscher (eds.), *Interacción entre gramática, didáctica y lexicografía*, 325–340. Berlin & Boston: De Gruyter.
Cuartero Otal, Juan. 2016b. Cómo se dice salir en alemán y otras serias dificultades para la lexicografía contrastiva. In Andreu Castell (ed.), *Sintaxis y diccionarios: La complementación en alemán y en español*, 161–197. Berlin: Lang.
Cuenca, María Josep & Joseph Hilferty. 1999. *Introducción a la lingüística cognitiva*. Barcelona: Ariel.
Czechowska, Natalia & Anna Ewert. 2011. Perception of motion by Polish-English bilinguals. In Vivian Cook & Benedetta Bassetti (eds.), *Language and bilingual cognition*, 287–314. New York: Psychology Press.
Danesi, Marcel. 1988. The development of metaphorical competence: A neglected dimension in second language pedagogy. In Albert N. Mancini, Pablo Giordano & Pier Raimondo Baldini (eds.), *Italiana: Selected papers from the proceedings of the third annual conference of the American association of teachers of Italian*, 1–10. River Forest, IL: Italiana.
De Bot, Kees. 2015. Multi-competence and dynamic/complex systems. In Vivian Cook & Li Wei (eds.), *The Cambridge handbook of linguistic multi-competence*, 125–141. Cambridge: Cambridge University Press.
De Knop, Sabine. 2017. German motion expressions without motion verbs. Paper presented at the Thinking, Doing, Learning Conference (TDL3), Ludwig-Maximilians-Universität, Munich.
De Knop, Sabine, Frank Boers & Antoon de Rycker (eds.). 2010. *Fostering language teaching efficiency through cognitive linguistics*. Berlin & New York: Mouton de Gruyter.
De Knop, Sabine & Teun de Rycker (eds.). 2008. *Cognitive approaches to pedagogical grammar*. Berlin & New York: Mouton de Gruyter.
De Knop, Sabine & René Dirven. 2008. Motion and location events in German, French and English. In Sabine de Knop & Teun de Rycker (eds.), *Cognitive approaches to pedagogical grammar: A volume in honour of René Dirven*, 295–324. Berlin & New York: Mouton de Gruyter.
De Knop, Sabine & Françoise Gallez. 2011. Manner of motion: A priviledged dimension of German expressions. *International Journal of Cognitive Linguistics* 2(1). 1–16.
De Knop, Sabine & Gaëtanelle Gilquin (eds). 2016. *Applied Construction Grammar*. Berlin & New York: Mouton de Gruyter.
Delbeque, Nicole. 1996. Towards a cognitive account of the use of the prepositions *por* and *para* in Spanish. In Eugene H. Casad (eds.), *Cognitive linguistics in the redwoods: The expansion of a new paradigm in linguistics*, 249–318. Berlin & New York: Mouton de Gruyter.
Duden. 2006. *Die Grammatik*. Manheim: Duden.
Elliott, Elisabeth & Lisa Yountchi. 2009. Total physical response and Russian multi- and unidirectional verbs of motion: A case study in acquisition. *Slavic and East European Journal* 53(3). 428–450.

Ellis, Nick C. 2003. Constructions, chuncking and connectionism. The emergence of second language. In Catherine Doughty and Michael Long (eds.), *The Handbook of Second Language Acquisition*, 63–103. Oxford: Blackwell.

Ellis, Nick C. 2008. Usage-based and form-focused language acquisition: The associative learning of constructions, learned attention and the limited L2 endstate. In Peter Robinson and Nick C. Ellis (eds.), *Handbook of cognitive linguistics and second language acquisition*, 372–405. London: Routledge.

Ellis, Nick C. & Teresa Cadierno. 2009. Constructing a second language: Introduction to the special section. *Annual Review of Cognitive Linguistics* 7. 197–220.

Ellis, Rod. 1994. *The study of second language acquisition*. Oxford: Oxford University Press.

Engberg-Pedersen, Elisabeth & Frederikke Blytmann-Trondhjeim. 2004. Focus on action in motion descriptions. The case of West-Greenlandic. In Sven Strömqvist and Ludo Verhoeven (eds.), *Relating events in narrative: Typological and contextual perspectives*, 59–88. New York: Psychology Press.

Engemann, Helen, Henriette Hendriks, Maya Hickmann, Efstathia Soroli & Coralie Vincent. 2015. How Language impacts memory of motion events. *Cognitive Processing – International Quarterly of Cognitive Science* 16(1). 209–213.

Enguita Utrilla, José María 2000. Aragón, panorama lingüistico. In Inés Carrasco (ed.), *El español y sus variedades*, 95–125. Málaga: Ayuntamiento de Málaga.

Enguita Utrilla, José María 2008. Spanish and historical dialect in Aragon. *International Journal of the Sociology of Language* 193/194. 79–89.

Evans, Reid. 2015. Typology in the classroom: Fostering motion-event awareness in Spanish-speaking ELLs. *Colombian Applied Linguistics Journal* 17(1). 11–24.

Fábregas, Antonio. 2007. An exhaustive lexicalization account of directional complements. *Nordlyd: Tromsø Working Papers on Language and Linguistics* 34(2). 165–199.

Fauconnier, Gilles. 1994. *Mental spaces: Aspects of meaning construction in natural language*. Cambridge: Cambridge University Press.

Fernández, Eva M., Ricardo A. De Souza & Agustina Carando. 2017. Bilingual innovations: experimental evidence offers clues regarding the psycholinguistics of language change. *Bilingualism: Language and Cognition* 20(2). 251–268.

Ferrari, Giacomo, and Monica Mosca. 2010. Some constructions of path: from Italian to some classical languages. In Giovanna Marotta, Alessandro Lenci, Linda Meini & Francesco Rovai (eds.), *Space in language. Proceedings of the Pisa international conference*, 317–338. Pisa: ETS.

Filipović, Luna. 2007a. *Talking about motion: A crosslingual investigation of lexicalization patterns*. Amsterdam: John Benjamins.

Filipović, Luna. 2007b. Language as a witness: Insights from cognitive linguistics. *International Journal of Speech, Language and the Law* 14(2). 245–267.

Filipović, Luna. 2010a. Typology meets witness narratives and memory: Theory and practice entwined in cognitive linguistics. In Elżbieta Tabakowska, Michał Choiński & Łukasz Wiraszka (eds.), *Cognitive linguistics in action: Theory to application and back*, 269–291. Berlin & New York: Mouton de Gruyter.

Filipović, Luna. 2010b. Thinking and speaking about motion: Universal vs. language-specific effects. In Giovanna Marotta, Alessandro Lenci, Linda Meini & Francesco Rovai (eds.), *Space in language. Proceedings of the Pisa international conference*, 235–348. Pisa: University of Pisa.

Filipović, Luna. 2011. Speaking and remembering in one or two languages: Bilingual vs. monolingual lexicalization and memory for motion events. *International Journal of Bilingualism* 15(4). 466–485.

Filipović, Luna. 2013. Constructing causation in language and memory: Implications for access to justice in multilingual interactions. *Journal of Speech, Language and the Law* 20. 1–19.

Filipović, Luna. 2017a. Applied language typology: Applying typological insights in professional practice. *Languages in Contrast* 17(2). 255–278.

Filipović, Luna. 2017b. Applying language typology: Practical applications of research on typological contrasts between languages. In Iraide Ibarretxe-Antuñano (ed.), *Motion and space across languages: Theory and applications*, 399–417. Amsterdam & Philadelphia: John Benjamins.

Filipović, Luna. 2019a. Evidence-gathering in police interviews: Communication problems and possible solutions. *Pragmatics and Society* 10(1). 9–31.

Filipović, Luna. 2019b. *Bilingualism in action. Theory and practice*. Cambridge: Cambridge University Press.

Filipović, Luna & Sharon Geva. 2012. Language-specific effects on lexicalization and memory of motion events. In Luna Filipović & Kasia Jaszczolt (eds.), *Space and Time across Languages, disciplines and cultures (Vol. II): Language, culture and cognition*, 269–282. Amsterdam & Philadelphia: John Benjamins.

Filipović, Luna & John A. Hawkins. 2013. Multiple factors in second language acquisition: The CASP model. *Linguistics* 51(1). 145–176.

Filipović, Luna & John A. Hawkins. 2019. The Complex Adaptive System Principles model for bilingualism: Language interactions within and across bilingual minds. *International Journal of Bilingualism* 23(6). 1223–1248.

Filipović, Luna & Alberto Hijazo-Gascón. 2018. Interpreting meaning in police interviews: Applied language typology in a forensic linguistics context. *VIAL . Vigo International Journal of Applied Linguistics* 15. 67–104.

Filipović, Luna & Iraide Ibarretxe-Antuñano. 2015. Motion. In Ewa Dąbrowska & Dagmar Divjak (eds.), *Handbook of Cognitive Linguistics*, 527–545. Berlin & New York: Mouton de Gruyter.

Filipović, Luna & Ivana Vidaković. 2010. Typology in the L2 classroom: Second language acquisition from a typological perspective. In Martin Pütz & Laura Sicola (eds.), *Inside the learner's mind: Cognitive processing in second language acquisition*, 269–291. Amsterdam & Philadelphia: John Benjamins.

Fillmore, Charles. 1977. Scenes-and-Frames Semantics. In A Zampolli (ed.), *Fundamental Studies in Computer Science*, 55–88. Amsterdam: North Holland Publishing.

Fillmore, Charles. 1983. How to know whether you are coming or going. In Gisa Rauh (ed.), *Essays on Deixis*, 219–227. Tübingen: Narr.

Flecken, Monique. 2011. Event conceptualization by early bilinguals: Insights from linguistic and eye tracking data. *Bilingualism: Language and Cognition* 14(1). 61–77.

Folli, Raffaella. 2001. *Constructing Telicity in English and Italian*. Oxford: Oxford University dissertation.

Galvan, Dennis & Sarah Taub. 2004. The encoding of motion information in American Sign Language. In Sven Strömqvist & Ludo Verhoeven (eds.), *Relating events in narrative: Typological and contextual perspectives*, 191–218. New York: Psychology Press.

Gallez, Françoise. 2015. Constructions verbales exprimant un déplacement en allemand – Approches linguistique et didactique. *SOLAGRAM: Revue de Didactique de la Grammaire* 1 https://scolagram.u-cergy.fr/ (accessed 9 April 2021)

Gathercole, Virginia. 1977. A study of the comings and goings of the speakers of four languages: Spanish, Japanese, English and Turkish. *Kansas Working Papers in Linguistics* 2. 61–94.

Gathercole, Virginia. 1978. Towards a universal for deictic verbs of motion. *Kansas Working Papers in Linguistics* 3. 72–88.

Geeraerts, Dirk & Hubert Cuyckens (eds.). 2008. *The Oxford handbook of cognitive linguistics*. Oxford: Oxford University Press.

Geeraerts, Dirk, Gitte Kristiansen & Yves Peirsman (eds). 2010. *Advances in cognitive sociolinguistics*. Berlin & New York: Mouton de Gruyter.

Gennari, Silvia, Steven Sloman, Barbara Malt & W. Tecumseh Fitch. 2002. Motion events in language and cognition. *Cognition* 83(1). 49–79.

Goddard, Cliff. 1997. The semantics of coming and going. *Pragmatics* 7(2): 147–162.

Goldberg, Adele. 1995. *Constructions: A construction grammar approach to argument structure*. Chicago: University of Chicago Press.

Goldberg, Adele & Devin Casenhiser. 2008. Construction learning and second language acquisition. In Peter Robinson & Nick C. Ellis (eds.), *Handbook of cognitive linguistics and second language acquisition*, 197–215. London: Routledge.

Gómez Vicente, Lucía. 2013. L'expression métaphorique de l'évènement émotionel en français (L1) et en espagnol (L1/L2): les images schéma haut/bas et dedans/dehors. Analyse descriptive et proposition didactique. *Recherches en didactique des langues et des cultures: Les cahiers de l'ACEDLE* 10(1). 81–102.

González Davies, María. 2004. *Multiple voices in the translation classroom: activities, task and projects*. Amsterdam & Philadelphia: John Benjamins.

González Davies, María. 2007. Translation: why the bad press? A natural activity in an increasingly bilingual world. *Humanising Language Teaching* 9(2).

Gonzálvez-García, Francisco. 2009. The family of object-related depictives in English and Spanish: Towards a usage-based, constructionist analysis. *Language Sciences* 31(5). 663–723.

Gonzálvez-García, Francisco. 2019. Exploring the pedagogical potential of vertical and horizontal relations in the constructicon: the case of the family of subjective-transitive constructions with decir in Spanish. *IRAL. International Review of Applied Linguistics in Language Teaching* 57(1). 121–145.

Goschler, Juliana. 2009. Typologische und konstruktionelle Einflüsse bei der Kodierung von Bewegungsereignissen in der Zweitsprache. *NLK-Proceedings: 10 Norddeutsches Linguistisches Kolloquium (NLK2009 Greifswald)*, 40–65.

Goschler, Juliana. 2013. Motion events in Turkish-German contact varieties. In Juliana Goschler and Anatol Stefanowitsch (eds.), *Variation and change in the encoding of motion events*, 115–132. Amsterdam & Philadelphia: John Benjamins.

Goschler, Juliana & Anatol Stefanowitsch. 2009. Pfad und Bewegung im gesprochenen Deutsch: Ein kollostruktionaler Ansatz. In Thomas Stolz, Esther Ruigendijk & Jürgen Trabant (eds.), *Linguistik in Nordwesten*, 103–115. Bochum: Brockmeyer.

Gras, Pedro. 2011. *Gramática de construcciones en interacción. Propuesta de un modelo y aplicación al análisis de estructuras independientes con marcas de subordinación en español*. Barcelona: Universitat de Barcelona dissertation.

Gras, Pedro. 2016. Revisiting the functional typology of insubordination. Insubordinate que-constructions in Spanish. In Nicholas Evans & Honoré Watanabe (eds.), *Insubordination*, 113–144. Amsterdam: John Benjamins.

Grinevald, Colette. 2011. On constructing a working typology of the expression of path. *Cahiers de Faits de Langue* 3. 43–70.
Grosjean, François. 1989. Neurolinguists, beware! The bilingual is not two monolinguals in one person. *Brain and Language* 36. 3–15.
Grosjean, François. 2008. *Studying Bilinguals*. Oxford: Oxford University Press.
Grosjean, François. 2010. *Bilingual: Life and reality*. Cambridge, MA: Harvard University Press.
Grosjean, François. 2012. An attempt to isolate, and then differentiate, transfer and interference. *International Journal of Bilingualism* 16(1). 11–21.
Gullberg, Marianne. 2009a. Reconstructing verb meaning in a second language. How English speakers of L2 Dutch talk and gesture about placement. *Annual Review of Cognitive Linguistics* 7. 221–244.
Gullberg, Marianne. 2009b. Gestures and the development of semantic representations in first and second language acquisition. *Language, Interaction and Acquisition* 1. 117–139.
Gullberg, Marianne. 2011. Thinking, speaking and gesturing about motion. In Aneta Pavlenko (eds.), *Thinking and speaking in two languages*, 143–169. Clevedon: Multilingual matters.
Gullberg, Marianne, Henriette Hendriks & Maya Hickmann. 2008. Learning to talk and gestures about motion in French. *First Language* 28(2). 200–236.
Han, ZhaoHong & Teresa Cadierno (eds). 2010. *Linguistic relativity in SLA: Thinking for speaking*. Bristol: Multilingual matters.
Harr, Anne-Katharina. 2012. *Language-specific factors in first language acquisition: The expression of motion events in French and German*. Berlin & Boston: De Gruyter Mouton.
Hasko, Victoria. 2010. The role of thinking for speaking in adult L2 speech: The case of (non) unidirectionality encoding by American learners of Russian. In ZhaoHong Han & Teresa Cadierno (eds.), *Linguistic relativity in SLA: Thinking for speaking*, 34–58. Bristol: Multilingual matters.
Hatim, Basil & Ian Mason. 1990. *Discourse and the translator*. London: Routledge.
Helms-Park, Rena & Vedran Dronjic. 2016. Cross-linguistic lexical influence: Cognate facilitation. In Rosa Alonso Alonso (ed.), *Cross-linguistic influence and second language acquisition*, 71–92. Bristol: Multilingual Matters.
Hendriks, Henriette, Maya Hickmann & Annie-Claude Demagny. 2008. How adult English learners of French express caused motion: A comparison with English and French natives. *Acquisition et interaction en langue étrangère (AILE)* 27. 15–41.
Herdina, Philip & Ulrike Jessner. 2002. *A dynamic model of multilingualism: Perspectives of change in psycholinguistics*. Clevedon: Multilingual Matters.
Hickmann, Maya. 2006. The relativity of motion in first language acquisition. In Maya Hickmann & Stephane Robert (eds.), *Space across languages: Linguistic systems and cognitive categories*, 281–308. Amsterdam: John Benjamins.
Hickmann, Maya, Helen Engemann, Efstathia Soroli, Henriette Hendriks & Coralie Vincent. 2017. Expressing and categorizing motion in French and English: Verbal and non-verbal cognition across languages. In Iraide Ibarretxe-Antuñano (eds.), *Motion and space across languages. Theory and applications*, 61–94. Amsterdam & Philadelphia: John Benjamins.
Hickmann, Maya & Henriette Hendriks. 2006. Static and dynamic location in French and English. *First Language* 26(1). 103–35.
Hickmann, Maya & Henriette Hendriks. 2010. Typological constraints on the acquisition of spatial language in French and English. *Cognitive Linguistics* 21(2). 189–215.
Hijazo-Gascón, Alberto. 2011a. *La expresión de eventos de movimiento y su adquisición en segundas lenguas*. Zaragoza: Universidad de Zaragoza dissertation.

Hijazo-Gascón, Alberto. 2011b. Las metáforas conceptuales como estrategias comunicativas y de aprendizaje. Una aplicación didáctica de la lingüística cognitiva. *Hispania. A Journal devoted to the teaching of Spanish and Portuguese* 94(1). 142–154.

Hijazo-Gascón, Alberto. 2017. Motion events contrasts in Romance languages: Deixis in Spanish as a second language. In Iraide Ibarretxe-Antuñano (ed.), *Motion and space across languages: Theory and applications*, 301–328. Amsterdam & Philadelphia: John Benjamins.

Hijazo-Gascón, Alberto. 2018. Acquisition of motion events in L2 Spanish by German, French and Italian speakers. *The Language Learning Journal* 46(3). 241–262.

Hijazo-Gascón, Alberto. 2019. Translating accurately or sounding natural? The interpreters' challenges due to semantic typology and the interpreting process. *Pragmatics and Society* 10(1). 72–94.

Hijazo-Gascón, Alberto, Teresa Cadierno & Iraide Ibarretxe-Antuñano. 2016. Learning the placement caused motion construction in L2 Spanish. In Sabine De Knop & Gaëtanelle Gilquin (eds.), *Applied Construction Grammar*, 185–210. Berlin & Boston: De Gruyter.

Hijazo-Gascón, Alberto, Teresa Cadierno & Iraide Ibarretxe-Antuñano. 2019. Los eventos de movimiento en la adquisición de español como lengua extranjera. In Iraide Ibarretxe-Antuñano, Teresa Cadierno & Alejandro Castañeda Castro (eds.), *Lingüística cognitiva y español LE/L2*, 322–339. London: Routledge.

Hijazo-Gascón, Alberto & Iraide Ibarretxe-Antuñano. 2013a. Las lenguas románicas y la tipología de los eventos de movimiento. *Romanische Forschungen* 125(4). 467–494.

Hijazo-Gascón, Alberto & Iraide Ibarretxe-Antuñano. 2013b. Same family, different paths: Intra-typological differences in three Romance languages. In Juliana Goschler & Anatol Stefanowitsch (eds.), *Variation and change in the encoding of motion events*, 30–54. Amsterdam: John Benjamins.

Hijazo-Gascón, Alberto & Iraide Ibarretxe-Antuñano. 2010. Tipología, lexicalización y dialectología aragonesa. *Archivo de Filología Aragonesa* 66. 181–215.

Hijazo-Gascón, Alberto & Iraide Ibarretxe-Antuñano. 2012. ¿Qué puede aportar el aragonés a la tipología semántica? *Alazet: Revista de filología* 24. 43–58.

Hijazo-Gascón, Alberto, Iraide Ibarretxe-Antuñano & Julia Guelbenzu-Espada. 2013. Clasificando los verbos de movimiento. ¿Qué piensan los hablantes? In José Francisco Val, José Luis Mendívil-Giró, María del Carmen Horno, Iraide Ibarretxe-Antuñano, Alberto Hijazo-Gascón, Javier Simón & Isabel Solano (eds.), *De la unidad del lenguaje a la diversidad de las lenguas*, 361–368. Zaragoza: Prensas Universitarias de Zaragoza.

Hijazo-Gascón, Alberto & Reyes Llopis-García. 2019. Applied cognitive linguistics and foreign language learning. Introduction to the special issue. *IRAL. International Review of Applied Linguistics in Language Teaching* 57(1). 1–20.

Hoffmann, Dorothea. 2012. Path salience in motion descriptions in Jaminjung. In Luna Filipović & Kasia Jaszczolt (eds.), *Space and time in languages and cultures: Linguistic diversity*, 459–480. Amsterdam & Philadelphia: John Benjamins.

Hohestein, Jill, Ann Eisenberg & Letitia Naigles. 2006. Is he floating across or crossing afloat? Cross-influence in L1 and L2 in Spanish-English bilingual adults. *Bilingualism: Language and Cognition* 9. 249–261.

Holme, Randal. 2009. *Cognitive linguistics and language teaching*. Basingstoke: Palgrave Macmillan.

Huang, Shuanfan & Michael Tanangkingsin. 2005. Reference to motion events in six western Austronesian languages. *Oceanic Linguistics* 44(2). 307–340.

Huang, Yan. 2006. *Pragmatics*. Oxford: Oxford University Press.
Huber, Judith. 2017. The early life of borrowed path verbs in English. In Iraide Ibarretxe-Antuñano (ed.), *Motion and space across languages: Theory and applications*, 177–204. Amsterdam & Philadelphia: John Benjamins.
Iacobini, Claudio. 2008. Presenza e uso dei verbi sintagmatici nel parlato. In Monica Cini (ed.), *I verbi sintagmatici in italiano e nelle varietà dialettali. Stato dell'arte e prospettive di ricerca*, 103–120. Frankfurt: Peter Lang.
Iacobini, Claudio. 2009. The role of dialects in the emergence of Italian phrasal verbs. *Morphology* 19(1). 15–44.
Iacobini, Claudio. 2012. Grammaticalization and innovation in the encoding of motion events. *Folia Linguistica Historica* 46(2). 359–386.
Iacobini, Claudio. 2015. Particle-verbs in Romance. In Peter O. Müller, Ingeborg Ohnheiser, Susan Olsen & Franz Rainer (eds.), *Word-formation. An international handbook of the languages of Europe*, 626–658. Berlin & New York: Mouton de Gruyter.
Iacobini, Claudio & Benjamin Fagard. 2011. A diachronic approach to variation and change in the typology of motion event expression. A case study: From Latin to Romance. *Cahiers de Faits de Langue* 3. 151–171.
Iacobini, Claudio & Francesca Masini. 2007a. The emergence of verb-particle constructions in Italian: Locative and actional meanings. *Morphology* 16(2). 155–188.
Iacobini, Claudio & Francesca Masini. 2007b. Verb-particle constructions and prefixed verbs in Italian: Typology, diachrony and semantics. In Geert Booij, Bernard Fradin, Angela Ralli & Sergio Scalise (eds.), *On-ine Proceedings of the Fifth Mediterranean Morphology Meeting (MMM5) (Fréjus 15–18 September 2005)*, 157–184. Bologna: University of Bologna.
Iacobini, Claudio & Carla Vergaro. 2014. The role of interference in motion event encoding/decoding: A cross-linguistic inquiry into English and Italian. *Lingue e linguaggio* 2. 211–240.
Ibarretxe-Antuñano, Iraide. 2004a. Motion events in Basque narratives. In Sven Strömqvist & Ludo Verhoeven (eds.), *Relating events in narrative: Typological and contextual perspectives*, 89–111. New York: Psychology Press.
Ibarretxe-Antuñano, Iraide. 2004b. Language typologies in our language use: The case of Basque motion events in adult oral narratives. *Cognitive Linguistics* 15(3). 317–349.
Ibarretxe-Antuñano, Iraide. 2004c. Motion events in second language acquisition: Spanish and Basque. Paper presented at the EUROSLA Conference, Universidad del País Vasco – Euskal Herriko Unibertsitatea.
Ibarretxe-Antuñano, Iraide. 2004d. Dicotomías frente a continuos en la lexicalización de eventos de movimiento. *Revista Española de Lingüística* 34(2). 481–510.
Ibarretxe-Antuñano, Iraide. 2005. Leonard Talmy. A windowing to conceptual structure and language. Part 1: Lexicalisation and typology. *Review of Cognitive Linguistics* 3. 325–47.
Ibarretxe-Antuñano, Iraide. 2006a. *Sound symbolism and motion in Basque*. Munich: Lincom Europa.
Ibarretxe-Antuñano, Iraide. 2006b. Interview: Leonard Talmy. A windowing onto conceptual structure and language. Part 2: Language and congition: Past and future. *Annual Review of Cognitive Linguistics* 4. 253–268.
Ibarretxe-Antuñano, Iraide. 2009. Path salience in motion events. In J Guo, E Lieven, N Budwig, S Ervin-Tripp, K Nakamura & Seyda Özçalışkan (eds.), *Cross-linguistic approaches to the psychology of language: Research in the tradition of Dan Isaac Slobin*, 403–414. New York: Psychology Press.

Ibarretxe-Antuñano, Iraide. 2010. Semantic typology, motion events and the Frog Stories. Paper presented at the 6th International Conference on Language Acquisition, Universitat de Barcelona.
Ibarretxe-Antuñano, Iraide. 2012. Placement and removal events in Basque and Spanish. In Anetta Kopecka & Bhuvana Narasimhan (eds.), *The events of putting and taking. A cross-linguistic perspective*, 123–143. Amsterdam & Philadelphia: John Benjamins.
Ibarretxe-Antuñano, Iraide. 2015. Going beyond motion events typology: The case of Basque as a verb-framed language. *Folia Linguistica Acta Societatis Linguisticae Europaeae* 49(2). 307–352.
Ibarretxe-Antuñano, Iraide (ed.). 2017a. *Motion and space across languages: Theory and applications*. Amsterdam & Philadelphia: John Benjamins.
Ibarretxe-Antuñano, Iraide. 2017b. Motion and semantic typology: A hot old topic with exciting caveats. In Iraide Ibarretxe-Antuñano (ed.), *Motion and space across languages. Theory and applications*, 13–38. Amsterdam & Philadelphia: John Benjamins.
Ibarretxe-Antuñano, Iraide, Teresa Cadierno & Alejandro Castañeda Castro (eds.), 2019. *Lingüística cognitiva y español LE/L2*. London: Routledge.
Ibarretxe-Antuñano, Iraide, Teresa Cadierno & Alberto Hijazo-Gascón. 2014. La expresión de los eventos de colocación en danés y español. *Scripta* 18(34). 63–84.
Ibarretxe-Antuñano, Iraide, Teresa Cadierno & Alberto Hijazo-Gascón. 2016. The role of force dynamics and intentionality in the reconstruction of L2 verb meanings: A Danish-Spanish bidirectional study. *Review of Cognitive Linguistics* 14(1). 136–60.
Ibarretxe-Antuñano, Iraide & Fátima Cheikh-Khamis. 2019. How to become a woman without turning into a Barbie: Change-of-state verb constructions and their role in Spanish as a foreign language. *IRAL. International Review of Applied Linguistics in Language Teaching* 57(1). 97–120.
Ibarretxe-Antuñano, Iraide & Luna Filipović. 2013. Lexicalization patterns and translation. In Ana Rojo & Iraide Ibarretxe-Antuñano (eds.), *Cognitive linguistics and translation*, 253–284. Berlin & New York: Mouton de Gruyter.
Ibarretxe-Antuñano, Iraide & Alberto Hijazo-Gascón. 2011. Variación intratipológica y diatópica en los eventos de movimiento. In Carsten Sinner, Sara Gómez Seibane & Carmen Isasi (eds.), *La expresión del tiempo y espacio y las relaciones espacio-temporales en el español norteño*, 135–159. San Millán de la Cogolla: Cilengua.
Ibarretxe-Antuñano, Iraide & Alberto Hijazo-Gascón. 2012. Variation in motion events: Theory and applications. In Luna Filipović & Kasia Jaszczolt (eds.), *Space and time across languages and cultures*, 349–372. Amsterdam & Philadelphia: John Benjamins.
Ibarretxe-Antuñano, Iraide & Alberto Hijazo-Gascón (eds.) 2015. *New horizons in the study of motion: Bringing together applied and theoretical perspectives*. Newcastle upon Tyne: Cambridge Scholars Publishing.
Ibarretxe-Antuñano, Iraide, Alberto Hijazo-Gascón & María-Teresa Moret-Oliver. 2017. The importance of minority languages in motion event typology. In Iraide Ibarretxe-Antuñano (ed.), *Motion and space across languages: Theory and applications*, 123–150. Amsterdam & Philadelphia: John Benjamins.
Ibarretxe-Antuñano, Iraide & Javier Valenzuela (eds.), 2012. *Lingüística cognitiva*. Barcelona: Anthropos.
Ibarretxe-Antuñano, Iraide & Javier Valenzuela. 2021. *Lenguaje y cognición*. Madrid: Síntesis.
Ijaz, I. Helene. 1986. Linguistic and cognitive determinants of lexical acquisition in a second language. *Language learning* 36(4). 401–451.

Inagaki, Shunji. 2001. Motion verbs with goal PPs in the L2 acquisition of English and Japanese. *Studies in Second Language Acquisition* 23. 153–170.

Instituto Cervantes. 2006. *Plan curricular del Instituto Cervantes: Niveles de referencia para el español*. Madrid: Biblioteca Nueva.

Jackendoff, Ray. 1983. *Semantics and cognition*. Cambridge, MA: MIT Press.

Jackendoff, Ray. 1987. *Consciousness and the computational mind*. Cambridge, MA: MIT Press.

Jackendoff, Ray. 1990. *Semantic structures*. Cambridge, MA: MIT Press.

Jarvis, Scott. 2000. Methodological rigor in the study of transfer. Identifying L1 influence in the interlanguage lexicon. *Language learning* 50(2). 245–309.

Jarvis, Scott. 2007. Theoretical and methodological issues in the investigation of conceptual transfer. *VIAL. Vigo International Journal of Applied Linguistics* 4. 43–71.

Jarvis, Scott. 2010. Comparison-based and detection-based approaches to transfer research. In Leah Roberts, Martin Howard, Muiris Laoire & David Singleton (eds.), *Eurosla Yearbook 10*, 169–192. Amsterdam & Philadelphia: John Benjamins.

Jarvis, Scott. 2015. The scope of transfer research. In Liming Yu & Terence Odlin (eds.), *New perspectives on transfer in second language learning*, 17–49. Bristol: Multilingual matters.

Jarvis, Scott & Aneta Pavlenko. 2008. *Cross-linguistic infuence in language and cognition*. London: Routledge.

Jessen, Moiken. 2014a. *The expression of motion in L2 Danish by Turkish and German learners. The role of inter- and intratypological differences*. Odense: University of Southern Denmark dissertation.

Jessen, Moiken. 2014b. The expression of Path in L2 Danish by German and Turkish learners. *VIAL. Vigo International Journal of Applied Linguistics* 11. 81–109.

Jessen, Moiken & Teresa Cadierno. 2013. Variation in the categorization of motion events by Danish, German, Turkish and L2 Danish speakers. In Juliana Goschler & Anatol Stefanowitsch (eds.), *Variation and change in the encoding of motion events*, 133–159. Amsterdam & Philadelphia: John Benjamins.

Jessner, Ulrike, Manon Megens & Stefanie Graus. 2016. Cross-linguistic influence in third language acquisition. In Rosa Alonso Alonso (eds.), *Cross-linguistic influence and second language acquisition*, 193–214. Bristol: Multilingual matters.

Kellerman, Eric. 1977. Toward a characterization of the strategy of transfer in second language learning. *Interlanguage Studies Bulletin* 2. 58–145.

Kellerman, Eric. 1978. Transfer and non-transfer: Where are we now? *Studies in Second Language Acquisition* 2. 37–57.

Kellerman, Eric. 1995. Cross-linguistic influence: Transfer to nowhere? *Annual Review of Applied Linguistics* 21. 47–77.

Kellerman, Eric & Anne-Marie van Hoof. 2003. Manual accents. *International Journal of Applied Linguistics* 41. 251–269.

Kita, Sotaro & Asli Özyürek. 2003. What does cross-linguistic variation in coordination of speech and gesture reveal? Evidence for an interface representation of spatial thinking and speaking. *Journal of Memory and Language* 48. 16–32.

Khalifa, Jean-Charles. 2001. Linguistique et traduction: Le cas des verbes de déplacement. *Anglophonia* 10. 199–213.

Koch, Peter & Wulf Oesterreicher. 1994. Schriftlichkeit und Sprache. In Hartmut Günther & Otto Ludwig (eds.) *Schrift und Schriftlichkeit / Writing and its use – Ein interdisziplinäres*

Handbuch internationaler Forschung / An interdisciplinary handbook of international research, 587–604. Berlin & New York: Mouton de Gruyter.

Kopecka, Anetta. 2004. *Étude typologique de l'expression de l'espace: Localisation et déplacement en français et en polonais*. Lyon: Université Lumière Lyon 2 dissertation.

Kopecka, Anetta. 2006a. The semantic structure of motion events in French: Typological perspectives. In Maya Hickmann & Stephane Robert (eds.), *Space in Languages: Linguistic Systems and Cognitive Categories*, 83–101. Amsterdam & Philadelphia: John Benjamins.

Kopecka, Anetta. 2006b. From a satellite- to a verb-framed pattern: A typological shift in French. Unpublished paper. Max Planck Institute for Psycholinguistics.

Kopecka, Anetta. 2009. L'expression du déplacement en français: L'interaction des facteurs sémantiques, aspectuels et pragmatiques dans la construction du sens spatial. *Langages* 173. 54–75.

Kopecka, Anetta. 2013. Describing motion events in Old and Modern French: Discoursive effects of a typological change. In Juliana Goschler & Anatol Stefanowitsch (eds.), *Variation and change in the coding of motion events*, 163–184. Amsterdam: John Benjamins.

Kopecka, Anetta & Bhuvana Narasimhan (eds.), 2012. *The events of putting and taking. A cross-linguistic perspective*. Amsterdam & Philadelphia: John Benjamins.

Kristiansen, Gitte & René Dirven (eds.) 2008. *Cognitive sociolinguistics. Language variation, cultural models, social systems*. Berlin & New York: Mouton de Gruyter.

Lado, Robert. 1957. *Linguistics across cultures*. Ann Arbor: University of Michigan Press.

Lakoff, George & Mark Johnson. 1980. *Metaphors we live by*. Chicago: Chicago University Press.

Lam, Yvonne. 2009. Applying cognitive linguistics to teaching the Spanish prepositions por and para. *Language Awareness* 18(1). 2–18.

Lamiroy, Béatrice. 1983. *Les verbes de mouvement en français et en espagnol. Etude comparée de leurs infinitives*. Amsterdam & Philadelphia: John Benjamins.

Langacker, Ronald W. 1987. *Foundations of cognitive grammar. Vol. 1*. Stanford, CA: Stanford University Press.

Lantolf, James & Larysa Bobrova. 2014. Metaphor instruction in the L2 Spanish classroom: Theoretical argument and pedagogical program. *Journal of Spanish Language Teaching* 1 (1). 46–61.

Lapesa, Rafael. 1968. *Historia de la lengua española*. Madrid: Escelicer.

Larrañaga, Pilar, Jeanine Treffers-Daller, Françoise Tidball & Mari Carmen Gil Ortega. 2011. L1 transfer in the acquisition of manner and path in Spanish by native speakers of English. *International Journal of Bilingualism* 16(1). 117–138.

Larsen-Freeman, Diane & Michael Long. 1991. *An introduction to second language acquisition research*. London: Routledge.

Lemmens, Maarten & Julien Perrez. 2010. On the use of posture verbs by French-Speaking learners of Dutch. A corpus-based study. *Cognitive Linguistics* 21(3). 315–347.

Leonardi, Vanessa. 2010. *The role of pedagogical translation in second language acquisition*. Bern: Peter Lang.

Levin, Beth. 1993. *English verb classes and alternations: A preliminary investigation*. Chicago: Chicago University Press.

Levin, Beth & Malka Rappaport Hovav. 1995. *Unaccusativity: At the syntax-lexical semantics interface*. Cambridge, MA: MIT Press.

Levin, Beth & Malka Rappaport Hovav. 2005. *Argument realization*. Cambridge: Cambridge University Press.
Levinson, Stephen C. 1983. *Pragmatics*. Cambridge: Cambridge University Press.
Levinson, Stephen C. 2003. *Space in language and cognition: Explorations in cognitive diversity*. Cambridge: Cambridge University Press.
Lewandowski, Wojciech. 2014. Deictic verbs: Typology, thinking for speaking and SLA. *SKY Journal of Linguistics* 27. 43–65.
Lewandowski, Wojciech. 2018. A typological approach to the encoding of motion events. In María de los Ángeles Gómez González & J. Lachlan Mackenzie (eds.), *The construction of discourse as verbal interaction*, 45–74. Amsterdam: John Benjamins.
Lewandowski, Wojciech & Jaume Mateu. 2016. Thinking for translating and intra-typological variation in satellite-framed languages. *Review of Cognitive Linguistics* 14(1). 185–208.
Lewandowski, Wojciech & Seyda Özçalışkan. 2021. How language type influences patterns of motion expression in bilingual speakers. *Second Language Research* 37(1). 27–49.
Lewis, Tasha N. 2012. The effect of context on the L2 thinking for speaking development of path gestures. *L2 Journal* 4. 247–268.
Li, Peiwen, Søren Eskildsen & Teresa Cadierno. 2014. Tracing an L2 learner's motion constructions over time: A usage-based classroom investigation. *The Modern Language Journal* 98(2). 612–628.
Liste-Lamas, Elsa. 2015. German directional adverbs with *hin-* and *her-*: A preliminary study on their acquisition by L1 speakers of Spanish. In Iraide Ibarretxe-Antuñano & Alberto Hijazo-Gascón (eds.), *New horizons in the study of motion: Bringing together applied and theoretical perspectives*, 10–31. Newcastle upon Tyne: Cambridge Scholars Publishing.
Liste-Lamas, Elsa. 2016a. Path encoding in German as a Foreign Language: Difficulties encountered by L1 Spanish learners. In Juliana Goschler & Susanne Niemeier (eds.), *Yearbook of the German Cognitive Linguistics Association*, 47–65. Berlin & New York: Mouton de Gruyter.
Liste-Lamas, Elsa. 2016b. Über einige Merkmale der Wegkodierung im Deutschen als Fremdsprache bei Lernern mit Spanisch als L1. In Ferran Robles i Sabater, Daniel Reimann & Raúl Sánchez Prieto (eds.) *Sprachdidaktik Spanisch-Deutsch. Forschungen an der Schnittstelle von Linguistik und Fremdsprachendidaktik*, 33–47. Tübingen: Narr.
Littlemore, Jeannette. 2001. An empirical study of relationship between cognitive style and the use of communication strategy. *Applied Linguistics* 22(2). 241–265.
Littlemore, Jeannette. 2009. *Applying cognitive linguistics to second language learning and teaching*. Basingstoke: Palgrave Macmillan.
Littlemore, Jeannette & Constanze Juchem-Grundman (eds.) 2010. Applied cognitive linguistics in second language learning and teaching. [Special issue]. *AILA Review* 23.
Llopis-García, Reyes. 2010. Why cognitive grammar works in the L2 Classroom: A case study of mood selection in Spanish. *AILA Review* 23. 72–94.
Llopis-García, Reyes. 2015. Las preposiciones y la metáfora del espacio: Aportaciones y potencial de la lingüística cognitiva para su enseñanza. *Journal of Spanish Language Teaching* 2(1). 51–68.
Llopis-García, Reyes & Alberto Hijazo-Gascón (eds.), 2019. Applied cognitive linguistics to L2 acquisition and learning: Research and convergence. [Special Issue]. *IRAL. International Review of Applied Linguistics in Language Teaching* 51(1).
Llopis-García, Reyes, Juan Manuel Real Espinosa & José Plácido Ruiz Campillo. 2012. *Qué gramática enseñar. Qué gramática aprender*. Madrid: Edinumen.

Long, Michael. 1991. Focus on form: A design feature in the language teaching methodology. In Kees de Bot, Ralph Ginsberg & Claire Kramsch (eds.). *Foreign language research in cross-cultural perspectives*, 39–52. Amsterdam & Philadelphia: John Benjamins.

Lowie, Wander & Marjolyn Verspoor. 2004. Input versus tansfer? The role of frequency and similarity in the acquisition of L2 prepositions. In Michele Achard & Susanne Niemeier (eds.), *Cognitive linguistics, second language acquisition and foreign language teaching*, 77–95. Berlin & New York: De Gruyter Mouton.

Lübke, Barbara & Victoria Vázquez-Rozas. 2011. In Carsten Sinner, Elia Hernández Socas & Christian Bahr (eds.), *Tiempo, espacio y relaciones espacio-temporales: Nuevas aportaciones de los estudios contrastivos*, 115–129. Frankfurt: Peter Lang.

Lucy, John A. 1992. Linguistic relativity. *Annual Review of Anthropology* 26. 291–312.

Lucy, John A. 2016. The implications of linguistic relativity for language learning. In Rosa Alonso Alonso (ed.), *Cross-linguistic influence and second language acquisition*, 53–70. Bristol: Multilingual matters.

Lyons, John. 1977. *Semantics*. Cambridge: Cambridge University Press.

MacWhinney, Brian. 1991. *The CHILDES project: Tools for analyzing talk*. Hillsdale, NJ: Erlbaum.

Madlener, Karin, Katrin Skoruppa & Heike Behrens. 2017. Gradual development of constructional complexity in German spatial language. *Cognitive Linguistics* 28(4). 757–798.

Maldonado, Ricardo. 1999. *A media voz: Problemas conceptuales del clítico se en español*. Mexico: Instituto de Investigaciones Filológicas, Universidad Nacional Autónoma de México.

Maldonado, Ricardo. 2019. Una aproximación cognitiva al clítico se. In Iraide Ibarretxe-Antuñano, Teresa Cadierno & Alejandro Castañeda Castro (eds.), *Lingüística cognitiva y español LE/L2*, 145–167. London: Routledge.

Malt, Barbara, Silvia Gennari, Mutsumi Imai, Eef Ameel, Naoaki Tsuda & Asifa Majid. 2008. Talking about walking: Biomechanics and the language of locomotion. *Psychological Science* 19. 232–240.

Martín Zorraquino, María Antonia. 2004. La situación lingüística de Aragón. In Emilio Ridruejo (ed.), *Las otras lenguas de España*, 181–222. Valladolid: Universidad de Valladolid.

Martín Zorraquino, María Antonia & José María Enguita Utrilla. 2000. *Las lenguas de Aragón*. Zaragoza: Caja de Ahorros de la Inmaculada.

Martínez-Vázquez, Montserrat. 2001. Delimited events in English and Spanish. *Estudios Ingleses de la Universidad Complutense* 9. 31–59.

Martínez-Vázquez, Montserrat. 2013. Intralinguistic variation in the expression of motion events in English and Spanish. *Lingue e linguaggi* 9. 143–156.

Masini, Francesca. 2005. Multi-word expressions between syntax and the lexicon: The case of Italian verb-particle constructions. *SKY Journal of Linguistics* 18. 145–173.

Masini, Francesca. 2008. Verbi sintagmatici e ordine delle parole. In Monica Cini (ed.), *I verbi sintagmatici in italiano e nelle varietà dialettali. Stato dell'arte e prospettive di ricerca*, 81–102. Frankfurt: Peter Lang.

Matras, Yaron & Jeannette Sakel. 2007. *Grammatical borrowing in cross-linguistic perspective*. Berlin & New York: Mouton de Gruyter.

Matsumoto, Yo. 1996. *Complex predicates in Japanese. A syntactic and semantic study of the notion of 'word'*. Stanford, CA: CSLI Publications.

Matsumoto, Yo. 2003. Typologies of lexicalization patterns and event integration: Clarification and reformulations. In Shuji Chiba (ed.), *Empirical and theoretical investigations into language: A Festschrift for Masaru Kajita*, 403–418. Tokyo: Kaiakusha.

Matsumoto, Yo, Kimi Akita & Kiyoko Takahashi. 2017. The functional nature of deictic verbs and the coding patterns of deixis: An experimental study in English, Japanese and Thai. In Iraide Ibarretxe-Antuñano (ed.), *Motion and space across languages. Theory and applications*, 95–122. Amsterdam & Philadelphia: John Benjamins.

Mayer, Mercer. 1969. *Frog, where are you?* New York: Dial Press.

McNeill, David. 1992. *Hand and mind: What gestures reveal about thought*. Chicago: Chicago University Press.

McNeill, David. 2000. Growth points, catchments, and contexts. *Cognitive Studies: Bulletin of the Japanese Cognitive Science Society* 7: 22–36.

McNeill, David. 2005. *Gesture and thought*. Chicago: Chicago University Press.

McNeill, David. 2009. Imagery for speaking. In Jiansheng Guo, Elena Lieven, Nancy Budwig, Susan Ervin-Tripp, Keiko Nakamura & Seyda Özçalışkan (eds.), *Cross-linguistic approaches to the psychology of language: Research in the tradition of Dan Isaac Slobin*, 403–414. Mahwah, NJ: Lawrence Erlbaum.

McNeill, David & Susan Duncan. 2000. Growth points in thinking for speaking. In David McNeill (ed.), *Language and gesture*, 141–161. Cambridge: Cambridge University Press.

Mendikoetxea, Amaya. 1999. Construcciones inacusativas y pasivas. In Ignacio Bosque & Violeta Demonte (eds.), *Gramática descriptiva de la lengua española*, 1575–1629. Madrid: Espasa.

Mendo Murillo, Susana. 2019. El significado de las preposiciones en la enseñanza del español LE/L2. El caso de *por* y *para*. In Iraide Ibarretxe-Antuñano, Teresa Cadierno & Alejandro Castañeda Castro (eds.), *Lingüística cognitiva y español LE/L2*, 254–270. London: Routledge.

Miller, George A., & Philip Johnson-Laird. 1976. *Language and perception*. Cambridge: Cambridge University Press.

Miquel López, Lourdes & Jenaro Ortega Olivares. 2014. Actividades orientadas al aprendizaje explícito de recursos gramaticales en niveles avanzados de E/LE. In Alejandro Castañeda Castro (ed.), *Enseñanza de gramática avanzada de ELE. Criterios y recursos*, 89–169. Madrid: SGEL.

Molés-Cases, Teresa. 2016. *La traducción de los eventos de movimiento en un corpus paralelo alemán-español*. Frankfurt: Peter Lang.

Moliner, María. 2007. *Diccionario de uso del español*. Madrid: Aguilar.

Montero Gálvez, Sonia. 2019. Una aproximación cogntiva al valor referencial y cuantificador de los artículos. In Iraide Ibarretxe-Antuñano, Teresa Cadierno & Alejandro Castañeda Castro (eds.), *Lingüística cognitiva y español L2/LE*, 73–95. London: Routledge.

Montero-Melis, Guillermo & Emanuel Bylund. 2017. Getting the ball rolling: The cross-linguistic conceptualization of caused motion. *Language and Cognition* 9(3). 446–472.

Montero-Melis, Guillermo, Sonja Eisenbeiss, Bhuvana Narasimhan, Iraide Ibarretxe-Antuñano, Sotaro Kita, Anetta Kopecka & Friederike Lüpke. 2017. Satellite- vs. verb-framing underpredicts nonverbal motion categorization: Insights from a large language sample and simulations. *Cognitive Semantics* 3. 36–61.

Montrul, Silvina. 2001. Agentive verbs of manner of motion in Spanish and English as second languages. *Studies in Second Language Acquisition* 2. 171–206.

Morimoto, Yuko. 2001. *Los verbos de movimiento*. Madrid: Visor Libros.

Mosca, Monica. 2007. *Spatial language in spoken italian dialogues. A cognitive linguistics perspective*. Pisa: Università degli studi di Pisa dissertation.

Mosca, Monica. 2009. Variazione dei costrutti di movimento: Prolegomena ad una classificazione basata sull'elaborazione di un corpus di dialoghi. In Monica Mosca (ed.), *Linguistica e modelli tecnologici di ricerca. Atti del XL congresso internazionale degli studi Vercelli, 21–23 Settembre 2006*, 327–343. Roma: Bulzoni.

Mosca, Monica. 2010. *Eventi di moto in italiano tra sintassi e semantica. Uno studio cognitivo empirico*. Pisa: Pisa University Press.

Mosca, Monica. 2017. Latin to ancient Italian motion constructions: A complex typological shift. In Iraide Ibarretxe-Antuñano (ed.), *Motion and space across languages. Theory and applications*, 151–176. Amsterdam & Philadelphia: John Benjamins.

Muñoz, Carmen & David Singleton. 2011. A critical review of age-related research on L2 ultimate attainment. *Language Teaching* 44(1). 1–35.

Muñoz-Carrasco, Meritxell. 2015. *La trasferencia bidireccional inglés-español en las situaciones de movimiento*. Madrid: Universidad Nebrija dissertation.

Muñoz-Carrasco, Meritxell & Teresa Cadierno. 2019. Mr Bean exits the garage driving or does he drive out of the garage? Bidirectional transfer in the expression of path. *IRAL. International Review of Applied Linguistics in Language Teaching* 57(1). 45–69.

Naigles, Letitia & Paula Terrazas. 1998. Motion verb generalizations in English and Spanish. Influences of language and syntax. *Psychological Science* 9. 363–369.

Narasimhan, Bhuvana & Marianne Gullberg. 2011. The role of input frequency and semantic transparency in the acquisition of verb meaning: Evidence from placement verbs in Tamil and Dutch. *Journal of Child Language* 38(3). 504–532.

Navarro, Samuel & Elena Nicoladis. 2005. Describing motion events in adult L2 Spanish narratives. In David Eddington (ed.), *Selected proceedings of the 6th conference on the acquisition of Spanish and Portuguese as first and second languages*, 102–107. Somerville, MA: Cascadilla Proceedings Project.

Negueruela, Eduardo, James Lantolf, Stephanie Rehn Jordan & Jaime Gelabert. 2004. The "private function" of gesture in second language speaking activity: A study of motion verbs and gesturing in English and Spanish. *International Journal of Applied Linguistics* 14: 113–147.

Nicoladis, Elena, Frank Brisard & Eve Clark. 2002. Encoding motion in gestures and speech: are these differences in bilingual children's French and English? Space in language. location, motion, path and manner. In *Space in language. Location, motion, path and manner. The proceedings of the 31st Stanford child language research forum*, 60–68. Stanford, CA: CSLI Publications.

Nikitina, Tatiana. 2008. Pragmatic factors and variation in the expression of spatial goals: The case of into vs. in. In Anna Asbury, Jakub Dotlacil, Berit Gehrke & Rick Nouwen (eds.), *Syntax and semantics of spatial P*, 175–195. Amsterdam & Philadelphia: John Benjamins.

Noonan, Michael. 2003. Motion events in Chantyal. In Erin Shat & Uwe Seibert (eds.), *Motion, direction, and location in languages. In honor of Zygmunt Frajzyngier*, 211–234. Amsterdam & Philadelphia: John Benjamins.

Odlin, Terence. 1989. *Language transfer: cross-linguistic influence in language learning*. Cambridge: Cambridge University Press.

Odlin, Terence. 2003. Cross-linguistic influence. In Catherine Doughty & Michael Long (eds.), *The handbook of second language acquisition*, 435–486. Oxford: Blackwell.

Odlin, Terence. 2010. Conclusion: On the interdependence of conceptual transfer and relativity studies'. In ZhaoHong Han & Teresa Cadierno (eds.), *Linguistic relativity in second language acquisition. Thinking for speaking*, 183–194. Bristol: Multilingual Matters.

Odlin, Terence. 2015. Language transfer and the link between comprehension and production. In Liming Yu & Terence Odlin (eds.), *New perspectives on transfer in second language learning*, 207–225. Bristol: Multilingual Matters.

Odlin, Terence. 2016. Was there really ever a contrastive analysis hypothesis? In Rosa Alonso Alonso (eds.), *Crosslinguistic influence in second language acquisition*, 1–23. Bristol: Multilingual Matters.

Odlin, Terence & Scott Jarvis. 2004. Same source, different outcomes: A study of Swedish influence on the acquisition of English in Finland. *The International Journal of Multilingualism* 1(2). 123–40.

Odlin, Terence & Liming Yu. 2015. Introduction. In Liming Yu & Terence Odlin (eds.), *New perspectives on transfer in second language learning*. Bristol: Multilingual Matters.

Oh, Kyung-ju. 2003. *Language, cognition, and development: Motion events in English and Korean*. Berkeley, CA: University of California, Berkeley dissertation.

Ortega, Lourdes. 2010. The bilingual turn in SLA. Paper presented at the American Association for Applied Linguistics Conference, Atlanta, GA.

Ortega, Lourdes. 2013. SLA for the 21st century: Discipline progress, transdisciplinarity relevance and the bi/multilingual Turn. *Language Learning* 63(1). 1–24.

Ortega, Lourdes. 2014. Ways forward for a bi/multilingual turn in SLA. In Stephen May (ed.), *The multilingual turn. Implications for SLA, TESOL, and bilingual education*, 32–54. London: Routledge.

Otheguy, Ricardo & Ofelia García. 1993. Convergent conceptualizations as predictors of degree of contact in U.S. Spanish. In Ana Roca & John Lipski (eds.), *Spanish in the United States*, 135–154. Berlin & New York: Mouton de Gruyter.

Özçalışkan, Seyda. 2009. Learning to talk about spatial motion in language-specific ways. In Jiansheng Guo, Elena Lieven, Nancy Budwig, Susan Ervin-Tripp, Keiko Nakamura & Seyda Özçalışkan (eds.), *Cross-linguistic approaches to the psychology of language: Research in the tradition of Dan Isaac Slobin*, 263–276. New York: Psychology Press.

Özçalışkan, Seyda. 2015. Ways of crossing a spatial boundary in typologically distinct languages. *Applied Psycholinguistics* 36(2). 485–508.

Özçalışkan, Seyda & Dan I. Slobin. 2003. codability effects on the expression of manner of motion in Turkish and English. In Sumru Özsoy, Didar Akar, Mine Nakipoglu-Demiralp, E. Eser Erguvanli-Taylan & Ayhan Aksu-Koç (eds.), *Studies in Turkish linguistics. Proceedings of the tenth international conference in Turkish linguistics. August 16–18, 2000*. 259–270. Istanbul: Bogaziçi University.

Özçalışkan, Seyda, Lauren J. Stites & Samantha N. Emerson. 2017. Crossing the road or crossing the mind: How differently do we move across physical and metaphorical spaces in speech and gesture. In Iraide Ibarretxe-Antuñano (ed.), *Motion and space across languages. Theory and applications*, 257–278. Amsterdam & Philadelphia: John Benjamins.

Öztürk, Özge & Anna Papafragou. 2005. The acquisition of evidentiality in Turkish. *University of Pennsylvania Working Papers in Linguistics* 11(1). 1–14.

Özyürek, Asli, Sotaro Kita & Shanley Allen. 2001. *Tomato man movies: Stimulus kit designed to elicit manner, path and causal constructions in motion events with regard to speech and gestures*. Nijmegen: Max Planck Institute for Psycholinguistics.

Özyürek, Asli, Sotaro Kita, Shanley Allen, Reyhan Furman & Amanda Brown. 2005. How does linguistic framing of events influence co-speech gestures? Insights from cross-linguistic variations and similarities. *Gesture* 5(1/2). 219–240.

Papafragou, Anna, Christine Massey & Lila Gleitman. 2002. Shake, rattle, "n" roll: The representations of motion in language and cognition. *Cognition* 84. 189–219.

Papafragou, Anna, Christine Massey & Lila Gleitman. 2006. When English proposes what Greek presupposes: The cross-linguistic encoding of motion events. *Cognition* 98(3). 75–87.

Pavlenko, Aneta (ed.) 2011. *Thinking and speaking in two languages*. Clevedon, UK: Multilingual Matters.

Pavlenko, Aneta. 2014. *The bilingual mind and what it tells us about language and thought*. Cambridge: Cambridge University Press.

Pedersen, Johan. 2014. Variable type framing in Spanish constructions of directed motion. In Hans C. Boas & Francisco Gonzálvez-García (eds.), *Romance perspectives on Construction Grammar*, 269–304. Amsterdam: John Benjamins.

Perdue, Clive. 2000. Organising principles of learner varieties. *Studies in Second Language Acquisition* 22(3). 299–305.

Perek, Florent & Martin Hilpert. 2014. Constructional tolerance: Cross-linguistic differences in the acceptability of non-conventional uses of constructions. *Constructions and Frames* 6(2). 266–304.

Piquer-Píriz, Ana María. 2008. Reasoning figuratively in early EFL: Some implications for the development of vocabulary. In Frank Boers & Seth Lindstromberg (eds.), *Cognitive Linguistic approaches to teaching vocabulary and phraseology*, 219–240. Berlin & New York: Mouton de Gruyter.

Piquer-Píriz, Ana María & Rafael Alejo-González (eds.) 2016. Applying cognitive linguistics. Figurative language in use, constructions and typology. [Special Issue]. *Review of Cognitive Linguistics* 14(1).

Piquer-Píriz, Ana María & Rafael Alejo-González (eds.) 2018. *Applying cognitive linguistics: Figurative language in use, constructions and typology*. Amsterdam & Philadelphia: John Benjamins.

Porquier, Rémy. 2001. "Il m'a sauté dessus", "Je lui ai couru après": Un cas de postposition en français. *Journal of French Language Studies* 11. 123–134.

Porquier, Rémy. 2003. "Gli corro dietro/je lui cours après". A propos d'une construction verbale spécifique en italien et en français. In Alvaro Rocchetti & Mathée Giacomo-Marcellesi (eds.), *Il verbo italiano. Studi diacronici, sincronici, contrastivi, didattici*, 491–500. Roma: Bulzoni.

Porroche Ballesteros, Margarita. 2004. Estudio de una elaboración humorística del español hablado en Aragón. In José María Enguita Utrilla (ed.), *Jornadas sobre la variación lingüística en Aragón a través de sus textos*, 205–225. Zaragoza: Institución Fernando el Católico.

Pourcel, Stephanie. 2005. *Relativism in the linguistic representation and cognitive representation of motion events across verb-framed and satellite-framed languages*. Durham: University of Durham dissertation.

Pourcel, Stephanie & Anetta Kopecka. 2005. Motion expression in French: Typological diversity. *Durham and Newcastle Working Papers in Linguistics* 11. 139–153.

Pütz, Martin & Susanne Niemeier (eds.) 2001. *Applied cognitive linguistics I: Theory and practice*. Berlin & Boston: De Gruyter Mouton.

Pütz, Martin, Susanne Niemeier & René Dirven (eds.) 2001. *Applied cognitive linguistics II: Language pedagogy*. Berlin & Boston: De Gruyter Mouton.

Pütz, Martin, Justyna A. Robinson & Monika Reif. 2014. *Cognitive sociolinguistics*. Amsterdam & Philadelphia: John Benjamins.

Ragnasdóttir, Hrafnhildur & Sven Strömqvist. 2004. Time, space and manner in Icelandic and Swedish. In Sven Strömqvist & Ludo Verhoeven (eds.) *Relating events in narrative: Typological and contextual perspectives*, 113–141. New York: Psychology Press.

Real Academia Española (RAE). 2001. *Diccionario de la lengua española*. Madrid: Espasa-Calpe.

Real Academia Española (RAE). 2009. *Nueva gramática de la lengua española*. Madrid: Espasa-Calpe.

Regier, Terry & Paul Kay. 2009. Language, thought and color: Whorf was half right. *Trends in Cognitive Sciences* 13(10). 439–446.

Ricca, Davide. 1993. *I verbi deittici di movimento in Europa: Una ricerca interlinguistica*. Firenze: La Nuova Italia.

Ringbom, Håkan. 1976. What differences are there between Finns and Swedish-speaking Finns learning English? In Håkan Ringbom & Rolf Palmer (eds.) *Errors made by Finns and Swedish-speaking Finns in the learning of English*, 1–13. Åbo: Åbo Akademi University.

Ringbom, Håkan. 1978. The influence of the mother tongue on the translation of lexical items. *Interlanguage Studies Bulletin* 3. 80–101.

Ringbom, Håkan. 2016. Comprehension, learning and production of foreign languages: The role of transfer. In Rosa Alonso Alonso (ed.) *Cross-linguistic influence and second language acquisition*, 38–52. Bristol: Multilingual Matters.

Roberson, Debi & Jules Davidoff. 2000. The categorical perception of colors and facial expressions: The effect of verbal interference. *Memory & Cognition* 28(6). 977–986

Robinson, Peter & Nick C. Ellis (eds.) 2008. *Handbook of cognitive linguistics and second language acquisition*. London: Routledge.

Rojo, Ana & Paula Cifuentes-Férez. 2017. On the reception of translations: Exploring the impact of typological differences on legal contexts. In Iraide Ibarretxe-Antuñano (ed.) *Motion and space across languages: Theory and applications*, 367–398. Amsterdam & Philadelphia: John Benjamins.

Rojo, Ana & Iraide Ibarretxe-Antuñano (eds.) 2013. *Cognitive linguistics and translation: Advances in some theoretical models and applications*. Berlin & New York: Mouton de Gruyter.

Römer, Ute, Matthew Brook O'Donnell & Nick C. Ellis. 2014. Second language learner knowledge of verb-argument constructions: Effects of language transfer and typology. *The Modern Language Journal* 98(4). 952–975.

Ruiz Campillo, José Plácido. 2005. Instrucción indefinida, aprendizaje imperfecto. Para una gestión operativa del contraste imperfecto/indefinido. *Mosaico* 15. 9–17.

Sánchez Cuadrado, Adolfo. 2016. *Aprendizaje formal de ELE mediante actividades cooperativas de traducción pedagógica con atención a la forma*. Granada: Universidad de Granada dissertation.

Sánchez Cuadrado, Adolfo. 2019. Foco en la forma y traducción pedagógica en español LE/L2: El caso de la pasiva perifrástica. In Iraide Ibarretxe-Antuñano, Teresa Cadierno & Alejandro Castañeda Castro (eds.) *Lingüística cognitiva y español LE/L2*, 300–321. London: Routledge.

Schmiedtová, Barbara & Monique Flecken. 2008. The role of aspectual distinctions in event encoding: Implications for second language acquisition. In Sabine de Knop & Teun de Rycker (eds.) *Cognitive approaches to pedagogical grammar*, 357–384. Berlin & New York: Mouton de Gruyter.

Schuhardt, Hugo. 1971[1884]. *Slawo-deutsches und Slawo-italienisches*. Munich: Wilhem Fink.

Schultze-Berndt, Eva. 2000. *Simple and complex verbs in Jaminjung: A study of event categorisation in an Australian language*. Wageningen: Ponsen & Looijen.

Schultze-Berndt, Eva. 2007. On manner and paths of refining Talmy's typology of motion events via language documentation. In Peter Austin, Oliver Bond & David Nathan (eds.) *Proceedings of the conference on language documentation and linguistic theory*, 223–233. London: SOAS.

Schwarze, Christoph. 1985. Uscire e andare fuori: Struttura sintattica e semantica lessicale. In Annalisa Franchi De Bellis & Leonardo Savoia (eds.), *Sintassi e morfologia della lingua italiana d'uso. Teoria ed applicazioni destrittive. SLI XXIV*, 355–371. Roma: Bulzoni.

Schwarze, Christoph. 2008. I verbi sintagmatici: Prospettive di ricerca. In Monica Cini (ed.), *I verbi sintagmatici in italiano e nelle varietà dialettali. Stato dell'arte e prospettive di ricerca*, 209–223. Frankfurt: Peter Lang.

Sebastián, Eugenia & Dan I. Slobin. 1994. Development of linguistic forms: Spanish. In Ruth A. Berman & Dan I. Slobin (eds.), *Relating events in narrative: A cross-linguistic developmental study*, 239–284. Hillsdale, NJ: Lawrence Erlbaum.

Selinker, Larry. 1972. Interlanguage. *International Review of Applied Linguistics* 10. 209–231.

Serratrice, Ludovica. 2007. Referential cohesion in the narratives of bilingual English-Italian children and monolingual peers. *Journal of Pragmatics* 39. 1058–1087.

Sharwood Smith, Michael & Eric Kellerman (eds.) 1986. *Cross-linguistic influence in second language acquisition*. New York: Pergamon Press.

Simone, Raffaele. 1996. Esistono verbi sintagmatici in italiano? *Cuadernos de Filología Italiana* 3. 47–61.

Simone, Raffaele. 2008. Verbi sintagmatici come costruzione e come categoria. In Monica Cini (ed.) *I verbi sintagmatici in italiano e nelle varietà dialettali. Stato dell'arte e prospettive di ricerca*, 13–30. Frankfurt: Peter Lang.

Sinha, Anjani Kumar. 1972. On the deictic use of "coming" and "going" in Hindi. *Papers from the eight regional meeting of the Chicago Linguistic Society*, 351–358.

Slobin, Dan I. 1991. Learning to think for speaking: Native language, cognition, and rhetorical style. *Pragmatics* 1. 7–26.

Slobin, Dan I. 1993. Adult language acquisition: A view from child language study. In Clive Perdue (ed.) *Adult language acquisition: Cross-linguistic perspectives*, 239–252. Cambridge: Cambridge University Press.

Slobin, Dan I. 1996a. From "thought and language" to "Thinking for speaking". In John J. Gumperz and Stephen C. Levinson (eds.) *Rethinking linguistic relativity*, 70–96. Cambridge: Cambridge University Press.

Slobin, Dan I. 1996b. Two ways to travel: verbs of motion in English and Spanish. In M Shibatani & Sandra A. Thompson (eds.) *Grammatical constructions: Their form and meaning*, 195–219. Oxford: Oxford University Press.

Slobin, Dan I. 1997a. The universal, the typological, and the particular in acquisition. In Dan I. Slobin (ed.) *The cross-linguistic study of language acquisition. Volume 5: Expanding the contexts*, 1–39. Mahwah, NJ: Lawrence Erlbaum.

Slobin, Dan I. 1997b. Mind, code, and text. In Joan Bybee, John Haiman & Sandra A. Thompson (eds.) *Essays on language function and language type. Dedicated to T. Givón*, 437–467. Amsterdam & Philadelphia: John Benjamins.

Slobin, Dan I. 2000. Verbalized events. A dynamic approach to linguistic relativity and determinism. In Susanne Niemeier & René Dirven (eds.), *Evidence for linguistic relativity*, 107–138. Amsterdam & Philadelphia: John Benjamins.

Slobin, Dan I. 2003. Language and thought online: Some consequences of linguistic relativity. In Dedre Gentner & Susan Goldin-Meadow (eds.) *Language in mind: Advances in the investigation of language and thought*, 157–191. Cambridge, MA: MIT Press.

Slobin, Dan I. 2004. The many ways to search for a frog: Linguistic typology and the expression of motion events. In Sven Strömqvist & Ludo Verhoeven (eds.) *Relating events in narrative: Typological and contextual perspectives*, 219–257. New York: Psychology Press.

Slobin, Dan I. 2005. Relating narrative events in translation. In Dorit Ravid & Hava Bat-Zeev Shyldkrot (eds.) *Perspectives on language and language development. Essays in honor of Ruth A. Berman*, 115–130. Dordrecht: Kluwer.

Slobin, Dan I. 2006. What makes manner of motion salient? Explorations in linguistic typology, discourse and cognition. In Maya Hickmann & Stephane Robert (eds.) *Space in languages: Linguistic systems and cognitive categories*, 59–82. Amsterdam: John Benjamins.

Slobin, Dan I. 2008. From S-language and V-language to PIN and PIV. Paper presented at the workshop Human Locomotion across Languages, Max Planck Institute for Psycholinguistics.

Slobin, Dan I. & Nini Hoiting. 1994. Reference to movement in spoken and signed languages: Typological considerations. In Susanne Gahl, Andy Dolbey & Christopher Johnson (eds.) *Proceedings of the 20th annual meeting of the Berkeley Linguistics Society*, 487–503. Berkeley, CA: Berkeley Linguistics Society.

Slobin, Dan I., Iraide Ibarretxe-Antuñano, Anetta Kopecka & Asifa Majid. 2014. Manners of human gait: A cross-linguistic event-naming study. *Cognitive Linguistics* 25. 701–741.

Soroli, Efstathia. 2012. Variation in spatial language and cognition: Exploring visuo-spatial thinking and speaking cross-linguistically. *Cognitive Processing-International Quarterly of Cognitive Science* 13(1). 333–337.

Soroli, Efstathia & Maya Hickmann. 2010. Spatial language and cognition in French and English: Some evidence from eye-movements. In Giovanna Marotta, Alessandro Lenci, Linda Meini & Francesco Rovai (eds.), *Space in language: Proceedings of the Pisa International Conference*, 581–597. Pisa: ETS.

Soroli, Efstathia & Annemarie Verker. 2017. Motion events in Greek. Methodological and typological issues. *CogniTextes* 15(1). DOI: https://doi.org/10.4000/cognitextes.889

Spreafico, Lorenzo. 2008a. Tipologie di lessicalizzazione degli eventi di moto nelle lingue dell'area linguistica Carlomagno. In Emanuela Cresti (ed.), *Prospettive nello studio del lessico italiano: Atti del IX congresso SILFI, Firenze, 14–17 Giugno 2006*, 367–372. Florence: Firenze University Press.

Spreafico, Lorenzo. 2008b. Tipologie di lessicalizzazioni avverbiali in alcune lingue d'Europa. In Monica Cini (ed.) *I verbi sintagmatici in italiano e nelle varietà dialettali. Stato dell'arte e prospettive di ricerca*, 61–81. Frankfurt: Peter Lang.

Stam, Gale. 2006. Thinking for speaking about motion: L1 and L2 speech and gesture. *International Review of Applied Linguistics* 44. 143–169.

Stam, Gale. 2010. Can an L2 speaker's patterns of thinking for speaking change? In ZhaoHong Han & Teresa Cadierno (eds.), *Linguistic relativity in second language acquisition. Thinking for speaking*, 59–83. Bristol: Multilingual Matters.

Stam, Gale. 2015. Changes in thinking for speaking: A longitudinal case study. *The Modern Language Journal* 99. 83–99.

Stefanowitsch, Anatol & Stefan Th. Gries. 2003. Collostructions: Investigating the interaction of words and constructions. *International Journal of Corpus Linguistics* 9(1). 97–129.

Stefanowitsch, Anatol & Stefan Th. Gries. 2005. Covarying collexemes. *Corpus Linguistics and Linguistic Theory* 1 (1). 1–46.

Stolova, Natalya. 2008. From satellite-framed Latin to verb-framed Romance. Late Latin as an intermediary stage. In Roger Wright (ed.), *Latin vulgaire-latin tardif VIII. Actes du VIIIe colloque international sur le latin vulgaire et tardif. Oxford, 6–9 Settembre 2006*, 253–262. Zürich: Olms-Weidmann.

Stolova, Natalya. 2015. *Cognitive linguistics and lexical change. Motion verbs from Latin to Romance*. Amsterdam & Philadelphia: John Benjamins.

Stošić, Dejan. 2001. Prendre par le sentier à travers le bois ou comment "à travers" (se) fraie un chemin. Presentation at International Conference Prépositions et conjonctions de subordination, 29–31 May 2001. Timisoara, Romania: 207–218.

Strömqvist, Sven & Ludo Verhoeven (eds.) 2004. *Relating events in narrative. Typological and contextual perspectives*. New York: Psychology Press.

Suárez-Campos, Laura & Alberto Hijazo-Gascón. 2019. La metáfora conceptual y su aplicación a la enseñanza de español como lengua extranjera. In Iraide Ibarretxe-Antuñano, Teresa Cadierno & Alejandro Castañeda Castro (eds.), *Lingüística cognitiva y español LE/L2*, 235–252. London: Routledge.

Suárez-Campos, Laura, Alberto Hijazo-Gascón & Iraide Ibarretxe-Antuñano. 2019. Metaphor and Spanish as foreign language. In Ana María Piquer-Píriz & Rafael Alejo-González (eds.) *Metaphor in foreign language instruction*, 79–98. Berlin & New York: Mouton de Gruyter.

Talmy, Leonard. 1985. Lexicalization patterns: Semantic structure in lexical forms. In Timothy Shopen (ed.) *Language typology and syntactic description. Vol. 3: Grammatical categories and the lexicon*, 36–149. Cambridge: Cambridge University Press.

Talmy, Leonard. 1991. Path to realization: A typology of event conflation. *Proceedings of the Seventeenth Annual Meeting of the Berkeley Linguistic Society*, 480–519.

Talmy, Leonard. 2000a. *Toward a cognitive semantics. Vol. I: Concept structuring systems*. Cambridge, MA: MIT Press.

Talmy, Leonard. 2000b. *Toward a cognitive semantics. Vol. II: Typology and process in concept structuring*. Cambridge, MA: MIT Press.

Talmy, Leonard. 2007. Lexical Typologies. In Timothy Shopen (ed.), *Language typology and syntactic description*, 66–168. Cambridge: Cambridge University Press.

Talmy, Leonard. 2009. Main verb properties and equipollent framing. In Jiansheng Guo, Elena Lieven, Nancy Budwig, Susan Ervin-Tripp, Keiko Nakamura & Seyda Özçaliskan (eds.) *Cross-linguistic approaches to the psychology of language: Research in the tradition of Dan Isaac Slobin*, 289–402. New York: Psychology Press.

Talmy, Leonard. 2012. Main verb properties. *International Journal of Cognitive Linguistics* 3(1). 1–24.

Tesnière, Lucien. 1959. *Élements de syntaxe structurale*. Paris: Klincksieck.

Treffers-Daller, Jeanine. 2012. Grammatical collocations and verb-particle constructions in Brussels French: A corpus linguistic approach to transfer. *International Journal of Bilingualism* 16(1). 53–82.
Tyler, Andrea. 2008. Cognitive linguistics and second language instruction. In Peter Robinson & Nick C. Ellis (eds.), *Handbook of cognitive linguistics and second language acquisition*, 456–488. London: Routledge.
Tyler, Andrea. 2012. *Cognitive linguistics and second language learning: Theoretical basics and experimental evidence*. London: Routledge.
Tyler, Andrea & Vyvyan Evans. 2003. *The semantics of English prepositions: Spatial scenes, embodied meaning and cognition*. Cambridge: Cambridge University Press.
Valenzuela, Javier & Ana Rojo. 2008a. What can language learners tell us about constructions? In Sabine de Knop & Teun de Rycker (eds.), *Cognitive approaches to pedagogical grammar. Volume in honour of René Dirven*, 197–229. Berlin & New York: Mouton de Gruyter.
Valenzuela, Javier & Ana Rojo. 2008b. On the existence of constructions in foreign language learners. In Rafael Monroy Casas & Aquilino Sánchez Pérez (eds.), *25 años de lingüística en España: Hitos y retos*, 907–912. Murcia: Editum.
Verde, Erica. 2014. *Investigating Miami English-Spanish bilinguals' treatment of English deictic verbs of motion*. Miami: Florida International University MA thesis.
Viberg, Åke. 1988. Cross-linguistic perspectives on lexical acquisition: The case of language-specific semantic differentiation. In Kirsten Haastrup & Åke Viberg (eds.), *Perspectives on lexical acquisition in a second language*, 175–208. Lund: Lund University Press.
Vicario, Federico. 1997. *I verbi analitici in friulano*. Milan: Franco Angeli.
Vulchanova, Mila, Liliana Martínez & Valentin Vulchanov. 2012. Distinctions in the linguistic encoding of motion: Evidence from a free naming task. In Mila Vulchanova & Emile van der Zee (eds.), *Motion encoding in language*, 11–44. Oxford: Oxford University Press.
Wälchli, Bernhard. 2006. Lexicalization patterns in motion events revisited. Unpublished manuscript.
Weinreich, Uriel. 1953. *Languages in contact. Findings and problems*. New York: Linguistic Circle of New York.
White, Benjamin J. 2012. A conceptual approach to the instruction of phrasal verbs. *Modern Language Journal* 96(3). 419–438.
Whorf, Benjamin L. 1956. *Language, thought, and reality*. Boston: MIT Press.
Wienold, Götz & Christoph Schwarze. 2002. *The lexicalization of movement concepts in French, Italian, Japanese and Korean: Towards a realistic typology*. Konstanz: Fachbereich Schprachwissenschaft Universität Konstanz.
Wieselman Schulman, Bari. *A cross-linguistic investigation of the speech-gesture relationship in motion events descriptions*. Chicago: University of Chicago dissertation.
Wilkins, David. 2004. The verbalization of motion events in Arrente. In Sven Strömqvist & Ludo Verhoeven (eds.), *Relating events in narrative: Typological and contextual perspectives*, 143–157. New York: Psychology Press.
Wilkins, David & Deborah Hill. 1995. When "go" means "come": Questioning the basicness of basic motion verbs. *Cognitive Linguistics* 6. 209–60.
Willet, Thomas. 1988. A cross-linguistic survey of the grammaticization of evidentiality. *Studies in Language* 12. 51–97.
Woerfel, Till J. Nesta. 2018. *Encoding motion events. The impact of language-specific patterns and language dominance in bilingual children*. Berlin & New York: Mouton de Gruyter.

Yip, Virginia & Stephen Matthews. 2007. *The bilingual child. Early development and language contact*. Cambridge: Cambridge University Press.

Yiu, Carine Yuk-man. 2014. *The typology of motion events: An empirical study of Chinese dialects*. Berlin & New York: Mouton de Gruyter.

Yoshinari, Yuko. 2015. Describing motion events in Japanese L2 acquisition: How to express deictic information. In Iraide Ibarretxe-Antuñano & Alberto Hijazo-Gascón (eds.), *New horizons in the study of motion events: Bringing together applied and theoretical perspectives*, 32–65. Newcastle upon Tyne: Cambridge Scholars Publishing.

Zlatev, Jordan & Peerapat Yangklang. 2004. A third way to travel: The place of Thai in motion event typology. In Sven Strömqvist & Ludo Verhoeven (eds.), *Relating events in narrative. Typological and contextual perspectives*, 159–90. New York: Psychology Press.

Zubizarreta, María Luisa. 2007. A compositional analysis of manner-of-motion verbs in Italian. In José Camacho, Nydia Flores-Ferrán, Liliana Sánchez, Viviane Déprez & María José Cabrera (eds.), *Romance Linguistics 2006: Selected papers from the 36th Linguistic Symposium on Romance Languages (LSRL), New Brunswick, March-April 2006*, 311–28. Amsterdam & Philadelphia: John Benjamins.

Zubizarreta, María Luisa & Eunjeong Oh. 2007. *On the syntactic composition of manner and motion*. Cambridge, MA: MIT Press.

Subject index

Adverbial pronoun 76, 121, 169–170, 174–175, 188
Applied Language Typology 263, 273, 279
Arabic 28, 95, 129
Aragonese 57, 77–80, 110, 120, 124, 127, 129, 155–156, 159, 164, 173, 217, 280

Basque 28, 32, 48, 56–57, 67, 72, 79–80, 124, 139, 155, 159, 164, 167, 194
Bilingualism 2, 14, 131, 150, 157
Boundary-crossing 41–44, 49, 51, 53, 58, 61, 63–64, 66–67, 78, 81, 92, 94–95, 98–102, 136, 139–140, 151, 159, 170–171, 178, 184–188, 215, 219, 227, 233, 237–238, 255, 259, 264, 268–269

CASP 14, 271
Catalan 28, 57, 67, 74–77, 79–80, 84, 108, 110, 112, 120–121, 124, 127, 129, 209, 280
Cause 24–25, 26, 45, 52, 74, 86, 125, 128, 132–133, 136, 160, 212–213, 217, 219, 261, 265–267
Caused-motion 60, 68
Chinese *See* Mandarin Chinese
Cline 40, 58, 114, 124, 139, 152, 155, 190, 218, 267, 280
Cognitive Linguistics 2, 12–13, 15–20, 30, 85, 158, 274–275
Complete Path construction 56, 121
Complex Path 36–37, 56, 80, 258
Conceptual transfer 12
Conformation 24, 48, 51, 111, 128
cross-linguistic influence 6, 9–12, 17, 21, 28, 61–63, 65, 69–71, 134, 219, 221–223, 227, 229, 231, 237, 240, 244–245, 247, 253, 255, 259–261, 263, 268, 270, 272, 277

Danish 18, 28, 54, 63, 66–69, 70, 106, 134, 151–152, 159, 169, 219, 241–242, 271
Deictic center 24, 217, 253, 281

Deictic motion verbs 81, 104, 125–126, 131, 171, 207–208, 211, 275
Deixis 24, 48, 51, 58, 64, 103–104, 111, 125, 128, 131, 160, 167, 207–208, 210–211, 217, 253, 264, 266–267, 278
Dutch 8, 12, 28, 38, 58, 61, 68, 70, 88, 106, 111, 134, 157, 209

English 11–12, 16–17, 20, 24, 26–28, 32–33, 42, 44, 52, 54, 56–57, 61–62, 78, 85, 108, 121, 123, 126, 269, 271
Equipollently-framed 47, 49–51, 57

Figure 24, 27, 41, 45, 50–51, 55, 68, 86, 118, 134, 148, 152, 168, 195
First language acquisition 28, 32, 38, 50, 59, 132, 147, 149
Focus on Form 263, 273–276
Force dynamics 23, 46, 48, 68, 98–99, 133
Forensic 134, 278
French 48, 58, 61, 76, 78–81, 84, 88, 90–93, 95, 103, 105, 107–108, 111, 117–119, 123–124, 154, 160, 165–166, 171, 177, 184, 188–189, 191–193, 195, 237–239, 255
– Belgian French 109, 157
– Brussels French 157
– Canadian French 157
– Old French 119–120, 159, 216, 266
Friulan 77–78, 109–111, 125, 165, 280

German 41, 44, 58, 68, 70, 72, 87, 105, 109, 111, 128, 132, 138, 154, 157, 159, 165, 168, 170–171, 175–179, 184–185, 187, 189–190, 192–193, 195, 235–240
– Standard German 58, 72, 78, 80
– Swiss German 58, 72, 78, 80, 140, 148, 154, 159, 267
Gesture 39, 58, 60–62, 64, 70, 87, 134, 281
Goal of motion 36, 56, 120, 125–127, 130–132, 136, 147
Greek 44, 56, 67, 111, 127, 141, 165, 275

Ground 15, 24, 34, 36–37, 42, 45, 56–57, 63, 66, 74, 80, 86–87, 118, 148, 153–154, 159, 167, 169, 171–172, 174, 186, 189, 191–196, 198–203, 206, 211–212, 216–218, 220, 227, 238–240, 243–244, 246–250, 252–253, 259–260, 264, 268, 270, 272

Ideophone 52, 57, 72, 79, 156
Intentionality 68, 97, 133–135
Interpreting 59, 225, 277
Intra-typological 20–21, 41, 53–54, 58, 60, 66–68, 70–73, 80–81, 89, 117, 125, 129, 131, 133, 136, 138, 141, 151, 153, 159–161, 168, 170, 184, 186, 188–189, 191, 193–194, 196, 207, 209–213, 215–219, 255, 257, 259, 261, 263–270, 280
Italian 57, 67, 72, 76, 78–79, 88–92, 99, 103, 106–110, 112–113, 117, 123–125, 139, 141, 157, 159–160, 162, 165–166, 168–173, 176, 184, 187–189, 191–193, 237–239, 253, 255
– Bergamasque 110
– Piedmontese 110, 113, 156
– Sicilian 109–110
– Trentino 110, 116, 157
– Tuscan 109–110, 156

Japanese 32, 48, 51–52, 57, 61, 64, 66, 70–72, 95, 127–128, 139, 209, 271

Latin 1, 7, 26, 28, 44, 54, 73–75, 76, 81, 110–112, 117, 120–122, 129, 136, 142, 153, 159, 165, 169, 173, 215, 230, 266, 275
Lexicalization patterns 25, 28, 31, 33, 42, 45, 49, 52, 62, 64, 66, 71, 77, 122, 138, 140, 149–151, 162, 259–261

Mandarin Chinese 26, 28, 50
Manner verb 38, 41–43, 49–51, 65, 78, 88, 92–93, 97, 99, 133, 141, 149, 152, 167, 176–177, 179, 184, 186–187, 233, 237–238, 240
Mediation 263, 277–278

Motion 22, 24–25, 26, 27, 32, 51, 56, 74, 81–82, 86, 104, 106, 136, 172, 178, 227, 258, 267–268
Multicompetence 3, 71

Path verb 41, 44, 49–50, 55, 88, 92, 128, 144, 167, 173, 175–176, 184, 186–188, 238–239
Pedagogical translation 21, 275–278
Portuguese 28, 38, 75–76, 80–81, 108, 120, 125, 127, 129, 165, 209, 280–281
Prefix 65, 74–75, 111, 119, 121, 143–144, 192, 212
Pseudo-satellite 46, 103, 117, 121, 124–125, 160, 175, 191, 211, 259, 265
Psychotypology 13, 63, 242, 258, 271

Re-thinking-for-speaking 12, 17, 70, 134, 240, 259, 261
Rhaeto-Romance 72, 74, 77–78, 80, 109, 125, 157, 159
Rhetorical style 28, 31–33, 37–39, 54, 59, 65, 73, 92, 102, 119, 138, 148–149, 153, 158, 160, 192, 213, 216–217, 234, 237–238, 240, 242, 245, 256, 259–261, 265–266, 268, 270, 272–273, 277, 281
Romanian 75–76, 80–81, 95, 109–110, 125, 280–281
Romansch 58, 77–80, 110, 121, 148, 154–155, 190, 280

Salience
– Manner salience 58, 139, 154, 280
– Path salience 58, 124, 139, 267, 280
Sardinian 76, 81, 112, 156, 165, 280
Satellite 28, 38, 214, 220, 268
Satellite-framed 2, 20, 27–28, 29, 31–33, 36–40, 43, 45–58, 60, 64–66, 69–70, 72–73, 75, 77–80, 101, 103, 105, 107, 110, 112, 116–119, 122–125, 139–142, 147–154, 159–162, 169, 171–172, 176–179, 183–184, 189, 192–193, 195–196, 209, 211–212, 214, 216–217, 219–220, 237, 240, 246, 253, 257–258, 263, 265–269, 280

Satellization 63, 169, 241–242
Second language acquisition 1–2, 4, 13, 15–16, 59–60, 64, 67, 69, 268, 272
Semantic typology 2, 17, 20, 40, 72, 81, 92, 136, 142, 157, 263
Serbo-Croatian 28, 53–54, 65, 124, 126–127, 153, 159
Spanish 26, 34, 37–38, 47–48, 57–58, 63, 71–72, 75–76, 79, 81–85, 105, 108, 110, 113, 116, 120–121, 123, 135–137, 152, 157, 159, 162, 164, 167, 170, 173–174, 177, 179, 181, 184, 188–189, 191–195, 203, 205–206, 208–209, 236, 238–240, 253
– Classical Spanish 129
– L2 Spanish 61, 67–68, 70, 219–220, 223–224, 227–228, 230, 232–234, 236–237
– Old Spanish 75, 112, 140
– Spanish fom the Basque Country 267
– Spanish from Aragón 58, 155, 164, 194, 211, 217, 260, 267, 281
– Spanish from Argentina 58, 155, 189, 193, 205, 211, 217, 260, 281
– Spanish from Chile 58, 155, 193, 206
– Spanish from Madrid 58, 189, 193, 205, 211, 217, 260, 281
– Spanish from the Basque Country 58, 155, 194, 217
Swedish 28, 32, 54, 68, 106, 159

Teaching 21, 219, 263, 273–276, 279
Thinking-for-speaking 9, 11–12, 17, 20, 29–32, 39–40, 51, 55, 59–60, 62, 64–67, 69–70, 81, 117, 131, 136–139, 142, 147, 154, 158, 162, 208, 218, 236, 245, 252, 261, 263, 266, 268, 281–282
Transfer
– Conceptual transfer 2, 11–12, 20–21, 61, 66–67, 69–70, 219–221, 257, 268–269, 271
– Negative transfer 7, 9–10, 14–15, 21, 253
– Positive transfer 10, 14–15, 21, 66, 270–271
– Transfer to nowhere 8–9, 256, 261, 270–271
– Transfer to somewhere 8
Translation 37–38, 59, 102, 149, 225, 263, 275–277
Turkish 28, 30–32, 38–39, 43, 46–47, 62, 66, 93, 124, 127, 136, 141, 150–152, 159, 209
Typological shift 73–74, 81, 119–120, 124, 266

Vector 24, 48, 51, 111, 128
Venitive 128, 131, 207–211, 217, 253, 264, 270, 281
Verb-framed 2, 20, 28–29, 32–34, 36–41, 43, 45–53, 55–58, 60, 62–64, 67, 69–70, 72–77, 79, 81–82, 92, 95–96, 99–101, 103, 105, 112, 117–119, 122, 124, 133, 135–141, 145, 150–152, 159–160, 162, 171, 177, 179, 181, 183, 185, 188, 193–195, 203, 209, 211, 213–216, 218–220, 236–238, 241, 246, 253, 257–258, 263–264, 266–268, 280
Verb-particle constructions 81, 103, 114, 156, 190

Witness testimony 279

Author index

Achard, Michele 15
Acquaroni, Rosana 18
Aguiló-Mora, Francisca 274
Ahlqvist, August 7
Aikhenvald, Alexandra 31
Akita, Kimi 48, 57, 72, 128–129
Alcina, Juan 82
Alejo-González, Rafael 16
Alferink, Inge 68
Alhmoud, Zeina 17
Allen, Shanley 163
Alonso Alonso, Rosa 63
Alonso Raya, Rosario 17
Alonso-Aparicio, Irene 17
Ameka, Felix 49, 50
Amenta, Luisa 109
Andersen, Roger 8
Andriá, Maria 67, 280–281
Annamalai, Elay 126
Antonopoulou, Eleni 127
Arnal Purroy, María Luisa 173
Asher, James 274
Asher, Nicholas 98
Athanasopoulos, Panos 59, 69

Baciu, Ileana 95
Badia Margarit, Antoni 120
Baicchi, Annalisa 99, 139
Bally, Charles 22, 142
Bamberg, Michael 31, 143, 148, 162, 168
Bartra, Anna 120
Bassetti, Benedetta 59
Beavers, John 44–45, 95, 98, 122
Behrens, Heike 148
Berlin, Brent 29
Berman, Ruth A. 28, 31, 136–137, 147, 162–163, 170, 178, 226
Bernardo Carrasco, José 161
Bernini, Giuliano 110, 117, 157
Berthele, Raphael 57–58, 72, 77–80, 98, 110, 125, 140, 144, 146, 151, 154, 159, 168, 175–176, 267, 280
Bialystok, Ellen 4
Blecua, José Manuel 82

Blytmann-Trondhjem, Frederikke 57
Bobrova, Larysa 18
Boers, Frank 15–16
Bohnemeyer, Juergen 53, 122
Boroditsky, Lera 30, 59
Bowerman, Melissa 30, 128
Brisard, Frank 61
Brown, Amanda 69, 71, 164, 224
Brown, Penelope 55, 72, 159, 167
Brown, Roger W. 5
Bühler, Karl 125
Bylund, Emanuel 18, 40, 68–69, 71

Cadierno, Teresa 12–13, 16–19, 54, 59–60, 62–64, 66–71, 88, 134–136, 151, 159, 167–168, 219, 241–242, 259, 261, 269, 271, 273–274, 280–281
Calderero Hernández, José Fernando 161
Calduch, Carme 277
Cameron, Lynn 18
Campos, Héctor 84
Carando, Agustina 267
Cardini, Filippo-Enrico 101–103, 139, 218
Carreres, Ángeles 277
Carroll, Mary 68, 141
Casenhiser, Devin 19
Castañeda Castro, Alejandro 16–17
Cerruti, Massimo 113
Chafe, Wallace 31
Cheikh-Kamis, Fátima 19
Chen, Liang 50
Chevalier, Gisèle 157
Choi, Soojung 30, 62, 69–70, 128
Chui, Daniel 131
Cifuentes Honrubia, José Luis 22, 84, 167–168, 280
Cifuentes-Férez, Paula 59, 85, 87, 167–168, 277, 280
Cini, Monica 103, 156
Clark, Eve 61
Colasacco, Marina Anna 67, 132, 275
Cook, Vivian 3, 6, 59, 71
Cordin, Patrizia 110, 116, 157
Council of Europe 225, 263, 277–278

Coventry, Kenny 17, 59
Croft, William A. 44–45, 52, 96, 122
Cuartero Otal, Juan 87, 95, 145–146
Cuenca, Maria Josep 19
Cuyckens, Hubert 13
Czechowska, Natalia 66

Danesi, Marcel 18
Davidoff, Jules 29
de Bot, Kees 3
de Knop, Sabine 15–16, 19, 146–148, 274
de Rycker, Antoon 16
de Rycker, Teun 15
de Souza, Ricardo 267
Delbeque, Nicole 17
Demagny, Annie-Claude 68, 132
Dirven, René 15, 158, 274
Dronjic, Vedran 9
Duden 142
Duncan, Susan 162

Eisenberg, Ann 61
Elliott, Elisabeth 274
Ellis, Nick C. 12–15, 17, 70, 259, 271, 274
Ellis, Rod 6–7, 10, 228, 241
Engberg-Pedersen, Elisabeth 57
Engemann, Helen 141
Enguita Utrilla, José María 164
Eskildsen, Søren 62
Essegbey, James 49, 50
Evans, Reid 274
Evans, Vyvyan 17
Ewert, Anna 66

Fábregas, Antonio 22, 45, 91
Fagard, Benjamin 73, 100–101, 117, 139
Fauconnier, Gilles 16
Fernández, Eva M. 267
Ferrari, Giacomo 73
Filipović, Luna 14–15, 41, 44, 46, 53–54, 58,
    65, 69, 71–72, 122, 124, 126–127,
    134–135, 138, 153, 159, 263, 271–273,
    277–279
Fillmore, Charles 16, 126, 128
Flecken, Monique 68–69
Folli, Raffaella 89, 92

Gallez, Françoise 147–148
Galvan, Dennis 58
García, Ofelia 1
Gathercole, Virginia 126–127, 129–130, 208,
    217, 253, 261, 264–265
Geeraerts, Dirk 13, 158
Gennari, Silvia 40, 43
Geva, Sharon 138
Gilquin, Gaëtanelle 19
Gleitman, Lila 40, 56
Goddard, Cliff 126
Goldberg, Adele 19
Gómez Vicente, Lucía 18
González Davies, María 275–276
Gonzálvez-García, Francisco 19
Goschler, Juliana 62, 126, 144–146, 150
Gras, Pedro 19
Graus, Stefanie 4
Gries, Stefan Th 144
Grinevald, Colette 53, 122
Grosjean, François 3, 71
Guelbenzu-Espada, Julia 87, 168
Guijarro-Fuentes, Pedro 17, 59
Gullberg, Marianne 11, 39, 60, 68–71, 87,
    134, 140–141, 164, 224, 280–281
Guo, Jiangsheng 50

Han, ZhaoHong 18, 59
Harr, Anne-Katharina 140–141, 146, 150
Hasko, Victoria 65, 70
Hatim, Basil 275
Hawkins, John A. 14–15, 271
Helms-Park, Rena 9
Hendriks, Henriette 39, 68, 99, 132–133,
    135, 140–141
Herdina, Philip 4
Hickmann, Maya 68, 99, 132–133, 140–141
Hijazo-Gascón, Alberto 16–17, 18, 19, 46,
    57–58, 67–68, 77–79, 87, 102–103, 110,
    120–121, 124, 127, 129, 132, 134–135,
    139–140, 155–156, 159, 168, 194, 204,
    206, 212, 217, 220, 246, 251, 260, 267,
    274, 278, 280–281
Hilferty, Joseph 19
Hill, Deborah 126
Hilpert, Martin 267

Hoffmann, Dorothea 51
Hohestein, Jill 61
Hoiting, Nini 41, 43, 49, 58, 84, 93, 184–185
Holme, Randal 16
Huang, Shuanfan 57
Huang, Yan 125
Huber, Judith 153

Iacobini, Claudio 45, 73, 99–103, 108–113, 115–117, 139, 156
Ibarretxe-Antuñano, Iraide 13, 16, 18–19, 22, 25, 28, 41, 45–46, 48–49, 51, 56–59, 67–68, 72, 77–80, 87, 102–103, 110, 120–122, 124, 127, 133–135, 138–140, 153, 155–156, 159, 163, 167–168, 194, 204, 206, 212, 217–218, 246, 251, 260, 267, 270, 274, 277–278, 280
Ijaz, I. Helene 12
Inagaki, Shunji 61
Instituto Cervantes 224, 225

Jackendoff, Ray 22, 85, 94
Jarvis, Scott 2, 7–8, 9, 10, 11, 12, 18, 21, 59, 68, 71, 219–223, 259–261, 270–272
Jessen, Moiken 67, 151, 159
Jessner, Ulrike 4
Johnson Laird, Philip 126
Johnson, Mark 16, 18, 29
Juchem-Grundmann, Constanze 16

Kay, Paul 29–30
Kellerman, Eric 6, 8–9, 12–13, 61, 63, 70, 256, 258, 261, 270
Khalifa, Jean-Charles 140
Kita, Sotaro 39, 163
Koch, Peter 80
Kopecka, Anetta 68, 91, 98, 117–120, 122, 133, 140–141, 153, 159, 168, 175, 210–211, 216, 266
Kristiansen, Gitte 158

Lado, Robert 7
Lagüéns Gracia, Vicente 173
Lakoff, George 16, 18, 29
Lam, Yvonne 17

Lamiroy, Béatrice 89, 140
Langacker, Ronald W. 16
Lantolf, James 18, 62, 69–70
Lapesa, Rafael 83
Larrañaga, Pilar 64, 99, 219, 269
Larsen-Freeman, Diane 161
Lemmens, Maarten 68
Lenneberg, Eric H. 5
Leonardi, Vanessa 275–277
Levin, Beth 22, 44–45, 98
Levinson, Stephen C. 30, 125
Lewandowski, Wojciech 64, 66, 129–131, 151–152, 281
Lewis, Tasha 64
Li, Peiwen 62
Lindstromberg, Seth 15
Liste-Lamas, Elsa 62, 126, 143, 146
Littlemore, Jeannette 16, 18
Llopis-García, Reyes 16–17, 19
Long, Michael 157, 161
Low, Graham 18
Lowie, Wander 17
Lübcke, Barbara 149
Lucy, John A. 29–30
Lyons, John 125

MacWhinney, Brian 166, 226
Madlener, Karin 148
Maldonado, Ricardo 17
Malt, Barbara 47
Martín Zorraquino, María Antonia 164
Martínez, Liliana 152
Martínez-Vázquez, Montserrat 95, 97
Masini, Francesca 45, 103, 106–107, 109–116, 139
Mason, Ian 275
Massey, Christine 40, 56
Mateu, Jaume 120, 151–152
Matras, Yaron 157
Matsumoto, Yo 48, 52, 122, 128–129
Matthews, Stephen 10
Mayer, Mercer 31, 162
McNeill, David 39, 138, 162
Megens, Manon 4
Mendikoetxea, Amaya 82–83

Mendo Murillo, Susana 17
Miller, George A. 126
Miquel López, Lourdes 274
Molés-Cases, Teresa 98, 149
Moliner, María 167
Montero Gálvez, Sonia 17
Montero-Melis, Guilermo 40
Montrul, Silvina 18, 61
Moret-Oliver, María-Teresa 77, 79, 110, 121, 124, 156, 159, 212, 280
Morimoto, Yuko 22, 89, 91, 94
Mosca, Monica 73–74, 112–113, 122, 139, 156, 168
Muñoz, Carmen 5
Muñoz-Carrasco, Meritxell 64, 99

Naigles, Letitia 18, 61, 95, 138
Narasimhan, Bhuvana 68, 133
Navarro, Samuel 63
Negueruela, Eduardo 61, 69, 219, 274
Nichols, Johanna 31
Nicoladis, Elena 61, 63
Niemeier, Susanne 15
Nikiforidou, Niki 127
Nikitina, Tatiana 22
Noonan, Michael 45, 56
Noriega-Sánchez, Maria 277

Ochsenbauer, Anne-Katharina 148–150
Odlin, Terence 6–7, 9
Oesterreicher, Wulf 80
Oh, Eunjeong 88–92, 98
Oh, Kyung-ju 47
Ortega, Lourdes 4, 17, 21, 220, 259, 272
Ortega Olivares, Jenaro 17, 274
Otheguy, Ricardo 1
Özçalışkan, Seyda 32, 38–39, 43, 46, 48, 64, 66, 159
Öztürk, Özge 31
Özyürek, Asli 39, 163
O'Donnell, Matthew Brook 271, 274

Papafragou, Anna 31, 40, 56
Pavlenko, Aneta 1–2, 5, 9–12, 18, 20, 59, 219, 258, 271
Pedersen, Johan 97–98, 102

Peirsman, Yves 158
Perdue, Clive 6
Perek, Florent 267
Perrez, Julien 68
Philips, Webb 30, 59
Piquer-Píriz, Ana María 16, 18
Porquier, Rémy 45, 107–108, 140
Porroche Ballesteros, Margarita 164
Pourcel, Stephanie 98, 120, 140, 152
Pütz, Martin 15, 158

Ragnasdóttir, Hrafnhildur 54, 153
Rappaport Hovav, Malka 22
Real-Espinosa, Juan Manuel 17
Regier, Terry 30
Reif, Monika 158
Ricca, Davide 127, 129–130
Ringbom, Håkan 8, 13
Roberson, Debi 29
Robinson, Justyna A. 158
Robinson, Peter 12, 15, 17, 66, 70, 259, 261
Rojo, Ana 19, 59, 277
Römer, Ute 271, 274
Ruiz Campillo, José Plácido 17
Ruiz, Lucas 18, 70, 136, 168

Sablayrolles, Pierre 98
Sakel, Jeannette 157
Sánchez Cuadrado, Adolfo 276, 277
Schmidt, Lauren A. 30, 59
Schmiedtová, Barbara 68
Schuhardt, Hugo 7
Schultze-Berndt, Eva 51
Schwarze, Christoph 103–105, 109, 112, 117, 139
Sebastián, Eugenia 88, 136–138, 155, 167–168, 193, 246
Selinker, Larry 3
Serratrice, Ludovica 162
Simone, Raffaele 109, 122, 139
Singleton, David 5
Sinha, Anjani Kumar 126
Skoruppa, Katrin 148
Slobin, Dan I. 2, 12, 17, 20, 28–34, 36–38, 40–41, 43–44, 46–51, 53–54, 57–60, 69, 73, 78, 84, 88, 93, 99, 122, 136–139,

147–148, 153–155, 159, 162–163,
167–168, 170–171, 176, 178–179,
183–185, 189, 191, 193, 205–206, 208,
214–216, 252, 257–258, 260–261, 263,
267, 273, 277, 280
Spreafico, Lorenzo 103, 110
Stam, Gale 18, 62, 281
Stefanowitsch, Anatol 126, 144–146
Stocker, Ladina 151
Stolova, Natalya 73–76, 121, 123, 129, 159,
169, 280
Stošić, Dejan 91
Strömqvist, Sven 28, 32, 54, 153, 162, 170,
178, 226
Suárez-Campos, Laura 19

Takahashi, Kiyoko 48, 128–129
Talmy, Leonard 2, 12, 16–17, 20, 22–27, 29,
40, 42, 44–46, 48–52, 55–57, 73, 78,
82, 84–85, 87, 89, 92–93, 103, 121–123,
128, 132, 136, 138–140, 142, 144, 154,
170, 174, 189, 207–208, 242, 253, 258,
261, 263–264, 266
Tanangkingsking, Michael 57
Taub, Sarah 58
Terrazas, Paula 95, 138
Tesnière, Lucien 22, 52, 84, 140, 142
Tham, Shiao-Wei 44–45, 98
Treffers-Daller, Jeanine 157
Tyler, Andrea 16–17

Valdés, Berenice 59
Valenzuela, Javier 13, 19

van Hoof, Anne-Marie 61, 70
Vázquez Rozas, Victoria 149
Verde, Erica 131
Vergaro, Carla 102
Verhoeven, Ludo 28, 32, 162, 170, 178, 226
Verspoor, Marjolyn 17
Viberg, Åke 68
Vicario, Federico 77, 80, 109–110, 125, 159
Vidaković, Ivana 55, 64–65
von Stutterheim, Christiane 68
Vulchanov, Valentin 152
Vulchanova, Mila 152

Wälchli, Bernhard 52
Weinreich, Uriel 6–7
White, Benjamin J. 275
Whorf, Benjamin L. 5, 29–30
Wienold, Götz 139
Wieselman Schulman, Bari 39
Wilkins, David 58, 126
Willet, Thomas 31
Woerfel, Till J. Nesta 140–141, 150

Yangklang, Peerapat 49–50, 88, 167
Yip, Virginia 10
Yiu, Carine Yuk-man 58
Yoshinari, Yuko 64
Yountchi, Lisa 274
Yu, Liming 6–7

Zlatev, Jordan 49–50, 88, 167
Zubizarreta, María Luisa 88, 90–92, 98

www.ingramcontent.com/pod-product-compliance
Lightning Source LLC
Chambersburg PA
CBHW031420150426
43191CB00006B/336